THIS AMERICAN RIVER

EDITED BY W. D. WETHERELL

THIS AMERICAN RIVER

Five Centuries of Writing about the Connecticut

UNIVERSITY PRESS OF NEW ENGLAND

Hanover and London

University Press of New England, One Court St., Lebanon, NH 03766

Printed in the United States of America

5 4 3 2 1

LIBRARY OF CONGRESS CATALOGING-IN-PUBLICATION DATA

This American river : five centuries of writing about the Connecticut / edited by W. D. Wetherell.

p. cm.

ISBN 1-58465-111-3 (cloth : alk. paper)

1. Connecticut River—Description and travel. 2. Connecticut River—History. 3. Connecticut River—Poetry. I. Wetherell, W. D., date–

F12.C7 T47 2002

974—dc21 2002004182

CONTENTS

INTRODUCTION

Rivers and anthologies have a lot in common. Composed of disparate elements that ultimately trend in the same direction; alternating between stretches of wild exuberance and placid intervals that reflect a quieter, more pensive mood; liable at times to flood and roil, and other times to run easier and clearer; harnessed now to a utilitarian purpose, now to an impressionistic one, anthologies and rivers—when it comes to human understanding—wend their way toward the sea. And further. A good anthology, like a good river, maintains its identity throughout its entire length, never mind the varied swerves, the surprising oxbows, the chaotic rapids that occur throughout.

This linkage is especially strong when it comes to the Connecticut River, the river I love, the river that flows past my home. At first glance there is little in common between the fast upper reaches flowing through farmland and forest and the lower stretches flanked by interstates, and yet, follow it from its source to the Sound, watch long enough, and the essential wholeness of the river becomes plain. Much of this comes from the surprisingly *secret* character the river has almost everywhere along the four hundred miles of its reach. People glimpse it from the highway on their way to work or view it from the distance in the course of an afternoon's hike, the sinuous line at the bottom of a pretty valley, but neither experience prepares you for the richness of the river once you're actually on it in a small boat—the way it flows through its countryside, its suburbia, its cities as a secret channel of beauty and quiet that most valley dwellers, even now, hardly suspect is there.

The same is true for the large, extraordinarily rich body of writing that runs parallel to the river through the four hundred years it's been known to western man: hardly any readers know it's there.

There has never been a full-length anthology devoted to writing about the Connecticut River until this one (nor, for that matter, many devoted to *any* American river): the writings form a resource that has been neglected for far too long, just as the river was neglected and undervalued for generations. The river, after all, is the centerpiece of New England and has been for the five centuries its banks have been settled. Its geographical reach alone, on a New England scale, is immense; the river basin drains

11,260 miles, representing one third of New Hampshire, Connecticut, and Massachusetts, and an ever larger percentage of Vermont. In the early days, it was the main avenue of transportation for interior New England, the route to the sea, the access to the busy commerce of Long Island Sound. Rich in natural resources, extraordinarily fertile, the river valley has always been the center of New England agriculture, while the water power of the river and its tributaries was a prime ingredient in shaping the Industrial Revolution. It was on the Connecticut that the steamboat was invented, the first submarine launched. It was and remains a river of education, with famous riverside universities extending from Wesleyan in the south to Dartmouth in the north. Its history has a river-like unity, settlements flowing over the years from Connecticut through Massachusetts to the northern two states, with a population nourished by the same democratic ethic that governed them when the white population was centered on a small, fragile stretch of river, the upper reaches all but unknown. Indeed, as some of the writers will demonstrate, the Connecticut River has at least as strong a claim as Massachusetts Bay to being the birthplace of American democracy.

And this brings up another point. The Connecticut is a very *American* river, one that could stand as the easternmost paradigm for a score of others right across the continent. Discovered early by the whites; thought of primarily as an avenue to riches; settled slowly at first; fought for bitterly along its entire reach; a transportation corridor in the early days, first for barges and scows, then later (being conveniently level) for trains and highways; polluted early, then gradually restored; the cause of many destructive floods; scene of the longest, most epic log drive in the country's history—the Connecticut has all the accoutrements of a major American river, with one vital exception: because of those infamous sandbars, there is no major city at its mouth, a difference that has led in turn to many differences along the entire river.

The Connecticut, two centuries ago, formed the natural link between all the towns and people within its reach. This linkage broke down over the years as people became less dependent on the river, less aware of it, less caring; but the feeling of unity—of the Connecticut River Valley as one comprehensible, interconnected whole—is coming back again, and not just in the literal sense, either.

A river is a better metaphor than most, though it's often used in two very contradictory senses. There's the river as a divide, a barrier, a border or gulf: the river Styx between life and death in classic myth, "one last river to cross" from the Negro spiritual, "crossing the Rubicon" and all that implies. These images all suggest how divisive in the human imagination that thin watery line can seem. Strong images—and yet how much stronger is the opposite usage, the river as a symbol of continuity, linkage, and connection. "The round river" is the phrase Aldo Leopold came up with in trying to explain ecology, the interconnectedness of life. "And he showed me a pure river of water of life, clear as a crystal, proceeding out of the throne of God," is the way the Bible says the same thing . . . and there are dozens of similar phrases that stress and glorify the wholeness of a river, how it links together not just the intimately connected (*connected, Connecticut*—the very words suggest each other) miles of a single watershed, but the equally vital, equally real watershed of generations, cultures, and epochs revealed in the writing this anthology contains.

Anyone compiling an anthology has to choose between two different approaches—the dry, painstakingly correct kind that focuses primarily on the historical record and tries to include *everything,* or a much more personal, selective, and entertaining kind of approach (slapdash some might say—but this is a word I approve of, its bright, watery sound), where the editor, having read everything on the subject he or she can find, shares with the reader what he has enjoyed the most. It's the second of these approaches this book will follow.

Writers have found many ways to pay homage to the Connecticut through the centuries, and this anthology gathers the best, most readable of these, the ones that give the sense of the river in all its variety. This criterion forms the principal basis for a selection's inclusion: that it must somehow cling to, emphasize, and reflect the river and its valley, never stray so far from its banks (and, as in a flood, the narrative will indeed do some straying) that it can't easily swing back. While I was doing the reading, quite often scenes or descriptions would suddenly come alive off the page, speak directly to my imagination, and thus force their way into this book. It was that way with the description of Lafayette's visit to America in 1824, the image of people standing on the banks, waving handkerchiefs in tribute to their aged hero as he sailed down from Hartford. It was that way when my daughter found Sylvia Plath's poem, "Above the Oxbow," and the phrase "The sunken grizzled-back of the Connecticut." It was that way when, laughing out loud, I discovered that the infamous novel *Peyton Place,* that byword for small-town sin, takes place on the banks of the Connecticut.

And since it is a personal selection, it's only fitting to say a few words about my own connection to the river. One of my earliest memories is of sitting in a car on my way to our family vacation in Vermont, driving along the Connecticut (could it have been near Springfield, Massachusetts, on the old Route 5?) and seeing men removing sandbags in the sunny aftermath of Hurricane Carol—being impressed by the heavy, burlap color of the bags, the way their limp dampness seemed to suggest the residue of a dark and furious power. Much later, trying to find my way as a novelist, I took a temporary job as a tour director on bus tours of New England; we would have lunch our first day out of New York at the old Black Swan restaurant at the river's mouth in Old Saybrook, and, in the five or so minutes it took us to find a parking space, I'd try telling my tourists something of the river's history, improvising as I went along.

At various times I've lived in all four states the river traverses; for the past twenty years, I've lived with my family in the Upper Valley near the northern end of ancient Lake Hitchcock, a musket shot from the river's banks. Almost every morning I stroll to the edge of our meadow and look down at the beautiful line—not quite a curve, but the sinuous beginning of a curve—the river makes between the Vermont hills and the smaller, steeper ridges here in New Hampshire. I spend a great deal of time on the river, probably more than anyone else in this village. I fish the headwaters, fish the tailwaters, canoe on it, kayak, swim, even sail, and feel whole on its water in a way I seldom feel whole anywhere else. I've written about it frequently—books that purport to be about fly fishing but are written more like love letters to a river, wearing my heart on my sleeve. Even in novels that ostensibly have nothing to do with rivers, let alone the Connecticut, I've managed to sneak it in. The idea for this anthology first came as a way of giving back to the river something of value to match all the beauty, joy, and solace I've received.

Me and the Connecticut—brothers, allies, pals. It's the kind of feeling a river leaves in you, the endless downstream flow of it being such an obvious metaphor for time's own inevitable rhythm. Here in New England this note is played even more explicitly than elsewhere. Thinking back on its history, remembering the Puritans who settled here with their burden of piety and guilt, it's hard not to picture the Connecticut being born old, and living through the centuries, not toward senescence, but toward a much delayed and much welcome youth.

And maybe this explains the fellow feeling—that here at the beginning of the twenty-first century, the Connecticut River has at last reached a mature middle age, and so it's no wonder I identify with its complicated intermingling of freshness and hope, pollution and neglect—those alternations between wild surges of energy and lazier, more introspective driftings. "Old Man," Faulkner called the Mississippi, but it's different on the Connecticut, and if either one of us, river or man, is headed toward old age, I'm the one, and the Connecticut—cherished, protected, and valued as the irreplaceable treasure it is—is on its way toward a well-deserved youth, when it will flourish as the centerpiece of the first region in America that puts aside greed as its only ethic and ugliness as its only aesthetic and recovers this beautiful wonder world that on first try we spoiled.

A few words as to method. When I first decided to compile the anthology, I went immediately to those writings I had stumbled upon in the course of many years' reading, to see whether they were as good as I remembered; often, as in the case of Francis Parkman's description of the Deerfield raid, they were even better. Next, I began reading more systematically, scouring libraries in the valley, and soliciting suggestions from people who know the river even better than I do. I eventually came up with over a hundred possible selections, which, with much difficulty, I whittled down to a manageable number. To give a sense of the full richness of the riverine writings, I've included a chapter called "Gleanings," with brief excerpts from fine works I couldn't include at full length.

There were some surprises, some disappointments. The Connecticut has generated more poetry than I suspected, much of it bad, but some of it surprisingly good. There was a noticeable lack of personal essays; for essayists, the Connecticut is something of a neglected subject, perhaps because it was polluted for so many years and essayists had to look elsewhere for inspiration. I read many town histories and they're inevitably disappointing as regards the river; they're often too busy with tracing the pattern of settlement to remember the town's central geographical fact. Conservation writing, alas, tends to be dry and full of technical jargon, or purple and full of pious platitudes, though arguably the most important single piece of writing regarding the Connecticut River is the dry terminology of the 1965 federal Clean Water Act, which made federal funds available for sewage treatment plants. The river tended to come alive in unexpected places—Dickens' description of his riverboat ride from Springfield to Hartford, or the rough-hewn logging ballads collected by Robert Pike.

The anthology sticks mainly to the Connecticut proper, the main stem, and only occasionally strays to the tributaries; many of these, like the White River in Vermont, or the Farmington in Connecticut, could support anthologies of their own. In organizing the book, I decided upon thematic groupings and worried less about chronology, so almost every chapter sweeps forward through the years. Attempts were made to contact the copyright holders of all the material, even though some of these publishers have long since ceased operation; a few times permission to reprint was denied, but for the most part publishers and authors have been very cooperative, and this anthology reflects their generous assistance.

Most of the selections have been shortened, both for reasons of space and to sharpen their focus on the river itself. One of the goals of the anthology is to send readers to the original works to explore even further.

Phil Pochoda of the University Press of New England saw the potential of this anthology right from the start, and has been wonderfully supportive throughout. Erin Wetherell, my daughter, has worked as my research associate and has helped with Internet research on one hand, scissors and paste work on the other. Thanks go to the following, many of whom recommended selections, and some of whom, including my fishing partners of so many years now, Ray Chapin and Tom Ciardelli, have helped me learn more about the river over the years. Adair Mulligan. Steve Long. Ellen Wicklum. Edmund Delaney. Tim Miner. Jere R. Daniell. Jim Lee. John Marshall. Syd Lea. Bill Schomburg. John Connolly. Matthew Wetherell. Betsey Eaton. Maria Graham. Sarah Putnam. Richard Pult. Leslie Cohen. Bill Macleish.

THIS AMERICAN RIVER

Chapter 1

FROM THE SOURCE TO THE SEA

As New England rivers flow, the Connecticut is long—410 miles from the sandbar at its mouth to the sweet, small springs that spawn it.
—*The Connecticut River* by Evan Hill

Three hundred and fifty miles from Mountain to Sea.
—*The Connecticut River* by Edwin Bacon

Its length is 335 miles.
—*The Connecticut River Valley* by Lyman S. Hayes

Up and down the 407-mile length of the Connecticut.
—"On the Connecticut River" by Bill McKibben

A handful of narrative accounts of the Connecticut River have blended together history, natural history, geology, and culture. Almost every author who has tried his or her hand at this task takes a crack at describing the river from its source to the sea, tying her narrative logic to the downstream current (I found no descriptions that go the other way, from the sea to the source). My favorite is from Edwin M. Bacon's epic treatment published in 1906, The Connecticut River. *Mr. Bacon, when his prose gets going, senses the valley's majesty like no one else, and he captures a sense of the river that is now all but lost.*

Over the years only a few writers have deliberately specialized in writing about the Connecticut. One of these is Ellsworth S. Grant, and his introduction to the history of the river, appearing in American Heritage in 1967, is the best general overview of the river's history I know.

As demonstrated by this chapter's epigraphs, there has long been some dispute about one very important Connecticut River fact: just how long is the river, anyway?

The Beautiful River

EDWIN M. BACON

SPRINGING FROM A MOUNTAIN pool and highland rivulets on the ridge of the great Appalachian chain which separates the waters of New England and Canada, the Connecticut winds and curves and bows its gracious way, with here a dashing fall and there a sweep of rapids, down its long, luxurious Valley, through four states, three hundred and sixty miles to the sea. River and Valley in their great sweep from the headwaters to Long Island Sound, though changed in aspect through the building up of towns and cities along the way, and the intrusion of other practical but not always æsthetic works of man, constitute "almost a continuous succession of delightful scenery" now as in President Dwight's time. The predominating beauty of the River is sweet and winsome, rather than proud and majestic. It has its grand moods, but these are brilliant flashes which serve to enhance the exquisiteness of its gentler mien. The Valley's charm is found in the frequency and magnitude of the fertile meadows or intervals,—intervals of common speech,—off-spreading from the River's sides; the procession of splendid terraces rising between intervening glens; and the continuous mountain frame, comprised in the irregular outline of trap and sandstone ranges on either side, interrupted only by the entrance of tributary streams.

From its mountain fastnesses the River "loiters down like a great lord," as Dr. Holmes has imagined, "swallowing up the small proprietary rivulets very quietly as it goes, until it gets proud and swollen, and wantons in huge luxurious oxbows . . . and at last overflows the oldest inhabitants, running in profligate freshets . . . all along the lower shores." In its downward course it flows between New Hampshire and Vermont to their southern bounds; crosses the length of Massachusetts between the "heart of the Commonwealth" and the beautiful Berkshire region; and passes on the eastern side of Connecticut state to the finish.

The Valley's bounding summits on the east are the mountain area of the Appalachian system which extends through New Hampshire, embracing the White Mountain range, and passes in the spurs and ridges of that range through Massachusetts and Connecticut toward Long Island Sound; and on the west, the extension of the Appalachian system through

From Edwin M. Bacon, *The Connecticut River* (New York: G. P. Putnam's Sons, 1907).

Vermont in the Green Mountains—their eastern chain continuing in the Berkshire Hills and the lesser highlands of Massachusetts and Connecticut. Between these primary ranges on either side the Valley expands and contracts, varying greatly in breadth in its sweep from north to south from less than twenty miles to upward of fifty. . . .

The fountain-head of "The Beautiful River" is hidden in the primeval forest, in a remote and solitary region, at the extreme northern point of New Hampshire, near the top of the mountain ridge that marks the Canadian line. It is a mountain pond, or miniature lake, of only a few square acres, lying less than eighty feet below the summit of the elevation known as Mount Prospect, and twenty-five hundred and fifty-one feet above the sea. Surrounded by dense growths of evergreen, the region is rarely penetrated. "Almost the only sound that relieves the monotony of the place," says Joshua H. Huntington in the *Geology of New Hampshire,* "is the croaking of the frogs; and this must be their paradise." This pool is the uppermost of four basins which constitute the River's headwaters, and bears the prosaic name of Fourth Lake. Its outlet is a silvery rill, tumbling along the mountain-side, and flowing down to a second lake half a mile directly south of the Canadian bound. This lake lies at a height of twenty hundred and thirty-eight feet. In prosaic fashion also it is denominated Third Lake—or sometimes Sophy Lake. It is a lake in fact, with an area of three-quarters of a square mile, set in the heart of the mountain forest. On all sides except the south, where is its greatest width, the hills rise almost from its shore. Beside the growth of spruce, firs, and cedar of immense size about it, Professor Huntington remarks its subalpine vegetation. From its outlet, at the southeast corner, the highland stream, now of somewhat larger growth, flows southward to the next basin, Second Lake, six and a half miles below. On its way, five miles or so from Third Lake, the growing stream receives a tributary from the east, also rising near the Canadian boundary, nearly as large as itself. Second Lake, a romantic piece of water, two and three-quarters miles in length, and at its widest a little more than a mile, with shores of graceful contour, deserves a happier name. Its height above the sea is eighteen hundred and eighty-two feet. Near its northern border it receives, besides our highland stream, two tributaries, coming one from the northeast, the other from the northwest. Its forest-framed outlet is on the southwest side. Thence our stream proceeds southwesterly four miles to the fourth basin, First or Connecticut Lake, increasing in beauty as it goes. Twenty rods down from Second Lake the young River drops in a little fall of eighteen feet. Then it descends gradually for a while with here and there deep eddies. Then it grows more rapid, and then for half a mile it dashes between precipitous rocky walls in a series of wild cascades. Then it moves on with gentler flow. Then again with swifter current, and with added volume from two tributary brooks coming down from north and west, it enters the basin.

Connecticut Lake, chief of the River's headwaters, lies sixteen hundred and eighteen feet above sea-level. Picturesquely irregular in outline, its shores in large part with forest fringes broken by green intervals, it is a handsome lake of fine proportions, as becomes a progenitor of so fair a stream. It extends four miles in length, has a breadth at its widest of two and three-quarters miles, and contains nearly three square miles. The neighboring hills are thick with deciduous trees, particularly the maple mingled with the spruce and fir. In the autumn, while the trees are aglow with their rich tints, the heights are often white from the frozen mist that clings to the spears of the evergreen foliage; and so a rare picture is presented, embracing, as Professor Huntington limns it, the blue waters of the lake, the belt of deciduous forest with their gorgeous colors, the dark bands of the evergreens, and the snow-white summits. From the shape of Connecticut Lake Timothy Dwight called it "Heart Lake." But his name did not hold. More poetical and yet more fitting were it called "Metallak," so perpetuating the name of the last of the Abenaquis, "the final hunter of the Coo-ash-ankes over the territory of his fathers," in which it lies.

Now full formed the River emerges from the rocky outlet of this limpid basin, falling abruptly about thirty-seven feet. For the first two and a half miles of its course it is almost a continual rapid, averaging perhaps ten rods in breadth. Then it drops into a more tranquil mood and glides gently along for some four miles, winding west and southwest. Then, and with a sweeping bend in the upper part of the township of Stewartstown (The Stuart of Timothy Dwight's writing), receiving along the way two fair-sized tributaries and lesser streams, it flows again more rapidly to the meeting of the bounds of New Hampshire, Vermont, and Canada. Here, joined by another tributary, Hall's Stream, which comes down from the north and makes the west bound of New Hampshire and Canada, it swings into its long serpentine course, separating New Hampshire and Vermont, southward, through romantic country.

From Connecticut Lake to the meeting of the bounds, or, more exactly, to the mouth of Hall's Stream, at Canaan, Vermont, a distance of about eighteen miles, its descent is set down as five hundred and eighty-three feet. Accordingly at this point its height above the sea is ten hundred and thirty-five feet. Thence the drop becomes very gradual for fifty miles, to the point where the upper section of the Upper Valley ends—at the head of the Fifteen Miles Falls, in Dalton, New Hampshire side,—the descent being only two hundred and five feet in all.

Following the River's downward course from source to mouth the terrace system distinguishing its banks is of first interest. These formations of modified drift, shaped during the formative geological period by action or contraction of the River and incoming tributaries, occur in spaces or "basins" separated by ridges, through which the river has cut or deepened gorges, or connected by the highest terraces. The terraces rise from the River in successive magnificent steps, three, four, five, and sometimes more in number: the lower consisting of the rich alluvial meadows or intervals; the highest being, as the geologists define, remnants of ancient flood-plains annually overflowed by the glacial river at the end of the Champlain period, as are the alluvial meadows now, and varying in height to two hundred feet above the River's present surface.

Dr. Edward Hitchcock, the third president of Amherst College, and first of all geologists to explore the River scientifically, enumerated twenty-two of these terrace-basins from the headwaters to the Sound.

We cannot do better than follow his lines in a rapid survey through their course of the features of the River and the Valley.

Five "basins" are defined in the upper section of the Upper Valley. Along this entire reach, below West Stewartstown and Canaan, the fertile intervals extend on both sides, varying from a half-mile to a mile or more in width. The terraces in the first basin are most developed at the end, in West Stewartstown, and opposite in Canaan. In the narrower second basin, extending only about five miles (to Leamington, Vermont side, and Colebrook, New Hampshire side) some terraces appear of unusual height. At Leamington, Vermont's Monadnock, extending to the river, uplifts its green crown. In the third basin, also short (from Colebrook to Columbia, or Bloomfield, Vermont side), two tributaries, the Mohawk River and Sims's Stream, enter the River from New Hampshire. The fourth basin (from Bloomfield to Guildhall, Vermont, and Northumberland, New Hampshire), with a length of eighteen miles, exhibits a beautiful succession of terraces, particularly fine at Guildhall. Near the northern bound of this basin, the Nulhegan River, part of the uppermost Indian route to Canada, comes in from Vermont at a point below the town of Brunswick; and at the south end of the basin, the Upper Ammonoosuc, from the New Hampshire side, at Northumberland. The fifth basin, another short one (Guildhall to Lunenburg, Vermont, and Lancaster, New Hampshire), advances into the old Coös country, so called by the Indians from the crookedness of the River passing through: the "Garden of New England," as characterized by Major Robert Rogers, with a soldier's eye for beauty, when he penetrated the then primitive region with his Rangers in the French and Indian war times. Lunenburg and Lancaster on their terraced banks are approached through broad meadows, the channel at length widening and gliding with a placid surface. In its meanderings by Lancaster the river's drop is said to be less than two feet in a flow of some ten miles. As illustrative of its twistings in this lovely reach, the local historian tells how in hunting days a sportsman might, at one point, "stand in New Hampshire, fire across Vermont, and lodge his ball in New Hampshire again." On the Lancaster line, Israel's River, rising in cataracts in the White Mountains, empties into the stream; and at Dalton, just below Lancaster, is Israel's companion, John's River, having started from the mountain town of Jefferson, through which Israel's also flows: both named for old-time hunters, Israel and John Glines, brothers, each of whom had a hunting-camp on them.

South of Lancaster the base of the White Mountains pushes the channel twenty miles westward. The Gardner Mountains range, crossing the Valley, and occupying the angle of the bend at Dalton, makes the Fifteen-Miles Falls, over twenty miles in length. These rapids, beginning at Dalton in a great eddy, continue through the long romantic passage excavated by the River, to Monroe, New Hampshire side, and Barnet, Vermont, finishing at Barnet in a pitch of a few feet, known as McIndoe's Falls, from a Scotch lumberman established here among the earliest settlers in the region. From the head of the rapids, or from the mouth of John's River, the descent is rapid, three hundred and seventy feet in twenty miles. The altitude of the foot of McIndoe's Falls above the sea is four hundred and thirty-two feet.

The Fifteen-Miles Falls, heading the lower section of the Upper Valley in New Hampshire and Vermont, occupy the sixth and seventh of Dr. Hitchcock's basins. From their foot this section of the Valley is comparatively level, and again with a southerly course. About a mile below McIndoe's Falls the Passumpsic River empties into the stream from its picturesque run down the Vermont hills. From the mouth of the Passumpsic to the Massachusetts line, a direct distance of one hundred and eighteen miles, our River's flow is one hundred and thirty-seven miles, with an average descent of two feet to the mile. The Fifteen-Miles falls separate the old Coös country into the Upper and Lower Coös.

Below McIndoe's Falls the hills recede and the broad alluvial meadows again intervene and form the particular features of the eighth basin, which extends from McIndoe's Falls to South Ryegate, Vermont side. In the succeeding five basins (Ryegate to Norwich, Vermont, and Hanover, New Hampshire) a succession of intervals, rising terraces, and mountain views delight the eye. These basins comprise a distance of about thirty miles. The terraces are especially marked in the upper part, at Newbury and Bradford, Vermont, and Haverhill, New Hampshire; and at the lower end in Hanover, providing Dartmouth College with a beautiful seat. The most extensive intervals are between Newbury, Vermont, and Haverhill, New Hampshire side, and between Bradford, Vermont, and Piermont, New Hampshire,—the region of the Lower Coös. Within this reach they are at greater breadth than at any other point in the Valley. At Newbury Wells River enters the stream; at Bradford, Wait's River; and just above Haverhill (from Bath), the Lower Ammonoosuc: all important tributaries. Between the mouths of Wells and Wait's Rivers the intervals spread from half a mile to a mile in width, the River twisting through them in Haverhill and Newbury in little and great oxbows. East of Haverhill, Moosilauk, the southwest extension of the White Mountains, towers four thousand seven hundred and ninety feet above the River. The hills back of Haverhill rising in procession to this rugged peak appear in full view from the opposite banks of Newbury. Midway between Haverhill and Hanover, Mount Cuba, in Orford, trending toward the River, with an altitude of two thousand nine hundred and twenty-seven feet above the sea, enriches the landscape.

Features more varied characterize the fourteenth basin, which extends from Norwich to Mount Ascutney, in Wethersfield, Vermont, the highest elevation lying wholly in the Valley. Between Hanover and the railroad centre of White River Junction are the Upper White-River Falls, at "Wilder's," splendid as a spectacle and practical as the motive-power for great paper-mills, transforming wood pulp into newspaper stock. At White River Junction the White River, the largest stream in Vermont on the east side of the mountains, produces as it enters some interesting terraces. At Lebanon, on the New Hampshire side, the Mascomy River comes in; and below, from the Vermont side, the Quechee, or Otto Quechee, at North Hartland: both contributing to the Quechee or Sumner Falls, two miles down from its mouth. Terraces beautify the banks of Lebanon and North Hartland, and of Cornish and Windsor on either side below. The triple-crowned Ascutney finishing this basin, sweeps close to the River, a graceful cone, independent of any range, and rising three thousand one hundred and sixty-eight feet above the sea. From near its top down quite to its base three deep valleys course, in size resembling one another, whence comes its Indian name, which signifies "three brothers." The next two basins, extending between Ascutney and Bellows Falls, about twenty-five miles, show terraces in fullest form at the upper part, most notably in Wethersfield, the little village south of Ascutney's base, North Charlestown, New Hampshire side, and Springfield, Vermont. Four tributaries enter in these reaches; Sugar River, at Claremont and Little Sugar, at North Charlestown, from New Hampshire; and Black

River at Springfield and Williams River at Rockingham, from Vermont,—the latter the historic junction where, three miles above Bellows Falls, the "Deerfield captives" of 1703–4 held their first Sunday service; in commemoration of which the river was afterward named for John Williams, the minister.

At Bellows Falls the aspect changes and the loitering stream becomes a foaming torrent in a narrow strait. Here Kilburn Peak, rising abruptly twelve hundred feet and pressing close on the east side, and steep hills crowding in on the west side, bound this gorge, through which the River, not more than forty rods in width, hurries in whirling rapids with spirit and dash. Entering with a plunge at the brink over a ledge of gneiss which cuts the current into two channels, it rushes and leaps in zigzags to a grand finish in a great eddy nearly fifty feet below. It is an animated spectacle indeed, but scarcely meeting the exuberant description of Samuel Peters, the romancing historian of Connecticut, a hundred and more years ago, who told of the tops of the bounding hills "intercepting the clouds," and of the water consolidated by pressure and swiftness "between the pinching rocks to such a degree of induration that an iron bar cannot be forced into it!" The village of Bellows Falls perched on "the island" and the steep west banks, its terraces among the highest in the Valley, adds to the charm of the surrounding landscape. The blemishes in the picture, from an æsthetic point of view, are the factories crowding on the River's edge below the gorge. These, however, are endurable blemishes, for they bring employment, comfort, and wealth to this favored town. The first bridge that ever spanned the River was built here. This great feat was accomplished in 1785, and gave added distinction to the place.

In the next basin, extending to Brattleborough, seventeen miles, the River resumes its tranquil flow. In this reach terraces are beautifully developed along the first five miles of Westminster, adjoining Bellows Falls. From the Westminster side Saxton's River enters the winding stream; and at Walpole, opposite, Cold River, after flowing around Kilburn Peak. The intervals here broadening on both sides give these rural towns a lovely river fringe. As Brattleborough is approached the Valley again narrows till it becomes almost a defile, and at this elevated terraced town the River passes through another gorge. This strait is made by the closing in of the precipitous Wantastiquet Mountain, thirteen hundred and sixty feet high, on the New Hampshire side, and of the west-side hills culminating in the crest of the Green Mountains. Toward either end of the village, north and south, two tributaries join the River but a mile apart, thus producing some remarkable and complicated terraces. These tributaries are West River, of considerable size, and Whetstone Brook, a brawling stream, both in picturesque setting. Attractive terraces also appear north of Wantastiquet, on the New Hampshire side, in Chesterfield opposite Brattleborough and Dummerston. Far across the Valley, twenty miles off on the eastern bound, grand Monadnock, in the charming hill town of Dublin, is discerned rising in majestic isolation to its altitude of more than three thousand feet.

The eighteenth basin, beginning at Brattleborough, extends past the remainder of New Hampshire and Vermont and penetrates Massachusetts for twenty miles or so. Terraces reappear numerously in the northern part of Vernon, the lowest Vermont town; and along Hinsdale, the New Hampshire town opposite Vernon. At Hinsdale the Ashuelot, the last New Hampshire tributary, enters the River with a royal sweep, having cut its narrow channel through mountain ranges. To the mouth of the Ashuelot, within four miles of the Massachusetts line, our River has coursed from its source two hundred and eight miles, with a descent from Connecticut Lake of fourteen hundred and twelve feet. At this point the River lies two hundred and six feet above the ocean level. Its whole length in New Hampshire, following its principal bends, is in round figures two hundred and thirty-six miles, the distance in the direct course being two hundred and one miles.

At the Massachusetts line the primary mountains crowd down, again narrowing the Valley. Across this state the Valley's stretch from north to south is nearly fifty miles, with a varying but averaging width of about twenty miles. It broadens toward the south and narrows at the southern end as at the north, between close-pressing hills.

The River enters Massachusetts meandering in long graceful curves through the border town of Northfield, the east-side village rising from the meadows in broad terraces, a picture of quiet beauty as seen in the summer sunshine from the car windows of a railroad train on the opposite bank. The eighteenth basin continues a few miles farther down, ending at the mouth of Miller's River, the first Massachusetts tributary, which flows into the stream in the southeast corner of the west-side town of Gill. Westward of this basin, rising in high ridges between Gill and the adjoining town of Greenfield, a range of greenstone appears, which, trending southward, enters the Valley and extends along its central parts through Massachusetts, twice crossing the river; and thence continuing in the chain that, lower down, cuts across the State of Connecticut and terminates in West Rock, at New Haven. This interior mountain range, with the River's magnificent curves and superb ox-bows and frequent meanders between deep meadows and terraced banks, diversifies the scenery and gives to much of the Valley in Massachusetts a charm of its own distinct from the beauties of other parts.

Through this region, extending from Northfield across the two states to New Haven, where the River had its earlier outlet in the Sound, lie the "new red sandstone" formations in which were found, some sixty years ago, between the strata of the bed, those marvellous fossil footprints of ancient bipeds, the discussion of which by savants of that time gave a great new zest to geological research in the Valley. Ages back, they say, before the globe was fit for man, these strange creatures roamed the shores of the estuary which then was here, and left their impress in the mud clay, the rock in its plastic state, on the slopes and shallow bottom when the tide was out. So Dr. Hitchcock, first to examine scientifically and describe these triassic tracks, recorded. Huge birds were they, as he portrayed, four times as large as the African ostrich. They reached in height twelve feet and more, in weight four hundred to eight hundred pounds, and had a stride of from thirty to sixty inches. With them were other gigantic races, for the high temperature which then prevailed was seemingly favorable to a giant-like development of every form of life. The footprints, thousands of which Dr. Hitchcock examined, were found in the bottom of the Valley in places scattered between Gill, in Massachusetts, and Middletown, in Connecticut, a linear distance of about eighty miles. Dr. Hitchcock's theory was that the colossal birds passed over the surface in flocks, as indicated by rows of tracks found in certain localities, among them the southeast part of Northampton. . . .

The nineteenth basin extends from the Miller's River junction in Gill to the conical peak of Mount Toby, or Mattawampe, in Sunderland, east side, in which the interior range reappears at its first crossing of the River. At the beginning of this reach of only eight or ten miles the River's course is sharply turned to the northwest. Thus it runs for about a mile between picturesque banks. Then bending westerly it flows in that direction for two miles, through a "horse race" and "the narrows," Gill lying on the north and the town of Montague on the south. In the narrows it turns again abruptly northward. After a mile or so in rapids it plunges over a rocky precipice at Turner's Falls. Then making a great semi-circle, or bow, of three miles in extent, it resumes its southward way, and so approaches the basin's end. Along this roving course numerous terraces appear on either side, some of considerable extent. Greenfield on its hills lies on the north and west of the great bow. At the upper bend Falls River, coursing down the side of Greenfield from the north, enters the stream. Next south of Greenfield beautiful Deerfield lies, back of a deep strip of meadow extending the town's full length, while the symmetrical stretch of Deerfield Mountains continues the interior range from the Gill and Greenfield ridges. At the town's north end Deerfield River empties into our stream, having come down from the Green Mountains and the Berkshire Hills through its own rich valley, bringing along with it Green River from Greenfield, which it receives near its mouth. At the south end, or in South Deerfield, the bluff Sugarloaf peaks, in which the Deerfield chain culminates, stand out boldly, with Mount Toby looming high on the opposite side of the River.

In the twentieth basin the Valley widens, and here the striking characteristics of the terraces are their width. Along the plains and over the rising banks spread on either side the historic towns of Hadley and Hatfield; Amherst back of Hadley, and Northampton, the "Meadow City," fair seats of colleges. Opposite Northampton, in South Hadley, the River circling through the splendid gorge between, Mount Holyoke lifts its graceful front. Here the interior range makes its second crossing, and attains its highest elevation in Mount Tom, on the Northampton side, eleven hundred and twenty feet above the sea. Thence the slopes of this range, called in this part the Holyoke range, trend southward with the River's course to the lower Massachusetts line. At Northampton, Mill River, a pretty feature of the rural city, joins the stream.

The twenty-first is the longest of all the basins, its extent being fifty-three miles through the remainder of Massachusetts and across Connecticut state to Middletown, with a varying width of from three to ten miles. In the Massachusetts part the River has an average width of twelve hundred feet, and expands to the greatest breadth before the Connecticut state line is met. All along this reach the terrace system is finely developed, although the terraces do not average high. The highest reach is the gorge terrace south of Mount Holyoke, two hundred and ninety-eight feet above the sea. Below Mount Holyoke South Hadley Falls break the River's course. On the west side lies the busy mill city of Holyoke, with its remarkable hydraulic works. On the east side again, below South Hadley, Chicopee, also a city of mills, occupies the River's banks. Just above the city the Chicopee River with its branches,—bringing the waters of Swift, Ware and Quaboag rivers from the eastward,—contributes to our stream by several mouths. Next below, the city of Springfield rises on a succession of terraces. Here another Mill River enters the stream, on its downward course furnishing water-power for the United States arsenal, and passing through lower portions of the city. On the opposite bank in West Springfield, with the Agawam or Westfield River, flowing down from the Berkshires, emptying into our river by two mouths. Next appear the rural towns of Agawam on the west, and Longmeadow on the east, both extending to the Connecticut State line. From either side several picturesque brooks drop into the River along the way. The most important of these, Pecowsic and Longmeadow Brooks, enter respectively at the north and the south parts of Longmeadow township.

At Springfield the River has descended to a point only forty feet above the sea-level. Here and from Holyoke above it has become of sufficient depth to float vessels of considerable size. At Longmeadow it has its greatest width, for a mile or more expanding to twenty-one hundred feet from bank to bank.

Crossing the Connecticut State line the Enfield Dam is soon reached. Thence the course is through the Enfield Rapids for five and a quarter miles, over a rocky bed, in parts between bluff banks, to Windsor Locks. Part way down King's Island, its west side a rock bluff, divides the channel. Opposite Windsor Locks, on the east side, is Warehouse Point, the landmark of earliest colonial times, which happily has retained its old name. Below Windsor Locks lies "ancient Windsor," now in three towns on either side of the River. At East Windsor the Scantic River joins our stream; at South Windsor, Stoughton's Brook and Podunk River; and at Old Windsor, the Tunxis, or Farmington River, the latter, the principal tributary in this state, having its rise on the east slope of the Green Mountains, and approaching its mouth through the Talcott range, part of the Valley's west bounding summits in this region. Over the plains and hills next below Old Windsor spreads the "Charter City" of Hartford, with the tall yellow dome of the State Capitol high above the mass of roofs, glistening in the sun. Here Park River, the "Little River" of earlier days, contributes to the stream. Opposite, on the east side, lies East Hartford, connected by a bridge with the parent city.

In the reach, ten miles in length, from the foot of Enfield Rapids to Hartford, the River has run with slight curvatures directly south, averaging fifteen hundred feet in width, through intervals from a third of a mile to a mile wide, which are overflowed in seasons of freshets. Below Hartford the course becomes more irregular. Here the changes in the River's bed, constantly going on through the wearing of the alluvial banks on the bends, are especially marked. Along by old Wethersfield the River is said now to flow diagonally across the bed it had two centuries ago, through the shifting of the clay and sand forming its banks from one part of a bend to another; an island of more than a mile in length that then divided the channel having completely disappeared in the process. In another section, six miles below Hartford, the same authority (Charles L. Burdette in the *Memorial History of Hartford County*) states that in a quite recent period, within twelve years of his writing (1885), the River was moved its whole width to the eastward. Between Old Wethersfield and Glastonbury, on the east side, great bends are now made in the crooked course. At South Glastonbury Roaring Brook drops into the stream. From the south end of Wethersfield the course resumes the southward direction and continues between fertile intervals close backed by hills, alongside the towns of Rocky Hill and Cromwell on the west, and Portland, with its quarries, on the east. Then another sharp turn is made, and the stream swings with a long sweep southwestward to Middletown, receiving in this generous bend another tributary, Sabethe River, from the west.

The last basin, from Middletown to the Sound, extends by the River's winding way, about thirty-eight miles. At Middletown the River is half a mile in width, winding yet in "delightful prospects," as Timothy Dwight found it. Below Middletown the primary mountains again close in, making a deep ravine through which, with occasional small openings of meadows, the River courses, eastward, south, and southwestward, to its finish. From the bend in which Middletown lies the run is directly east for about five miles. In this reach the river makes the "Straits," a narrow pass through high ranges, of about a mile in length, in which the stream is contracted to a breadth in places of but forty rods. Below, at Middle Haddam, a sharp turn is taken southward. So the course continues for about three and a half miles, when another bend is made eastward, between Haddam on one side and East Haddam on the other. At East Haddam, Salmon River, the last tributary of note, enters from the hills in a little cataract. From East Haddam the course takes a generally southeastward direction, with numerous windings, to the Sound. Along the way, in the upper parts between hilly banks sloping downward to the River, old towns of historic flavor are passed on either side. Between Essex and Old Lyme the channel broadens perceptibly; and again at the mouth by Old Saybrook.

The entrance to the Sound is marked picturesquely as well as practically by a dazzling white lighthouse on Saybrook Point, and another at the end of a jetty from the same west side.

The Mainstream of New England

ELLSWORTH S. GRANT

"A RIVER IS THE most human and companionable of all inanimate things," wrote the famous clergyman-educator Henry van Dyke. "It has a life, a character, a voice of its own." Everyone, therefore, has his

From Ellsworth S. Grant, "The Mainstream of New England," *American Heritage* (April 1967).

favorite stream, from Father Tiber to the mighty Pedernales. Ancient man revered and deified great rivers like the Ganges and the Nile, and along them have grown trade, settlement, and civilization.

The Connecticut River, to be sure, is neither one of the longest nor in any way the most ancient of this great company, but it fits van Dyke's description like a glove. Some artists have thought it compares for beauty, in places, with the Hudson and the Rhine. It is the only body of water which runs the full length of New England, some four hundred miles from mountain lakes near the Canadian border to Long Island Sound. Once the hunting and fishing grounds of peaceful river Indians—among them the Podunks, Wongunks, and others—then a trading post for the enterprising Dutch, and finally a new territory for land-hungry English settlers, the Connecticut River valley saw many firsts in the history of the new land. Most of these occurred along the seventy miles of riverway within what is now the state of Connecticut. Here were born both the Puritan divine Jonathan Edwards and the inventor of the steamboat, John Fitch; the first cigars, the first canal, the first vessel to engage in the West Indian trade, the first American-built warship (the Oliver Cromwell, out of Essex), the first bicycle factory, all these came into being along the Connecticut. The valley is also the home of the oldest continuously published daily newspaper in America, the Hartford Courant (originally the Connecticut Courant), which dates back to 1764. Perhaps the most significant, this is the place where, in drawing up the Fundamental Orders of Connecticut, the founders of the colony brought to birth the world's first written constitution which created a representative government.

The little colony of Connecticut had an impact upon the development of the United States far beyond its size and population. In the nineteenth century, that keen observer of America Alexis de Tocqueville summed up this fact in a speech to Americans celebrating the Fourth of July in Paris in 1835. Recounting, in his heavily accented English, an illuminating experience he had had in the gallery of the House of Representatives in Washington, he recalled:

> . . . I held up one map of the Confederation in my hand. Dere was von leetle yellow spot dey called Connect-de-coot. I found by the Constitution he was entitled to six of his boys to represent him on dat floor. But ven I make de acquaintance personelle with de member, I find dat more than tirty of the Representatif on dat floor was born in Connect-de-coot. And then ven I was in the gallery of the House of the Senat, I find de Constitution permits Connect-de-coot to send two of his boys to represent him in dat Legislature. But once more . . . I find nine of de Senator was born in Connect-de-coot . . . the leetle yellow spot . . . make de clock-peddler, de school master, and de senator. De first, give you time: the second, tell you what you do with him; and de sird make your law and your civilization.

In his recollection of Tocqueville's remarks, quoted here, the Congregationalist historian William S. Fowler may have made the accent a bit theatrical, but the sentiments are undoubtedly genuine.

But let us return to where the story begins: the river was called the Quinnehtukqut by the Indians, meaning "long estuary" or "long tidal river," because the tide rises and falls as far north as the Enfield rapids, almost at the Massachusetts line, sixty miles from its mouth. The Connecticut twists and eddies through stretches of woods, meadows, and marshes that delight the eye of the modern adventurer as much as they must have pleased the Dutch explorer Adriaen Block when he sailed upstream in 1614. Block had been preparing to return to Holland from the island of Manhattan with a cargo of furs when his ship burned. He and his crew then built the *Onrust* (the name means "unrest" or "restless") and continued along the coast to the Connecticut, which he called De Versche, "the Freshwater" river. (The explorer is memorialized by Block Island, just outside the point where long Island Sound meets the Atlantic.)

In the state to which it gave its name the river varies in width from 600 to 2,100 feet; it is creased with shifting shoals that have always made navigation difficult for all but vessels with the shallowest draft, while the sand bar at its exit into the sound—formed by the conflux of river and tidal currents—prevents any great port from rising at its mouth. The historian Benjamin Trumbull once observed that "as its banks are generally low, it forms and fertilizes a vast tract of the finest meadow," the unique sandy soil of which proved ideal for growing the Indian plant called tobacco, still an important crop in the Connecticut Valley. Especially in the last thirty miles of its course the river is an impressive spectacle: the rugged cliffs of the Middletown Straits, the gentle hills that turn purple in the twilight, the tree-covered islets, and everywhere the quiet villages with their tall white church spires and gracious homes built by river captains and merchants.

Immense schools of fish once populated the river. Salmon were so plentiful in colonial days that it was prohibited to feed them to bond servants more than thrice weekly. During the spawning season, one legend has it, a man with snowshoes could cross the river on their backs. In Old Saybrook's South Cove one Elias Tully caught 3,700 salmon in one haul. Herring, striped bass, and shad also ran in great numbers. The latter sold for as little as a penny apiece, and people who would eat them were considered of pretty mean estate. Indians fertilized their cornfields with shad, but later the ingenious colonists found a market for them by salting and packing the fish in hogsheads and shipping them as far as Portugal.

What attracted the white man to the Connecticut River valley was, first of all, trade and, soon after, land. Block's voyage upstream as far as the Enfield rapids had resulted in the exchange of goods for beaver pelts which the Indians had brought downriver in their long narrow dugouts. But no sooner had the Dutch erected—in 1633—a little fort and trading post called House of Hope, just below the present site of Hartford, than the English, both by sea and land, descended upon the valley. At the same time that the Pequots, a warlike division of the Mohegan, were making the initial sale of riverfront property to the Dutch (for, it is said, "1 piece of duffel . . . , 6 axes, 6 kettles, 18 knives, one sword blade, 1 pr. of shears, some toys, and a musket"). Podunk sachems were journeying to Boston and Plymouth to solicit English settlers with promises of corn and beaver skins and glowing descriptions of the "exceeding fruitfulness of the country." What the Indians along the river wanted was protection against the hostile neighboring Pequots. The bait was taken when, in the fall of 1633, William Holmes and his followers settled at what became Windsor, Connecticut.

During the next few years groups from Massachusetts led by Thomas Hooker and others made settlements along the river at Hartford and Wethersfield. Thus was established the nucleus of the Connecticut colony. One eminent historian, Charles M. Andrews, maintains, in the face of some skepticism, that "every acre . . . was honestly obtained." In any case, the land was worthless to the unwarlike river tribes without the Englishman's musket. Soon the settlers and their Indian friends had to contend with and later decimate the Pequots. Eventually most of the red men disappeared before the onslaught of the white man's diseases and the conversion of their hunting and fishing paradise into a land of villages and cultivated fields. Now the English had only the Dutch to deal with.

Considering their different objectives, it was inevitable that the English in their new settlements and the Dutch in their little fort would clash. Rarely on the frontier have agricultural and trading societies been able to live peacefully together. Out of this confrontation came the word that is now universally applied to citizens of the United States, "Yankee." It probably derives from the Dutch diminutive of Jan, Janke (Johnny in English), and then, as now, one of the implications of the term was "rascal" or "brigand." It was a common nickname among the Dutch buccaneers along the Spanish Main. Thus it was natural for the Dutch traders to brand the Englishmen who coveted the rich meadowland around their post *janke* pirates.

With families to feed, the Yankee newcomers soon commenced to encroach on Dutch territory, planting life-giving corn and other crops. The Dutch were too few and the English multiplying too fast for the struggle to be even; unable to resolve their legal claims and unwilling to risk open warfare, the Hollanders finally sailed downriver for good in 1654. A hundred years later the Yankee, by then a trader par excellence, was the butt of jokes everywhere he appeared. But he always bore proudly the nickname which had come to connote, in addition to "rascal," one who was shrewd, inventive, and practical. . . .

One of the warmest debates over American history has been centered around the question of whether or not Thomas Hooker's concept of government and the Fundamental Orders which he persuaded the Connecticut colonists to adopt in 1639 were really democratic. It is undoubtedly too much to claim that they were democratic in the modern sense of the word. Hooker's departure from Massachusetts was primarily motivated by a desire, not to abolish the Puritan state, but to found a less rigidly theocratic one of his own. Hooker's ideas were much closer to our modern notions than were those prevalent in Massachusetts Bay. "The foundation of authority," Hooker theorized, "is laid, firstly, in the free consent of the people." Even if by "people" Hooker meant the "admitted inhabitants" and freemen who were competent, church-going Congregationalists and land owners, his scheme was much more inclusive than that of the Boston theocrats who limited the control of government to those few church members who were, in their eyes, "spiritually elect."

Affairs in Connecticut towns were initially conducted by committees appointed in a meeting of the whole electorate; later this function was taken over by elected town officers, subsequently called selectmen. In practice, a very few men—ministers, merchants, and lawyers from the leading families, the so-called Standing Order—controlled the government well into the nineteenth century. Town meetings were held monthly, called at nine in the morning by the beating of a drum or the blowing of a trumpet from the top of the meeting house. Since the same building was used for both religious and civic functions, practically speaking Church and State were one until the constitution of 1818 disestablished the Congregational Church as the state-supported religion. But the town meeting survives: 118 of Connecticut's 169 towns retain this form of self-rule.

The next settlement after the three original river towns was Saybrook, which played a leading role in the river's history because of its strategic location near the mouth. In 1635 a group of Puritan lords, having obtained a grant from Robert Rich, Earl of Warwick, to the Saybrook territory, sent over a tough but fair-minded soldier and military engineer, Lion Gardiner, at a salary of 100 pounds per annum, to build a fort and take charge of the defenses of the colony. In April, 1636, during an Indian siege, a son was born to Gardiner and his Dutch wife, the first recorded birth of a white child in the colony. William Fiennes, First Viscount of

Saye and Sele, and Robert Greville, Lord Brooke, and their fellow adventurers hoped to make Saybrook a Puritan refuge from royal persecution. But though a number of prominent Puritans were interested in the scheme, only George Fenwick and his lovely redheaded lady, Alice, ever came to claim their share of the land. The Fenwicks' dream of building a manor house was shattered by the marauding Pequots, while the fickle sandbar at the river's mouth spoiled their plan of making Saybrook Point a port.

Finally, in 1644, Fenwick sold the fort to the General Court at Hartford. The terms required the colonists to pay him twopence per bushel for "all graine that shall be exported out of this River for ten yeares ensueing," sixpence per hundredweight for "Biskett," and twenty shillings for each hogshead of beaver. Later, the terms were changed to a flat payment of 180 pounds annually, one third in good wheat, one third in peas, and one third in rye or barley. After Lady Fenwick's death in 1645 George Fenwick returned to England. But Lion Gardiner bought an island off the tip of Long Island, named it after himself, and thus established a manor which has remained in the Gardiner family to this day.

The deal between Fenwick and the General Court at Hartford was typical of the barter system which the Yankees used from the beginning along the river highway and, in time, refined to the highest degree. The first building erected at the confluence of the Farmington and Connecticut rivers, at Windsor in 1633, was the Plymouth trading house, which in prefabricated form had been transported over water by William Holmes from Plymouth, Massachusetts.

William Pynchon, at Springfield, Massachusetts, was the first Englishman to establish a thriving river trade; because of the rapids at Enfield he built, in 1636, a warehouse just above Windsor, where he could unload his shallops and pinnaces and move the goods overland to Springfield or transfer the cargo to flatboats poled by a dozen stout men who, their labors eased by ample consumption of West Indian kill-devil, braved the rapids and reached Springfield by water. Pynchon's trade with the Indians was mostly in pelts, which he shipped to Boston. In fact beaver skins were such a common medium of exchange that when merchants struck the first coins or tokens, long before the issuance of government currency, that specie bore a crude image of the valuable little animal and the coins were popularly called beavers.

It was not long before Indian maize, tobacco, and other crops were being exported, not only to Massachusetts but after 1650 to England and the West Indies. Sailing masters found that the voyage upriver was in many ways more hazardous and certainly more frustrating than the ocean passage to the Indies. It usually took as long to sail from Saybrook to Wethersfield, two weeks, as to reach the mouth of the river from the land of rum and sugar. There was no dependable channel, there were no markers, no cuts through the sand bars—and no sailing was allowed on the Sabbath; they had to contend against strong tidal currents and fickle southwest winds impeded by the hills. To beat to windward in such a narrow body of water was nigh impossible. Frequently, a vessel had to be towed by the crew, who carried a line ashore or who "walked" the ship by kedging an anchor upstream. Captain Lord of Glastonbury, in his sloop *Speedwell,* took twenty-six days to cover the ten miles from Glastonbury to Rocky Hill and wrote in his journal: "We can neither warp, tow, nor sail, and I feare me we never schalle." Next to the big bar at Saybrook, which had only six feet of water over it, the greatest obstacle in the seventeenth century was the double oxbow bend at Wethersfield, with its 180 degree turns, which forced river captains to anchor below Hartford for days and weeks at a time—and, incidentally, made Wethersfield the leading port of the period. Nature solved this problem in 1698, when a spring flood almost straightened the course of the river.

The colonists' dependence upon the river as the main artery of trade and travel for two centuries stimulated the growth of a prosperous shipbuilding industry. The first ship was launched at Wethersfield in 1649. She was the *Tryall,* built by Thomas Deming, whose yard was to keep busy until the middle of the nineteenth century. By 1700 small shipyards from Saybrook to Windsor were turning out vessels up to 100 tons. They started copying the chunky, high-pooped English design, but soon turned to building the distinctive river sloops with their sharply raked masts and long bowsprits set at a sharp angle. Sometimes they were rigged with a square topsail and topgallant and carried an enormous square foresail to run before the wind.

Although seaworthy, the river sloops were hard to handle. Even so, often sailed by only a man and a boy, with livestock on deck, they made regular trips to the Caribbean, where they cruised from island to island, bartering Connecticut produce. They then returned to river wharves, where they became floating stores. Advertising their wares in the *Courant,* the owners offered to exchange them for salt pork, wheat, lumber, tobacco, onions, horses, and cloth, which they carried south on their next voyage. Rum was by far their leading import, and tippling was so prevalent that an early almanac contained this ditty:

Ill husbands now in taverns sit
And spend more money than they git.
Calling for drink, and drinking greedy
Tho many of them poor and needy—

While their sloops were venturing to distant horizons, the colonists had to find ways of crossing the river itself in order to carry on their daily tasks. There was no bridge until 1808. Cable-operated ferries quickly appeared. The first was Bissell's at Windsor in 1648; it was operated by the family for three generations. For a while the Hartford ferry used a horse on a treadmill—enclosed in a cage to prevent contact with passengers—which turned a paddlewheel amidships. On a 1794 map of the state six ferries appear; as many as fifteen existed from time to time, including private ones like that of gunmaker Sam Colt (the largest employer on the river), which transported employees from the Colt armory across to East Hartford. (There are still two ferries in operation.) The Chester-to-Hadlyme ferry was originally a sailboat belonging to a man named Warner, who presented it to his son as a wedding present with the stipulation that if he earned more than thirty dollars a year in tolls, the excess must be returned to his father. When a traveller wished to cross there, he blew on a tin horn attached to a large maple tree near the landing.

By the middle of the eighteenth century shipbuilding on the river had reached its peak, and it continued to prosper almost without interruption for another hundred years, despite two wars and the introduction of competing forms of transportation. Over seventy vessels, locally built and owned, and employing nearly 500 men in their crews, were in service in the mid-seventeen-hundreds. Haddam had "nine great shippes" on her ways at one time, Essex thirty. At this time the sloops were giving way to larger craft like the new schooners and brigs. An English officer visiting Hartford in 1764 wrote in his journal: "Here they build vessels, for the Lumber Trade to the West Indies, from 100 to 150 tons, and float them down in Freshes, in Spring and Fall." When the Revolution came, the town of Essex gave the colonies their first homemade warship, the 24-gun *Oliver Cromwell,* built by Uriah Hayden. Her twelve-foot draft made her the largest craft to cross the Saybrook bar, and before being captured by the British three years later she succeeded in taking nine prizes. In the course of the war, the Connecticut navy comprised thirteen vessels, in addition to nearly three hundred commissioned privateers. The river itself was defended by the fort at Old Saybrook, with a battery of six guns and a twenty-man garrison.

After the victory of the colonies, river commerce revived. The increasingly larger and heavier ships plying the Connecticut forced merchants to do something about the main obstacle to more profitable cargoes—the lack of a dependable channel from Hartford to the mouth. In 1773 the first real move to improve navigation had been made by the assembly when, goaded by the Hartford merchant Jeremiah Wadsworth, it had voted to raise money by lottery for marking the Saybrook bar. Still, the average depth was less than six feet. In 1784 one of Wadsworth's captains advised him that he had brought a load of salt to New London and there engaged two small craft to carry about a thousand bushels to Hartford, and he hoped this action would "lighten the ship so she will go over Saybrook Bar with a common Tide." Even at high tide loaded sloops and schooners could not reach Hartford under sail. At great expense and delay it was often necessary to warp them across the sand bars or unload their cargoes into lighters below Middletown. As a result of Wadsworth's petition to the legislature, the Union Company was chartered in 1800 to deepen the river bed below Hartford, to construct wharves, and to collect tolls to pay for their improvements.

The War of 1812, highly unpopular in New England, brought about a coastal blockade and caused the Connecticut River merchants severe hardships. During the conflict English men-of-war boldly invaded the river, set fire to Essex, and burned twenty-three ships. To reduce their risks, the Hartford merchants entered into partnerships, taking shares in various vessels and adventures. There was even joint underwriting of ship insurance, at 5½ or 6 per cent interest, with individual liability commonly limited to 100 pounds. These experiences were an important factor in making Hartford a world insurance capital.

The river merchants were the center of the power structure of this period; they made up what Vernon Parrington called "a small, interlocking directorate [that] controlled religion, business, and politics." Staunch Federalists, good Congregationalists, they were the bulwark of a social system that did not change until the Industrial Revolution. Their fortunes, based in most instances on smaller ships, were not as impressive as those of the great Massachusetts shipping moguls with their ocean ports; but in proportion to the total population of the colony there were more shipping fortunes. Called the "river gods," these shipowners and merchants supplied the American armies of several wars, helping to make Connecticut famous as the arsenal of the nation.

A new era arrived suddenly for the Connecticut in 1815, when the steamboat *Fulton* churned upriver between the scows and sloops cluttering the channel and docked in Hartford for thousands to see. Rigged as a sloop, in case sails were needed—as indeed they were—she made a dreadful din with her wood-fired engine, which gave off sharp, staccato blasts of steam. The *Courant* enthused: "Indeed it is hardly possible to conceive that anything of its Kind can exceed her, in elegance and convenience." She was designed by Robert Fulton, the man popularly acknowledged to be the inventer of the steamboat, despite the fact that John Fitch, a native of Windsor who died by his own hand in penury, had successfully used steam to propel vessels seventeen years before Fulton. "The day will come," Fitch had prophesied, "when some more powerful man will get fame and riches from my invention; but nobody will believe that poor John Fitch can do anything worthy of attention."

Four years after the *Fulton*'s debut a steamboat was launched at Hartford and functioned as a towboat along the river. There quickly followed regular steamboat service thrice weekly on the *Enterprize* of Captain James Pitkin, who advertised that passengers could be landed "at any place on the river at their pleasure." The *Oliver Ellsworth,* in 1824, was the first of a long line of "floating palaces" that cruised the river in the next half century. Built by the Connecticut Steam Boat Company, she was 112 feet long, 24 feet in beam, had an eight-foot draft, and weighed nearly 230 tons. Her 44-horsepower engine enabled her to average eight knots. Sleeping 62 persons and carrying 400 passengers, at five dollars apiece, she made three trips a week between Hartford and New York, the approximately 140-mile voyage sometimes taking as little as eighteen hours. This same year, "amidst the salute of cannon and the shouts of thousands of gratified and grateful spectators," the aged Marquis de Lafayette left Hartford aboard her during his last, triumphal visit to America.

Travel on the early side-wheelers, with their crude cross-head engines and undependable copper boilers, was at best a hazardous undertaking. Three years later, when in the sound about four miles from Saybrook light at seven thirty in the evening, the *Oliver Ellsworth*'s boiler exploded, and the steam injured several persons and killed a fireman. She managed to sail into Saybrook, whence an excited postrider galloped to Hartford, burst in upon the legislature sitting in the old statehouse, and shouted: "The Eliver Ollsworth . . . biled her buster!" Not long after, the *New England* blew up at Essex, killing or maiming fifteen out of seventy people aboard. Despite these disasters, the number of steamboats on the river increased sharply after 1840. River traffic, although the railroad whistle was already sounding its death knell, was then at its peak, and three competing steamboat lines served New York. In 1846 there were over 2,000 arrivals and departures of sail and steam vessels at Hartford's twenty-odd wharves, even though the town's population was barely 13,000.

In the 1820's the Enfield rapids limited traffic above Hartford to flatboats carrying less than ten tons, and Hartford's merchants were frustrated by their inability to make the fullest use of the river for trade northward with Massachusetts, New Hampshire, and Vermont. Further, their business was threatened by the granting of a charter, in 1822, to a New Haven group to build the Farmington Canal, paralleling the river route. The ditch, which was actually built (and is now a weed-grown freight railroad track), headed north, bypassing all the river ports some miles to the west, and finally joined the Connecticut at Northampton, Massachusetts. In 1824 the Hartford interests formed the Connecticut River Company and obtained a charter for the purpose of improving upstream navigation above Hartford. . . .

Thus encouraged, the merchants proceeded with the building of the Enfield canal, a six-mile-long, seventy-foot-wide ditch to get around those rapids, deep enough to accommodate large flatboats and steamboats up to seventy-five tons. (In 1795, with the construction of the canal at South Hadley, Massachusetts, to bypass the Hadley Falls, the Connecticut had become the first river in the United States to be so improved.) Four hundred Irishmen arrived as workmen, their worldly goods tied in red bandannas, and in 1829 the Enfield canal opened to traffic. Fifteen boats passed through the first day, including Thomas Blanchard's new stern-wheeler *Vermont*. Soon stern-wheelers were chugging daily between Hartford and Springfield, going up through the canal and down over the rapids. Tolls were one dollar per passenger and fifty cents per ton of freight. . . .

In the years before the Civil War river steamers were transporting more than ordinary passengers and goods. With abolitionst sentiment strong in New England, many a shipowner, like Jesse G. Baldwin of Middletown, Connecticut, found room on his vessel for runaway slaves and thereby made the river a link to the underground railroad. Steamboats bringing southern cotton to Connecticut mills not infrequently carried fugitives, and Old Lyme was an active underground railroad center. In Hartford the most prominent abolitionist was Francis Gillette, a United States senator and father of the famous actor William Gillette. At his Nook Farm, which later became the focus of the city's intellectual life and where Charles Dudley Warner, Harriet Beecher Stowe, Joseph Hawley, and Mark Twain were to live, Gillette gave food and shelter to dark-skinned travellers who came and went in secrecy. The slave trade never played a significant role in Connecticut's economy. In 1784 the legislature had provided for gradual emancipation of the 6,500 slaves then in the state; by 1830, there were only 23 slaves left out of a Negro population of some 8,000 and in 1848 the legislature abolished slavery.

After the Civil War, thanks to the excellent steamboat service, the river developed into a popular resort area for the carriage trade of New York City. The Haddams in particular attracted summer visitors. At East Haddam was Goodspeed's Hotel, one of the many enterprises of an unusual Yankee fireball by the name of William Goodspeed, who was, besides being a hotel-keeper, a successful shipbuilder, merchant, and banker. To capture and hold the tourists arriving by steamboat at his hotel, he conceived the idea of an opera house ornately decorated in the manner of a steamer saloon. Finished in 1877, Goodspeed's Opera House was an instant success. Entire shows were brought from Broadway, often for a one-night stand. Josh Billings, Bloodgood's Minstrels, and orators of note, such as Henry Ward Beecher, all played Goodspeed's. The large drop curtain depicted the steamer *State of New York*—the last and most elegant of the side-wheelers—passing below East Haddam. Ironically, in 1881 the *State of New York* struck a hidden snag and was beached with a big hole in her bottom at almost the identical spot shown on the curtain. A promoter at heart, Goodspeed was more than equal to the occasion. He raced to the balcony of the Opera House which overlooked the river and instructed the captain of the ferryboat *Goodspeed* to bring the 150 passengers to see the show at his expense and to spend the night at his hotel. It is said that the next day he offered a twin bill: *Uncle Tom's Cabin* at the Opera House and a visit to the wrecked steamer. Her wreck forced the Hartford & New York Steamboat Company into receivership, and from then on, in diminishing numbers and elegance, the steamboat continued to fight a losing battle against the railroad and the highway, until the *Hartford* made its last trip during the early 1930's. Goodspeed's Opera House has recently been beautifully restored, and operates as a theatre, but the great passenger steamers whistle up no more. . . .

Today, beneath the fine new skyline at Hartford and through a maze of superhighways, the river runs almost forgotten. Here no docks remain, only a few old pilings and bulkheads that give mute testimony to what used to be, and the dikes shut out any view of the stream itself. Worse than man's neglect of the river has been his abuse of it, especially of this upper section, where the tide is almost imperceptible, and where no cleansing salt water sweeps in from ocean and sound. The Connecticut has earned the unsavory reputation of being dirty, smelly, and unfit for man, fish, or bird. Concern over the river's condition was expressed as early as 1884 by J. B. Olcott of South Manchester, who wrote: "A land with its rivers running filth instead of pure water, is like a body with its veins running filth instead of pure blood . . . Hartford sits nervously in the lap of what was once one of the fairest and sweetest, and is now one of the filthiest valleys in the world." . . .

Between Essex and the entrance the marshes remain a naturalist's paradise, even though the onslaught of civilization has reduced them to two thirds of their former size. Here, on land washed twice a day by salty tides, muskrats scamper through waist-high grasses and bulrushes;

sandpipers poke about in search of insects; and wild duck and heron and osprey make their seasonal visits. Slip down in a sailboat past the marshes, the little towns, and the neat lighthouses, and you are in Long Island Sound, still pulsing with the same currents that carried in Adriaen Block over three and a half centuries ago. What vast changes all that time has seen!

Chapter 2

RIVER OF WAR

I now at Number Four Remain
Tho Tis Again my will
I hope I shall no enemy meet
But what I wound or kill
—verse etched on a powder horn by Jonathan Hobart (1757)

For anyone who loves the Connecticut River today, who admires its pastoral beauty, it takes a strenuous act of imagination to remember that for nearly two centuries it was a river of war, fought over bitterly, not only whites versus Native Americans, but whites versus whites. From the bloody Pequot War of 1637, through the hit and run raids of the French and Indian wars, to the War of 1812, the Connecticut, as a central and strategic corridor, was the scene of repeated fighting, in contests that were by no means as one-sided as were subsequent Indian wars that occurred as the Europeans moved west. Indeed, if you count several half-comic postludes, you could make an argument that the river-of-war period didn't end until 1945 (when German P.O.W.s were still held at Camp Stark, on a Connecticut tributary)—and, for that matter, anyone living in the Upper Valley during the 1980s remembers the chart that newspaper editors loved to print, showing how far the circle of destruction would spread from a nuclear bomb dropped on the I-89 bridge where it crossed the river in West Lebanon, New Hampshire.

Bloody history makes for good reading, of course; this is one of the largest chapters in the anthology and I could easily triple its length, so deep are the resources here. It's hard not to include everything Francis Parkman wrote about the river (including a youthful memoir of bushwhacking across the upper river on a trip from Pittsburg to Maine); I've chosen his classic account of the raid on Deerfield in 1704.

If the literature of the Connecticut River has one characteristic and unique genre, one that's made an impact on American literature as a whole, it would have to be the "captivity narrative," wherein a white man or woman—captured by the French and Indians in one of their raids, brought to Canada, returned again after much hardship—recounts the story of their abduction. These narratives were the eighteenth-century equivalent of the best seller; and why not, since they had everything—violence, savagery, bravery, sexual titillation, and the powerful metaphor of a Christian being taken to hell and back. One of the most remarkable stories is Susanna Johnson's, included here: she was taken captive at Charlestown, New Hampshire, Fort Number Four, in August 1754.

Robert Rogers of Rogers's Rangers fame, led an infamous raid on the Indian village at St. Francis in Quebec in 1759. Considered a brave and daring feat at the time, it's now seen as just another brutal example of the white man's genocidal policy. Whichever interpretation is true, there is no doubt that his escape was dramatic enough, including as it did an epic raft trip from the mouth of the Ammonoosuc down the Connecticut to Fort Number Four in order to rescue his starving men.

The Connecticut River has a prominent place in the history of war's technology, since it was the birthplace of the world's first submarine. During the Revolution, the Connecticut River towns supplied privateers to fight for the patriot cause, but otherwise escaped the kind of destruction that was visited upon areas just east and west of it. This changed during the War of 1812 and the all-but-forgotten British raid on Essex. Since it was such a one-sided defeat for the Americans, very little has ever been written about it; included here is the British captain's boastful account and the local paper's embarrassed response.

The Indian Stream Republic, the illegitimate "country" made out of the headwaters in the first third of the nineteenth century, had a brief little war of its own; Edwin Bacon gives a good summary, while Daniel Doan explains the complexity that led to the crisis—the fact that for many years absolutely no one understood the geography of the headwaters: which river flowed where.

The Deerfield Raid

FRANCIS PARKMAN

ABOUT MIDWINTER THE GOVERNOR of Canada sent another large war-party against the New England border. The object of attack was an unoffending hamlet, that from its position could never be a menace to the French, and the destruction of which could profit them nothing. The aim of the enterprise was not military, but political. "I have sent no war-party towards Albany," writes Vaudreuil, "because we must do nothing that might cause a rupture between us and the Iroquois; but we must keep things astir in the direction of Boston, or else the Abenakis will declare for the English." In short, the object was fully to commit these savages to hostility against New England, and convince them at the same time that the French would back their quarrel.

The party consisted, according to French accounts of fifty Canadians and two hundred Abenakis and Caughnawagas,—the latter of whom, while trading constantly with Albany, were rarely averse to a raid against Massachusetts or New Hampshire. The command was given to the younger Hertel de Rouville, who was accompanied by four of his brothers. They began their march in the depth of winter, journeyed nearly three hundred miles on snow-shoes through the forest, and approached their destination on the afternoon of the 28th of February, 1704. It was the village of Deerfield,—which then formed the extreme northwestern frontier of Massachusetts, its feeble neighbor, the infant settlement of Northfield, a little higher up the Connecticut, having been abandoned during the last war. Rouville halted his followers at a place now called Petty's Plain, two miles from the village; and here, under the shelter of a pine forest, they all lay hidden, shivering with cold,—for they dared not make fires,—and hungry as wolves, for their provisions were spent. Though their numbers, by the lowest account, were nearly equal to the whole population of Deerfield,—men, women, and children,—they had no thought of an open attack, but trusted to darkness and surprise for an easy victory.

Deerfield stood on a plateau above the river meadows, and the houses—forty-one in all—were chiefly along the road towards the villages of Hadley and Hatfield, a few miles distant. In the middle of the place, on a rising ground called Meeting-house Hill, was a small square wooden

From Francis Parkman, *A Half-Century of Conflict* (Boston: Little, Brown and Company, 1893).

meeting-house. This, with about fifteen private houses, besides barns and sheds, was enclosed by a fence of palisades eight feet high, flanked by "mounts," or block-houses, at two or more of the corners. The four sides of this palisaded enclosure, which was called the fort, measured by all no less than two hundred and two rods, and within it lived some of the principal inhabitants of the village, of which it formed the centre or citadel. Chief among its inmates was John Williams, the minister, a man of character and education, who, after graduating at Harvard, had come to Deerfield when it was still suffering under the ruinous effects of King Philip's War, and entered on his ministry with a salary of sixty pounds in depreciated New England currency, payable, not in money, but in wheat, Indian-corn, and pork. His parishioners built him a house, he married, and had now eight children, one of whom was absent with friends at Hadley. His next neighbor was Benoni Stebbins, sergeant in the county militia, who lived a few rods from the meeting-house. About fifty yards distant, and near the northwest angle of the enclosure, stood the house of Ensign John Sheldon, a framed building, one of the largest in the village, and, like that of Stebbins, made bullet-proof by a layer of bricks between the outer and inner sheathing, while its small windows and its projecting upper story also helped to make it defensible.

The space enclosed by the palisade, though much too large for effective defence, served in time of alarm as an asylum for the inhabitants outside, whose houses were scattered,—some on the north towards the hidden enemy, and some on the south towards Hadley and Hatfield. Among those on the south side was that of the militia captain, Jonathan Wells, which had a palisade of its own, and, like the so-called fort, served as an asylum for the neighbors.

These private fortified houses were sometimes built by the owners alone, though more often they were the joint work of the owners and of the inhabitants, to whose safety they contributed. The palisade fence that enclosed the central part of the village was made under a vote of the town, each inhabitant being required to do his share; and as they were greatly impoverished by the last war, the General Court of the province remitted for a time a part of their taxes in consideration of a work which aided the general defence.

Down to the Peace of Ryswick the neighborhood had been constantly infested by scalping-parties, and once the village had been attacked by a considerable force of French and Indians, who were beaten off. Of late there had been warnings of fresh disturbance. Lord Cornbury, Governor of New York, wrote that he had heard through spies that Deerfield was again to be attacked, and a message to the same effect came from Peter Schuyler, who had received intimations of the danger from Mohawks lately on a visit to their Caughnawaga relatives. During the autumn the alarm was so great that the people took refuge within the palisades, and the houses of the enclosure were crowded with them; but the panic had now subsided, and many, though not all, had returned to their homes. They were reassured by the presence of twenty volunteers from the villages below, whom, on application from the minister, Williams, the General Court had sent as a garrison to Deerfield, where they were lodged in the houses of the villagers. On the night when Hertel de Rouville and his band lay hidden among the pines there were in all the settlement a little less than three hundred souls, of whom two hundred and sixty-eight were inhabitants, twenty were yeomen soldiers of the garrison, two were visitors from Hatfield, and three were negro slaves. They were of all ages—from the Widow Allison, in her eighty-fifth year, to the infant son of Deacon French, aged four weeks.

Heavy snows had lately fallen and buried the clearings, the meadow, and the frozen river to the depth of full three feet. On the northwestern side the drifts were piled nearly to the top of the palisade fence, so that it was no longer an obstruction to an active enemy.

As the afternoon waned, the sights and sounds of the little border hamlet were, no doubt, like those of any other rustic New England village at the end of a winter day,—an ox-sledge creaking on the frosty snow as it brought in the last load of firewood, boys in homespun snowballing each other in the village street, farmers feeding their horses and cattle in the barns, a matron drawing a pail of water with the help of one of those long well-sweeps still used in some remote districts, or a girl bringing a pail of milk from the cow-shed. In the houses, where one room served as kitchen, dining-room, and parlor, the housewife cooked the evening meal, children sat at their bowls of mush and milk, and the men of the family, their day's work over, gathered about the fire while perhaps some village coquette sat in the corner with fingers busy at the spinning-wheel, and ears intent on the stammered wooings of her rustic lover. Deerfield kept early hours, and it is likely that by nine o'clock all were in their beds. There was a patrol inside the palisade, but there was little discipline among these extemporized soldiers; the watchers grew careless as the frosty night went on; and it is said that towards morning they, like the villagers, betook themselves to their beds.

Rouville and his men, savage with hunger, lay shivering under the pines till about two hours before dawn; then, leaving their packs and their snow-shoes behind, they moved cautiously towards their prey. There was a crust on the snow strong enough to bear their weight, though not to prevent a rustling noise as it crunched under the feet of so many men. It is said that from time to time Rouville commanded a halt, in order that the sentinels, if such there were, might mistake the distant sound for rising and falling gusts of wind. In any case, no alarm was given till they had mounted the palisade and dropped silently into the unconscious village. Then with one accord they screeched the war-whoop, and assailed the doors of the houses with axes and hatchets. The hideous din startled the minister, Williams, from his sleep. Half-wakened, he sprang out of bed, and saw dimly a crowd of savages bursting through the shattered door. He shouted to two soldiers who were lodged in the house; and then, with more valor than discretion, snatched a pistol that hung at the head of the bed, cocked it, and snapped it at the breast of the foremost Indian, who proved to be a Caughnawaga chief. It missed fire, or Williams would, no doubt, have been killed on the spot. Amid the screams of his terrified children, three of the party seized him and bound him fast; for they came well provided with cords, since prisoners had a market value. Nevertheless in the first fury of their attack they dragged to the door and murdered two of the children and a negro woman called Parthena, who was probably their nurse. In an upper room lodged a young man named Stoddard, who had time to snatch a cloak, throw himself out of the window, climb the palisade, and escape in the darkness. Half-naked as he was, he made his way over the snow to Hatfield, binding his bare feet with strips torn from the cloak.

They kept Williams shivering in his shirt for an hour while a frightful uproar of yells, shrieks, and gunshots sounded from without. At length they permitted him, his wife, and five remaining children to dress themselves. Meanwhile the Indians and their allies burst into most of the houses, killed such of the men as resisted, butchered some of the women and children, and seized and bound the rest. Some of the villagers escaped in the confusion, like Stoddard, and either fled half dead with cold towards Hatfield, or sought refuge in the fortified house of Jonathan Wells.

The house of Stebbins, the minister's next neighbor, had not been attacked so soon as the rest, and the inmates had a little time for preparation. They consisted of Stebbins himself, with his wife and five children, David Hoyt, Joseph Catlin, Benjamin Church, a namesake of the old Indian fighter of Philip's War, and three other men,—probably refugees who had brought their wives and families within the palisaded enclosure for safety. Thus the house contained seven men, four or five women, and a considerable number of children. Though the walls were bullet-proof, it was not built for defence. The men, however, were well supplied with guns, powder, and lead, and they seem to have found some means of barricading the windows. When the enemy tried to break in, they drove them back with loss. On this, the French and Indians gathered in great numbers before the house, showered bullets upon it, and tried to set it on fire.

They were again repulsed, with the loss of several killed and wounded; among the former a Caughnawaga chief, and among the latter a French officer. Still the firing continued. If the assailants had made a resolute assault, the defenders must have been overpowered; but to risk lives in open attack was contrary to every maxim of forest warfare. The women in the house behaved with great courage, and moulded bullets, which the men shot at the enemy. Stebbins was killed outright, and Church was wounded, as was also the wife of David Hoyt. At length most of the French and Indians, disgusted with the obstinacy of the defence, turned their attention to other quarters; though some kept up their fire under cover of the meeting-house and another building within easy range of gunshot.

This building was the house of Ensign John Sheldon, already mentioned. The Indians had had some difficulty in mastering it; for the door being of thick oak plank, studded with nails of wrought iron and well barred, they could not break it open. After a while, however, they hacked a hole in it, through which they fired and killed Mrs. Sheldon as she sat on the edge of a bed in a lower room. Her husband, a man of great resolution, seems to have been absent. Their son John, with Hannah his wife, jumped from an upper chamber window. The young woman sprained her ankle in the fall, and lay helpless, but begged her husband to run to Hatfield for aid, which he did, while she remained a prisoner. The Indians soon got in at a back door, seized Mercy Sheldon, a little girl of two years, and dashed out her brains on the door-stone. Her two brothers and her sister Mary, a girl of sixteen, were captured. The house was used for a short time as a depot for prisoners, and here also was brought the French officer wounded in the attack on the Stebbins house. A family tradition relates that as he lay in great torment he begged for water, and it was brought him by one of the prisoners, Mrs. John Catlin, whose husband, son, and infant grandson had been killed, and who, nevertheless, did all in her power to relieve the sufferings of the wounded man. Probably it was in recognition of this charity that when the other prisoners were led away, Mrs. Catlin was left behind. She died of grief a few weeks later.

The sun was scarcely an hour high when the miserable drove of captives was conducted across the river to the foot of a mountain or high hill. Williams and his family were soon compelled to follow, and his house was set on fire. As they led him off he saw that other houses within the palisade were burning, and that all were in the power of the enemy except that of his neighbor Stebbins, where the gallant defenders still kept their assailants at bay. Having collected all their prisoners, the main body of the French and Indians began to withdraw towards the pine forest, where they had left their packs and snow-shoes, and to prepare for a retreat before the country should be roused, first murdering in cold blood Marah Carter, a little girl of five years, whom they probably thought unequal to the march. Several parties, however, still lingered in the village, firing on the Stebbins house, killing cattle, hogs, and sheep, and gathering such plunder as the place afforded.

Early in the attack, and while it was yet dark, the light of burning houses, reflected from the fields of snow, had been seen at Hatfield, Hadley, and Northampton. The alarm was sounded through the slumbering hamlets, and parties of men mounted on farm-horses, with saddles or without, hastened to the rescue, not doubting that the fires were kindled by Indians. When the sun was about two hours high, between thirty and forty of them were gathered at the fortified house of Jonathan Wells, at the southern end of the village. The houses of this neighborhood were still standing, and seem not to have been attacked; the stubborn defence of the Stebbins house having apparently prevented the enemy from pushing much beyond the palisaded enclosure. The house of Wells was full of refugee families. A few Deerfield men here joined the horsemen from the lower towns, as also did four or five of the yeoman soldiers who had escaped the fate of most of their comrades. The horsemen left their horses within Wells's fence; he himself took the lead, and the whole party rushed in together at the southern gate of the palisaded enclosure, drove out the plunderers, and retook a part of their plunder. The assailants of the Stebbins house, after firing at it for three hours, were put to flight, and those of its male occupants who were still alive joined their countrymen, while the women and children ran back for harborage at the house of Wells.

Wells and his men, now upwards of fifty, drove the flying enemy more than a mile across the river meadows, and ran in headlong pursuit over the crusted snow, killing a considerable number. In the eagerness of the chase many threw off their overcoats, and even their jackets. Wells saw the danger, and vainly called on them to stop. Their blood was up, and most of them were young and inexperienced.

Meanwhile the firing at the village had been heard by Rouville's main body, who had already begun their retreat northward. They turned back to support their comrades, and hid themselves under the bank of the river till the pursuers drew near, when they gave them a close volley and rushed upon them with the war-whoop. Some of the English were shot down, and the rest driven back. There was no panic. "We retreated," says Wells, "facing about and firing." When they reached the palisade they made a final stand, covering by their fire such of their comrades as had fallen within range of musket-shot, and thus saving them from the scalping-knife. The French did not try to dislodge them. Nine of them had been killed, several wounded, and one was captured.

The number of English carried off prisoners was one hundred and eleven, and the number killed was according to one list forty-seven, and according to another fifty-three, the latter including some who were smothered in the cellars of their burning houses. The names, and in most cases the ages, of both captives and slain are preserved. Those who escaped with life and freedom were, by the best account, one hundred and thirty-seven. An official tabular statement, drawn up on the spot, sets the number of houses burned at seventeen. The house of the town clerk, Thomas French, escaped, as before mentioned, and the town records, with other papers in his charge, were saved. The meeting-house also was left standing. The house of Sheldon was hastily set on fire by the French and Indians when their rear was driven out of the village by Wells and his men; but the fire was extinguished, and "the Old Indian House," as it was called, stood till the year 1849. Its door, deeply scarred with hatchets, and with a hole cut near the middle, is still preserved in the Memorial Hall at Deerfield.

Vaudreuil wrote to the minister, Ponchartrain, that the French lost two or three killed, and twenty or twenty-one wounded, Rouville himself being among the latter. This cannot include the Indians, since there is proof that the enemy left behind a considerable number of their dead. Wherever resistance was possible, it had been of the most prompt and determined character.

Long before noon the French and Indians were on their northward march with their train of captives. More armed men came up from the settlements below, and by midnight about eighty were gathered at the ruined village. Couriers had been sent to rouse the country, and before evening of the next day (the 1st of March) the force at Deerfield was increased to two hundred and fifty; but a thaw and a warm rain had set in, and as few of the men had snow-shoes, pursuit was out of the question. Even could the agile savages and their allies have been overtaken, the probable consequence would have been the murdering of the captives to prevent their escape.

In spite of the foul blow dealt upon it, Deerfield was not abandoned. Such of its men as were left were taken as soldiers into the pay of the province, while the women and children were sent to the villages below. A small garrison was also stationed at the spot, under command of Captain Jonathan Wells, and thus the village held its ground till the storm of war should pass over.

We have seen that the minister, Williams, with his wife and family were led from their burning house across the river to the foot of the mountain, where the crowd of terrified and disconsolate captives—friends, neighbors, and relatives—were already gathered. Here they presently saw the fight in the meadow, and were told that if their countrymen attempted a rescue, they should all be put to death. "After this," writes Williams, "we went up the mountain, and saw the smoke of fires in town, and beheld the awful desolation of Deerfield; and before we marched any farther they killed a sucking child of the English."

The French and Indians marched that afternoon only four or five miles,—to Greenfield meadows,—where they stopped to encamp, dug away the snow, laid spruce-boughs on the ground for beds, and bound fast such of the prisoners as seemed able to escape. The Indians then held a carousal on some liquor they had found in the village, and in their drunken rage murdered a negro man belonging to Williams. In spite of their precautions, Joseph Alexander, one of the prisoners, escaped during the night, at which they were greatly incensed; and Rouville ordered Williams to tell his companions in misfortune that if any more of them ran off, the rest should be burned alive.

The prisoners were the property of those who had taken them. Williams had two masters; one of the three who had seized him having been shot in the attack on the house of Stebbins. His principal owner was a surly fellow who would not let him speak to the other prisoners; but as he was presently chosen to guard the rear, the minister was left in the hands of his other master, who allowed him to walk beside his wife and help her on the way. Having borne a child a few weeks before, she was in no condition for such a march, and felt that her hour was near. Williams speaks of her in the strongest terms of affection. She made no complaint, and accepted her fate with resignation. "We discoursed," he says, "of the happiness of those who had God for a father and friend, as also that it was our reasonable duty quietly to submit to his will." Her thoughts were for her remaining children, whom she commended to her husband's care. Their intercourse was short. The Indian who had gone to the rear of the train soon returned, separated them, ordered Williams to the front, "and so made me take a last farewell of my dear wife, the desire of my eyes and companion in many mercies and afflictions." They came soon after to Green River, a stream then about knee-deep, and so swift that the water had not frozen. After wading it with difficulty, they climbed a snow-covered hill beyond. The minister, with strength almost spent, was permitted to rest a few moments at the top; and as the other prisoners passed by in turn, he questioned each for news of his wife. He was not left long in suspense. She had fallen from weakness in fording the stream, but gained her feet again, and, drenched in the icy current, struggled to the farther bank, when the savage who owned her, finding that she could not climb the hill, killed her with one stroke of his hatchet. Her body was left on the snow till a few of her townsmen, who had followed the trail, found it a day or two after, carried it back to Deerfield, and buried it in the churchyard.

On the next day the Indians killed an infant and a little girl of eleven years; on the day following, Friday, they tomahawked a woman, and on Saturday four others. Their apparent cruelty was in fact a kind of mercy. The victims could not keep up with the party, and the death-blow saved them from a lonely and lingering death from cold and starvation. Some of the children, when spent with the march, were carried on the backs of their owners,—partly, perhaps, through kindness, and partly because every child had its price.

On the fourth day of the march they came to the mouth of West River, which enters the Connecticut a little above the present town of Brattleboro'. Some of the Indians were discontented with the distribution of the captives, alleging that others had got more than their share; on which the whole troop were mustered together, and some changes of ownership were agreed upon. At this place, dog-trains and sledges had been left, and these served to carry their wounded, as well as some of the captive children. Williams was stripped of the better part of his clothes, and others given him instead, so full of vermin that they were a torment to him through all the journey. The march now continued with pitiless speed up the frozen Connecticut, where the recent thaw had covered the ice with slush and water ankle-deep.

On Sunday they made a halt, and the minister was permitted to preach a sermon from the text, "Hear, all people, and behold my sorrow: my virgins and my young men are gone into captivity." Then amid the ice, the snow, the forest, and the savages, his forlorn flock joined their voices in a psalm. On Monday, guns were heard from the rear, and the Indians and their allies, in great alarm, bound their prisoners fast, and prepared for battle. It proved, however, that the guns had been fired at wild geese by one of their own number; on which they recovered their spirits, fired a volley for joy, and boasted that the English could not overtake them. More women fainted by the way and died under the hatchet,—some with pious resignation, some with despairing apathy, some with a desperate joy.

Two hundred miles of wilderness still lay between them and the Canadian settlements. It was a waste without a house or even a wigwam; except here and there the bark shed of some savage hunter. At the mouth of White River, the party divided into small bands,—no doubt in order to subsist by hunting, for provisions were fast failing. The Williams family were separated. Stephen was carried up the Connecticut; Samuel and Eunice, with two younger children, were carried off in various directions, while the wretched father, along with two small children of one of his parishioners, was compelled to follow his Indian masters up the valley of the White River. One of the children—a little girl—was killed on the next morning by her Caughnawaga owner, who was unable to carry her. On the next Sunday, the minister was left in camp with one Indian and the surviving child,—a boy of nine,—while the rest of the party were hunting. "My spirit," he says, "was amost overwhelmed within me." But he found comfort in the text, "Leave thy fatherless children, I will preserve them alive." Nor was his hope deceived. His youngest surviving child,—a boy of four,—though harshly treated by his owners, was carried on their shoulders or dragged on a sledge to the end of the journey. His youngest daughter—seven years old—was treated with great kindness throughout. Samuel and Eunice suffered much from hunger, but were dragged on sledges when too faint to walk. Stephen nearly starved to death; but after eight months in the forest, he safely reached Chambly with his Indian masters. Of the whole band of captives, only about half ever again saw friends and home. Seventeen broke down on the way and were killed; while David Hoyt and Jacob Hix died of starvation at Coos meadows, on the upper Connecticut. During the entire march, no woman seems to have been subjected to violence; and this holds true, with rare exceptions, in all the Indian wars of New England. This remarkable forbearance towards female prisoners, so different from the practice of many Western tribes, was probably due to a form of superstition, aided perhaps by the influence of the missionaries.

The Captivity of Mrs. Johnson

SUSANNA JOHNSON

AT THE AGE OF FOURTEEN, in 1744, I made a visit from Leominster to Charlestown to visit my parents. Through a long wilderness from Lunenburg to Lower Ashuelot, now Swanzey, we travelled two days: a solitary house was all the mark of cultivation that occurred on the journey. Guided by marked trees, we travelled cautiously through the

From Colin G. Calloway, comp., *North Country Captives* (Hanover, N.H.: University Press of New England, 1992).

gloomy forest where now the well-tilled farms occupy each rod of ground. From Ashuelot to Charlestown the passage was opposed, now by the Hill of Difficulty, and now by the Slough Despond. A few solitary inhabitants, who appeared the representatives of wretchedness, were scattered on the way.

When I approached the town of Charlestown, the first object that met my eyes was a party of Indians holding a war dance: a cask of rum, which the inhabitants had suffered them to partake of, had raised their spirits to all the horrid yells and feats of distortion which characterize the nation. I was chilled at the sight, and passed tremblingly by. At this time Charlestown contained nine or ten families, who lived in huts not far distant from each other. The Indians were numerous, and associated in a friendly manner with the whites. It was the most northerly settlement on Connecticut River, and the adjacent country was terribly wild. A saw mill was erected, and the first boards were sawed while I was there. The inhabitants commemorated the event with a dance, which took place on the new boards. In those days there was such a mixture on the frontiers of savages and settlers, without established laws to govern them, that the state of society cannot be easily described; and the impending dangers of war, where it was known that the savages would join the enemies of our country, retarded the progress of refinement and cultivation. The inhabitants of Charlestown began to erect a fort, and took some steps towards clearing their farms; but war soon checked their industry.

Charlestown

In the year 1740 the first settlement was made in the town of Charlestown, then known by the name of No. 4, by three families, who emigrated from Lunenburg, by the name of Farnsworth: that part of New Hampshire west of Merrimack River was then a trackless wilderness. Within a few years past instances have been known of new townships, totally uninhabited, becoming flourishing and thick-settled villages in the course of six or seven years. But in those days, when government was weak, when savages were on our borders and Frenchmen in Canada, population extended with timorous and tardy paces: in the course of twelve years the families increased only to twenty-two or three. The human race will not flourish unless fostered by the warm sunshine of peace.

During the first twenty years of its existence as a settled place, until the peace between Great Britain and France, it suffered all the consternation and ravages of war; not that warfare which civilized nations wage with each other, but the cruel carnage of savages and Frenchmen. Sometimes engaged in the duties of the camp, at others sequestering themselves from surrounding enemies, they became familiar with danger, but not with industrious husbandry.

In the year 1744 the inhabitants began to erect a fort for their safety. When the Cape Breton war commenced the Indians assumed the hatchet and began their depredations on Charlestown on the 19th of April, 1746, by burning the mills and taking Captain John Spafford, Isaac Parker, and Stephen Farnsworth prisoners. On the 2nd of May following Seth Putnam was killed. Two days after Captain Payne arrived with a troop of horse, from Massachusetts, to defend the place. About twenty of his men had the curiosity to view the place where Putnam was killed, and were ambushed by the Indians. Captain Stevens, who commanded a few men, rushed out to the fort to their relief: a sharp combat ensued, in which the Indians were routed. They left some guns and blankets on the field of action; but they carried their dead off with them, which is a policy they never omit. Ensign Obadiah Sartwell was captured; and Samuel Farnsworth, Elijah Allen, Peter Perin, Aaron Lyon, and Joseph Massy fell victims to Indian vengeance.

On the 19th of June a severe engagement took place. Captain Brown, from Stow, in Massachusetts, had previously arrived with some troops; a party of his joined a number of Captain Stevens's soldiers to go into the meadow after their horses. The dogs discovered an ambush, which put them into a posture for action and gave them the advantage of the first fire. This disconcerted the savages, who, being on higher ground, overshot and did but little damage to the English. The enemy were routed, and even seen to drag several dead bodies after them. They left behind them guns, spears, and blankets, which sold for forty pounds, old tenor. During the time Captain Josiah Brown assisted in defending the fort Jedediah Winchel was killed; Samuel Stanhope,Cornet Baker, and David Parker were wounded. During this summer the fort was entirely blockaded, and all were obliged to take refuge within the picket. On the 3d of August one Philips was killed within a few feet of the fort as he accidentally stepped out: at night a soldier crept to him with a rope, and he was drawn into the fort and interred. In the summer of the year 1746 Captain Ephraim Brown, from Sudbury, arrived with a troop of horse to relieve Captain Josiah Brown. The Sudbury troop tarried about a month, and were relieved by a company commanded by Captain Winchester, who defended the place till autumn, when the inhabitants, fatigued with watching and weary of the dangers of the forest, deserted the place entirely for about six months. In the month of August, previous to the evacuation, the Indians, assisted by their brethren the French, were very troublesome and mischievous: they destroyed all the horses, hogs, and cattle. An attack was made on the fort which lasted two days. My father at this time lost ten cattle; but the people were secured behind their wooden walls, and received but little damage.

In this recess of the settlement of No. 4 the Indians and French were icelocked in Canada, and the frontiers suffered only in apprehension. In March, 1747, Captain Phinehas Stevens, who commanded a ranging party of about thirty men, marched to No. 4 and took possession of the fort. He found it uninjured by the enemy; and an old spaniel and a cat, who had been domesticated before the evacuation, had guarded it safely through the winter, and gave the troops a hearty welcome to their tenement.

Captain Stevens was of eminent service to the infant settlement. In 1748 he moved his family to the place, and encouraged the settlers by his fortitude and industry. In the early part of his life, when Rutland suffered by savage vengeance, when the Rev. Mr. Williard was murdered, he was taken prisoner and carried to St. Francis. This informed him of the Indian customs and familiarized him with their mode of warfare. He was an active, penetrating soldier, and a respectable, worthy citizen.

In a few days after the fort was taken possession of by Captain Stevens's troops a party of five hundred French and Indians, commanded by Monsieur Debelcie, sallied from their den in Canada and made a furious attack on the fort. The battle lasted five days, and every strategem which the French policy or Indian malice could invent was practised to reduce the garrison. Sometimes they made an onset by a discharge of musketry; at others they discharged fire arrows, which communicated fire to several parts of the fort. But these were insufficient to daunt the courage of the little band that were assailed. Their next step was to fill a car with combustibles, and roll it against the walls, to communicate fire; but the English kept up such a brisk, incessant fire that they were defeated in the project. At length the monsieurs, tired with fighting, beat a parley. Two Indians, formerly acquainted with Captain Stevens, came as negotiators, and wished to exchange some furs for corn: this Captain Stevens refused, but offered a bushel of corn for each hostage they would leave to be exchanged at some future day. These terms were not complied with; and on the fifth day the enemy retreated, at which time the soldiers of the garrison honored them with as brisk a discharge as they could afford, to let them know that they were neither disheartened nor exhausted in ammunition. The garrison had none killed; and only one, by the name of Brown, was wounded.

Perhaps no place was ever defended with greater bravery than this fort during this action. Thirty or forty men, when attacked, by five hundred, must have an uncommon degree of fortitude and vigilance to defend themselves during a siege of five days. But Captain Stevens was equal to the task, and will be applauded by posterity. After the battle he sent an express to Boston with the tidings. Governor Charles Knowles happened then to be at Boston, and rewarded Captain Stevens with a handsome sword; in gratitude for which the place was afterwards called Charlestown.

In November, 1747, a body of the troops set out from the fort to return to Massachusetts. They had not proceeded far before the Indians fired on them. Isaac Goodale and Nathaniel Gould were killed, and one Anderson taken prisoner. From this period until the end of the Cape Breton war the fort was defended by Captain Stevens. Soldiers passed and repassed to Canada; but the inhabitants took sanctuary in the fort, and made but little progress in cultivation. During the Indian wars, which lasted till the year 1760, Charlestown was noted more for its feats of war than a place of rapid improvement. Settlers thought it more prudent to remain with their friends in safety than risk their scalps with savage power. Since that period it has become a flourishing village, and contains all that a rural situation affords of the useful and the pleasant. Numerous farms and stately buildings now flourish where the savage roamed the forest. The prosperity of the town was greatly promoted by the Rev. Bulkely Olcott, who was a settled minister there about thirty-two years. In the character of this good man were combined the agreeable companion, the industrious citizen, and the unaffected Christian. During the whole of his ministry his solicitude for the happiness of his parishioners was as conspicuous in the benefits they received from his assistance as in their sincere attachment to his person. As a divine he was pathetic, devout, and instructive, and may with propriety be said to have

> Shown the path to heaven, and led the way.

He was highly respected through life. In June, 1793, he died, much lamented.

Removal to Charlestown, &c.

In May, 1749, we received information of the cessation of arms between Great Britain and France. I had then been married about two years, and Mr. Johnson's enterprising spirit was zealous to remove to Charlestown. In June we undertook the hazardous and fatiguing journey. We arrived safe at the fort, and found five families, who had ventured so far into the woods during hostilities. But the gloomy forest and the warlike appearance of the place soon made me homesick. Two or three days after my arrival orders came from Massachusetts to withdraw the troops. Government placed confidence in the proffered peace of Frenchmen, and withdrew even the appearance of hostility. But French treachery and savage malice will ever keep pace with each other. Without even the suspicion of danger, the inhabitants went about their business of husbandry. The day the soldiers left the fort Ensign Obadiah Sartwell went to harrow some corn, and took Enos Stevens, the fourth son of Phinehas Stevens, Esq., to ride horse: my father and two brothers were at work in the meadow. Early in the afternoon the Indians appeared and shot Ensign Sartwell and the horse, and took young Stevens a prisoner. In addition to this my father and brothers were in the meadow, and we supposed they must be destroyed. My husband was gone to Northfield. In the fort were seven women and four men: the anxiety and grief we experienced were the highest imaginable. The next night we despatched a post to Boston to carry the news of our disaster; but my father and brothers did not return. The next day but one my husband and five or six others arrived from Northfield. We kept close in the garrison, suffering every apprehension for ten or twelve days, when the sentry from the box cried out that troops were coming: joyful at the relief, we all mounted on the top of the fort, and among the rest discovered my father. He, on hearing the guns, supposed the fort was destroyed, left his team in the meadow, and made the best of his way to Northfield with my two brothers. The soldiers were about thirty in number, and headed by Major Josiah Willard, of Fort Dummer. Enos Stevens was carried to Montreal; but the French commander sent him back directly by the way of Albany. This was the last damage done the frontiers during the Cape Breton war. . . .

Situation until August 31, 1754

Some of the soldiers who arrived with Major Willard, with the inhabitants who bore arms, were commanded by Captain Stevens the rest of the year 1749 and part of the following spring; after which the inhabitants resided pretty much in the fort until the spring or fall of the year 1752. They cultivated their lands in some degree, but they put but little confidence in the savages.

The continuation of peace began by degrees to appease the resentment of the Indians, and they appeared to discover a wish for friendly intercourse. The inhabitants in No. 4 and its vicinity relaxed their watchfulness and ventured more boldly into their fields. Every appearance of hostility at length vanished. The Indians expressed a wish to traffic; the inhabitants laid by their fears, and thought no more of tomahawks or scalping knives. Mr. Johnson now thought himself justified in removing to his farm, a hundred rods distant from the fort, which was then the uppermost settlement on Connecticut River. He pursued his occupation of trade, and the Indians made frequent visits to traffic their furs for his merchandise. He frequently credited them for blankets and other necessaries, and in most instances they were punctual in payment. During the year 1753 all was harmony and safety; settlements increased with tolerable rapidity; and the new country began to assume the appearance of cultivation.

The commencement of the year 1754 began to threaten another rupture between the French and English; and as the dividing line between Canada and the English colonies was the object of contention, it was readily seen that the frontier towns would be in imminent danger. But as immediate war was not expected, Mr. Johnson thought that he might risk the safety of his family while he made a tour to Connecticut for trade. He set out the last of May; and his absence of three months was a tedious and a bitter season to me. Soon after his departure every body was "tremblingly alive" with fear. The Indians were reported to be on their march for our destruction; and our distance from sources of information gave full latitude for exaggeration of news before it reached our ears. The fears of the night were horrible beyond description; and even the light of day was far from dispelling painful anxiety. While looking from the windows of my log house and seeing my neighbors tread cautiously by each hedge and hillock lest some secreted savage might start forth to take their scalp, my fears would baffle description. Alarms grew louder and louder, till our apprehensions were too strongly confirmed by the news of the capture of Mr. Malloon's family on Merrimack River. This reached us about the 20th of August. Imagination now saw and heard a thousand Indians; and I never went round my own house without first looking with trembling caution by each corner to see if a tomahawk was not raised for my destruction.

On the 24th of August I was relieved from all my fears by the arrival of my husband. He brought intelligence from Connecticut that a war was expected the next spring, but that no immediate danger was contemplated. He had made preparations to remove to Northfield as soon as our stock of hay was consumed and our dozen of swine had demolished our ample stores of grain, which would secure his family and property from the miseries and ravages of war. Our eldest son, Sylvanus, who was six years old, was in the mean time to be put to school at Springfield. Mr. Johnson brought home a large addition to his stores, and the neighbors made frequent parties at our house to express their joy for his return; and time passed merrily off by the aid of spirit and a ripe yard of melons. As I was in the last days of pregnancy, I could not join so heartily in their good cheer as I otherwise might. Yet in a new country pleasure is often derived from sources unknown to those less accustomed to the woods. The return of my husband, the relief from danger, and the crowds of happy friends combined to render my situation peculiarly agreeable. I now boasted with exultation that I should, with husband, friends, and luxuries, live happy in spite of the fear of savages.

On the evening of the 29th of August our house was visited by a party of neighbors, who spent the time very cheerfully with watermelons and flip till midnight. They all then retired in high spirits except a spruce young spark, who tarried to keep company with my sister. We then went to bed with feelings well tuned for sleep, and rested with fine composure till midway between daybreak and sunrise, when we were roused by neighbor Labarree's knocking at the door, who had shouldered his axe to do a day's work for my husband. Mr. Johnson slipped on his jacket and trousers and stepped to the door to let him in. But by opening the door he opened a scene terrible to describe. "Indians! Indians!" were the first words I heard. He sprang to his guns; but Labarree, heedless of danger, instead of closing the door to keep them out, began to rally our hired men up stairs for not rising earlier. But in an instant a crowd of savages, fixed horribly for war, rushed furiously in. I screamed and begged my friends to ask for quarter. By this time they were all over the house—some up stairs, some hauling my sister out of bed; another had hold of me; and one was approaching Mr. Johnson, who stood in the middle of the floor to deliver himself up. But the Indian, supposing that he would make resistance and be more than his match, went to the door and brought three of his comrades, and the four bound him. I was led to the door, fainting and trembling. There stood my friend Labarree bound. Ebenezer Farnsworth, whom they found up chamber, they were putting in the same situation; and, to complete the shocking scene, my three little children were driven naked to the place where I stood. On viewing myself I found that I, too, was naked. An Indian had plundered three gowns, who, on seeing my situation, gave me the whole. I asked another for a petticoat; but he refused it. After what little plunder their hurry would allow them to get was confusedly bundled up, we were ordered to march. After going about twenty rods we fell behind a rising ground, where we halted to pack the things in a better manner: while there a savage went back, as we supposed, to fire the buildings. Farnsworth proposed to my husband to go back with him, to get a quantity of pork from the cellar to help us on our journey; but Mr. Johnson prudently replied, that, by that means, the Indians might find the rum, and in a fit of intoxication kill us all. The Indian presently returned with marks of fear in his countenance, and we were hurried on with all violence. Two savages laid hold of each of my arms, and hurried me through thorny thickets in a most unmerciful manner. I lost a shoe and suffered exceedingly. We heard the alarm guns from the fort. This added new speed to the flight of the savages. They were apprehensive that soldiers might be sent for our relief. When we had gone a mile and a half my faintness obliged me to sit. This being observed by an Indian, he drew his knife as I supposed, to put an end to my existence. But he only cut some band with which my gown was tied, and then pushed me on. My little children were crying, my husband and the other two men were bound, and my sister and myself were obliged to make the best of our way with all our might. The loss of my shoe rendered travelling extremely painful. At the distance of three miles there was a general halt. The savages, supposing that we as well as themselves might have an appetite for breakfast, gave us a loaf of bread, some raisins, and apples which they had taken from the house. While we were forcing down our scanty breakfast a horse came in sight, known to us all by the name of Scoggin, belonging to Phinehas Stevens, Esq. One of the Indians attempted to shoot him, but was prevented by Mr. Johnson. They then expressed a wish to catch him, saying, by pointing to me, for squaw to ride. My husband had previously been unbound to assist the children; he, with two Indians, caught the horse on the banks of the river. By this time my legs and feet were covered with blood, which being noticed by Mr. Labarree, he, with that humanity which never forsook him, took his own stockings and presented them to me, and the Indians gave me a pair of moccasons. Bags and blankets were thrown over Scoggin, and I mounted on top of them, and on we jogged about seven miles to the upper end of Wilcott's Island. We were there halted and prepared to cross the river. Rafts were made of dry timber. Two Indians and Farnsworth crossed first; Labarree, by signs, got permission to swim the horse; and Mr. Johnson was allowed to swim by the raft that I was on, to push it along. We all arrived safe on the other side of the river about four o'clock in the afternoon. A fire was kindled, and some of their stolen kettles were hung over it and filled with porridge. The savages took delight in viewing their spoil, which amounted to forty or fifty pounds in value. They then with a true savage yell gave the war whoop and bade defiance to danger. As our tarry in this place lasted an hour, I had time to reflect on our miserable situation. Captives, in the power of unmerciful savages, without provision and almost without clothes, in a wilderness where we must sojourn as long as the children of Israel did for aught we knew; and, what added to our distress, not one of our savage masters could understand a word of English. Here, after being hurried from home with such rapidity, I have leisure to inform the reader respecting our Indian masters. They were eleven in number, men of middle age except one, a youth of sixteen, who in our journey discovered a very mischievous and troublesome disposition. According to their national practice, he who first laid hands on a prisoner considered him as his property. My master, who was the one that took my hand when I sat on the bed, was as clever an Indian as ever I saw. He even evinced, at numerous times, a disposition that showed he was by no means void of compassion. The four who took my husband claimed him as their property; and my sister, three children, Labarree, and Farnsworth had each a master. When the time came for us to prepare to march I almost expired at the thought of leaving my aged parents, brothers, sisters, and friends, and travel with savages through a dismal forest to unknown regions, in the alarming situation I then was in, with three small children. The eldest, Sylvanus, was but six years old; my eldest daughter, Susanna, was four; and Polly, the other, two. My sister Miriam was fourteen. My husband was barefoot, and otherwise thinly clothed. His master had taken his jacket, and nothing but his shirt and trousers remained. My two daughters had nothing but their shifts, and I only the gown that was handed me by the savages. In addition to the sufferings which arose from my own deplorable condition, I could not but feel for my friend Labarree. He had left a wife and four small children behind to lament his loss and to render his situation extremely unhappy. With all these misfortunes lying heavily upon me, the reader can imagine my situation. The Indians pronounced the dreadful word "munch," march; and on we must go. I was put on the horse; Mr. Johnson took one daughter; and Mr. Labarree, being unbound, took the other. We went six or eight miles and stopped for the night. The men were made secure by having their legs put in split sticks, somewhat like stocks, and tied with cords, which were tied to the limbs of trees too high to be reached. My sister, much to her mortification, must lie between two Indians, with a cord thrown over her and passing under each of them. The little children had blankets; and I was allowed one for my use. Thus we took lodging for the night with the sky for a covering and the ground for a pillow. The fatigues of the preceding day obliged me to sleep several hours, in spite of the horrors which surrounded me. The Indians observed great silence, and never spoke but when really necessary; and all the prisoners were disposed to say but little. My children were more peacable than could be imagined; gloomy fear imposed a deadly silence.

History of our Journey through the Wilderness till we came to the Waters that enter Lake Champlain

In the morning we were roused before sunrise: the Indians struck up a fire, hung on their stolen kettles, and made us some water gruel for breakfast. After a few sips of this meagre fare I was again put on the horse, with my husband by my side to hold me on. My two fellow-prisoners took the little girls, and we marched sorrowfully on for an hour or two, when a keener distress was added to my multiplied afflictions. I was taken with the pangs of childbirth. The Indians signified to us that we must go on to a brook. When we got there they showed some humanity by making a booth for me. Here the compassionate reader will drop a fresh tear for my inexpressible distress; fifteen or twenty miles from the abode of any civilized being, in the open wilderness, rendered cold by a rainy day, in one of the most perilous hours, and unsupplied with the least necessary that could yield convenience in the hazardous moment. My children were crying at a distance, where they were held by their masters, and only my husband and sister to attend me. None but mothers can figure to themselves my unhappy fortune. The Indians kept aloof the whole time. About ten o'clock a daughter was born. They then brought me some articles of clothing for the child which they had taken from the house. My master looked into the booth and clapped his hands with joy, crying, "Two moneys for me! two moneys for me!" I was permitted to rest the remainder of the day. The Indians were employed in making a bier for the prisoners to carry me on, and another booth for my lodging during night. They brought a needle and two pins, and some bark to tie the child's clothes, which they gave my sister, and a large wooden spoon to feed it with. At dusk they made some porridge, and brought a cup to steep some roots in, which Mr. Labarree had provided. In the evening I was removed to the new booth. For supper they made more porridge and some johnny cakes. My portion was brought me in a little bark. I slept that night far beyond expectation.

In the morning we were summoned for the journey, after the usual breakfast of meal and water. I, with my infant in my arms, was laid on the litter, which was supported alternately by Mr. Johnson, Labarree, and Farnsworth. My sister and son were put upon Scoggin and the two little girls rode on their masters' backs. Thus we proceeded two miles, when my carriers grew too faint to proceed any farther. This being observed by our sable masters, a general halt was called, and they imbodied themselves for council. My master soon made signs to Mr. Johnson that if I could ride on the horse I might proceed, otherwise I must be left behind. Here I observed marks of pity in his countenance; but this might arise from the fear of losing his two moneys. I preferred an attempt to ride on the horse rather than to perish miserably alone. Mr. Labarree took the infant, and every step of the horse almost deprived me of life. My weak and helpless condition rendered me, in a degree, insensible to every thing. My poor child could have no sustenance from my breast, and was supported entirely by water gruel. My other children, rendered peevish by an uneasy mode of riding, often burst into cries; but a surly check from their masters soon silenced them. We proceeded on with a slow, mournful pace. My weakness was too severe to allow me to sit on the horse long at a time. Every hour I was taken off and laid on the ground to rest. This preserved my life during the third day. At night we found ourselves at the head of Black River Pond. Here we prepared to spend the night. Our supper consisted of gruel and the broth of a hawk they had killed the preceding day. The prisoners were secured as usual, a booth was made for me, and all went to rest. After encampment we entered into a short conversation. My sister observed, that, if I could have been left behind, our trouble would have been seemingly nothing. My husband hoped, by the assistance of Providence, we should all be preserved. Mr. Labarree pitied his poor family; and Farnsworth summed the whole of his wishes by saying, that, if he could have got a layer of pork from the cellar, we should not be in fear of starvation. The night was uncommonly dark, and passed tediously off.

In the morning, half chilled with a cold fog, we were ordered from our places of rest, were offered the lean fare of meal and water, and then prepared for the journey. Every thing resembled a funeral procession. The savages preserved their gloomy sadness. The prisoners, bowed down with grief and fatigue, felt little disposition to talk; and the unevenness of the country, sometimes lying in miry plains, at others rising into steep and broken hills, rendered our passage hazardous and painful. Mr. Labarree kept the infant in his arms and preserved its life. The fifth day's journey was an unvaried scene of fatigue. The Indians sent out two or three hunting parties, who returned without game. As we had in the morning consumed the last morsel of our meal, every one now began to be seriously alarmed; and hunger, with all its horrors, looked us earnestly in the face. At night we found the waters that run into Lake Champlain, which was over the height of land. Before dark we halted; and the Indians, by the help of their punk, which they carried in horns, made a fire. They soon adopted a plan to relieve their hunger. The horse was shot, and his flesh was in a few moments broiling on embers; and they, with native gluttony, satiated their craving appetites. To use the term politeness, in the management of this repast, may be thought a burlesque; yet their offering the prisoners the best parts of the horse certainly bordered on civility. An epicure could not have catered nicer slices, nor in that situation served them up with more neatness. Appetite is said to be the best sauce; yet our abundance of it did not render savory the novel steak. My children, however, ate too much, which made them very unwell for a number of days. Broth was made for me and my child, which was rendered almost a luxury by the seasoning of roots. After supper countenances began to brighten. Those who had relished the meal exhibited new strength, and those who had only snuffed its effluvia confessed themselves regaled. The evening was employed in drying and smoking what remained for future use. The night was a scene of distressing fears to me; and my extreme weakness had affected my mind to such a degree that every difficulty appeared doubly terrible. By the assistance of Scoggin I had been brought so far; yet so great was my debility that every hour I was taken off and laid on the ground, to keep me from expiring. But now, alas! this conveyance was no more. To walk was impossible. Inevitable death, in the midst of woods one hundred miles wide, appeared my only portion. . . .

I am now in the winter of life, and feel sensibly the effects of old age. I live on the same spot where the Indians took us from in 1754; but the face of Nature has so changed that old savage fears are all banished. My vacant hours I often employ in reflecting on the various scenes that have marked the different stages of my life. When viewing the present rising generation, in the bloom of health and enjoying those gay pleasures which shed their exhilarating influence so plentifully in the morn of life, I look back to my early days, when I, too, was happy and basked in the sunshine of good fortune. Little do they think that the meridian of their lives can possibly be rendered miserable by captivity or a prison: as little, too, did I think that my gilded prospects could be obscured: but it was the happy delusion of youth; and I fervently wish there was no deception. But that Being who "sits upon the circle of the earth and views the inhabitants as grasshoppers" allots all our fortunes.

Although I have drunk so largely from the cup of sorrow, yet my present happiness is a small compensation. Twice has my country been ravaged by war since my remembrance. I have detailed the share I bore in the first: in the last, although the place in which I live was not a field of bloody battle, yet its vicinity to Ticonderoga and the savages that ravaged the Coos country rendered it perilous and distressing. But now no one can set a higher value on the smiles of peace than myself. The savages are driven beyond the lakes, and our country has no enemies. The gloomy wilderness, that forty years ago secreted the Indian and the beast of prey, has vanished away, and the thrifty farm smiles in its stead: the Sundays, that were then employed in guarding a fort, are now quietly devoted to worship; the tomahawk and scalping knife have given place to the sickle and ploughshare; and prosperous husbandry now thrives where the terrors of death once chilled us with fear.

My numerous progeny often gather around me to hear the sufferings once felt by their aunt or grandmother, and wonder at their magnitude. My daughter Captive still keeps the dress she appeared in when brought to my bedside by the French nurse at the Ticonderoga hospital, and often refreshes my memory with past scenes when showing it to her children. These things yield a kind of melancholy pleasure.

Instances of longevity are remarkable in my family. My aged mother, before her death, could say to me, "Arise, daughter, and go to thy daughter; for thy daughter's daughter has got a daughter;" a command which few mothers can make and be obeyed.

And now, reader, after sincerely wishing that your days may be as happy as mine have been unfortunate, I bid you adieu.

CHARLESTOWN, June 20, 1798

Rangers on the River

MAJOR ROBERT ROGERS

Number Four, NOV. 5, 1759.
TO GEN. AMHERST.

I cannot forbear making some remarks upon the difficulties and distresses, which attended the expedition under my command, against the village of St. Francis, situated within three miles of the river St. Lawrence in the heart of Canada about half way between Montreal and Quebec. While we kept the water, it was found extremely difficult to pass undiscovered by the enemy, who were cruising in great numbers upon the Lake, and had prepared certain vessels armed with all manner of mischievous

From Robert Rogers, *Reminiscences of the French War* (Concord, Mass.: Luther Roby Publisher, 1831).

implements to decoy English parties on board, and destroy them. But we escaped their designs, and landed at Missisqui bay in ten days. Here I left my boats and provisions sufficient to carry us back to Crown Point, under the charge of two trusty Indians;—who were to remain there until we came back, unless the enemy should discover the boats, in which case, they were to follow my track, and bring the intelligence. The second day after this, they joined me at night, informing that 400 French had discovered my boats, and that 200 of them were now following my track. This caused us some uneasiness. Should the enemy overtake us, and we have the advantage in an encounter, they would be immediately reinforced, while we could expect no assistance, being so far advanced beyond our military posts, our boats and provisions likewise being taken, cut off all hope of retreat by the rout we came; but after due deliberation, it was resolved to accomplish our object at all events, and return by Connecticut River. Lieut. McMullen was despatched by land to Crown Point to desire Gen. Amherst to relieve us with provisions at Ammonoosuck river, at the extremity of the Coos intervales; that being the way we should return if we ever should return. We now determined to out-march our pursuers, and destroy St. Francis, before we were overtaken. We marched nine days through a spruce bog, where the ground was wet and low, great part of it being covered with water a foot deep. When we encamped at night, we cut boughs from the trees, and with them, constructed a kind of hammocks to secure ourselves from the water. We uniformly began our march a little before day and continued it until after dark at night. The tenth day after leaving the Bay brought us to a river fifteen miles north of St. Francis, which we were compelled to ford against a swift current. The tallest men were put up stream, and holding by each other, the party passed over with the loss of several guns, which were recovered by diving to the bottom. We had now good marching ground, and proceeded to destroy the town as before related; which would in all probability, have been effected with no other loss but the Indian who was killed in the action, had not our boats been discovered, and our retreat that way cut off.

This tribe of Indians was notoriously attached to the French, and had for a century past harrassed the frontiers of New England, murdering people of all ages and sexes, in the most barbarous manner, and in times of peace, when they had no reason to suspect their hostile intentions.

They had within my own knowledge during the six years past, killed and carried away more than 600 persons. We found 600 scalps hanging upon poles over the doors of their wigwams.

It is impossible to describe the dejected and miserable condition of the party; on arriving at the Coos intervales. After so long a march over rocky barren mountains, and through deep swamps, worn down with hunger and fatigue, we expected to be relieved at the intervales, and assisted in our return. The officer despatched to the General reached Crown Point in nine days, and faithfully discharged his commission; upon which, the General immediately ordered Lieut. Stevens to Number Four, and to proceed thence with provisions up the river, to the place I had designated; there, to wait so long as there were any hopes of my return. The officer thought proper to remain but two days, and returned carrying with him all the provisions, about two hours before our arrival. We found a fresh fire burning in his camp, and fired guns to bring him back, which he heard, but would not return supposing we were an enemy.

In this emergency I resolved to make the best of my way to Number Four, leaving the remainder of the party now unable to proceed any further, to obtain such wretched subsistence as the wilderness afforded, until I could relieve them, which I promised to do in ten days.

Capt. Ogden, myself and a captive Indian boy, embarked upon a raft of dry pine trees. The current carried us down the stream in the middle of the river, where we kept our miserable vessel, with such paddles as could be split, and hewn with small hatchets. The second day we reached White River falls; and very narrowly escaped running over them. The raft went over, and was lost; but our remaining strength enabled us to land and march by the falls. At the foot of them, Capt. Ogden and the Ranger killed some red squirrels and also a partridge, while I attempted to construct another raft. Not being able to cut the trees, I burnt them down, and burnt them at proper lengths. This was our third day's work after leaving our companions. The next day we floated down to Wattoquichie falls, which are about fifty yards in length. Here we landed, and Capt. Ogden held the raft by a wythe of hazle bushes, while I went below the falls, to swim in, board and paddle it ashore; this being our only hope for life, as we had not strength sufficient to make a new raft, should this be lost. I succeeded in securing it; and next morning we floated down within a short distance of Number Four. Here we found several men cutting timber, who relieved and assisted us to the Fort. A canoe was immediately despatched up the river with provisions, which reached the men at Coos in four days after, which according to my agreement, was the tenth after I left them. Two days afterwards, I went up the river with two other canoes, to relieve others of my party who might be coming that way. . . .

One of the Rangers instead of more important plunder, placed in his knapsack a large lump of tallow, which enabled him to fare comfortably on his return, while many of his comrades, who had secured more valuable articles, perished with hunger.

Birthplace of the Submarine

ELLSWORTH S. GRANT

ALTHOUGH UNQUESTIONABLY THE OUTSTANDING mechanical genius of the American Revolution, David Bushnell has long been one of his country's unsung heroes. The father of submarine warfare, from his own fertile brain he designed and built *Turtle,* the first practical "water machine," armed with underwater bombs, to be used as a weapon of war. Early on young David determined a farmer's life was not for him. An omnivorous reader, his inquiring mind turned to anything mechanical or mathematical, and he longed for more education than the village school offered. After his father's death and his mother's remarriage, Bushnell moved into the Saybrook home of Elias Tully, whose ancestor had compiled the first American almanac, and prepared to enter Yale College. He did so in 1771 in his 31st year, twice the age of most of his classmates, who included Nathan Hale and Joel Barlow.

There he astonished his fellow students one day by demonstrating that gunpowder could burn under water. His wooden bottle containing two ounces of powder, sunk to the bottom of a pond and ignited by an external fuse, exploded with a glorious roar and massive concussion that lifted a waterspout high above the surface. The idea of a "sub-marine" had already occurred to him, but he realized that, if such a craft were to attach a mine to the bottom of an enemy vessel, the operator would need time to escape if he wanted to live. Accordingly, he made a clockwork mechanism inside the mine that enabled the operator to regulate the exact moment of detonation[:] the first time bomb.

The flames of hostility between the thirteen American colonies and the mother country were intensifying. The Boston Massacre, the Boston Tea Party and the battles at Lexington and Concord had outraged the patriots of Connecticut. During his final college vacation, Bushnell rushed back to Saybrook where he persuaded his husky younger brother, Ezra, to help him put together both the mine and the submarine. David paid for the materials out of his own pocket, subcontracting the making of the clockwork mechanism and the water pumps. Yale closed its doors early in response to General Washington's call to arms, and by the end of July, David and Ezra were working feverishly to finish their project.

From Ellsworth S. Grant, *Thar She Goes!* (Essex, Conn.: Fenwick Productions, 2000).

Now they took into their confidence two close friends, David's tutor at Yale, the Reverend John Lewis and Dr. Benjamin Gale of Killingworth, a pastor and physician. On August 3, Lewis dispatched a long letter, written entirely in Latin, to Dr. Ezra Stiles in Newport, who became president of Yale three years later, saying, "This man is the inventor of a machine which is now made and almost perfected for the destruction of the fleet in the harbor of Boston. . . ." Gale followed with an eyewitness account of the curious vessel in operation which he communicated to Benjamin Franklin in Philadelphia. Describing *Turtle* in detail, he concluded, "It is all Constructed with Great Simplicity and upon Principles of Natural Philosophy and I Conceive is not Equaled by any thing I ever heard of or Saw, Except Dr. Franklin's Electrical Experiments."

Dr. Franklin responded promptly by coming to Saybrook en route to Boston for a demonstration. With Dr. Gale, he was conveyed by boat to the mouth of the river, where they could observe *Turtle* in action. One legend states that Mrs. Bushnell was also present and fainted away when Ezra, who had agreed to be the operator, disappeared under the surface of the Lyme marshes! Properly impressed, Franklin must have carried the news to Boston, for soon many were whispering about "the famous water machine from Connecticut." General Israel Putnam and Colonel David Humphreys became two of the inventor's staunchest supporters.

A Tory spy, none other than the Killingworth postmaster, who opened and copied all of Gale's correspondence, informed the British governor of New York, William Tryon. The latter, tongue in cheek, advised the commander-in-chief of the English fleet: "The great news of the day with us is now to Destroy the Navy, a certain Mr. Bushnell has completed his Machine. . . ."

Meanwhile, Bushnell, delayed by malfunctioning water pumps, had to postpone his plan to attack the British men-of-war in Boston. In February 1776, he rode up to Lebanon to acquaint Governor Trumbull and the Council of Safety with his efforts. Moved by its great potential and the desperation of the times, the council voted to advance him £60, which was soon conveyed to Saybrook by Lieutenant Matthew Griswold, a resident of Lyme.

By summertime, the Bushnell brothers were ready. A gigantic British fleet had assembled off New York, including Admiral Howe's 64-gun flagship *Eagle*. Opposing this impressive array of power was the rag-tag Continental Army of 28,000 men, cheered only by the Declaration of Independence being circulated throughout the colonies. David and Ezra, loading their mines and underwater craft aboard a small sloop, sailed westerly up Long Island Sound and, unobserved by the British, arrived at their destination in August.

Bad luck, however, plagued them. Ezra succumbed to a fever, forcing his brother to load his equipment back aboard his sloop and return home, where he put three new volunteers through a crash training program. On August 22, the Battle of Long Island dealt a disastrous blow to the Americans. Bushnell immediately returned with *Turtle* to New York. After a few delays, the submarine was brought around to the tip of Manhattan, where she would be sheltered by the two 32-pound guns of Whitehall Battery.

The anxious patriots selected the night of September 6, as suitable for the attack on the British fleet, because the moon was a mere crescent, the weather clear, the tidal currents not too strong and the waters of the harbor relatively calm. Bushnell had already selected Sergeant Ezra Lee of Lyme as the best prepared to carry out *Turtle*'s ambitious and specific mission of blowing up *Eagle* as she lay at anchor just north of Staten Island. The intrepid young operator was joined at the Battery wharf by Bushnell, Israel Putnam, Colonel David Humphreys, Lee's brother-in-law, Brigadier Samuel Parsons of Lyme and a few others. General George Washington and some aides are reputed to have viewed the proceedings from the vantage point of a Broadway rooftop, hoping to witness the thrilling spectacle of the British battleship bursting asunder.

Lee's orders were to maneuver *Turtle,* either above or below the surface of the bay, out to its target. Then he was to descend to the keel of the enemy vessel, into which he would firmly insert a prepared screw. Attached to the screw was a short line tied to the mine, which he would set to explode within the hour. After accomplishing this task, he was to make his way back to the Battery as fast as possible.

Sergeant Lee climbed into *Turtle* and cast off from the wharf at exactly 11 P.M., the whale boats towing him as near the fleet as they dared. Submerging under *Eagle,* he tried twice without success to insert the screw into the ship's hull and then abandoned his mission because of the oncoming daylight. He retreated upriver as fast as he could go, a four-mile trip that took him past Governor's Island, where the enemy observed him. Seeing a barge launched to intercept him, he let loose the mine. The sailors took flight, to Ezra's infinite joy, and rowed back to shore. An American whaleboat then towed Lee in, at which point there was a tremendous explosion in the water. General Putnam, thrilled by the sight of the mine bursting, is reputed to have shouted: "God curse 'em, that'll do it for them!" But of course the world's first submarine attack had already failed. After two more unsuccessful attacks, Bushnell gave up his grand scheme.

In mid-1779 Bushnell, having abandoned any further bold experiments, was inducted into the Corps of Sappers and Miners as a captain-lieutenant, and he served until the end of the hostilities. He was mustered out with a land bounty of 400 acres and five years' pay. Connecticut still owed him for his patriotic services between 1777 and 1779, but the General Assembly, disregarding his pioneering work, deigned to pay less than a third of his bill. Galled, discouraged and weakened by a strange malady, Bushnell suddenly disappeared from Saybrook in the summer of 1787. The strangely secretive and moody inventor was never seen again in the town of his birth. Rumors spread that he had perished in the French Revolution, had died in the poorhouse or even committed suicide. Most people simply forgot his existence.

Actually, David Bushnell lived to a ripe old age. Deciding to assume a new identity and an academic career, with the support of Yale friends, he settled down in the little town of Warrenton, Georgia. For the rest of his life he kept secret his past exploits. Until his death in 1826, he was known only as Dr. David Bush, professor of medicine, at Franklin College, the first land-grant college in America.

The Essex Raid

CAPTAIN RICHARD COOTE AND THE *CONNECTICUT GAZETTE*

His Majesty's Sloop *Borer*
Off Saybrook 9th April 1814
Sir,

I have the honor to acquaint you that in obedience to your Order of the 7th instant, directing me to take charge of a detachment of Boats belonging to the Squadron under your command for the purpose of taking or destroying a number of Vessels building and equipping as Privateers and Letters of Marque in Connecticut River, I proceeded to His Majesty's sloop under my command on the evening of that day to put those Orders in Execution, and I have now the pleasure of informing you that thro' the

From the report of Captain Richard Coote, commanding officer of H.M.S. *Borer*, 9 April 1814, and the article in the *Connecticut Gazette,* 13 April 1814.

steady and indefatigable exertions of the Officers and Men who you did me the honor of placing under my Orders, the Service has been accomplished in a more effectual way than my most sanguine hopes could have led me to expect.

The *Borer* anchored off Saybrook bar at 1/4 before 10, and the Boats, consisting of a Barge, Pinnace and Gig, under Lieuts Pyne, Parry and Acting Lieut Fisher from *La Hogue,* a Barge from the *Maidstone* under Lt. Siddon, a Barge from the *Endymion* under Lieut Fanshaw, and the *Borers* Gig, with the Seamen and Marines selected for the expedition under their respective Officers immediately proceeded up the River.

The wind being Northerly, and a very [undecipherable] outset of the Current (notwithstanding its being flood tide) prevented us from making [undecipherable] a progress as we desired, but even this difficulty tended in the end to render our operations more deliberate, the first object being that of destroying a Battery on the West Side of the Entrance, a division landed for that purpose, and meeting no opposition in entering the Fort from which was found the Guns had been removed.

The distance from the Entrance of the River to Petty Pogue where the Vessels lay is only 6 miles; we did not arrive at that place till 1/2 past 3 in the morning of the 8th, on approaching it we found the town alarmed, the Militia all on the alert, and apparently disposed with the assistance of one 4 lb. Gun to oppose our landing, however after the discharge of the Boats' Guns, and a volley of Musketry from our Marines, they prudently ceased firing and gave us no further interruption.

The Marines were formed immediately on landing and under the skilful direction of Lieut Lloyd of that Corps, took up such a position as to command the principal Street and to cover the Seamen which employed in their respective Duties.

The Vessels alongside the Wharf were then warped out into the Stream, and those on the Stocks and aground near the Town were instantly burned.

As the day opened many others were seen on Slips and at Moorings higher up the River, and those were as promptly set fire to by a small detachment under Lieuts Pyne and Fanshaw to whom we are greatly endebted for the serious damage the Enemy has sustained in this respect.

Several Stores were found to contain large quantities of Cable, Cordage, Sails & Spirits which were either destroyed or removed to the *Young Anaconda* Brig and *Eagle* Schooner, each ready for sea and which I at first deemed practicable to bring out, and the object of the expedition being fully accomplished by every Vessel within 3 Miles of the Town being either destroyed or in our possession, the party were at 10 o'clock embarked with the most perfect order and regularity in presence of a very numerous population, not an execution to the character of discipline and sobriety having arisen tho' surrounded by temptations and even urged by the inhabitants to indulge in Liquor.

At 11 AM we weighed with the Brig *Anaconda* and *Eagle* Schooner and proceeded with them and the Boats some distance down the River, the Wind however blowing strong directly up, and the Channel being extremely narrow, the former grounded with a falling Tide, and I so perceived from the preparations which were making to annoy us on all sides, that it would be expedient to destroy both these Vessels, the Party were accordingly all removed to the *Eagle,* and before we lost sight of the Brig we had the satisfaction of seeing her burnt to the Water's edge. I then determined to defer our retreat 'till after dark, as tho' at the Schooner's present Anchorage, we were exposed to a fire of Musquetry from a Wood within half Musquet Shot, by far the greatest preparations were making on the banks of a still narrower part of the River which we had got to pass, I here received a communication from the Military Officer Commanding in that district of which I have the honor to enclose herewith a Copy.

My reply was verbal, and merely expressed my Surprise at such Summons, assuring the bearer that tho' sensible of their humane intentions, we set their power to detain us at defiance.

Every arrangement being made for effecting our retreat, at 7 o'clock the *Eagle* was set on fire, and the Boats formed in regular Order, commenced dropping down the River, here a brisk fire was opened from the Wood which had partially annoyed us during the day, but where they had prudently concealed their Cannon 'till darkness rendered it impossible for us to get possession of them, this encounter I am sorry to say deprived us of the lives of two valuable Marines, and wounded one Seaman in the *Maidstone's* Boat, but did not in any degree disturb the regularity of our movements.

The most formidable preparations were made near the town of Lyme and on the opposite bank of the river which is there not more than 3/4 of a mile wide, here they were provided with several pieces of Cannon, and from my own observation confirmed by Major Ely's statement, I feel confident that their Military Force amounted to many hundred men.

By waiting 'till the Night became dark, and by then allowing the Boats to drop down the Stream silently, we got nearly abreast of this part of the passage unobserved.

Every precaution within the Compass of their Military Skill had here been taken to arrest our progress, large fires were alight on each side to show the situation of the Boats, and Vessels filled with armed Men were anchored in the River, all these commenced a brisk but ill directed fire at the same instant, and from the short space which separated the Parties, I have reason to suppose it must have proved much more destructive to their friends than to their Enemies, for tho' I believe no Boat escaped without receiving more or less shot, by a degree of good fortune which I can only ascribe to providential care, on our side there was only one Man wounded, at ½ past 8 we were abreast of the lowest Fort, and that which we had found dismantled on the preceding Evening, guns however had been provided for this Fort also during the day, and here they made final and equally ineffectual effort to detain us. The Boats passed in triumph leaving our Enemies to lament, their acknowledgement of being provided with a force which they had the leisure of a whole day to collect in one of the most populous parts of America, from which they thought it impossible for us to escape. . . .

I have the honor to be, Sir,
With every Sentiment of Respect
Your very humble Servant
(Signed) RICHARD COOTE, Commander

To/
The Hon'ble T. B. Capel
Captain HM Ship *La Hogue*
& Senior Officer off New London

DISASTER OF PETTIPAUGE

It is with grief and mortification, we perform the task of announcing to our readers, that on Friday morning last, four of the enemy's barges and two launches commanded by Capt. Coote of the brig BORER, with 800 men proceeded up Connecticut River to Pettipauge Point, and destroyed upward of twenty sail of vessels, without sustaining, probably, the loss of a single man.

We have ascertained on the unfortunate stop the following facts. The boats first landed at the fort at Saybrook, where they found neither men nor cannon; from thence they proceeded directly to Pettipauge Point; landed at 4 o'clock in the morning and were paraded in the principal street before the least alarm was given. The inhabitants were, it may well be supposed, in great consternation; but Capt. Coote informed them that he was in sufficient force to effect the object of his expedition, which was to burn the vessels; and that if his party were not fired upon, no harm should fall upon the persons of the inhabitants, or the property unconnected with the vessels, and a mutual understanding of that purport was agreed to. The enemy immediately after commenced the act of burning the vessels. Such as exposed the buildings on the wharves they hauled into the stream.

A party of 14 men in the meantime were sent a quarter of a mile above the point, who put fire to several vessels which were on the stocks. At ten o'clock they left the shore entirely, and took possession of a brig and a schooner, which were built for privateers; these they attempted to beat down the river, but the brig getting on shore they burnt her, and the schooner was so light as to be unmanageable.

They continued in her and the boats alongside, until about dusk, when Lieutenant Bray with a field piece from Killingworth, commenced firing on them. After the second shot they left the schooner and took shelter under a small island opposite the point, and at half past 8 o'clock it being very dark made their escape from the river. Their conduct towards the inhabitants was unexceptionable, except that some clothes and plate were taken by a person supposed to be an American, who it was conjectured acted as a pilot and guide; and had frequently been there with fish for sale. This wretch, without orders, destroyed a large new cable by cutting it with an axe.

Notwithstanding the enemy were on shore at 4 o'clock in the morning, it was half past 12 P.M. before the express arrived here with the information, although a report of the fact was brought by stage at 11. Every exertion was immediately made to send a force sufficient for the object; a body of marines from the squadron, a company of infantry from Fort Trumbull, and a part of Capt. French's militia company of artillery with a field piece, and a considerable number of volunteers were soon in motion. A part of the marines and volunteers in carriages, and Capt. French with his detachment and field piece, arrived at the River at 4 o'clock, at which time a respectable body of militia, infantry and artillery, occupied the banks on both sides, in the momentary expectation that the enemy would attempt to descend.

It was, however, soon perceived that it was not their intention to attempt going out before dark; and that the only chance of taking or destroying them was by a joint attack by land and water. Timely measures for this purpose were prevented by the want of water craft, a misfortune which could not be remedied in the very short period required. A strong freshet, an ebb tide, and thick mist, enabled the enemy to escape down the river unheard, and unseen, except by a very few who commenced a fire, which was followed at random by many who discerned no object to direct their aim. The troops from the garrison and Marines on foot did not arrive until the British had escaped.

Thus ended an expedition achieved with the smallest loss to the enemy, and the greatest in magnitude of damage that has occurred on the seaboard since the commencement of the War.

Indian Stream Republic

EDWIN M. BACON

PITTSBURG WAS THE ORIGINAL "Indian Stream Territory" which has a record as an independent republic as late as the eighteen-thirties. The region was a magnificent Indian hunting-ground and lay unexplored till 1787, when a party of Canadian surveyors penetrated it. Shortly after it was drawn into the limits of New Hampshire by a survey of 1789. Then two former Rangers journeyed up to it from the Lower Coös on a prospecting trip. They came upon the broad intervals at the mouth of Indian Stream late in September when the bordering woods in autumn ripeness were flaming with gorgeous hues, and were enraptured. After a month of hunting and trapping in the game-filled forests, they returned bearing rich spoil and flattering reports. The next summer, joined by a few others, they came up again to attempt a settlement; and "pitches" were made on the meadows. As winter approached, however, all went back to the Lower Coös. Thereafter only hunting parties roamed the country till about 1796, when the permanent settlement was promoted by other Valley-townsmen who had obtained a deed of the whole territory from a local Indian chief—an up-country King Philip.

At that time the region was in dispute, and many regarded it as a sort of *terra incognita* wholly outside of the jurisdiction of either New Hampshire or Canada. In the wake of the permanent settlers came troubled debtors and persons of easy morals who sought the remote district untrammeled by awkward laws as an asylum from pressing creditors or from punishment for crime. But the settlers themselves were of worthy stock. They cleared large farms up the River's sides and on the north of Connecticut Lake; built comfortable homes; and reared great families.

From Edwin M. Bacon, *The Connecticut River* (New York: G. P. Putnam's Sons, 1907).

Despite the mixed character of the community, affairs moved tranquilly for the first thirty years without any fixed system of local government, a mild form of vigilance committee law sufficing for the treatment of flagrant offences against the common peace. Then disorganizing features developed and the need of a local government of some sort for mutual protection became apparent; and accordingly, in the spring of 1829, the independent state was set up as "the United Inhabitants of the Indian Stream Territory." It was a unique political establishment, one of the smallest and most democratic in history. The "Centre School-House" was sufficient for the assembly of all the people at its inauguration. At the outset the "United Inhabitants" asserted their independence of both the United States and Great Britain. The frame of government comprehended three departments, representative, executive, and judicial. The representative department comprised the entire voting population, each member directly representing his own interests. The executive department was termed the "supreme council," and consisted of five persons, to be chosen annually. The judicial department was composed of justices of the peace elected by the people in their municipal capacity. The supreme council constituted a court of last appeal. Trial by jury was provided, the jury to consist of six persons. A code of laws was adopted at the first meeting of the legislative branch. A military company of forty men was formed for protection against "foreign invasion" and domestic violence.

This forest state with its novel government continued in fair working order for about five years. Then it fell to pieces. With no jail it could only resort to punishment by fine or by banishment. It lost the power to enforce the execution of its laws. Finally "treason crept in" and its destruction was complete. This was in 1835. Chaos followed. The people divided into two opposing parties, one invoking the protection of New Hampshire, the other of Canada. New Hampshire assumed a quasi jurisdiction over the territory by sending officers into it to serve processes issued by her courts. The Canada party resisted them. The sheriff of Coös County came up and appointed a resident deputy sheriff. At the same time he gave assurances of the protection of New Hampshire to all who were loyal to her, warning all others of the "consequences of treasonable acts." Shortly after a county magistrate of Lower Canada appeared with promises of the protection of Great Britain to all favoring Canadian jurisdiction, and with the added advice to the Canada party to resist the "encroachments" of the New Hampshire authorites. Several of the Canada party fortified their houses and armed themselves. Soon the gage was thrown down and war opened.

It was a short and decisive campaign of a single fight. On a certain crisp October morning the New Hampshire deputy sheriff awoke to find his house surrounded by a company of armed men from Canada headed by a Canadian sheriff, together with a band of the local Canada party. The deputy was seized on a Canadian warrant and hurried off on foot toward Canada. News of the capture was quickly spread to the River towns below. By noon a hundred or more mounted men had collected from the lower border towns, Clarksville, Stewartstown, Canaan, and Colebrook, variously armed with implements of warfare ranging from murderous farm tools to the regulation weapons of the militia. Immediately the improvised army started in hot pursuit. The invaders were overhauled a mile beyond the Canada line, and there fought. The skirmish, in which a few were hurt but none was killed, ended with the rescue of the prisoner and the inglorious rout of his captors. The rescued deputy was brought back to the safe haven of the country store at Canaan, and then the "army" quietly melted away. Subsequently the militia of the border towns were called to the assistance of the Coös County sheriff, but no further outbreak occurred. Peace came with the final establishment of the jurisdiction of New Hampshire. The more aggressive of the Canada party moved over the border, and those who remained accepted the situation philosophically. In 1840 the "Indian Stream Territory" disappeared from the map, and Pittsburg, with sixty ratable polls, took its place.

Boundary Confusion

DANIEL DOAN

IN THE YEAR 1755, with the French and English about to engage in the final struggle for North America, John Mitchell published a map in London. He called it the "Map of British and French Dominions in North America." Six feet four inches by four feet four inches, clearly drawn, it became a standard reference until after the Revolution.

When Mitchell drew his map, the wilderness of the northern Connecticut valley extended south from the source a hundred and fifty miles to the most northerly English fort. The forests had for years sheltered the

Daniel Doan, excerpts from *Indian Stream Republic*, pp. 58–65 © 1977 by Donald Keith McDougal, reprinted by permission of University Press of New England.

Algonquian allies of the French in their raids on the English settlements. The most extended, official, upstream exploration in New Hampshire had been carried out by Captain Peter Powers at the head of a scouting party sent by Governor Benning Wentworth. Powers turned back several days' march from the crucial eastward bend of the river, which Mitchell had omitted.

Like other mapmakers of his time, Mitchell relied on "the best information" (as Blanchard described it on his later map) about the uninhabited areas. This information came from hunters, from trappers, from rangers in the service of the province, or from captives ransomed back from Canada. These men also contributed information derived from the Indians themselves. Thus, across the territory between the upper Connecticut and the Kennebec Rivers, Mitchell printed the caption, "Carriages from Norridgenaok to R. St. Francis." This suggested Indian canoe travel, for he meant portages between rivers and lakes; it contributed little to understanding the geography of the area, other than the idea that Indians somehow traveled the maze of projected rivers and lakes.

The map's serious error lay, for New Hampshire, in the arrangement Mitchell gave to the Connecticut at its source. The river did not run where he drew it on his map. He showed it leading north beyond the Forty-fifth Parallel—upstream—in a straight course, slightly east of the dwindling St. Francis river of Canada, to three lakes on three branches. His mistake had some accuracies in it. The river *did* have three lakes in this twenty miles, but joined by a single main channel. The river *did* flow into New England from the highlands, which tipped northern water into the St. Lawrence, but the river turned east, and much of the area was drained by the tributaries, eventually to be known as Hall's Stream, Indian Stream, and Perry Stream. The error might have been of no special consequence had not Benjamin Franklin, for the United States, and Richard Oswald, the British negotiator, referred to the map in preliminary discussions that led to the treaty concluding the Revolution.

There are other origins of the confusion. Twelve years before the shots fired at Lexington and Concord, the English king found himself, through the foolhardy but successful gamble of General Wolfe, in control of eastern North America. He issued a proclamation that established a northern boundary, east to west, between the old colonies and the provinces acquired by the conquest of Canada. This line was to be the forty-fifth degree of north latitude from the St. Lawrence River east across the northern end of Lake Champlain to the highlands dividing the waters of the St. Lawrence from those "which fall into the sea," namely, the Atlantic. No directions specified how to go from the Forty-fifth Parallel to the highlands in northern New Hampshire. None was needed; the territory was wilderness and all British. An unaccountable jog of twenty miles in the line had little importance.

Meanwhile, the provinces of New Hampshire and of New York began to quarrel over the territory that is now Vermont. Their conflicting claims went back to complications in original charters. New Hampshire's Governor Benning Wentworth granted townships as far west as Bennington and as far north as Maidstone. Under his direction, in March 1760 Joseph Blanchard of Dunstable surveyed up the Connecticut River on the ice from Charlestown, Old Fort Number Four, as far north as the present towns of Haverhill and Newbury in the section known as Lower Coos. Hubartes Neal continued the survey to Upper Coos above Fifteen Mile Falls, setting up markers of stones, blazing trees, and driving stakes in the riverbank six miles apart to indicate the townships. Governor Wentworth granted these surveyed towns to groups of men suitably equipped with money. He reserved land to himself, and had a tidy real estate business going.

New York objected so strenuously that the board of trade became involved. It established a north-south division between the provinces in 1762, the year after the king proclaimed the east-west lines of the northern boundary. The board decreed that the west bank of the Connecticut should separate the two provinces, from the boundary of the Province of Massachusetts Bay as far north as the Forty-fifth Parallel established by the king's proclamation.

Nobody knew exactly where this degree of latitude lay, though it formed so prominent a part of the proclamation, and though it appeared as a line on Mitchell's map. Obviously it lay midway between the equator and the north pole, but where was it on Lake Champlain? Where was it on the Connecticut River? Governor Wentworth's men had not surveyed that far upstream. What is more, nobody cared where it lay. Eight years passed before New York and Quebec undertook a joint survey. In 1771, under the direction of John Collins for New York and of Thomas Vallentine for Quebec, men began cutting a line through the wilderness.

On the first of October in the following year, 1772, John Collins wrote to Governor Tryon of New York from his camp on the Connecticut River. The completion of his work in that section, enhanced by the clear weather of October and by the red and yellow trees under a blue sky, put a note of satisfaction in his letter. He had fixed the boundary between New York and Quebec on the west bank of the Connecticut River, two miles and fifty chains on a direct line beyond the mouth of a small river flowing into the west side of the Connecticut, known as Hall's Brook.

Here, marking the eastern end of the survey that was to be known as the Vallentine-Collins Line, a cedar post became the focal point of a controversy, not between two or three of His Majesty's provinces, but between Great Britain and the United States of America, then a group of restless colonies. Probably John Collins supervised the setting of the cedar post. His name was carved on it. Besides marking the eastern end of New York's northern boundary, the post also indicated the spot at which the Forty-fifth Parallel intersected the Connecticut. Later determination that Vallentine and Collins had been north of the true latitude made no difference; it was accepted for thirty years before anyone questioned the astronomy of it. Today, because the international boundary negotiations of Webster and Ashburton settled on Hall's Stream, a granite monument stands in the approximate place of the cedar post, denoting the northeast corner of Vermont on the Canaan-Pittsburg town line. Maps show the Forty-fifth Parallel about a mile south.

At the time of the 1772 survey, no attempt was made to plot a route to the highlands, logically up the Connecticut River, or to follow the highlands east. New Hampshire, the province involved south of Quebec from there to the District of Maine, had no representative at the survey. This seems odd in view of a New Hampshire man's normal willingness to believe the Yorkers would steal him blind if given half a chance. Quebec, alone, could have surveyed on up the river to establish its claim on the route to the highlands, and to locate the highlands, a vague term in the king's proclamation. But wilderness was, after all, only wilderness, and for either side of the theoretical division, the forest and land came under the jurisdiction of His Majesty's government—if the moose and other furry inhabitants cared to know. More important was a survey at the head of that great north-south thoroughfare, Lake Champlain.

Boundaries to the highlands from other New England provinces had a similarly tentative quality about their northern ends. In 1764 the Province of Massachusetts Bay had sent a party to the Bay of Passamaquoddy in search of the St. Croix River, the eastern bound of its Maine lands. The line between New Hampshire and these Maine lands had been agreed on as the Piscataqua River at Portsmouth, then north from its source two degrees west, "till one hundred and twenty miles were finished from the mouth of Piscataqua harbor or until it meet with his majesty's other governments." Walter Bryant in 1741 measured and blazed about thirty miles of the line, but bad traveling and "alarms as to Indians" turned him back to the coast. Twenty-seven years later, in 1768, Isaac Ringe marked the line to Lake Umbagog but did not push on to the highlands, beyond which water flowed into the St. Lawrence.

These boundaries remained unchanged, except for annual growth of bark on blazed trees and for bushes springing up in the clearings around the stakes marking the miles. The colonies took more and more positive measures against England's policies, and embarked on their own independent troubles by revolution. The Continental Congress, clumsily prosecuting a war of doubtful outcome against a great power, yet looked ahead with sanguine forethought to a peace treaty. On August 14, 1779, it unanimously agreed to the north boundary that its peace commissioner must adhere to in negotiations. This would follow west from Nova Scotia, in the area now New Bruswick, along the same highlands designated in the king's proclamation of 1763. Here, more knowledgeable than the king's commissioners, the congressional committee specified the route across New Hampshire over the jog between the highlands and the forty-fifth degree of latitude, taken to be the line west along the survey by Vallentine and Collins. At the northwesternmost head of the Connecticut River, the line would turn down the middle of the river and follow it to the Forty-fifth Parallel. Here was a northern boundary for the United States (as well as for New Hampshire), to be demanded of Great Britain by a peace commissioner not yet appointed, in a treaty terminating a war not yet won, by a country that could scarcely claim the name of nation, in a territory never surveyed and most inaccurately mapped. Yet it was accepted: the detailed disputes came later.

Whoever the congressional expert coining the phrase "northwesternmost head of Connecticut River," he devised a term that was made for controversy. Had he described it as the source of Hall's Brook, the tributary running from the western end of the highlands, all would have come clear. Probably the British would have accepted it. They were in an accepting mood when, in 1782, Benjamin Franklin and John Jay met with the British peace commissioners, Richard Oswald and Henry Strachey, in France. After discussions about the boundary, Franklin and Oswald marked in red ink one of Mitchell's maps. Most certainly to them, the northwesternmost head of the Connecticut lay in the waters of Mitchell's western lake—which did not exist.

Rumors of this tentative claim by the United States—or of its intention to make the claim, for the negotiations had been secret—reached Canada, where the authorities realized that their new neighbor planned to seek a frontier on Hall's Brook, meaning the present Hall's Stream. Surveyor General Samuel Holland reported to Lieutenant Governor Alured Clarke that the idea of considering Hall's Brook as a frontier, instead of the Connecticut River, appeared to him new. The survey of 1772 by Vallentine and Collins crossed Hall's Brook to the Connecticut, and formed the boundary accepted by the provinces of New York and Lower Canada. Although Paris negotiations had been secret, as was the provisional treaty of 1782, this exchange in March 1783 indicates a knowledge of American plans and a suspicion of the outcome. The final treaty of September 3, 1783, did not clarify the problem, although a New Englander,

John Adams, had joined the negotiations. The treaty specified: "along the said highlands which divide the rivers that empty themselves in the River St. Lawrence from those that fall into the Atlantic Ocean, to the northwesternmost head of Connecticut River, thence down the middle of that river to the forty-fifth degree of north latitude; thence by a line due west . . ."

And so the treaty was signed. The fifty-nine-year controversy began. Without even considering all the complications the treaty caused, such as the Aroostook War of 1839 in Maine, it is clear that the treaty's wording could be interpreted to suit two claims north of New Hampshire. Great Britain continued to maintain that the treaty meant that beyond the cedar post, the Canadian boundary should be the Connecticut. This would put the northwesternmost head at a tributary of Third Lake. To Americans this was not northwest at all. They maintained that Hall's Stream was the boundary, and its source was the northwesternmost head of the Connecticut. For New Hampshire this meant about two hundred thousand acres.

But the dispute at first remained undefined. Six years went by before anyone found time to go into the woods and locate the treaty points. General Washington had become president under the new constitution by the time the New Hampshire legislature at last appointed commissioners to survey the state's northern bounds. In 1789, Jeremiah Eames, the surveyor, then of Northumberland, and Luther Fuller, an early explorer of the upper valley, prepared to set out in March, that good month for woods travel. With them would go Nathan Hoit, another commissioner, later to be one of the men listed in the deed from Philip, Indian chief, and a Mr. Cram. Thomas Eames went along to supplement the wilderness knowledge of Eames and Fuller.

Fuller's account of the expedition indicates no hesitation about where the northwesternmost head of the Connecticut might be. He was testifying for the state in 1836, but his story is borne out by an earlier deposition by Jeremiah Eames. Men such as the Eames brothers and Luther Fuller—wide-ranging hunters and surveyors, associates of the Indians, in that time and place—had no doubts as to the lay of the land. They went up Hall's Stream, with packs and snowshoes, perhaps with a hand sled to haul over the crust. Sixteen miles from the junction they blazed trees, scribed them, and took bearings. This was close to being the northwesternmost head of the Connecticut by the American interpretation of the treaty. They then ran a line east-northeast to the highlands betwen the St. Francis River and the Connecticut, where they blazed more trees in the depths of the forest. then they went home.

In the fall, the same group, again led by Jeremiah Eames, surveyed the eastern line of New Hampshire from Shelburne to the highlands, where water ran north. On a cloudy, stormy day, they blazed and marked a birch as the northeast corner of the state. They felled or girdled additional trees to mark the spot. Then they surveyed west with compass and chain for a total of seventeen miles, numbering a tree at each mile, till they reached their March line and a big fir tree on Hall's Stream. This was the final northwesternmost head of the Connecticut as they understood it, and so they carved "NH NW 1789" on the fir. Then they returned down Hall's Stream to Canaan and Stewartstown. Jeremiah kept a journal of his survey.

This was the fall when Nathaniel Wales and David Gibbs camped on Indian Stream to hunt and explore. Jeremiah and his party had surveyed around them.

The New Hampshire legislature made no prominent announcement that it had established the state's northern boundary. Had it instructed representatives at New York, the national capital at the time, to read excerpts from Jeremiah's journal, some national attention might have been given that section of the Canadian line, and future confusion eliminated.

Canada disregarded the survey, or did not know of it. Samuel Holland, Quebec's surveyor general, in 1792 sent a party to lay out a township east of Hall's Stream. Starting at the cedar post of Vallentine and Collins, the Canadian surveyors ran a line north to mark off Hereford in the west and the new township of Drayton on the east. Drayton would include the fertile valley of Indian Stream, where Wales and Gibbs had begun to clear land and raise crops.

The Canadian survey party did not disturb the New Hampshire men. Neither did the Canadians make objections to the survey of 1799, which Jeremiah made to lay out a township for the Eastman Company.

In the next twelve years further settlement continued by New Hampshire men: John Haynes, Nathaniel Perkins, and Ebenezer Fletcher, among others. Disliking the War of 1812, they found no satisfaction from the national government in the Treaty of Ghent. Its article five could be regarded as a slick taking of the American commissioners by the British. Ebenezer Fletcher in particular kept up with the news, and John Haynes learned of downriver events from his friend, Colonel Bedel. New Hampshire men wouldn't expect much of a Kentuckian, Henry Clay, but they figured that since he wanted the war, at least he could get more than article five out of the British, now that the war was won. John Quincy Adams ought to have known, as a Massachusetts man, that the head of the St. Croix River, on the border of Maine, had been agreed to in 1798 by both Great Britain and the United States. He ought to have been informed that New Hampshire had marked the northwesternmost head of the Connecticut River. All the same, both Clay and Adams as well as others signed the treaty, which declared that these points had not yet been established. It further expressed the nonsense—to a New Hampshire man—that the forty-fifth degree of north latitude had not been surveyed, when everyone knew that the cedar post, where the road from Canaan came to the brow of the hill on the way to Indian Stream, marked the eastern end.

Some of the settlers figured they were in Canada anyway—and glad of it. Others figured they were in New Hampshire—and anyone who doubted it, a fool. Still others figured they were in a secluded, untaxed valley, where a sheriff seldom bothered, or dared, to penetrate, and they wanted it left that way.

A New Hampshire gazetteer, which Eliphalet Merrill published in Exeter three years after the treaty, supported those who claimed New Hampshire had a northern boundary on the highlands north of the Connecticut. According to the declaration on the title page, *The Gazetteer* was compiled from information by the best authorites. Eliphalet Merrill noted the birch on the highlands toward Maine, marked "NE NH 1789" and a line extending seventeen miles, two hundred and seven rods, to the head of the northwesternmost branch of the Connecticut River, where a fir tree was inscribed as the northwest corner of New Hampshire, and down that river to the forty-fifth degree of latitude: Hall's Stream and the Vallentine-Collins line, of course. As that put the cedar post into New Hampshire, so much the better.

The settlers all went back to chopping trees, to raising wheat, corn, cattle, and offspring, back to trapping marten, making potash, building houses of lumber to replace their log houses, and to shooting bears and wolves. A commission had been appointed to meet at St. Andrews, New Brunswick, for surveying and mapping the boundary. Maybe something would come of it.

Chapter 3

EARLY TRAVELERS

Middletown, I think, is the most beautiful town of all. When I first came into the town, which was upon the top of a hill, there opened before me the most beautiful prospect of the river, and the intervals and improvements on each side of it, and the mountains, at about ten miles distant, both on the east and west side of the river. I went down this hill and into a great gate which led me right to the banks of the river. . . . I wish the Connecticut flowed through Braintree.
—John Adams in his diary, 1771

By the late 1700s, the Connecticut was peaceful enough that writers could begin looking at the river with a different focus, marveling at the wars it had passed through, excited about the new civilization that was springing up along its banks. Some of the most colorful "travels" in the valley occur from this period. John Ledyard, the Dartmouth dropout, made what is to this day the most famous voyage downriver, on his way to an adventurous, if tragically short, career as a world explorer; he died on an expedition to Africa in 1788 at the age of thirty-seven. (As Henry Beston notes: "John Ledyard had probably seen more of the vast world than any other being of his time.") My favorite account of his travels is by a young Henry Beston, the American nature writer whose later, more mature work includes the classic, The Outermost House.

Timothy Dwight was not only president of Yale College, not only the most prominent minister in New England, not only the most famous son of a family who had lived in the valley for nearly two centuries, but a travel writer with a very sharp eye; his Travels *is deservedly among the most celebrated writings connected to the river, and his lyrical summary of its beauty, its possibilities, remains the most ardent panegyric to the Connecticut ever written. The letters included here are from his trip of 1797.*

Visiting V.I.P.s were common in the eighteenth century in the valley, including the Marquis de Lafayette on his farewell visit to America in 1824. Charles Dickens came along in 1842 during his first American reading tour, and his trip resulted in a very characteristic piece of writing, with its delight in life's absurdities. Thoreau visited the Connecticut, too, but as shown by this excerpt from his journals, seemed homesick for Concord, and was not impressed.

Travelers have left, and continue to leave, interesting accounts right up to our own time. I've included Marguerite Allis's poignant conclusion to her book Connecticut River, *published in 1939. Ms. Allis also wrote two historical novels set on the Connecticut,* Not Without Peril, *about Fort Number Four, and* The Bridge, *set on the river in Middletown.*

John Ledyard Drops Out

HENRY BESTON

HERE WAS A MAN who was born with two great gifts, one the most precious in the world, the other most perilous. The first was an abounding physical vitality which made the casual business of being alive a divine adventure, the second, an imagination of the sort which refuses dicipline and runs away with the whole mind.

The adventure begins in the spring of the year 1772 with the farmers of the Connecticut Valley halting their ploughs in the furrow, and straightening up to stare at a certain extraordinary vehicle going north on the river road. This vehicle was nothing less than a two-wheeled sulky, then a rig almost unheard of outside the towns, and one never known to be used by travellers. A sulky with bundle baggage lashed behind, surely the driver must be an odd kind of rogue! Stopping at night-fall at a farm, the stranger met with close scrutiny by rural candle light. He was a fair-haired youth an inch or so under six feet tall, and of that "rangy" and powerful build which is as characteristic of American soil as Indian corn. His eyes, which were well spaced in a wide forehead, were grey-blue in

From Henry Beston, *The Book of Gallant Vagabonds* (New York: George H. Doran Co., 1925).

color, he had a good chin to face the world with, and something of a lean and eagle-ish nose. His name, he said, was John Ledyard, and he was on his way to become a missionary to the Indians.

This youth, John Ledyard, third of his name, had seen the light of day in the village of Groton, Connecticut; his father, a sea captain, had died young; legal mischance or a descent of happy relatives had deprived the young mother of her property, and John had been brought up in the house of his grandfather at Hartford. Then had come years at grammar school, the death of his grandfather, his virtual adoption by an uncle and aunt, and the attempt of these good folk to make a lawyer of him, which experiment had not been a success.

At twenty-one years of age, John presented something of a problem to his kinsmen. What was to be done with this great fair-haired youth who had neither money nor influential friends? Suddenly Destiny came down the Conecticut Valley with a letter.

The Reverend Eleazar Wheelock, founder of Dartmouth, wrote to John inviting him to the college. The passion of this good man's life was the evangelization of the dispossessed and incorrigible redskins; he visited them in their forlorn and dwindling encampments; he took their young men to be his pupils, and he had founded his college largely for the sake of training the sons of colonists to be Indian missionaries. Good Doctor Wheelock had been a friend of grandfather Ledyard's, and something or other had recalled to his mind the fair-haired boy who he had seen playing about the old man's house at Hartford. He would make a missionary of the lad, and send him forth to comfort the copper-skinned of the elect. A letter arrived offering John the status of a free pupil destined to the Indian field. Sulky and ancient nag were presently produced from somewhere, perhaps from John's own pocket, for he had just inherited a tiny legacy; the uncle and aunt waved farewell, a whip cracked in the air, and John and his sulky vanished over the hills and far away.

At Dartmouth College, he liked to act in plays, and clad in robes of Yankee calico, strutted about as the Numidian Prince, Syphax, in Mr. Addison's "Tragedy of Cato." A savour of old-fashioned rhetoric and magniloquence made its way from these plays into John's mind, and coloured his letters and his language all his life. He liked the out-of-doors, and on one occasion induced a group of comrades to climb with him to the top of a neighboring height, and spend the night on evergreen boughs strewn on the floor of deep holes dug in the snow. Doctor Wheelock nodded an enthusiastic consent; he saw in John's adventure fine training in hardship for his future missionaries! Letters of classmates paint Ledyard as restless, impatient of the dry bones of discipline, authoritative on occasion, and more a man with devoted cronies than one largely and carelessly popular. All other Dartmouth memories have faded in the epic glow of the adventurer's flight from his Alma Mater.

He came to college in a sulky, he left it an even more adventurous way. In the spring of 1773, the sound of the axe rings in the Dartmouth woods. Presently comes a shout, a great, crackling crash, and the sound and tremor of a heavy blow upon the earth. John Ledyard and his cronies have just felled a giant pine standing close by the bank of the Connecticut River. From this log, the home-spun undergraduates fashion a dug-out canoe, fifty feet long and three feet wide, a veritable barge of a canoe, and once the digging and hacking is done with, John himself weaves at the stern of the craft a kind of shelter-bower of willow wands. Word passes among the lads to be at the river early in the morning.

The spring in northern New England is no gracious and gradual awakening, it is shy, even timid, of approach, and there are times when the new leaves and petals have quite the air of children who have run out of the house on a winter's day. Then comes a sudden night of warmth and southwest wind, smells of wet earth and the sound of flooded streams fill all the dark, a rushing spirit of fertility shakes the land, and the rising sun reveals a world hurrying on to June. A dangerous spring in a Puritan land, for flesh and spirit are taken unawares, and swept off to the shrines of gods who have never made a covenant with man.

Such a spring it was, as the forest undergraduates gathered at the huge dug-out under the slanting light of early day, and watched their friend carry supplies to his canoe. John first put aboard a provender of dried venison and cornmeal, then a huge bearskin for a coverlet, and last of all two strangely assorted books, a Greek New Testament and the poems of Ovid. The truant Yankee sophomore steps into his canoe. A long halloo, a push all together, and the craft has slid off into the river, which, clear of ice and swollen by a thousand mountain streams, is rushing past their little college and on into the world. The current seizes the canoe; the wet paddle blade flashes in the cool sun; John masters the swirl with his strength and woodsman skill, and the future vagabond disappears on the way to his fantastic destiny. Little does the truant know that in January and February, 1787, a forlorn, penniless but indomitable traveller will accomplish one of the most amazing feats ever performed by mortal man, a fifteen hundred mile trudge through an unknown country deep in arctic snow and cold, and that the vagamond will be John Ledyard.

The mystery of his truancy remains to puzzle the world. For after all, why had he run away? In abandoning Dartmouth, he had locked behind him the one door to an education which had opened to him in his obscurity. John Ledyard's contemporaries said simply that the spring was racing in his blood, and that the born vagabond had been unable to control a vagabond urge. There is a world of truth in the reply, but not quite all the truth. The present day, with greater historical perspective, will have it that this fair-haired lad was not really a scion of the seaboard generations of transplanted Englishmen, but a son of the new, native-born, and native-minded culture which was springing up in the hearts of Americans during the last half of the eighteenth century. This lad is no spiritual kinsman of harsh and merciless Endecott; his place is with Daniel Boone and the lords of the frontier. But at Dartmouth, the seventeenth century sat in the seat of power, for, intellectually, Wheelock was a contemporary of Cotton Mather; the two dominies would have talked the same Canaanitish jargon, and shared an identical attitude to life. But young John was of different stuff, and, moreover, he was in certain ways, curiously modern. His flight from Dartmouth thus becomes a bit of vagabondage hiding an instincitive recoil, for had he accepted a missionary career, the seventeenth century would have claimed him forever for its own.

Down the Connecticut River floats the log canoe, carrying a young New Englander from theology under Oliver Cromwell to adventure under George the Third.

Dwight's Travels

TIMOTHY DWIGHT

Letter VI

Bellows Falls—Cavities worn in the rocks by the river—Canal—The first bridge over Connecticut River erected in this place by Colonel Enoch Hale—Governor's meadow

DEAR SIR,

Monday, September 25th, we set out for Charlestown, accompanied by Colonel Tyler, of Guilford in Vermont, who politely offered to point out to us whatever was interesting at Bellows Falls, three miles north of

From Timothy Dwight, *Travels in New England and New York* (New Haven: S. Converse, 1821).

the village of Walpole. These are the falls so fancifully described by Peters in that collection of extravagancies which he has been pleased to style "The History of Connecticut." They are certainly an interesting natural curiosity, although we did not find the water beneath them so hard as to be impervious to an iron crow. They are formed by four successive rifts, with the same number of rapids, and extend in a straight line three fourths of a mile; or, if measured on the circular course of the river, seven eighths. In this estimate include that part of the river which lies between the two ends of the canal to be described hereafter. All these rifts run from the foot of the Fall Mountain, the base of which at this spot terminates about forty rods eastward of the river. The rocks are very hard gray granite. In the northern and middle rifts there is nothing remarkable, but the southern has long been an object of peculiar attention. The waters of the Connecticut, which both above and below the falls are forty rods in breadth, are here contracted to the narrow compass of twenty feet; and, when the stream is very low, it is said, within that of six. The rapidity of the current may be conjectured from this fact.

An inquisitive traveler, while inspecting this ground, will want no argument to convince him that the river anciently had its channel about fifty rods, where the distance is greatest, westward of the place where it now runs. Here a canal is dug in its former bed to facilitate the transportation of boats around these falls. The bed of rocks, after crossing the present channel, takes a southwestern direction toward the lower end of the canal. Originally, the bed of the river was from fifteen to twenty feet higher than it is at present, as is unanswerably evident from the great number of excavations which it formerly wrought out in the rocks, chiefly on the western bank, which are now from ten to fifteen feet above the highest present watermark. The river now is often fuller than it probably ever was before the country above was cleared of its forests, the snows in open ground melting much more suddenly and forming much greater freshets than in forested ground. The river cannot, therefore, have risen to the height of these excavations by having a greater supply of water. Besides, excavations so deep, so large, and wrought in rocks so hard show with absolute certainty that the river ran at this level often and for a long period: a fact which no possible sources of its waters could have been the means of accomplishing had it customarily flowed at its present level.

These cavities are very numerous, both above and below the bridge. They are also of various forms, from that of a shallow dish to that of an iron pot, that of a barrel, and in one instance that of an inverted pear; and of various sizes, from the capacity of a pint bowl to that of perhaps two hogsheads. Their greatest depths we could not accurately estimate, because those which were deepest, as well as many others, were partially filled with water, gravel, and stones.

From these cavities and others like them, and generally from the depredations made by falls of water upon the rocks over which they fell, that class of infidels who have discernment exactly fitted to perceive, candor enough to love, and industry sufficient to point out petty objections against revelation have with no small triumph found here, in their own opinion, means of disproving the date assigned to the creation by Moses. . . .

On one of the rocks lying in the river below the bridge, we saw two rude Indian attempts at sculpture. They were very coarse copies of the human face: a circular figure cut in the rock serving for the outline, two round holes for the eyes, and an elliptical one for the mouth. For what purpose they were made in this place we were unable to divine. They are not visible except when the water is low.

I have observed that the bed of the river is lower than it was formerly. This change has been chiefly accomplished by the washing away of the earth, gravel, and stones which were of such a size as to yield to the force of the current. In consequence of this process, the stones and rocks of a larger size have gradually subsided. Even these, indeed, have been partially worn, but not so as to contribute perceptibly to any alteration in the channel. Where the bed of a river is a stratum of slate or limestone, very great changes often take place from the attrition of the stream and the influence of the atmosphere; but these rocks are of too firm a texture to be greatly affected by the efficacy of either.

On the western side of the river a canal was begun, and, in 1797, about two thirds finished, for the purpose of conveying boats around these falls. Its length is three fourths of a mile, its breadth at the bottom eighteen feet, at the top sixty, and its depth twenty. The expense at which it is dug, exclusive of the passage through the rocks mentioned above, is thirty dollars per rod. Through these rocks a way has been blown with great expense. The whole sum already laid out, as we were informed, is $45,000. A considerable addition must be made to this before the works can be completed.

In September 1803, October 1806, and May 1810, I visited this spot, and in all these instances found the canal answering in a good degree the purpose for which it was made. Boats of the size formerly mentioned in the account of the South Hadley Canal are safely and easily conveyed through it, as are also rafts of boards and timber. The water is thrown into it by a dam which crosses the river a little below its upper entrance. The whole number of locks, including a guard lock, is seven; six of these raise or lower the boats seven feet four inches each, or forty-four feet, the whole descent of the river at this place. In digging the canal the proprietors have availed themselves of the ancient bed of the river, and thus have saved a prodigious mass of labor. Indeed, without this advantage the attempt in all probability would not have been made.

Two sawmills, a gristmill, a papermill, and a carding machine are built near the lower end of the canal. All these are esteemed valuable property, as they stand in perfect safety from the ravages of the river, and are furnished with a never failing supply of water. The gristmill particularly is considered as the best and most profitable in this part of the country. It is questionable whether the canal will soon become proportionally profitable to the proprietors, although it cannot fail to be of considerable use to the community. . . .

There is a small hamlet, containing a few houses and stores, on the western side of the canal and on the island between that and the river.

Just below the principal fall was built in the year 1785, and in the year 1797 was still standing, the first bridge which was ever erected over Connecticut River. The builder was Colonel Enoch Hale. When he first formed the design, its practicability was generally denied, and the undertaker laughed at for seriously proposing so romantic a project. He was not, however, discouraged; but, meeting the common opinion and the ridicule with which it was expressed with that firmness which is indispensable to the success of new and difficult efforts, he began and completed the work in the year 1785. The spot was granted to him for this purpose by the legislature of New Hampshire, and the toll established by law. The project has been eminently useful to the public, but was not very profitable to himself. The want of a good road across the country prevented a great part of that traveling which has since been produced by the establishment of the turnpike last mentioned. He was, therefore, obliged to sell his property without reaping from it that reward which a generous mind instinctively wishes to ingenuity and public spirit. How often do the authors of ingenious and honorable undertakings experience this painful retribution!

Colonel Hale was probably the first man who seriously realized the practicability of erecting a bridge over this river. What is much more, he was the first man who proved that it could be done. It is curious to mark the progress of opinion concerning subjects originally so difficult as scarcely to become topics of reflection, and yet so interesting as to be objects of general desire. This river at Lancaster, one hundred and thirty-three miles north of this bridge, is thirty rods in breadth, and of considerable depth. The ice with which it is covered every winter is thick and strong; and the freshets are at times sudden and not unfrequently so great as to raise its waters from ten to twenty-five feet above their common level, and to spread them in various places, from half a mile to a mile and a half or two miles in breadth, over the intervals on its borders. Before a bridge had been actually built over, it, therefore, it was a very natural conclusion that no structure of this kind which the wealth of the inhabitants could conveniently furnish would be of sufficient strength to sustain the occasional violence of the stream. I have often heard this subject mentioned in the early periods of my life, and always as a thing which was indeed extremely desirable, but absolutely impracticable; an object of ardent wishes, but of no expectations. In such a situation, the man who with comprehensive views discerning all the difficulties sees also the means of surmounting them; whose energy not only prompts him to adventure, but invigorates him to overcome; and whose public spirit quickens him to use enterprises from which his heavy minded and parsimonious neighbors shrink with self-gratulation, begins, and in a sense creates, all the future success of such generous efforts, and deserves a grateful and permanent remembrance as a public benefactor.

Dr. Belknap, speaking of this bridge in 1792, says, "This is the only bridge across Connecticut River, but it is in contemplation to erect one thirty-six miles above, at the middle bar of White River Fall." There are now thirteen bridges over this river. The commencement of difficult enterprises is usually entered upon very slowly and reluctantly; their progress is often rapid beyond the most sanguine expectation.

In the year 1803, the bridge erected by Colonel Hale at the expense of thirty-seven hundred dollars had been taken down, and a new one built, under the direction of Mr. Geyer, a merchant of Boston and the present proprietor. I was not a little pleased with this structure. It is neat, light, and simple, and yet possesses great strength. Two sets of very long and very firm braces fastened near the center extend to the rocks on both sides of the river, and leave the passage for the water and the ice entirely clear, and the bridge perfectly secure. Its figure is a very obtuse arch. Wherever the ground will admit of this construction, it is the best within my knowledge, and combines neatness and strength with the least possible expense.

This bridge is said to be valuable property. . . .

These falls, though much less magnificent than those of South Hadley, have engrossed much more the attention of travelers. To see a river usually forty rods wide, and at all times deep enough to convey boats carrying twenty-five tons, run through a channel twenty feet in breadth is equally singular and surprising. The impression made by this extraordinary fact is not a little increased by the surrounding objects. The rapids above and below, the canal, the mills, the stores, and the neighboring hamlet; the rocks on both shores, piled together in absolute confusion, and fantastically worn into such a variety of forms; the very bridge on which the traveler stands; the beautiful house of Mr. Geyer; and the wild and rugged mountain hanging over it with its awful precipices leave an impression on the mind which it will be impossible for him to forget in the future periods of life.

I am, Sir, yours, etc.

Letter X

Lyme—Orford—Piermont—Haverhill

DEAR SIR,

Thursday, September 28th, we left Dartmouth, and proceeded to Haverhill through Lyme, Orford, and Piermont: twenty-eight miles. The road for a country so newly settled was good.

Of Lyme, the township immediately above Hanover, we saw very little, as the road passes along the foot of the hills and very near the river. The journey was, however, pleasant and romantic, the river, bordered in several places by small intervals, being frequently in sight and forming a cheerful contrast to the solemnity of the forest.

The township of Lyme, which is extensively settled and well cultivated, is said to be excellent land. A mine has been lately discovered here, which, we were told, yields good steel immediately from the ore, or with very little preparation.

Lyme was incorporated in 1761, and in 1775 contained 252 inhabitants; in 1790, 816; in 1800, 1,318; and in 1810, 1,670: all included in one congregation.

Orford lies immediately north of Lyme, and contains a village on the road. It is built on a beautiful plain bordered by intervals on the west. The hills on both sides of the river near the center of the expansion approach each other so as to form a kind of neck; and, with a similar approximation at the two ends, give the whole the appearance of a double amphitheater, or of the numerical figure 8. The greatest breadth of each division is about a mile and a half, and the length of each between two and three miles. On the western side of the river, and at the northern end of each division, rises a fine, bold bluff: the southern, named Coney's; the northern, Sawyer's mountain. I was informed that a gentleman in the neighborhood had measured Coney's mountain and found the height of it to be 450 above the surface of the river. Sawyer's mountain is little, if at all, inferior. Both are very noble objects, being perpendicular cliffs of gray granite, terminating almost immediately on the road. In a part of the country where precipices are uncommon, the effect produced by these remarkable promontories on the landscape is exquisite.

Orford is chiefly built on a single street extending between two or three miles along the river. The houses stand all along at moderate distances, and near the center are built more compactly. Generally they do not rise above mediocrity; a few are of a better class. The intervals, particularly in the southern part of the expansion, are rich. Soap rock, a soft kind of magnesian stone, freestone, and a gray rock said to make excellent millstones (granite, I presume) are all found in Orford.

In this township there are two mountains, one of which is named *Mount Cube,* from a dog which bore that name and was killed upon it by a bear. The other was named *Mount Sunday* from the following fact. Seven men, one of them a Mr. Palmer, went into the eastern part of the township and, in the language of the country, *were lost,* that is, they became wholly uncertain of the course which they were to pursue in order to regain their habitations. Palmer insisted that it lay in a direction really eastward, although he believed it to point Westward. His companions, judging more correctly, determined to take the opposite course. In their progress, they passed over this mountain. The day on which they ascended it was the Sabbath, and the mountain has from this circumstance derived a name which it will probably retain so long as the posterity of the English colonists inhabit this country. The six men returning home and not finding Palmer went again in search of him. In a place two miles eastward of the spot where they had left him, they found him engaged in a contest with a bear which had attacked hm the preceding evening on his way. As the bear was advancing toward him, he was fortunate enough to procure a club, with which he had been able to defend himself until he made good his retreat to a neighboring tree. The bear followed him as he ascended the tree, but his club enabled him to keep the animal at bay until his companions came up and delivered him from the impending destruction.

I presume you will wonder at my mentioning these trifling incidents. I have mentioned them because they are trifles. The names of mountains, rivers, and other distinguished natural objects, both here and in England, have often seemed to me strange and inexplicable. The little incidents which I have mentioned furnish, I suspect, a probable explanation of this enigmatical subject in a great proportion of cases. Events, sometimes more and sometimes even less significant than these, have, I am persuaded, been the origin of a great part of those odd appellations given to so many of the objects in question. Among the proofs that this opinion is just, the oddity and the vulgarity of the appellations and the speedy oblivion into which the causes of them have fallen are to me satisfactory. . . .

Orford is a pretty settlement. The inhabitants are said to be sober, industrious, and well behaved. The township was incorporated in 1761, includes one congregation, and in the year 1775 contained 222 inhabitants; in 1790, 540; in 1800, 988; and in 1810, 1265.

Piermont is a rough and generally unpleasant piece of ground. The soil also appears to be lean and unpromising. From Bradford, opposite to it, there are seen, however, some rich and handsome lands, particularly some beautiful intervals belonging to this township. Piermont was incorporated in 1764. In 1775, the number of inabitants was 168; in 1790, 426; in 1800, 670; and in 1810, 877: all included in one congregation.

Haverhill lies immediately north of Piermont. This is a well-appearing town, built in a manner somewhat scattered for several miles along the road. The site is a handsome elevation overlooking the adjacent country many miles north and south, and not less than six or seven from east to west. The prospect is charming. The soil is loam mixed with gravel, and suited to every species of cultivation: yet, for a reason which I could not divine, the apple trees appeared less thrifty than in the country below and than I afterwards found them in the opposite township of Newbury. In many instances they were decaying as if with age; yet, they were probably of less than thirty years standing.

Haverhill is a half-shire town in the county of Grafton, which begins on the river at the southern boundary of Lebanon, and extends to the northern line of the state: more than one hundred and fifty miles. The courthouse is a decent building and stands on a pretty square, which, however, some individual has miserably deformed by building on it a merchant's store and a stable. On this square there are several neat houses, and a little northward a handsome church. From the street the ground slopes with unusual elegance to the west, and is succeeded by a chain of intervals. . . .

. . . Haverhill Upper Street [is] inferior to any other which we had hitherto passed. I was unable to account for the existence of a settlement on this hopeless soil until I came to the brow of the plain. Here I discovered a succession of rich intervals, extending along the river several miles and furnishing a most inviting field to industrious agriculture. The inhabitants of the plain were, I presume, allured to this spot by so tempting an object, but they must have been sadly disappointed. From the skirts of this settlement we discovered several houses whose brilliant appearance plainly showed that their owners had preoccupied all these fruitful lands, and left the inhabitants of the plain to derive their subsistence from the parsimonious grounds in their neighborhood.

Haverhill was incorporated in the year 1763. The number of its inhabitants in 1775 was 365; in 1790, 552; in 1800, 805; and in 1810, 1,105: included in one congregation. There is in this township a quarry of freestone and a bed of iron ore.

I am, Sir, yours, etc.

Letter VIII

DEAR SIR,

New England villages, and in peculiar degree those of the tract under consideration, are built in the following manner.

The local situation is pitched on as a place in itself desirable, as a place where life may be passed through more pleasantly than in most others, as a place, not where trade compels, but where happiness invites to settle. Accordingly the position of these towns is usually beautiful. The mode of settlement is such as greatly to enhance the pleasure intended. The body of inhabitants is composed of farmers: and farmers nowhere within my knowledge of a superior character for intelligence and good manners. The mechanics, the class next in numbers, have their full share of this character, and usually aim at a higher degree of respectability than in most parts of the country. Of both sorts a considerable number merit the appellation of gentlemen. A more than common proportion of men liberally and politely educated reside in the towns of this valley, and the pleasures of intellectual and refined society are here enjoyed to a considerable extent.

To this character of the inhabitants, the manner of locating and building these towns is happily suited. The town plat is originally distributed into lots containing from two to ten acres. In a convenient spot on each of these, a house is erected at the bottom of the courtyard (often neatly enclosed) and is furnished universally with a barn and other convenient outbuildings. Near the house there is always a garden replenished with culinary vegetables, flowers, and fruits, and very often also prettily enclosed. The lot on which the house stands, universally styled the home lot, is almost of course a meadow, richly cultivated, covered during the pleasant season with verdure, and containing generally a thrifty orchard. It is hardly necessary to observe that these appendages spread a singular cheerfulness and beauty over a New England village, or that they contribute largely to render the house a delightful residence.

The towns in this valley, taken together, are better built than an equal number in any other part of the United States, unless perhaps on the eastern coast of Massachusetts where the wealth of the inhabitants is greatly superior. Most generally they are built of wood, and are neater, lighter, and pleasanter dwellings than those of brick or stone. As they stand at a distance from each other, they are little exposed to fire except from within, and accordingly are very rarely consumed. Both they and the public buildings are usually painted white. No single fact except the universal verdure and the interspersion of streams contributes equally to the sprightly, cheerful appearance of any country.

In this valley the principal commerce of the country within twenty miles of the river is carried on, and a great part of their mechanical business is done. Here the newspapers circulated throughout this region are printed, and the bookstores kept by which the inhabitants are supplied. Here also, the great body of information concerning this and other countries is first received and disseminated, and here fashions of all kinds are first adopted from abroad and diffused throughout the vicinity.

In this region poverty in its absolute sense is scarcely known. Those who are here styled poor possess usually both the necessaries and comforts of life. The paupers maintained by the public, compared with the whole number of inhabitants, are probably not more than one out of three or four hundred. Every man, with hardly an exception, lives on his own ground and in his own house. Every man, therefore, possesses an absolute, personal independence, derived from his earliest ancestor, and secured by the government under which he lives. It was born with him, and therefore sits upon him easily and naturally. The ancestor from who he derived it, he respects. The government by which it is secured, he loves and venerates, and is ever ready to defend. Life here is therefore seen in all its pleasing, rural forms, and in these forms is seen with uncommon advantage.

The intercourse of the inhabitants is invited and cherished by all the facts already mentioned. To these may be added the goodness of the roads and the inns, and the salubrity of the climate. The time has not been long passed since the roads on the hills were almost universally too rough to be traveled for pleasure. At that time the roads in this valley were generally good throughout a great extent. Hence the inhabitants were allured to a much more extensive intercourse with each other than those in any other part of New England except along the eastern coast. For the same reasons a multitude of strangers have at all times been induced to make this valley the scene of their pleasurable traveling. The effects of this intercourse on the minds and manners of the inhabitants I need not explain.

Beauty of landscape is an eminent characteristic of this valley. From Hereford Mountain to Saybrook, it is almost a continued succession of delightful scenery. No other tract within my knowledge, and from the extensive information which I have received, I am persuaded that no other tract within the United States of the same extent, can be compared to it with respect to those objects which arrest the eye of the painter and the poet. There are indeed dull, uninteresting spots in considerable numbers. These, however, are little more than the discords which are generally regarded as necessary to perfect the harmony. The beauty and the grandeur are here more varied than elsewhere. They return oftener; they are longer continued; they are finished by a hand operating in a superior manner. A gentleman of great respectability, who had traveled in England, France and Spain, informed me that the prospects along the Connecticut excelled those on the beautiful rivers in these three counties in two great particulars: the forests and the mountains (he might, I believe, have added the intervals also), and fell short of them in nothing but population and the productions of art. It is hardly necessary to observe that both these are advancing with a rapid step (perhaps sufficiently rapid) toward a stronger resemblance to European improvement.

The first object, however, in the whole landscape is undoubtedly the Connecticut itself. This stream may perhaps, with as much propriety as any in the world, be named the beautiful river. From Stewart to the Sound, it uniformly sustains this character. The purity, salubrity, and sweetness of its waters; the frequency and elegance of its meanders; its absolute freedom from all aquatic vegetables; the uncommon and universal beauty of its banks, here a smooth and winding beach, there covered with rich verdure, now fringed with bushes, now crowned with lofty trees, and now formed by the intruding hill, the rude bluff, and the shaggy mountain, are objects which no traveler can thoroughly describe, and no reader adequately imagine. When to these are added the numerous towns, villages, and hamlets almost everywhere exhibiting marks of prosperity and improvement, the rare appearance of decline, the numerous churches lifting their spires in frequent succession, the neat schoolhouses everywhere occupied, and the mills busied on such a multitude of streams, it may be safely asserted that a pleasanter journey will rarely be found than that which is made in the Connecticut Valley.

The Hero Returns

THE *AMERICAN SENTINEL*

IT BEING UNDERSTOOD THAT on Saturday, the 4th of September, General Lafayette might be expected in Middletown, measures were taken for his reception which had been adopted by the Court of Common Council. Thirteen guns at an early hour announced the day. At one o'clock, John Lawrence Lewis, Sherrif of the County of Middlesex had passed the northern line of the County and stood at Rocky Hill with a corps of cavalry in readiness to escort the General on the road to Middletown. But at that hour in Hartford he had not yet been conducted to the Senate.

Between two and three o'clock advice was received by express that the General was too fatigued to travel the whole distance by land, but he would embark on the *Oliver Ellsworth* to pass down the Connecticut River and would land at a settlement called Upper Houses if practicable about six o'clock which was about three miles from the landing in Middletown, along the right hand side of the Connecticut River. Sooner than was hoped after this information, the *Oliver Ellsworth* was seen coming from a point more than a league from the landing. On the instant this was made known by a salute of thirteen guns from the high ground near the river. General Lafayette was met by a deputation of thirteen distinguished citizens with the first Marshall and a squadron of cavalry commanded by Col. Richard Wilcox of the Eleventh Regiment stood in readiness to escort him, and he was supported by the citizens of the deptation to the elegant barouche which stood in waiting. With him was the chairman of the deputation and his son George Washington Lafayette followed in a second coach with another member of the deputation.

The arrival at the bridge which crosses the northern line of the city was announced by the salute of thirteen guns from the high ground near the head of Main Street. He was here received by a corps of artillery, riflemen and light artillery. Flags were displayed from various buildings and from the shipping in port.

He was received by the Mayor and deputation, and took a ride up Washington Street, down High Street and through Church Street, stopping to greet Commodore Thomas Macdonough, then embarked on the

From the *American Sentinel,* 8 September, 1824.

Oliver Ellsworth, being in Middletown about an hour, from six o'clock until seven. His carriage was easingly discerned as it was well known that the white horses, beautiful and spirited, the four in hand, drew the barouche which bore the General.

His son, George Washington Lafayette, remarked his father was sorry to make so hurried a departure, but he was several hours late and they could not keep the boat waiting any longer.

The banquet was not prolonged on the part of the corporation. One toast and only one was given. The company all standing, drank with plaudits: "To the benefactor and guest of the Empire of Freedom, General Lafayette!"

On his trip down the Connecticut, the houses were all illuminated and groups of girls and women in white were assembled at the river's edge to greet the boat as it went past.

The Connecticut River Is a Fine Stream

CHARLES DICKENS

THESE TOWNS AND CITIES of New England (many of which would be villages in Old England) are as favourable specimens of rural America as their people are of rural Americans. The well-trimed lawns and green meadows of home are not there; and the grass, compared with our ornamental plots and pastures, is rank, and rough, and wild: but delicate slopes of land, gently-swelling hills, wooded valleys, and slender streams abound. Every little colony of houses has its church and school-house peeping from among the white roofs and shady trees; every house is the whitest of the white; every Venetian blind the greenest of the green; every fine day's sky the bluest of the blue. A sharp dry wind and a slight frost had so hardened the roads when we alighted at Worcester, that their furrowed tracks were like ridges of granite. There was the usual aspect of newness on every object, of course. All the buildings looked as if they had been built and painted that morning, and could be taken down on

From Charles Dickens, *American Notes* (London: Chapman and Hall, 1842).

Monday with very little trouble. In the keen evening air, every sharp outline looked a hundred times sharper than ever. The clean cardboard colonnades had no more perspective than a Chinese bridge on a teacup, and appeared equally well calculated for use. The razor-like edges of the detached cottages seemed to cut the very wind as it whistled against them, and to send it smarting on its way with a shriller cry than before. Those slightly-built wooden dwellings, behind which the sun was setting with a brilliant lustre, could be so looked through and through, that the idea of any inhabitant being able to hide himself from the public gaze, or to have any secrets from the public eye, was not entertainable for a moment. Even where a blazing fire shone through the uncurtained windows of some distant house, it had the air of being newly lighted, and of lacking warmth; and instead of awakening throughts of a snug chamber, bright with faces that first saw the light round that same hearth, and ruddy with warm hangings, it came upon one suggestive of the smell of new mortar and damp walls.

So I thought, at least, that evening. Next morning, when the sun was shining brightly, and the clear church bells were ringing, and sedate people in their best clothes enlivened the pathway near at hand, and dotted the distant thread of road, there was a pleasant Sabbath peacefulness on everything which was good to feel. It would have been the better for an old church; better still for some old graves; but as it was, a wholesome repose and tranquillity pervaded the scene, which, after the restless ocean and the hurried city, had a doubly grateful influence on the spirits.

We went on next morning, still by railroad, to Springfield. From that place to Hartford, whither we were bound, is a distance of only five-and-twenty miles, but at that time of the year the roads were so bad that the journey would probably have occupied ten or twelve hours. Fortunately, however, the winter having been unusually mild, the Connecticut River was "open," or, in other words, not frozen. The captain of a small steamboat was going to make his first trip for the season that day (the second February trip, I believe, within the memory of man), and only waited for us to go on board. Accordingly, we went on board with as little delay as might be. He was as good as his word, and started directly.

It certainly was not called a small steamboat without reason. I omitted to ask the question, but I should think it must have been of about half a pony power. Mr. Paap, the celebrated Dwarf, might have lived and died happily in the cabin, which was fitted with common sash-windows like an ordinary dwelling-house. These windows had bright red curtains, too, hung on slack strings across the lower panes; so that it looked like the parlour of a Lilliputian public-house, which had got afloat in a flood or some other water accident, and was drifing nobody knew where. But even in this chamber there was a rocking-chair. It would be impossible to get on anywhere, in America, without a rocking-chair.

I am afraid to tell how many feet short this vessel was, or how many feet narrow; to apply the words length and width to such measurement would be a contradiction in terms. But I may state that we all kept the middle of the deck, lest the boat should unexpectedly tip over; and that the machinery, by some surprising process of condensation, worked between it and the keel: the whole forming a warm sandwich about three feet thick.

It rained all day, as I once thought it never did rain anywhere but in the Highlands of Scotland. The river was full of floating blocks of ice, which were constantly crunching and cracking under us; and the depth of water, in the course we took to avoid the larger masses, carried down the middle of the river by the current, did not exceed a few inches. Nevertheless, we moved onward dexterously; and, being well wrapped up, bade defiance to the weather, and enjoyed the journey. The Connecticut River is a fine stream; and the banks in the summer-time are, I have no doubt, beautiful: at all events, I was told so by a young lady in the cabin; and she should be a judge of beauty, if the possession of a quality include the appreciation of it, for a more beautiful creature I never looked upon.

After two hours and a half of this odd travelling (including a stoppage at a small town, where we were saluted by a gun considerably bigger than our own chimney), we reached Hartford, and straightway repaired to an extremely comfortable hotel: except, as usual, in the article of bedrooms, which, in almost every place we visited, were very conducive to early rising.

Mr. Thoreau Is Not Impressed

HENRY DAVID THOREAU

SEPT. 9, 1856. TUESDAY. 8 A.M.—Ascend the Chesterfield Mountain with Miss Frances and Miss Mary Brown.

The Connecticut is about twenty rods wide between Brattleboro and Hinsdale. This mountain, according to Frost, is 1064 feet high. It is the

From Bradford Torrey and Francis H. Allen, eds., *The Journal of Henry D. Thoreau* (Boston: Houghton Mifflin, 1906).

most remarkable feature here. The village of Brattleboro is peculiar for the nearness of the primitive wood and the mountain. Within three rods of Brown's house was excellent botanical ground on the side of a primitive wooded hillside. . . . But, above all, this everlasting mountain is forever lowering over the village, shortening the day and wearing a misty cap each morning. You look up to its top at a steep angle from the village streets. A great part belongs to the Insane Asylum. This town will be convicted of a folly if they ever permit this mountain to be laid bare. Francis [*sic*] B. says its Indian name is Wantastiquet. . . . The Connecticut, though unusually high (several feet more than usual), looks low, there being four or five or six rods of bare gravel on each side, and the bushes and weeds covered with clayey soil from a freshet. Not a boat to be seen upon it. The Concord is worth a hundred of it for my purpose.

The River's Challenge

MARGUERITE ALLIS

WE TOO MADE AN early start, back to Third Lake for a morning picture, through a sunrise as clear and beautiful as the sunset had been. Light wind rustled the lonely woodlands and ruffled the lovely waters. We got our picture of them, then chalet and the watershed—this side contributing to the Connecticut, the other to the Saint Lawrence. Then back through the frost-wet woods where, on that road scarcely wider than one of those pioneer bridle paths, we met a truckload of CCC boys going to work; it was they who were pushing Daniel's highway to the Canadian border. The driver nearly capsized them in an effort to give us all the road there was, and their mingled salutations and farewells, friendly, boisterous, but not ribald, sang after us. The headwaters of the River were cool silver. That mighty pine stood out against a sky where clean dawn still lingered. These were fine company for boys. Something

From Marguerite Allis, *Connecticut River* (New York: G. P. Putnam's Sons, 1939).

besides a highway was being built there in the wilderness, fourteen hundred feet above sea level and immeasurably above the abyss of idle "living on relief."

Swiftly we slid down the long incline to Colebrook, passing through the town this time and along the main highway on the New Hampshire side only to be more firmly convinced that the dirt road over in Vermont offered greater charms. We returned to it at the first bridge, eager to get a picture of Monadnock with the River winding about its feet, but the clouds came down and a fierce squall washed the windshield; the prophecy of the fair dawn had been false. Nevertheless we proposed to keep close to Fifteen Miles Fall *this* time, if we were let. We weren't. A great tree blocked the by-road—deliberately, as the torn-up surface beyond explained. Nothing to do but keep to the main road over the high ground through Lunenburg, a picturesque grouping of white houses about a tree-set meetinghouse on a hilltop; the pioneers had built nearer the River only to be driven up here, even as we were. Before we reached the Passumpsic it became evident that the hurricane had gone up that tributary into Canada; and when, above Barnet, we came back to the Connecticut its swollen waters were lashed by a fresh downpour through which we perceived vaguely the outlines of the power plant under the mighty Fifteen Mile Fall Dam. No water was coming over to add to the surfeit below, and if that "damnifying" had ruined our chances of seeing one of the loveliest stretches of the River, it had also prevented further innundation downstream. Another tributary practically leaped over our heads at McIndoe Falls. This way during the Revolution, when the British had the mouth of the River pretty well bottled up, you remember, a great deal of contraband was smuggled in from Canada.

Another old trail, used by the Saint Francis Indians, came down Wells River where, at its confluence with the Connecticut, you remember, the rangers expected to find supplies on the return from wiping out that tribe. The mill town that grew up here at the head of River navigation is a drab, uninteresting place today except for those reminders of an historic past. We pushed on to Newbury, transpontine neighbor of Haverhill and co-sufferer from hurricane. Undoubtedly a lovely village under normal conditions, we passed it up to search for that long covered bridge seen yesterday from a distance on the other side. It proved tantalizingly illusive. First we approached a bridge, only to find it a new steel span, replacing another covered bridge, lost in 1936. We crossed this thinking to see the older bridge from it—and didn't, so stopped at a shabby unpainted old house to inquire. For all it cried poverty, brilliant dahlias leaned against the crazy porch where the shred of a morning-glory vine clambered, and behind the shining windows freshly starched curtains quivered under a curious hand. Then the door swung wide on a rosy dumpling of an old woman, her comfortable middle pouched out by hands rolled in a gingham apron. She gave us new directions about that covered bridge, adding: "I'm a-putting up citron." Her eyes strayed away, and ours followed them to where a row of sugar maples had been decapitated as though by a giant scythe. Her eyes and ours met then, understandingly; that "sugar bush" in which the sap would never rise again, undoubtedly paid the taxes on that small meager farm. She only repeated: "I'm puttin' up citron." Then: "You got to do something to take up your mind." She was not asking for sympathy, although, God knows she had ours; she was only expressing the old pioneer spirit which may be down, but never gives up.

Back across the River we tried again for that covered bridge, this time landing in a cul de sac among farm buildings on an out-jetting terrace. From the gloom of the red barn emerged a stately old man in blue overalls who, as we appologized for the intrusion, put a companionable boot on the running board, pushed a straw hat off a heavy thatch of iron-gray hair, and regarded us out of splendid, somber dark eyes set in one of those hewn-granite faces bespeaking generations of New England forebears, as he explained, briefly and clearly, just how to reach that bridge, ending: "It's still there."

"So's your barn," we replied. "You're lucky."

"I don't know whether I am or not," he came back. "That pine"—he removed his boot and swung around, a little pulse beating quickly among the wrinkles of his eye corners. Following his glance, we saw it, then, the fallen giant. It must have towered head and shoulders above the surrounding pines torn by its crash. Ignoring these ruined others, he said: "It was a big tree when I was a boy. I used to look up at it and think it would still be there long after I was gone. Why, I wouldn't have taken any money for that pine! And now—" The firm mouth twitched.

With a feeling of intrusion on private grief, we murmured something inadequate and started the motor. Like thousands of other New Englanders, that farmer looked upon his tree as his friend. There are others who had looked upon their trees as old-age insurance. Many a young farmer of fifty years ago dared not marry until he had planted a woodlot, for hill farms are not rich like those on the pocconock. When he was no longer able to till his thin fields, those pines or hardwoods would be ready for market. Perhaps they were ready in the fall of 1938, and he told himself he was still good for a few more years of hard labor; the timber would be worth all the more for the waiting. Then, in the space of a few hours, that timber was a heap of kindling wood, scarcely worth salvaging for the stove. The old-age insurance of his wife and himself was gone.

Realization of countless tragedies like these weighted us down as we continued our search for that bridge. And found it, a long, sway-backed structure infinitely more impressive in its lack of repair than the better-kept, better-patronized Cornish-Windsor. A long bridge, an old bridge! Hundreds of trees had gone into its making. Hundreds of floods had threatened it—vainly. It stretched across the River, staunch and strong. Waters swirled beneath not many feet from its floor, and the bridge gave never a shudder, even as we thundered through the dark tunnel, turned, and thundered back again for the sake of hearing it give forth that loud challenge to the River.

Somehow that challenge seemed to epitomize the challenge the white man has always issued to the River, from the time he first persisted in building his towns on those off-drowned pocconocks to that latest scientific challenge issued on the Pittsburg Project. Always the story of the River has been a story of challenge—pioneer shallops sailing up; River-built barks sailing down; canals challenging white water; steamboats challening sailboats; railroads challenging steamboats; motors challenging railroads; the River challenging them all and the men who made them challengers. As man came here by and because of the River, so man struggles to remain here by and because of the River—fearing her, hating her, loving her, leaving her only to come back, unable to resist her spell, hoping he may subdue her, knowing she may subdue him—but knowing with an ever surer knowledge that without her he is nothing. What would New England be without the River? What, without New England would these United States ever have become? It's a challenging question.

Chapter 4

THE BUSY YEARS

I am an American. I was born and reared in Hartford, in the state of Connecticut—anyway, just over the river in the country. So I am a Yankee of the Yankees and practical; yes, and nearly barren of sentiment I suppose—or poetry, in other words. My father was a blacksmith, my uncle was a horse doctor, and I was both, along at first. Then I went over to the great arms factory and learned my real trade; learned all there was to it; learned to make everything: guns, revolvers, cannon, all sorts of labor-saving machinery.
—*A Connecticut Yankee in King Arthur's Court* by Mark Twain

During the nineteenth century, the Connecticut River was more thoroughly used *than at any time before or since. Not only were the first power dams operating then, fueling industry in growing, river-dependent cities like Holyoke, but major efforts were being made to use the river as a transportation corridor from the coast deep into the interior, with canals around the worst rapids. Much of this industry (Mark Twain wasn't exaggerating) concerned the design and manufacture of weaponry, with Colt Firearms located next to the river in Hartford and the famous Springfield armory set back no more than a musket shot from the banks.*

George Calvin Carter writes of the man who might have been the busiest along the river, Samuel Morey, the true inventor—his adherents claim with much justice*—of the steamboat. Melanothon Jacobus uses the story of the* Barnet *to epitomize steamboat history on the river. A veteran of the river rafts that used to float the upper river recalls those years, a Captain C. W. Bliss. John V. Goff writes of shipyard workers and owners, an example of local history at its best and most detailed, bringing back the days when the lower river was one of the centers of American shipbuilding. Scott Hastings, Jr., reminds us that the river worked in another* *sense—providing ice well into the twentieth century for the people who lived along it.*

This is the kind of chapter where the editor wishes he had more room. How nice, for instance, to include more on the river's stone industry, as summarized by W. Storrs Lee in his Yankees of Connecticut.

The one mineral that created the greatest extraterritorial pageantry was the brownstone from the Portland [Connecticut] quarries. In endless processions of barges, the blocks were ferried down the Connecticut during the nineteenth century—a major item of traffic on the river. Vast tonnages of the stone were transported to cities along the northeast seaboard, but principally it went to New York to alter the facade of the big American metropolis. For a generation Manhattan proudly put up a distinguished Connecticut front.

And wouldn't it be nice to hear more about the famous incident in Holyoke at the inauguration of its pride and joy, as quoted in Edmund Delaney's fine general history of the river, The Connecticut River.

In 1848, a group of investors constructed what at the time was the largest dam in the world, at Holyoke. The dam came to a disastrous end on the very day of its inauguration. As reported by the newly invented telegraph to its Boston sponsors:

10:00 A.M.—Gates just closed; water filling behind dam.
12: noon—Dam leaking badly.
2:00 P.M.—Stones of bulkhead giving way to pressure.
3:20 P.M.—Your old dam's gone to Hell by way of Willimansett.

And, for that matter, how good it would be to have more on the eponymous hero of the doggerel quoted in Walter Hard's The Connecticut.

And further, and further, and further still,
The steamboat winding through the vale,
While cannon roared through hill and dale:
For this is the day when Captain Nutt
Sailed up the fair Connecticut.

A busy century. The river worked hard.

Morey on the River

GEORGE CALVIN CARTER

THE MOREY STORY WOULD fill volumes if complete copies of all the available material were included. Year by year additional evidence is coming to light with reference to secret agreements, and promises on the part of the Livingston-Fulton interest, in which not a single agreement or promise was kept. Probably they felt justified in so doing by the pressure of the times and the mad scramble to be first in the field. But they were not the first. Captain Samuel Morey of Orford, New Hampshire, has that honor.

In recent years the Fultonians, confronted with ever increasing evidence damaging to the earlier popular conception, have been gradually abandoning their earlier positions, and one of them has recently gone as far as to state that Fulton never claimed to have invented the steamboat. This view is incorrect, for Fulton frequently made the claim over his signature, in speeches before groups, and in some of his legislative and court appeals.

It is a fair question, in view of the now admitted primacy of Morey, why more frequent or detailed mention is not made of him and his work, when the claims and deeds of others than Fulton are mentioned. The answer is probably found in the fact that Orford and Fairlee are far off the beaten track, and in such a case it is easier and less expensive to quote from others than to spend time, energy and money in original research.

As an illustration of the thoughtless and careless manner with which reference to Morey has been frquently made, examination of a large number of books and essays on the life of Fulton and the story of steam navigation reveals seven different spellings of Morey's name, while Orford is nearly always written "Oxford," and he is called "Morey (and with various spellings), of Vermont, New Hampshire, Connecticut, Massachusetts, Rhode Island, and New York," all indicating complete absence of any original or extensive research.

There is now no question but that Captain Samuel Morey successfully propelled a boat on Fairlee Pond by steam in 1790. The rest of that year and all of the years 1791 and 1792 were spent in further experimentation, both with boat and engine. In 1792 the experiments were made in quiet,

From George Calvin Carter, *Samuel Morey* (Concord, N.H.: Privately printed, 1945).

secluded curves and coves of the Connecticut River. In 1792 he was able to successfully battle the river current with a speed of four and a half miles an hour which, for conservatism, he called four miles per hour.

Then, in 1793, in order to prove that his engine would not lose power during winter storage, he arranged for a more extended trip up and down the river, with special reference to speed, steadiness and ease of handling on turns. The first trip of the season was taken on Sunday during church services, in order that his attention might not be distracted in handling the boat, on account of possible watchers on the shore. After this successful series of trips during the long church service, there were many others which were fully observed and reported upon by many prominent residents of that section. Captain Morey, in building his engines and his boats, did not have the benefit of European experimentation, or that of any others, but worked wholly from original ideas, and all of the fabricating and construction was done by himself with the assistance of his brother, Israel. So well was the plan conceived and carried out, that they both testified that none of the trips from 1790 to 1793 were with either "accident or incident." They did improve things a bit here and there, and made a large number of experiments which were of value only in proving that they had the right idea in the first place. Boilers and parts used have been found bearing dates from 1790 to 1793.

Other attempt before this by other inventors had resulted in failure and disaster, as well as in public ridicule and litigation. Beginning in a quiet, cautious way, Captain Morey wholly succeeded in 1790 under favorable conditions, and continuously, with increasing hazards, up to the time of his public announcement in 1793, not only without mechanical trouble of any kind, but without the slightest hint of litigation. In fact, he frequently stated that during his long life he had never been sued and had never found it necessary to bring legal action against anybody else.

Next came the salt water test. He personally directed the navigation of his boat from Hartford, Connecticut, to New York City at rate of between five and six miles an hour, and various other trips were arranged. Numerous notables were guests on these trips. One of his boats went from New York to Greenwich, and at this time Chancellor Robert R. Livingston, Judge Livingston, Edward Livingston and John Stevens were guest passengers. They were most enthusiastic in their praise of the boat and its equipment and made special mention of its maneuverability.

From the very start Morey had thought of experimenting with paddle wheels in various positions on the boat, and was encouraged to do this by Professor Silliman of Yale, who believed that some position would be found which would give greater power and speed. Morey's first boat had its paddle wheel at the prow. Later he tried one at the stern, and still later experimented with the side-middle position as well as locations both forward and aft of center. It was his conviction, after many experiments and paddle wheel position changes, that there was very little difference in the various plans, so as far as power, speed and handling were concerned, with this size boat.

In 1797, at the invitation of Dr. Allison and a group of men who wished to found a steamship line, Morey proceeded to Bordentown, New Jersey, and there built a suitable boat, running it repeatedly between Bordentown and Philadelphia with marked success. Dr. Allison stated that he took many people, or arranged for their passage, on these trips, and not a single untoward incident occurred. While they were organizing, three interlocking companies in which Dr. Allison and his friends had invested, collapsed by a series of unusual and unfortunate events, practically wiping out the entire group financially. There were no others to finance the plan, and what would have otherwise been the first steamship line in America, a line founded on the Morey patents, died at birth. . . .

Samuel Morey lived his entire life in the Connecticut River country. From the ox team-canoe-dugout-raft-rowboat days, to his father's ferry, then his own steamboat and the subsequent steamboat development, clear through to the successful operation of the lock and canal system. Of all this, he was an integral part.

He literally grew up with locks and canals, knew every problem connected with them, and it was a fitting thing that in due course of time, when all six of the units of the Lock and Canal system which made the Connecticut River navigable for so many miles were completed, that he should be put in direct charge of their mechanical operation. In his contract it was stated that he was to have charge of all six, beginning with Windsor Locks, Connecticut, on the south, to Olcott's Falls on the north.

One of the first acts of the Vermont legislature, then sitting at Windsor, was to grant a charter for the first navigation canal, with appropriate locks, in America. This was chartered in 1791, work commenced in 1792 and the first boat passed through in 1802. At one time difficulties were considered almost insurmountable on account of the great fall of the river, 52 feet, and the heavy rock ledges through which cuts must be made. Captain Morey was the local consulting engineer under the English engineer brought in by the English owners. It was Morey who rearranged the plans and overcame the difficulties.

Popular conception has sometimes regarded the Middlesex Canal as the first, but this is not correct. Colonel Loammi Baldwin, for whom the Baldwin apple was named because he also brought it out, on September

10, 1794, turned the first sod which began the construction of the Middlesex Canal from Boston to Lowell. The Canal was opened to traffic in 1804, two full years after the one at Bellows Falls had been in successful operation.

All of the capital for the construction of the locks and canals at Bellows Falls, chartered under the name of "Company for Rendering Connecticut River Navigable by Bellows Falls," was furnished by three brothers of London, England. They were John, Francis, and Hodgdon Anderson. The early settlers could not raise, what was for those days, a very large sum of money, and the Andersons preferred not to sell stock to outsiders, so they bore the entire cost of $105,338.13.

Traffic was heavy and the business was profitable. Large quantities of lumber went from points as far north as the Morey Mills at Fairlee and Orford to the rapidly growing communities in the lower Connecticut region, and into the New York City market. The tariff by the Falls was "for a long stick, 75 cents. For a short one, 50 cents. For two hhds. liquors, 70 cents. Salt, same."...

The strategic position and utilitarian aspect of the Bellows Falls Canal and Locks is indicated by the fact that although the railroads came up the valley in 1849 to 1850, and the transition from river to railroad transportation, for obvious reasons, was almost overnight, the Bellows Falls Canal continued in active operation until 1858.

At a location seven miles south of White River Junction, between the villages of Hartland and North Hartland, at what were known as Sumner's Falls, was the location of locks and canals authorized by the Vermont Legislature under the name "Company for Rendering Connecticut River Navigable by Water,—Quechee Falls." New Hampshire also gave a charter to the same company. The Falls were short, and consisted of two locks only, but served a very useful purpose.

February 23, 1792, the Massachusetts Legislature granted a charter to "The Proprietors of the Locks and Canals of the Connecticut River," to build at Turner's Falls and South Hadley Falls. There were many successful and important Dutch traders in the lower Connecticut Valley who conceived the idea of extensive commerce with the north country through the upper reaches of the river. Through their influence the necessary capital was obtained in Holland.

In 1794 it was deemed best to make two charters grow where only one grew before, and the long title named above was used exclusively by the project at South Hadley Falls, while that at Turner's Falls was built by "The Proprietors of the Upper Locks and Canals on the Connecticut River." The construction at South Hadley Falls was three and a half miles long, with eight locks, while that at Turner's Falls was three miles long with ten locks. The work was carried out efficiently and served a very useful purpose.

The well-thought-out and carefully engineered "works" at Windsor Locks, Connecticut, were based on a charter granted by the State of Connecticut in 1825. The locks were ready for the first boats in 1828. The natural drop of the river at this point is 30 feet in six miles. The rise and fall of the tides from Long Island Sound is clearly evident at this point. The Windsor Locks were the southern end of the chain of six canals over which Captain Samuel Morey had certain managerial jurisdiction, and this place also made a convenient point of departure for some of his trips to Hartford, New Haven, and New York.

The most northerly development and one nearest his own home in Orford was at Olcott's Falls, now Wilder, Vermont, not far from Dartmouth College in Hanover, New Hampshire. Chartered by Vermont, October 21, 1795, construction was held up until the New Hampshire Legislature passed a law June 12, 1797, entitled "An Act Granting Miles Olcott the Privilege of Locking White River Falls."

After an expenditure of about $40,000 the corporation advertised in 1810 that it was ready for the passage of boats and rafts. At this location, two miles north from White River Junction, there were two sections of two locks each. These were cut through the rock and soil at the New Hampshire end of the dam. All others between Vermont and New Hampshire were cut on the Vermont side. After serving well for many years, floods wiped out the last vestiges of what was once a noble utility, and in 1880 the power rights were purchased and a splendid new dam built.

The locks and canals on the Connecticut were so successful that many more were projected but most of them were never built, for lack of funds. It was agreed that an intricate system of inland water transportation was vital to the growth of the nation, but there simply wasn't money enough in the country to back up private promotions, and foreign capital, at first generously proffered, later became cautious and then withheld from further projects of this nature.

The War Department folks still held to their original view, that a very material extension of the Connecticut River System was vital to the nation, and in 1825 they sent an engineer of exceptional ability, and a corps of assistants, to carefully survey every possible route to Canada from Olcott's Falls to Barnet, Vermont. Enthusiasm ran high. Mass meetings and more mass meetings were held in key towns along the various proposed routes, bringing the best arguments to bear on the home town line, and accentuating the difficulties and objections to other plans.

One favored route was from Wells River, Vermont, to Groton, Marshfield, Plainfield, Montpelier, and down the Winooski River to Lake Champlain. Routes from White River and several other points to the one which was to start from Barnet, Vermont, were surveyed but did not meet the full approval of the army engineers. The latter did strongly approve the general plan and, as a connecting link to Boston, gave approval to a proposed line of locks and canals beginning at Concord, New Hampshire, going north to Franklin, thence up the Pemmigewasset River to Bristol. The seven-mile length of Pasquaney (Newfound Lake) was to be utilized, then through West Plymouth to Rumney and Wentworth, from which point there were two options, one reaching the Connecticut River at Haverhill, and the other at Orford, New Hampshire.

Naturally much pressure was brought upon Captain Morey to bring about the extension of the canal projects and to see to it that the New Hampshire-Vermont connecting link was at the Fairlee-Orford intersection. Even the Army Engineers tentatively offered the Captain a life position in connection therewith. Calmly but firmly he explained that he was unalterably opposed to the proposition. Admitting that the engineering difficulties in surmounting the extremely hilly country between the Connecticut and Montpelier could be overcome with money enough and years enough, to use his own expression, he did not believe in public projects that were not needed and would never pay. Secretly he foresaw the time when "steam would be applied to a carriage on a railroad" to such an extent as to supplant canals. He said the projected line would never be built, and it never has been constructed!

The Steamboat Story

MELANOTHON W. JACOBUS

AS THE FIRST QUARTER of the new century ran out, steamboating on the Connecticut River (as elsewhere) had progressed beyond the primary invention stage. It was not that steamboat design became static. On the contrary, many subsequent improvements—radical changes, even—appeared, but the steamboat as an instrument of waterborne transportation was an accepted fact. The size and shape of a ship

From Melanothon W. Jacobus, *The Connecticut River Steamboat Story* (Hartford: The Connecticut Historical Society, 1956).

were dictated by the depth and width of channels, lockage and dockage facilities, and the general purpose she was called upon to serve.

The story of up-river steamboating is an almost unbelievable one. Above Hartford there were all sorts of obstacles to navigation, but they did not daunt the steamboat enthusiasts who pulled and poled their craft over rapids and succeeded in getting at least one steamer as far north as Wells River, Vermont. Had projected plans for a canal link with Lake Memphremagog materialized, there might have been Connecticut River steamboats chugging across the Canadian border.

BARNET was the first of these up-river steamers, named confidently for that village in Vermont it was hoped she would reach. Barnet was understandably regarded as the head of navigation on the Connecticut; just above the village the river tumbles over the so-called Fifteen Mile Falls, whose name alone would be a damper to any serious boating beyond that point.

Her owners were the Connecticut River Company, an association formed in 1824 to promote river navigation in the interests of the bordering towns and regions, and in opposition to the canal development companies which were threatening to tap the same territory. Corporations for a complete canal from New Haven to Northampton had already been chartered—the Farmington Canal Company in Connecticut in 1822, and the Hampshire and Hampden Canal Company in Massachusetts in 1823—and plans for a canal on into Vermont, paralleling the river, were in the thought stage. There were two rival propositions here, with opinion about equally divided. Army engineers, who were making preliminary surveys for canals connecting the Connecticut River with Lake Memphremagog, incorporated this statement in a report in 1825.

"There exists much contrariety of opinion among intelligent men on the most feasible plan of forming an inland communication. Some are in favor of a canal independent of the river, and a respectable association of individuals in the town of Hartford (Connecticut) to whose disinterestedness and liberality, the public are indebted for the survey of the river, from McIndoes Falls (Barnet) to tide water, consider the most practicable plan is to improve the bed of the river, and to use steam vessels in towing up freight boats."

I wonder whether this disinterested association in Hartford was the Connecticut River Company!

Neither the building of a canal nor the improvement of a river was a light undertaking. The canal from New Haven to Northampton meant digging a 75-mile ditch with the hand tools of the time, and about 60 locks had to be provided to accommodate the 110-foot difference of elevation between the terminal towns. Against this the river people had to contend with freshets, floating debris, shifting bars and channels; and wherever a fall line did occur, heroic measures had to be taken to raise or lower the boats in a hurry. A by-pass canal and incline around the falls at South Hadley had been completed in 1795, and improved with locks in 1805, but between Hartford and Northampton there still were two mammoth barriers across the Connecticut—the Enfield rapids and the Willimansett falls.

These barriers notwithstanding, and with the prospect of some favorable legislation in the offing if its steamboat made good, the Connecticut River Company went forward and authorized the construction of BARNET. Her builders were Messrs. Brown and Bell of New York, who went to work right away. Building started 22 August, 1826; launching took place 26 September, just over a month later; and by mid-November her engine had been installed and she was towed to Hartford. BARNET was a small steamer, of course; 75 feet long, 14.5 feet beam, and she drew only 22 inches of water.

BARNET left Hartford on her northern venture 17 November, 1826, but her first try to climb the Enfield rapids failed. A combination of obstacles—wind, tide, and a loaded barge bound downstream—brought her to a standstill, and she had to return to Hartford that same day. It was a disappointing beginning, and I guess the canal advocates could not resist the chance to poke a little fun at the river company's show. The Connecticut *Courant* said "this circumstance has called forth a vast deal of wit and good feeling from some of our neighbors." (The "neighbors," no doubt, were folk from New Haven or Northampton, who might have a logical counter-interest in the canal.)

In two days her machinery was "strengthened" (whatever that means), and a second start was made on 19 November. With a scow lashed to each side, and thirty men poling, BARNET surmounted the rapids successfully and, in the words of the *Courant,* "reached Springfield in very good season," where she "was received with true neighborly kindness." What is more, the news of her arrival promptly emptied the court house of all but judge, jury, and counsel.

The engineers monkeyed some more with her machinery, but this did not delay the resumption of her voyage the next day. Enthusiastic onlookers pulled her up and over the Willimanset falls, and she negotiated the South Hadley by-pass canal and locks without incident. Somewhere along here BARNET tied up for a whole day on account of its being Thanksgiving, but she arrived at Northampton a little after noon on Friday. Saturday she pushed north and took a side trip up the Deerfield River where it was feared she might spend the winter because of ice, but milder weather the next week thawed things out, and she reached Brattleboro and Bellows Falls without any other notable delay.

The Bellows Falls *Intelligencer* of 1 December, 1826, took a long and confident forward look as it reported her coming:

> "The arrival of the Barnet at this place is an event which will form an interesting epoch in the History of the Connecticut river, and is only a small item in the list of improvements calculated to be carried into execution at some future period."

BARNET was too wide to pass through the locks at Bellows Falls so there could be no thought of her reaching her namesake town at that time—or ever, unless the locks were enlarged. (Isn't it strange that no one thought to measure the locks before the dimensions of BARNET were fixed upon?) But her journey as far as it went was a tremendous achievement. It is 125 miles from Hartford to Bellows Falls, and the elevation of the river there is 200 feet higher than it is in Hartford.

There was a celebration and a big dinner at the best hotel in town; indeed, that sort of welcome was routine. At almost every landing BARNET had been greeted with cannon, muskets, bells, cheers, speeches—all topped off with a feast where there would be toasts to BARNET, the Connecticut River, and such intangibles as Steam and New England Enterprise.

It was December, with a real threat of the river freezing over, and BARNET did not linger at Bellows Falls. She got away on the fourteenth and, without pressing at all, reached Brattleboro that night and docked at Hartford five days later. Her return touched off a real demonstration; the Connecticut *Courant* of 25 December had a long description, of which the following is a part:

> "On Tuesday last our citizens were gratified by the return of this boat from her late trip to Bellows Falls. Her arrival was welcomed by the discharge of cannon and the cheers of a numerous throng of persons assembled at the wharf. In the evening the gentlemen who accompanied the boat on her expedition, several passengers from Springfield and the adjacent towns on the river, and a large collection of our citizens partook of a supper provided for the occasion at Mr. Joseph Morgan's Coffee-House."

Even though the Company had certainly hurried the building of BARNET and had undertaken the up-river voyage without proper facilities at Enfield or Willimansett, its point—which was the feasibility of steamboat operation above tidewater—was pretty clearly proved. If the Company was not sure about it, the newspapers were. From the Boston *Daily Advertiser* there came this statement:

> "It ought not to be forgotten that this experiment was made under almost every disadvantage. The Barnet was built entirely since 22d August last. . . . Yet success

has followed the exertion, and when we look to the future, we can see nothing to limit our hope that they who live on the fertile banks of the Connecticut, which are more thickly settled than those of any river of the same size in the Union, may soon be favored with all the advantages which come from the cheap, safe, regular, and quick communication afforded by steam navigation. There is nothing in the character of the river to set bounds to the course of improvement, short of the entire accomplishment of the object proposed."

The Greenfield *Gazette*, which was partial to canals rather than river development, was frank to admit, when BARNET steamed that far, that "her arrival has afforded the highest degree of evidence that steam boats can navigate Connecticut River."

"The friends to an improved navigation of the Connecticut River cannot fail to be highly gratified with the result of the late experiment with the Steam Boat Barnet."

"Excluding those rapids where she could not ascend by her own power, an imperfect steam boat has been able to navigate the Connecticut, a greater distance, than the Hudson has yet been navigated with like power."

"She moves easily, with twice the speed of a canal boat. This speed . . . may be increased to 9 or 10 miles an hour."

And then, in a gesture to heal the wound somewhat:

"It would be ungrateful . . . to retort, or remember even, the spleen of the few interested and therefore active adversaries of the improvement of Connecticut river."

BARNET did not, of course, decide any issue between rivers and canals. Her mission was to demonstrate what could be done by a steamboat on the Connecticut River above the fall line, and this she did. Not for an instant did she shake the confidence of the canal contingent. 1826 saw no diminution of canal construction, canal contracts, or canal projects. Throughout the country enthusiasm for canals continued unabated. The Erie and the Chesapeake and Ohio canals were setting a fashion and a pace, and everywhere there was talk of this great system of overland transportation which would open up the inland resources of the nation. It was seen by some as a defense measure—a means of rushing troops to the border at a conservative twenty miles per day. In all seriousness, though, travel by canal was a serene and placid way of going places when the alternative was a jolting junket by stagecoach!

The case for the river had to be argued against an enthusiastic opposition which fervently believed that God made a river only to feed a canal. And there were practical difficulties as well. An open water fairway was often trapped with a hidden and shifting sand bar or a whirling eddy. The mirror surface of a river could suddenly be changed into an uncontrollable flood by melting snow or torrential rains. Where there were falls or turbulent rapids, some by-pass had to be built. The safe and successful navigation of a river meant a considerable outlay in so-called "river improvements," yet the people who foresaw a future for the steamboat on the Connecticut fervently believed all this could and should be done. With the slogan "Let the Connecticut River be damned—never choked" they hailed the success of BARNET's demonstration.

It would be rather nice to record here that her voyage to Bellows Falls and back was only the first of many BARNET made, but such was not the case. She almost, but not quite, dropped from sight. I have come across no references to her until late in the year 1827 when the Connecticut *Courant* of 5 November carried these melancholy lines:

"We regret to learn that the Steam-Boat Barnet, on her way from New York to this place [Hartford] last week, burst her boiler when off Milford Harbour, by which one person was killed."

The Rafting Gangs

C. W. BLISS

THE PRESENT CHANGES BEING made in the Bellows Falls canal, redeveloping it for electrical transmission, makes any early experiences of its use of particular importance and interest.

More than 25 years ago the following story of actual experiences with a rafting gang passing here were [sic] told to the writer by C. W. Bliss, then a well-known merchant of West Fairlee, Vt. In May of 1854, when a boy of 18, he made a trip down the Connecticut river in the capacity of cook for the raftsmen. He said:—

"The lumber was round logs cut sixty feet long. They were fastened together by two-inch planks at each end and in the middle of each log. Through these planks

From Lyman S. Hayes, *The Connecticut River Valley* (Rutland, Vt.: The Tuttle Company, 1929).

a wooden pin was driven into each log, making a solid mass about twelve feet wide and sixty long, which was called, in the river parlance, a 'box.' From the end of the planks, at each corner of the box, a stout hard wood pin stuck up fifteen inches or more, against which were braced oars for propelling and guiding the box, and over which could be placed short planks with holes in them, thus yoking the boxes securely together. Two boxes, side by side, and three in length, six in all, constituted a 'raft" or 'division,' and it was in this form that the trip down the river was made, except when it was necessary to 'break up the rafts' into boxes in order to pass through the different canals.

"There were eighteen rafts in our lot and we had eighteen men. It took two men to navigate each raft with rough oars at opposite corners and so the practice was for the men to take nine rafts as far down the river as possible and make connections with a north bound passenger train; then go back and bring the other nine down. A rough board shanty nearly covered one box. One end was used as dining room and kitchen, the other for sleeping purposes. An old elevated-oven stove was used in cooking. In the sleeping end, a liberal quantity of straw was thrown loosely on the logs on which the men slept with their clothes on. They lay in two rows with heads towards the sides of the raft and feet in the middle. I bought at different points white bread and I made brown bread, cooked potatoes, beans, tea and coffee. These constituted the whole bill of fare. The men were always sure to reach the raft on which was the shanty at meal time and at night. The rafts, when left at night, or at other times, were tied to trees on the shore.

"The lumber in the raft on which I shipped, was owned by an old man named Richardson from Orford, N. H., who accompanied us by train, coming aboard frequently. It came from much farther north than Orford and was to go to Holyoke, but not making a sale of it there, it was taken along to Middletown, Conn. I joined the party at the locks at what is now Wilder, just north of White River Junction, and left it at Holyoke, having hired out only to go this distance, and having become tired of it. It took three weeks and four days between those two points. My pay was $1 per day while the regular men had $1.50. One 'pilot' was among the men, who knew the channel of the river at all points, and he received $3 per day. An additional pilot was taken on at two different points, one called the 'Geese' and the other 'The Tunnel,' on account of the swiftness of the water and the dangerous rocks at both places. The pilots or 'swift-water men,' at each place knew the rocks perfectly and they took the head of the first raft, guiding that, the rest following in exactly the same course.

"When the rafts reached Bellows Falls, it took the men three days to break them up and get the one hundred and eight boxes through the locks and put them together again. One of these days was Sunday, but the river-men always had to work on Sunday the same as on other days. That day, I think there were at least five hundred people on the banks of the river and the canal watching our work. There was considerable competition between the men on the different rafts on the long stretch of still water above the dam to see which raft would get down to the canal first. As the river was broad and still for some miles, it gave them their best chance for sculling, but the movement was necessarily slow.

"After getting out of the lower locks at Bellows Falls, I remember seeing a number of small dwellings near the locks on the Vermont side. From one of these an old Irishman's cow had wandered down over the broad beach into the water in which she stood up to her body. The irate wife of the old man came down and called the cow loud and long, but she would not come ashore. The woman yelled a command to her 'old man' to come and drive the cow out. 'The divil a bit will I do it,' says he, and after soundly berating him for his neglect, she calmly gathered her skirts about her high enough to keep them from getting wet, and walked in, driving the cow home herself.

"Among the men was a large and powerful half-breed Indian named Sam Flint, who stood six feet four inches, and was very strong. He was a general favorite and in all cases when any of the boys went ashore, and it was thought there might be trouble from drinking otherwise, they wanted Sam to go to protect them. There were many places along the river where rough crowds gathered at saloons. As the raft was leaving the eddy at Bellows Falls, Sam made a misstep and landed in the river, but was readily pulled aboard again and worked with his wet clothes on until they were dried. No other man got a ducking during the trip."

Shipyard Owners and Workers

JOHN V. GOFF

THE NINETEENTH CENTURY DAWNED upon a special people building ships in the lower Connecticut River Valley, their craft tying each valley township to the world outside. Fishing, the coastal trade and overseas commerce were also dependent upon shipbuilding, for it was at the shipyards that ferries were launched to stitch the river links together and naval vessels constructed to win independence, save the young republic and preserve the Union. Hundreds of men worked together to build at least 4,000 wooden vessels in the lower valley [from Lyme to Windsor] before 1850, and it is the shipyards, the shipyard owners and ultimately the common shipyard worker upon whom we must focus to understand this ancient process that was so integral to the valley.

From Ellsworth S. Grant, *Thar She Goes* (Essex, Conn.: Fenwick Productions, 2000).

Middletown, on the west bank of the river and in the middle of the state, was the first to commence shipbuilding (1669) in the lower valley. In 1776, Middletown (pop. 5,000) was the greatest shipbuilding and commercial center between the two great cities of the nation, New York and Boston. Many of Middletown's vessels were built in Cromwell, north of the present city, and in Portland, across the river. Middletown ranked Timothy Southmayd and Middle Haddam noted Clark and Markham among its early nineteenth-century builders, while William Belcher, Captain Luther Smith and Captain Abijah Savage, each with separate shipyards, helped Cromwell put its name on the map after the Revolution. Portland was underway, following the launching of a 90-ton schooner at the George Lewis yard in 1741. Here too, Philip Gildersleeve, famed as a master carpenter of the ship *Connecticut* (1798), established a firm that succeeded the Lewis yard in 1838 and where two vessels were produced yearly for the next three generations. David and Daniel White and Charles and David Churchill operated two other early nineteenth-century Portland yards. Finally, one notes Elizur Abbey, credited with 35 pre-1853 vessels, distinguished for their grace and, unlike others, built to haul the region's cargo and brownstone. With at least 10 shipyards, it is easy to picture greater Middletown industriously converting its forests into seafaring vessels.

Like its northern counterpart, Saybrook also derived its shipbuilding strength from affiliated towns in its circumference, even though Lyme, Essex, Deep River and Westbrook, unlike Middletown's Portland, were all political subdivisions of the larger township. Lyme's shipbuilding capabilities in the eighteenth century were due to such men as Sterling and Edward and Samuel Hill, whose yards, respectively, were located in Hamburg, Lyme and on the Lieutenant River in Old Lyme. In the nineteenth century, Brockway and Henry T. Comstock each built yards in Lyme, while Reuben Champion launched into the Lieutenant River. Essex achieved particular fame for the region when John Tucker planted the industrial seed, c. 1720 and Uriah Hayden, master carpenter, built the warship *Oliver Cromwell* in 1776. If it is true that "No place on the river, except Middletown, turned out more craft in the early nineteenth century," certainly specific shipbuilders deserve special credit. Conklin, Jeremiah Gladding, David Mack, Parker, Uriah Hayden, Redfield and Parmelee, David Williams and Richard P. Wiliams all established shipyards in Essex before 1850. Along the intermediary route, Thomas Denison opened his yard in what is now Deep River, c. 1830. Not to be overlooked was Westbrook, producing ships after 1740 and, in the early nineteenth century, "All [of its] yards" were located on the Pochaug River and included the Ball and Calvin Hayden yards. Middletown yards may have been more prolific or productive than those in the Saybrook region, but over 20 have been recorded in the area at the mouth of the river, with one said to have been at Saybrook Point.

The towns between Middletown and Saybrook never equaled the larger center of output, but they nevertheless attracted the industry at Haddam, Middle Haddam, East Haddam, Killingworth, Higganum and Chester. The industry began anonymously in Haddam in the eighteenth century, while that at Middle Haddam commenced in 1763, where four years later the name of the region surrounding Middle Haddam was called "Chatham" after the English shipbuilding metropolis. Here Abel Shepard was a "most active eighteenth-century Middle Haddam shipbuilder." Jesse Hurd also maintained his yard in Chatham, c. 1780–1850, and Thomas Child, descendant of Higganum's James Child, built 237 vessels before 1851 "mostly in Middle Haddam."

Killingworth began launching vessels in the early eighteenth century under the direction of Robert Carter, and by 1831 a Killingworth historian would write that "For many years this has been a leading branch of business. Three yards are improved, all of which are on Indian River, a small stream which enters the harbor." He further stated that an average of five ships were built yearly at this time. Higganum launched a sloop in 1754 and here too two yards were maintained continuously after 1760, one being that of James Child. Chester was not without its shipbuilding activity "near the mouth of Chester Cove" after 1755 and, early in the eighteenth century, at a site "a mile westward." Such activity would seem to indicate that towns in the middle region, supporting probably at least 16 yards, were distinguished centers of shipbuilding in their own right.

Over 45 shipbuilding centers have been documented in this overview, suggesting that most towns with water frontage in the lower Connecticut River Valley were prominent building areas before the mid-nineteenth century. The grand extent to which they were established here may perhaps never be known in its entirety, although it has been said that in Essex "there wasn't a backyard but had a skeleton craft on the stocks." Two different authorities have noted that Middletown and Essex each had the capacity to produce 30 vessels at once. Although there may be errors in counting twice those few sites operating in later years as different yards under new management, it seems certain that this listing is far too scant. In any case, there can be little doubt that shipbuilding was a major industry in the lower Connecticut valley during the early nineteenth century.

Those who called themselves shipbuilders were major shareholders in the yard and personally directed the business. Early arrivals to the industry were James Child from Rhode Island in 1762 and Philip Gildersleeve from Long Island in 1776. By the nineteenth century, most of the yards were established, with their owners already long-time residents. The yards in this way became family legacies to be inherited by sons, or passed on to skilled mechanics who might be favored by the family.

The shipyard owner usually managed at least one other business in tandem, for the logical complements to the shipyard included facilities which would manufacture material for shipbuilding itself. Many yard owners such as Clark and Markham (Middle Haddam), Gildersleeve (Portland), Gladding and Wooster (Essex) and Comstock (Hadlyme) operated their own sawmills or lumber businesses. Jesse Hurd (Middle Haddam) maintained a ropewalk in addition to his shipyard, while his partner, John Stewart, manufactured oakum used for caulking ships. These were efficient business solutions whereby the shipbuilder both diversified his manufacture and assured himself of a steady supply of building materials.

The owner, too, often had the capability of providing other trade goods and services. The Sterlings (Lyme), for instance, ran a tanning and fulling mill as well as a shipyard; Brockway and Reuben Champion (both of Lyme) maintained ferries; and Jesse Hurt (Middle Haddam) operated a distillery. Uriah and Horace Hayden (Essex, East Haddam and New York) were merchants as well as shipbuilders and managed a store in Essex. Foodstuffs, like Hurd's rum and Hayden's flour, could easily be exchanged for work performed in the owner's shipyard and, additionally, it could and did become a product for overseas trade. Shipyard owners possessed the business sense and capital to allow them to operate their yards as elements of large profit-making systems.

In the shipyard, the owner held ultimate responsibility for all business. He neogiated contracts with clients and sometimes contributed physical labor. Jesse Hurd, for one, contracted to supply timber to shipbuilder Thomas Child (Middle Haddam) just as he would contract with any other client.

Yet the shipyard owner was more than a clerical administrator; he was a craftsman with intimate knowledge of the secrets of his trade. If his name was Noah Starkey or Thomas Denison (Essex and Deep River, respectively), he may have spent years as a subordinate shipyard worker. Jesse Hurd worked with his men "getting timber across [the] river," directed them in the yard and supervised particular operations such as 'salting the ship' built for Thomas and Gardiner Child in 1821. For this job he referred to "boiling trunnels," "salting," and putting on lots of varnish. Reuben Champion, who had only about 20 workers at most, called himself a common laborer on virtually every one of his jobs, indicating that he and Roger Williams were the few consistent common workers. The owner understood his craft fully because he was experienced in all its aspects, both mysterious and mundane, and was continually aware of how his individual actions related to both the success of his yard and the welfare of his community of workers.

The shipyard was a complex place where diverse tasks were coordinated. Most operations involved heavy manual labor performed by different "common workers." Records for the building of *Henry Hill* (David Williams yard, Essex, 1822) permit an inside glimpse into early nineteenth-century Connecticut River shipbuilding. Fifty-seven men were paid for her construction; 25 produced and brought materials to the site; and 20 more assembled and carved the ship from those materials. Unfortunately, services were not recorded for 12 of those 57 men. Product suppliers ranged from farmer/ship carpenters who cleared the land, provided rails for launching and lumber for knees, to artisans like Thomas Millard, figurehead carver and Benjamin Meigs, a block-and-spar maker. A local ship captain was also a product supplier, who was paid for "freight" on the transportation of materials. It was the special duty of the other shipyard workers to build *Henry Hill:* to convert lumber, plank, trunnels, treenails (rust-proof wooden pins), knees, iron and copper into her hull. Still others would finish her mahogany, rigging, sails, anchors, metal work, carved work, cordage and boats.

The workers were divided into three main categories: ship carpenters, ship joiners and caulkers. These distinctions made by the 1859 census taker of Middlesex County generally accord with early nineteenth-century shipyard and worker accounts. Ship carpentry probably included all the processes that went into the rough hull, which included the use of the saw, adze, auger and mallet. Caulkers used special mallets and chisel-like tools to force oakum into the seams of the hull and deck; coated with tar, the stuffed seams were then rendered waterproof. Ship joiners relied mostly on their collection of planes and were responsible for furnishing the vessel with cabins, stairs, doors and furniture. Other trades, such as painters and plumbers, were employed, but it was the ship carpenter, the ship joiner and the ship caulker who constituted the three basic classes of shipyard workers. Until new information suggests otherwise, it is reasonable to associate the work of the sawyer, borer and adze man with the function of ship carpenter.

Carpenters were usually paid a daily or monthly wage and were expected to perform a variety of tasks for the shipyard. Nathaniel Purple worked on *Alexander, Potosi, Hayden-Falcon* and *Chancellor* for Jesse Hurd, yet he was also paid for "cutting [timber]" and working with a crew felling in Cone's woods. Though ship joiners and caulkers ranged throughout the lower valley working for various yards, ship carpenters were apparently less transient. No cases of ship carpenters working for different yards at the same time has [*sic*] yet been discovered, which contrasts sharply with certain joiners (the Denisons and Parkers of Essex and Chester) and caulkers (the Stokes and Tookers of Westbrook and Essex) who performed their skills for different shipyards on a regular basis. Jedediah Post Jr., the only Valley ship carpenter whose mobile life is known in detail, did manage to work in four distinct localities during his lifetime. He left Westbrook to train in Madison, was later employed in New York and finally returned once more to Essex and Westbrook. In each place, however, he seems to have been strongly tied to one shipyard. Unlike the joiners and caulkers who plied specialized finishing trades to complete a vessel, the ship carpenter's job was essentially a stationary one. Jedediah Post Jr. is a case in point, for he worked for a single shipyard owner, continually laboring to convert rude timber into a succession of vessels ready for finishing.

Was the ship carpenter's task perceived as a skilled one? As stated, in about 1820, Post left the Westbrook locality to train for the occupation elsewhere. Most record keepers, however, grouped the ship carpenter with the adze man, sawyer and borer, rarely distinguishing between any of these skills. They were paid laborers and, as Stephen Thernstrom has observed, "laborer" was a large nineteenth-century category for society's bottom-rung workers, whose tasks required physical strength and no particular skill. Valley shipyard owners paid their carpenters for "labor" or, occasionally, "help," but none was specifically paid for "carpentry work." The terminology employed by these bookkeepers suggests that ship carpenters were looked upon in a vague and indifferent manner.

A remarkable ship carpenter was Richard Pratt, and he was the only one in the valley known to have kept a workbook of his own. He worked for more than one yard at the time. This should be understood in light of the fact that he worked during the valley's era of shipbuilding decline. Other evidence of unusual freedom and/or economic hardship, with its need to move on, exists, for we find him listed in another source with the additional occupation of cabinetmaker. Still, there is little doubt that his ship carpenter work was quite traditional in all respects. He labored "hewing plank" and "making spars . . . 10 hours per day" in 1853, while on another re-planking job he worked "splitting out" treenails and constructed a steam-box.

Boring was a major, if not a totally classifiable, task in ship construction, with the production of bits for hand augers a major industry in Chester and Essex villages. Ezra L'Hommedieu won fame for his double twist auger bit, which was a product of the lower Connecticut River Valley. Hole drilling was as fundamental to wooden shipbuilding as welding and riveting would be in later years. Holes were bored for iron rods to hold the knees (inner braces) to the frame of the vessel. Thousands were also required for treenails, to fasten planking to the exterior. Borers were usually paid for piecework. Richard Flood, a Hurd worker, for instance, was paid 3 shillings per hundred for the 2,300 treenails he bored in one vessel in 1802. James Myrick at the Lewis yard in Portland received 9 pence per hole for the 5,300 he sank into the cutter *Renown* in 1808. Yet, Ephrain Ufford was given a daily wage by Hurd in 1821 with his account listed as "hole borren 18 days = 1,146." Maritime joinery was more complex than domestic joinery, and because of the unusually large number of holes required in ship construction, boring probably emerged as a separate function, which it never did achieve in house construction.

Few absolute statements can be put forward concerning valley shipyard sawyers except to say that they were paid by both daily wage and piece work and for diverse and specific tasks. Solomon Bailey received 5 shilling 6 pence for every 80 feet of timber he sawed for Jesse Hurd in 1802. Yet he was given 1 shilling 8 pence for cutting boards, whether by quota or by day is not known, or 5 shillings per day for general work. Seth Eddy received $20.00 per month for "sawing" and other work at the Lewis yard in 1804 and Reuben Champion paid Daniel Carter for "sawyer's work at 75 cts." in 1821.

No shipyard bookkeeper has been found paying any worker specifically for adze work, dubbing or hewing. From a secondary source, however, it is apparent that this was the special task of James Lester (1791–1890) of the Sterling yard in Lyme. His job was to adze the exterior joints of the hull, working "something like 90 days on each hull, most of the time lying on his back." Though isolated workers received wages for boring, sawings and adzing, we have already noted that ship carpenters Nathaniel Purple and Richard Pratt worked "cutting" wood in the fores, "hewing plank," and shaping new parts for vessels and repairing the old. There can be little doubt that adzing, boring and sawing were close allies to, or facets of, the ship carpenter's trade.

The caulker's job was exceedingly demanding but potentially lucrative. Rational men might avoid the task because of its strenuous conditions, as described by Captain Nathaniel Cooper Johnson of Chatham, who ". . . began his career by working for his father in the shipyard, caulking on the underside of a vessel. After his first day at this grueling task, he told his father he had worked as long as he wanted on the underside of a vessel and hereafter he would get his living on deck. It was not long before he became a sailing master."

Caulking was probably grueling work because of the amount of hammering required; its occupational hazards are supposed to have included deafness. Yet, financial rewards often compensated for phsysical hardship.

Caulkers, for instance, received a wage of 9 and 10 shillings per day from Jesse Hurd in 1807 and 1815, when the average worker's wage was only 4 shillings per day. It is apparent that B. Bonfoy, Demon Brook, Benjamin P. Jones and Walter Clark (all caulkers) were a few of the highest paid workers in their day. On the other hand, subordinate caulkers (presumably children and apprentices) never did receive exceptional wages. Records show that a minority of caulkers were paid in systems other than the daily wage; i.e., in piece work and by the job rate, thereby confusing the historian's analytical task. Surviving account books and other references suggest, however, that the early nineteenth-century caulker's trade, if not trying, was at least financially rewarding.

Ship joiners had a happier compromise. Their wages were not outstanding—the leaders of Jeremiah Gladding's group received 6 or 7 shillings per day between 1798 and 1812—but their working conditions seem to have been exceptional. Their work required refined woodworking skills, unlike some carpentry and most caulking which required, primarily, strength or persistence in a repetitive task. They planed decks, paneled doors, built cabins, staircases and interior furniture and thus were paid a better-than-average wage to do clean, varied and creative work on what was often at least a level surface.

Ship joiners were a distinct and elite group in several respects. Some maintained the apprentice system, while others seem to have been especially prepared for certain types of private enterprise. Also, the vocation was perpetuated among just a few families in 1850. Josiah Gladding's account book (1798–1812) permits extraordinary glimpses into the workings of an early nineteenth-century valley ship joiner crew. His consisted of a master and a partner, at least two apprentices and "two boys," with graduated wages for all three levels. Clues to the existence of the apprentice system stem from one particular statement by Gladding in which he said, "August 18th 1803 Know [that] Jeremiah Gladding began to live with me and larn my trade." Under this arrangement, Jeremiah received after four years of apprenticeship his own set of tools, mostly planes, from his master, Josiah. Elevated to the position of master, a ship joiner might start a group of his own, a route which Jeremiah's fellow apprentice, Rufus Fordham, followed. The master's job included negotiating contracts with private clients and shipowners, keeping the group's account books and doing ship joinery like the rest. When contracts were slow in coming, the crew might shift to making furniture or working on buildings in the community. Such a list of work included making a linen chest and a large dovetailed chest for Abigail Lord, bedsteads for Rebecca Shipman, Mr. Ely and David Williams, window frames for David Williams II and a rope house for Gordon Smith, work for the meeting house in 1791 and the schoolhouse in 1812. Most work, however, was on a variety of craft identified by type, such as a "sconer" or "scuner," "brig," "cutter," "ship," "big ship," "vesil" and "boat," with the records giving the name of the client and date of work performed. Occasionally references actually describe the joiner work, such as "on the forepeak, deck, planing the mast," and "laying the cabin floor." Though Josiah Gladding's account book is principally a financial one, it also manifests a distinct image of the ship joiner's life. He worked in autonomous groups, structured an apprentice system and did building construction as well as ship joinery.

Ship joiners are also found to have been manufacturers and administrators as well as woodworkers. Josiah Gladding described the tools he sold to apprentice Jeremiah as "the tools I made you" in 1807 and he had previously manufactured tools for Eliakim Pratt, occupation unknown, which were largely an assortment of planes. No ship carpenter or caulker is known to have matched the dramatic advancement of Thomas and Eli Denison, who left the ship joinery trade to become owners of yards in Deep River. Actually, several yard owners came from ship joiner families. In Essex, there were Noah Starkey and Jeremiah Gladding, son of the "apprentice" Gladding. The younger Gladding, between leaving his family and becoming a shipyard owner, ran a plane factory in Deep River. Some joiner groups produced their own tools and capitalized on this manufacturing ability, while others benefited enough from the administrative training associated with the autonomy of the ship joiner's trade to manage shipyards of their own.

The 1850 census reveals that ship joinery was a select, family-monopolized business in the lower Connecticut River Valley. Middlesex County, which included 13 towns, had 132 ship carpenters and 28 caulkers, but only 17 ship joiners. The joiners belonged to just four families [:] the Gladdings, the Tripps, the Starkeys and the Denisons of Essex and East Hampton. Compared to other shipyard workers, ship joiners enjoyed a pleasant workplace and a differentiated status.

The shipyards were a training ground for others besides carpenters, joiners and caulkers. An example is Cicero Hayden, who at the age of 20 was a common worker on Uriah and Horace Hayden's schooner *Alert*. Six years later he was painting *Henry Hill* in the Williams yard in Essex. By the time he was an old man in 1850, he was established as a professional painter and left the shipyard entirely. Similarly, Jesse Pratt provided "labor" in the Willimas yard in 1822, but by 1850 he listed his occupation as house joiner. The shipyard, then, gave adequate vocational training for entering related trades. Richard Pratt and members of Josiah Gladdings's group, for instance, were proficient furniture makers. Some of Gladding's crew became toolmakers and Chatham's ship carpenter,

Nathaniel Purple, learned some elements of the housewright's trade. In the agrarian community, the shipyard probably served as a kind of urban center, which provided vocational training for many.

It is possible that ship carpenters and caulkers enjoyed professional training of an excellence that matched that of the ship joiner. After all, ship carpenter Jedediah Post Jr. trained for his occupation in Madison. Caulker Walter Clark left two work receipts suggesting that he had led a group much like Gladding's working with two boys, at least two apprentices and with one and an occasional extra partner in addition to himself, the master. Many caulkers, the four generations of Philip Tookers in Essex no less than Nathan Cooper Johnson, passed their skills on from father to son.

Probate records suggest that it was a rare shipyard owner who squeezed riches from his shipyard. On the other hand, mercantile pursuits often proved a reliable and valuable financial investment. Richard Hayden (Essex) was a master carpenter and George Cary (Chatham) was a common Hurd worker; yet both died wealthy with sizeable investments in a vessel and distillery.

Reuben Champion was described as a farmer at the time of his death and Jesse Hurd Jr. left a "Recpt for Making Ointment for Sheep," indicating that he, too, was familiar with husbandry. Other sources reveal that many, if not a majority, were farmers as well as shipyard workers, with agricultural holdings reflected in their probate data. Eli Denison Jr. [,] a ship joiner and shipyard-owner's son, accrued assets worth only $181 at the time of his premature death in 1820. Yet 80 percent of that was invested in property without a residence. Elias Hayden, sash worker, boat builder and master carpenter, died worth $2,891 in 1810. Again, 80 percent of his assets were invested in property, which included a 77.5-acre homestead. Geoge Cary managed to acquire an estate totaling $5,105 before his death in 1826, 44 percent of which was invested in a wood lot, lots, meadow, part of a pier and a fishing place, showing that these holdings also were largely agricultural.

Accounts describing the lives of the workers clearly illustrate that many retired to farming after a productive shipbuilding career. Westbrook's Jedediah Post Jr. has received significant historical attention because his son became a successful commander in the coasting trade. Post, born in 1807 and listed as a ship carpenter in the 1850 census, is said to have engaged almost continually in shipbuilding, built his own house in 1837 and farmed in his later years. Like Calvin Hayden, a yard owner and other workers such as William Lay and Horace Dee, he was one of Westbrook's leading agriculturists in 1850. It was a logical choice for him to "retire" to farming when, with a broken leg, he could no longer do ship carpentry in 1867. He farmed for the next nine years until his crippled condition worsened in 1876 and he called his prominent son home to manage the farm. In Portland, Jonathan Shepard, who painted a schooner at the Lewis yard in 1808, raised a family of ship carpenters and was living in a neighborhood of shipyard workers in 1850; he was then a professional farmer worth the prodigious sum of $4,000. Two-thirds of Essex's top agriculturists in 1850 are known to have worked in the shipyards earlier in their lives.

The impetus to farm was probably economic in origin; some shipyard workers followed the calling at the same time they worked in area shipyards. Initial investigation of materials pertaining to workers in three sets of valley archives has produced only two manuscrips written by shipyard workers. These were Sylvester Rowland (Lyme) and the Nathaniel Purple family (Chatham), both of whom avidly pursued farming careers. Sylvester Rowland, who worked for Reuben Champion in Lyme, c.1823, maintained a farm with Louis Peck for a year, starting April 1, 1823. Another instance of a shipyard worker actually engaging in agricultural activity during work pertains to Richard Pratt. During his normal workweek of May 11, 1846, he "Sit Net caught 4 shad" on Monday and "went bean polling" on Wednesday.

A rich fabric of detail reflects the life of the family of Nathaniel Purple, Chatham ship carpenter born in 1791. Like Rowland, Nathaniel Purple worked in at least one valley shipyard in the 1820s. He labored in Cone's woods December 1820, cut timber for the ship being built by Thomas and Gardiner Child in 1821 and worked on several vessels which included *Alexander,* 1820, ship *Potosi,* 1821, brig *Hayden-Falcon* and ship *Chancellor* in 1823. From the surviving probate data on his father, Josiah Purple, it is reasonable to assume that both shared a farming operation as well as a house.

A large majority of shipyard workers were family men. This fact is found in the demographic information from the post 1790 census which defeats all notions that workers were a transient, single lot. To date, shipyard and manuscript material has revealed the names of 196 early nineteenth-century valley workers, their names coming from several different shipyards and time periods. Of these, 90 worked at the Hurd yard in Middle Haddam in 1802–1825, 50 at the Williams yard in Essex in 1822, 25 at the Champion yard in Lyme 1823–1824 and 22 at the Lewis yard in Portland 1798–1808. The final nine were associated with Gladding's ship joiner crew in Essex and environs 1798–1812. Census information is available for 154 of these 196 men, showing that fully 75 percent remained in Connecticut long enough to appear on at least one census and only 14 individuals made but a single "ghost appearance" in the area. About 70 percent of all the workers in our sampling lived in a single area, appearing on two consecutive censuses taken 10 years apart.

Where were the homes of the shipyard workers located? Maps pinpointing them in the Connecticut River Valley can be produced, conceptually or physically, with the aid of the 1850 census. 1850 was the first year that the census taker both noted the occupation of each head of household and numbered the houses consecutively according to the route he walked through the community.

Rather than disperse themselves equally throughout the community, the shipyard workers tended to group themselves into distinct clusters of houses within the neighborhoods. The most prominent sizes of the clusters were groups of two or three houses in close proximity, although clusters of 11 houses were not uncommon, of which Portland was a unique example.

Statistically, in 1850, 73.6 percent of the 181 shipyard workers in these six communities lived in houses located in one type or another of 39 clusters. In Essex, the workers lived in houses at the end of New City Street, on Little Point Street, in the south middle portion of Main Street, at the end of Mack Lane and at the end of the aparallel lane nearby, on the shore at South Cove and were heavily clustered along, virtually, the full length of South Main Street.

In Portland, only half the cluster of 11 and the cluster of three have been located within the city's confines. The first was on the east side of Main Street south of the intersection that joins Summer Street. Here Sylvester Gildersleeve lived in the largest house in the middle of the semi-cluster and the Abbeys owned property immediately north of Summer Street. The intersection was one-fifth of a mile away from the Gildersleeve (formerly Lewis) shipyard to the west and four-fifths of a mile from the Congregational Church and heart of the cluster of three to the east.

Locating shipyard workers' houses in the lower Connecticut River Valley opens up avenues of research, since the evidence suggests that most workers—ship carpenters, anyway—lived within walking distance of the shipyard. Thus the houses in Essex were probably located near the New City yard, the Gladding yard and the Mack yard, with a majority of Essex shipyards fronting South and Middle coves. In Portland, Essex and Westbrook it is also apparent that the workers lived in particular sections of the town's Main Street.

For reasons not totally known, wooden shipbuilding all but died out in the Connecticut River Valley by 1850. Richard Pratt noted *City of Hartford, Rip Van Winkle* and three other large steamers plying the river before the Civil War. Perhaps the vessels simply became too large for the local shipyards to build or repair, or the local yards had totally depleted their natural resources. The advent of metal may have sounded the death knell on traditional methods of building vessels, or perhaps the valley population had discovered a cheaper form of transportation, such as the "Air Line Railroad." Possibly the entire valley lost its economic magnetism to other, greater "cities of the nation" such as Boston, New York and Providence. Whatever the reasons, signs of the demise were clear before 1850 with one historian noting that Middle Haddam shipbuilding "lags c.1840." This had been evident from our own exploration when we found that at one time Jesse Hurd and John Stewart were thought to have "employed most of the two hundred [local] inhabitants hewing and shaping hulls below the bluff." Yet manuscript sources reveal only 90 Hurd workers, while the census indicated only 50 of them lived in all of Chatham, East Haddam and Haddam in 1850.

A century and a half ago, the lower Connecticut River Valley was alive with the sound of men felling, hauling and shaping wood with tools as disparate as the ship carpenter's splitting chisel and the ship joiner's cross plane. Vessels slid down at least 60 ways in the Middletown district and Saybrook townships alone. Shipbuilders like Jesse Hurd and Reuben Champion kept their accounts and enterprises straight, while product suppliers, workers and finishers labored together to build all of the vessels launched in the lower valley. Each was affected in a unique way. Richard Pratt would probably remember his treenails and steambox, Ephraim Ufford his 1,146 holes, Daniel Carter his sawn timber and James Lester his adze work. Nathaniel Cooper Johnson left his caulker's high wage to men like Walter Clark and Philip Tooker; Rufus Fordham experienced the special satisfaction of becoming master of his own group of ship joiners and Jeremiah Gladding's son left the joiners' ranks to direct his own shipyard. This was an astonishing record, considering the small number of men engaged in so vital an enterprise. Without them our commerce would have been altered. There would have been no *Oliver Cromwell* or any of the other vessels that followed, fewer prosperous towns along the river and less of a contribution by Connecticut to our nation's mercantile greatness.

Cutting Ice at McIndoe Falls

SCOTT E. HASTINGS, JR.

IN NOVEMBER THE LAND gathered itself and turned inward against the cold. Ice crystals danced in the moon's glow as nights lengthened. Each morning skim ice, edging ponds and rivers, thickened and spread from the shore. Till the sun got up the world was rimed in white, each weed stalk, twig, and branch a delicate tracery of frost. Week by week Jack Frost extended his domain over the hours.

Sometimes, skating in the long January nights, we saw the northern lights. Far away beyond the Arctic Circle, shimmering curtains of green and red fire flickered eerily in the sky. In the growing cold, ice thickened deep on ponds and rivers. Now the harvest could begin.

H. P. Hood & Son, a Boston milk firm, owned a huge icehouse beside the railroad tracks adjacent to the Connecticut River in McIndoes. They used ice in shipping milk and they also sent tons of it to the Boston market. My father told me how, at age fourteen, he worked with his father during the winter of 1918, cutting ice for H. P. Hood & Son. Later, when he worked at the paper mill in East Ryegate, the men picked up a few extra dollars cutting ice for the mill during their time off shift. One way and another, Dad had a lot of experience at the ice trade.

Cutting began whenever the ice was thick enough, usually at the end of an intense cold snap in January or early February. For ten, maybe twenty, days in a row the morning temperature would have registered twenty to thirty degrees below zero. At those temperatures it was a foregone conclusion that a day of ice cutting began with a good breakfast. That first day, when they came in from morning chores and milking, Gramp crumbled a slice of Dill's Best and filled his pipe while Dad and Indian Joe helped themselves to cups of hot coffee and sat chatting quietly while Gram cooked breakfast, which began with bowls of hot oatmeal. Bacon and eggs came next, followed by fried potatoes with salt pork in milk gravy to pour over them. Toast with homemade jam, scalding coffee, and pie filled up the corners.

"Come on, boys," urged Gramp, "it's going to be almighty cold out there on the ice. Eat up! You'll need all the fuel you can carry."

After breakfast they dressed for the ice. Along the river, at that time,

From Scott E. Hastings, Jr., *Goodbye Highland Yankee* (Chelsea, VT: Chelsea Green, 1988). Copyright Scott E. Hastings.

there was a more or less standard cold-weather dress for outdoor work like logging and ice cutting. First came long, heavy woolen underwear. Then thick woolen pants, likely as not a pair of Johnson's, a light shirt and a heavy wool one, a sweater, scarf, and mackinaw or blanket-lined frock, and woolen mittens inside a pair of leather outsiders. Hats had visors and pull-down earflaps, though some men wore the toque and a few hardy souls only a felt hat. Often a pair of bib overalls went over everything under the coat. Footgear was a couple pair of light woolen socks worn inside felt boots and rubber overshoes. Some men wore woolen stockings and higher leather moccasins.

After thus fortifying themselves against the cold, Gramp got Pete out of his stall, put a work harness on him, and the three set off for the river. Looking down from the rise at the edge of the village, they saw dark figures of men moving about the ice, opening up the field for the day's work. The dull red of a blanket coat, the flash of a bright scarf, and the blue-painted sleds made colorful contrasts with the broad white expanse of ice. In the pale light of early morning the scene looked like a winter landscape by Brueghel.

A couple of horse-drawn bobsleds were already on the ice near the end of a loading channel. One of the teamsters smashed the night's skim of ice and stuck two spruce loading poles down into the water, hooking the upper ends to the back of his sled. Now he was ready to pull the cakes of ice up the poles and load his sled. Other workers drifted by twos and threes down the temporary road onto the ice. Some were itinerants and "floaters"—tramps and out-of-work men from the outside—anxious to turn a few dollars. Some of them were hard cases, not to be messed with. A knot of men huddled at a fire of slabs on the shore where, at noontime, lunches would be thawed and coffee boiled.

The ice was twenty inches thick. The crew had been cutting for a few days and the field was well established. Today a new section was being opened. The foreman sent Gramp over to lay it out and begin scoring the cakes with an ice plow. The job called for a considerable degree of skill and a good eye. Gramp was an acknowledged master. He turned his horse over to a big itinerant whose job it was to snake long strings of floating ice cakes out of the water onto the conveyor carrying them into the icehouse.

Dad and Indian Joe picked up a couple of the heavy cross-handled ice saws and went to sawing ice nearby. As the morning wore on Indian Joe gave Dad a nudge and pointed. They saw Gramp walking over to the man working with Pete. Gramp said something to him and the man turned his back. Gramp walked away and began scoring blocks again.

"What's going on?" Dad asked.

"That guy's abusing Pete," Gramp said. "I told him not to do it again or he'd be sorry."

Gramp was not a big man. He was, in fact, nowhere near the size of the itinerant. But he was strong and a good boxer. A few minutes later the man looked round sideways at him, grinned, and hit Pete a good lick across the rump. Gramp walked over, spun him around, and knocked him into the freezing, black water. Then he graped a pike pole, wound it into the heavy mackinaw, and dunked him a couple of times before dragging him back out on to the ice.

There was no fight left in him. Somebody helped him up to the boardinghouse for a change of clothes and a drink. The rest of the time he was there he was a good deal more caring for the horses.

Chapter 5

THE GREAT DRIVE

June 1: Went to school. Killed a snake near Mill Brook Bridge. The log drivers are wangin in Daley's pasture. The cook gave us the biggest cookies you ever saw.
—Diary of a ten-year-old boy, 1904

Log driving, like whaling and cowpunching, was a brutal job carried out by largely illiterate wage slaves, and yet, like the other two exploitive industries, it resulted in a romantic myth that has become an ingrained part of our culture. The log drive on the Connecticut River was said to be the longest in the history of the world, measured from where the trees were cut to where the logs were delivered, and it gives the river its myth, its color, its romance and swagger. That huge tracts of first-growth forest were destroyed, that huge areas of the river were polluted, that dozens of men drowned every spring—well, all this has been submerged in the myth, time has erased most of the scars, and what's remembered is the drama of it, the sheer guts, stamina, and shrewdness it took to float millions of huge logs from Pittsburg to Holyoke, on an ice-cold river in the worst days of spring.

Two remarkable writers devoted their careers to capturing the flavor of those days. Stewart White, born in Lemington, Vermont, right on the river (a town where logging is still the principal industry), joined the log drive as a young man; Robert F. Pike was old enough to know most of the men who led the drives, and took it as his personal mission to get their stories and ballads down before they disappeared. Pike's Tall Trees, Tough Men, is one of the genuine classics of Connecticut River writing. Full honor to them both, as well as to the dozens of local people up and down the river who, in town histories, in oral histories, have contributed their own recollections, often just of sitting on the bank every spring, watching the logs go down. This was the Connecticut River pageant, and reading about it today can still quicken the heart.

After the days of the long-log drives, paper companies still used to float pulp down to the mills, an era which a veteran of those days, Fred Cowan, keeps alive in his column in a Colebrook, New Hampshire, newspaper. The column I've included testifies to the fact that moving pulp, despite its shorter length, was no easy job and explains the fact behind the ghostly remains of the dam still visible at Lyman Falls.

Third Lake to Mt. Tom

STEWART H. HOLBROOK

THE CONNECTICUT TAKES FORM as a river after it leaves Third Lake. Although a few other ponds empty into it, Third Lake is generally recognized as the source, the Headwaters.

About the headwaters of a river there is something of the mystery of Genesis. I felt it long ago as a boy when I heard men who had been there speaking of the headwaters of the Connecticut. The word had magic. Though I desperately wanted to know, I did not think it proper to ask what "a headwaters" was like. I imagined it to be a sort of never-failing geyser, a lonely fountain spouting in one specific spot, and I let it go at that.

It seemed to me that the bold fellows who had seen a headwaters were in the select company of great explorers. They had been to the Source, and the Source was of necessity in some remote place, wholly inaccessible, even unknown save to a few God-enlightened men. Beyond the Source there was nothing, nothing at all. Here you had arrived at Genesis, and you stood to look in awe upon the First Cause, where Adam drank, Eve bathed, and Deity moved over the face of the waters and commanded this stream to flow and gather together with other waters and be called the seas. And the evening and the morning were the third day . . .

Years later I first came to see these headwaters of the Connecticut when I scaled pulpwood at Third Lake. I have since been back there

From Stewart H. Holbrook, *Yankee Loggers* (New York: International Paper, 1961).

many times. It is a fine spot to sit awhile and reflect on the people and places and events that have meant something in the life of this stream, which ranges the full length of Vermont and New Hampshire and then crosses Massachusetts and Connecticut to join Long Island Sound at Saybrook.

Where it leaves Third Lake, it is little more than a good brook, but with the aid of a head dam named for Win Schoppe, a famous boss of the drive, it carried the logs into Second Lake, then on to First Lake, where horse-powered headworks, and later gasoline tugs, moved them to First Lake Dam. Here almost in front of the enormous and ancient Lake House, the CVL's three-storied and gabled depot camp, the logs were sluiced into the wildly plunging river. From here on they were the nucleus of the main drive, the longest drive in New England.

Other drives might join it, one year or another, first from Perry and Indian streams in Pittsburg and from Halls Stream at Canaan–West Stewartstown; men were sent ahead to "tend out" at these places—to keep the sticks moving and to watch at the Beecher Falls and Canaan bridges lest jams occur. There was another reason for precaution against jams in this stretch: Canaan is on the border and was handy to two saloons known as "line houses." Delay of the drive here could present melancholy possibilities.

Above Canaan-Stewartstown one of the most dangerous spots had been passed. This was Perry Falls in Pittsburg, where the river ran like the milltail of hell; there for many years you could read, cut in the bark of trees, the names of Charles Seymour and Dan Sullivan and Jake Regan, three lads who had tried to ride out this white water and found it too fast. Yet there were dangers still ahead too, and over the years the river took a fearful toll. So here, where the drive began to enter the Upper Coos meadows, the company thoughtfully put a few sets of grappling irons into each of the wangan wagons.

The wangan train was an impressive caravan of great long wagons hauled by four or six horses each and loaded with tents, food, stoves, baking sheets, cant dogs, pike poles, chains, and almost everything else that could be needed to put the logs into the ultimate booms, including a monstrous supply of B & L plug chewing and smoking tobacco. The wagons had long blue bodies, CVL painted on their sides. The harness were trimmed with bright brass and bedecked with tassels as gaudy as the Frenchmen's red shirts. The whole shebang was called the "Mary Anne." I do not recall any circus parade that impressed me more than the caravan of the drive.

On occasion, and for reasons I never knew, the Mary Anne came down as a cookhouse tent on a raft; and one year she rammed head on against Colebrook bridge, sweeping everybody and everything on deck into the water. I heard that this floating Mary Anne was the idea of Tom Van Dyke. In any case, it did not become a usual thing.

The boss of the drive was always an important fellow. He had to be a man who knew some 150 miles of river like the palm of his hand. The Smarts, Bill and Frank, and Win Schoppe were among the best. On them depended the delivery of from 45,000,000 to 55,000,000 feet of logs, short or long; and it had to be done when the water was right. A drive left high and dry stayed high and dry for a year. Two "high-and-dries" were likely to make a common mortal man out of an imperious boss of the drive.

As the main drive proceeded south from Canaan-Stewartstown, it was either joined or followed by others. The winter cuts might come in from Willard Stream, the Mohawk, Simms Stream, even from Blodget Brook, and half a dozen more; and at North Stratford–Bloomfield, the Nulhegan and Paul Stream drives added notably to the mass of restless wood being herded toward the saws and the grinders. John O'Donnel of Bloomfield, who drove the 'Hegan eight seasons, started work there as a flagboy. Stationed on a high point above the stream, he had the job of watching the logs and running a flag up a pole to signal to the drivers below. "We had a sort of code system—to open or to close the gates, or maybe a wing was building up somewhere. All sorts of things," O'Donnel remembered, adding that the 'Hegan Telegraph could meet almost any emergency.

Perhaps the most dreaded water of the entire Conecticut was the Fifteen-Mile Falls, now deep dead water behind a dam. Though Logan's Rips at Fitzdale could be dangerous, the falls a few miles below were notoriously bad; and in the fifteen-mile stretch there were two spots responsible, legend had it, for a total of twenty deaths. One of these was Mulligan's Lower Pitch, the other the Seven Islands on the gravel beds at the lower end of the falls. Perley Hurd rated Mulligan's the worst spot on the Connecticut, but he said that nothing at all on the big stream could equal the speed and power of many places on the White River in Vermont, which brought the Champlain Realty's drive into the Connecticut farther south at White River Junction.

For many years the Champlain's cut on Phillips Brook arrived in the Connecticut by way of the Ammonoosuc, which also brought that company's cut on the Wild Ammonoosuc; the two streams, one running south, the other northwest, merged near Woodsville in the town of Haverhill.

It was the custom for many years to boom the river at Woodville–Wells River and hold the main drive briefly, then release it gradually. This tended to prevent jams in the Ox Bow, the snaky stretch over the Haverhill meadows, and it also made less work for the floating rear, which came along behind the main crew to clear stray sticks from the banks and sand bars. This operation was known as "sacking the rear."

Among rivermen Woodsville won the reputation as the liveliest town between North Stratford and North Walpole. This was partly because it boasted a well-defined red-light district, plus an adequate number of saloons, but also because it and adjoining Wells River village comprised one of the busiest railroad centers in northern New England. It was in Woodsville, too, that one Ed Smith, an obscure woodman, leaped from the sidewalk to crash through a plate-glass show window of Sargent's store and embrace a pretty wax dummy dressed in silk hose and corsets. The rain of jagged glass left Ed unscratched. It was the height of his career, for the next spring he was caught by a log at Perry Falls.

After the logs had passed the Ox Bow meadows, it was a short run to Wilder, Vermont, where a part of the drive had reached its goal and was held for International Paper's Wilder mill. A dam now makes a ten-mile-long lake of the Connecticut above Wilder. Just below the town a Champlain Realty drive arrived from the White River, heading for the paper plant at Bellows Falls with logs from the Green Mountains in the Granville region. Eight head dams kept them moving until they entered the Connecticut. Bill Smart was often boss of this drive.

At the Bellows Falls plant of International Paper was a dam across the Connecticut through which logs were sluiced. One spring Bert Ingersoll, a noted woods and river character from First Lake, was swept over the dam, but he managed to catch hold of an iron peg set into the cement. With what must have been herculean effort, he pulled himself back up to the boom and there he stood, so it is recalled, a good five minutes, looking down at the watery hole below. One of the drivers shouted at him:

"Bert, do you figure going back down there?"

"No, by God," shouted Ingersoll, "I'm just looking at my fingerprints on that iron."

Probably because the drivers usually remained several days at Bellows Falls, the nearby village of North Walpole developed a tradition for hospitality. One verteran says there were eighteen saloons open there on occasion and never less than a dozen. It was also the place where Old Colorado, politely known as a camp follower, set up shop in a tent. It was her custom, for more years than men can remember, to trail the main drive from First Lake to Bellows Falls. When the logs were all in, she returned home again.

Below Bellows the remaining drive soon passed into Massachusetts and on to the end of the line, the sawmills and paper plants near Holyoke. This final goal, however, was commonly referred to as Mount Tom, because of the modest geographic feature on the west side of the river.

Cleve Dore at Pittsburg recalls that he scaled logs in the old CVL sawmill at Mount Tom back in 1911. Two drives reached Mount Tom almost simultaneously that year as the 1910 drive got hung up. The mill sawed almost 80,000,000 feet in that one year. The sulphite mill at Mount Tom was probably the first mill in North America, and perhaps in the world, designed to run on sawmill leavings. Slabs and edgings from the sawmill used to be loaded into a cart holding about a cord and then pulled by a horse on a narrow-gauge track over to the pulpmill. This early Yankee venture in thrift is today an important conservation measure throughout the industry.

More than forty years after the last log was in, memories of the Long Drive on the Connecticut crowded one upon the other when I talked with some of the veterans. One of Frank B. Willson's first jobs was as scaler at Wildwood, and as clerk he came down with the Champlain drive on the Wild Ammonoosuc. Later, when he became a division manager, he engaged Nate Nutter, of Woodsville, who knew as much or more than Black Bill Fuller about horses, to go west to buy a hundred animals. Ed Hutchins, now of Rochester, Vermont, came to Champlain to work first at Wildwood, then moved to the White River, where he drove for many seasons. Herbert Watts recalls eight seasons on the Long Drive for the CVL and remembers Philo Van Dyke, a company official who made it a practice, when paying off a crew, to infuriate men until they struck him; whereupon he deducted ten dollars "for assault and battery." Watts thinks the best river boss he ever had was Win Schoppe, who drove rivers for both the CVL and Champlain.

Lewis Marshall, postmaster at North Stratford, once worked under Jigger Johnson and Jack Bruce at Dennis Pond, Vermont. He later worked under John Hinman at Phillips Brook and still later in International Paper's New York City and Albany offices. Hugh Grogan, who went far in Canadian International Paper before he retired recently, was reared in North Stratford and worked in the 'Hegan woods for CVL when Charlie Hadley was running things in the local office. Hugh went down on the Long Drive one year when Bill Smart was boss. Of all the river towns, he recalls North Stratford as the liveliest. "If the camps shut down in the winter," he remembers, "or if the logs jammed on the drive, our little village suddenly became a loud and busy metropolis, and often a violent one. I know. For two years I worked in the Grand Trunk depot, the right place to see the boys when they came to town."

Of Perley Hurd, former Champlain camp and drive boss, all who saw him in action are likely to say he was the cattiest-footed man that ever rode a log. There can be few who drove longer or on more streams. At fifteen he drove the Dead Diamond for Berlin Mills, now the Brown Company. At seventeen he got a job from Bill Smart and went down with the Long Drive. From then until the time when *all* drives had gone down, he was on one or another of them. For several seasons he took charge of sluicing the Nulhegan logs into the Connecticut; then he ranged—east to drive the Swift Diamond into the Magalloway, then into the Androscoggin and through the Thirteen-Mile Woods to Berlin; and west to the White River to take the logs to the Connecticut.

Because of his great energy and habit of quick decisions, Perley Hurd was much sought after to take charge of drives on the brooks and streams, where emergencies were the rule. The drive on a small stream was done quickly or never. In time Perley came to know them all. Besides those already mentioned, he took charge of driving the East, Black, and Yellow branches of the Nulhegan; Willard Stream, Clear Stream, the Mohawk River; both the Reed and the Montague branches of Blodgett Brook; Smith Brook; Cedar, Nash, and Paul streams; and he "boomed across Second Lake." How many seasons he went down on the Long Drive he could not remember. He said that Dan Bossie, whom he met on the Magalloway and elsewhere, was the "best man on a log" he ever saw. Many, however, have rated Perley Hurd himself by that title. One old-timer once saw him "leap right up straight and out of a bateau to land on a center jam in swift water."

During a week in summer of 1958 I ranged the Connecticut from below Bellows Falls to its headwaters at Third Lake. There was little or no evidence that thousands of men once filled this river with uncounted millions of logs and rode them sharpshod to the mills. It is now a quiet stream. No longer do its banks echo to the shouts of men in red shirts and bright-yellow greasers. Quiet is the right word.

The quiet takes me back fifty years to muse on the effect of the coming and the passing of the drive, which used to arrive bringing all the excitement of a circus. Our streets came suddenly to life. So did the river. Even a small jam was an event. Then, just as suddenly, the men, the horses, the bateaux, and the logs disappeared, leaving a void from which it took weeks to recover. Over on the wangan lot there were no cheery fires, no white tents. The river was empty, save for a few stray logs floating idly. The stream muttered and grumbled no longer. The village lights seemed to have gone out. Over all was an infinite hush one associates with funerals. The drive had gone down.

The Last Drive

ROBERT E. PIKE

THE CONNECTICUT RIVER DRIVE ended in a burst of glory. In the winter of 1914–1915 the C.V.L. had more than two thousand men in the woods, and the word went out that the long-log drive the next spring would be the last. It was the most exciting news that had hit the North Country since the Indian Stream War in 1835. Men talked about it in saloons and on street corners; they argued about it and fought about it; they said that it just couldn't be true. Many of them swore that logs would be driven down the Connecticut until the end of time. But before the ice went out, the rumor received official confirmation. The C.V.L. said that there would never be another saw-log rolled into the upper Connecticut.

Then everybody wanted to get onto the drive. It was the last chance for the young men to carve their names on the North Country totem pole of glory, so to speak, while the old-timers wanted to give it one more whirl. There were men in the border towns then who had gone down with every drive since 1868.

The C.V.L. did it up in style—more than five hundred men on drive, the greatest crew of rivermen who ever went down the Connecticut. Dan Bosse abandoned the Brown Company that spring, attracted by the lure of the last drive and the princely wage of four dollars a day. Bangor Tigers came all the way from Old Town, and some of the old ones among them had been with John Ross in 1876.

One night in April, 1915, the ice went out, and the next day the drive was under way. Forty million feet of logs massed at Second Connecticut Lake shot down the roaring river and in no time were spreading themselves quietly in the booms set to catch them on the choppy waters of First Connecticut Lake. There, fifteen million more came out of South Bay, and all of them were towed across the lake at night, when the wind was quiet, and sluiced through the dam into the channel below. Three million more came out of Perry Stream, and six from Deadwater Brook. And so, like a snowball, the drive grew and grew until, when it hit North Stratford, there were sixty-five million feet of logs in the river.

Two men were killed at Perry Falls that spring. "I saw one of them die," 'Phonse Roby told me. "There was a wing jam on both sides, and he was walking across the stream on a log wedged about a foot under water. He held his peavey dangling from his hand, on the up-stream side, and the current hit it just enough to throw him off balance. He fell into the stream, where the water was fast as a mill-race. He could swim some, and a log came along and he grabbed it by the middle and tried to hoist himself on top.

"If he'd only used his head and taken the log at one end, he could have held himself up until we pulled him out; but I suppose he was too scared to think, and he kept trying to wrestle that log, and it kept rolling out of his hands.

"The jam struck out into the stream a few rods below, and the current set in against it. I ran to beat hell over those logs and got out on the point and was all ready to pull him in when the cold water and the shock were too much for him, and he let go the log and went under. One of his hands came up as if he was waving good-bye—and that was the last of him."

But after a couple of men were lost at Perry Falls, the drive went merry as a wedding bell until it reached North Stratford. There the river was blocked by an ice jam, and the logs jammed behind it, rearing in huge piles, twenty and thirty feet high; the worst log jam ever seen, said Rube Leonard, who could remember them all, even the first one. For there were thirty-five million feet of logs in one bunch, sticking straight up and sideways, and every other way, a diabolical and inextricable mass.

They kept piling up, and the water backed up and flooded houses and barns and tore up the Grand Trunk Railroad tracks, and the Grand Trunk started a lawsuit, and there was hell to pay.

'Phonse Roby had charge of the drive that year, and Win Schoppe, one of the great names in the North Country, bossed the rear. They got all the men down at the great jam, and they worked day and night. Finally, after many days, they had picked and dynamited the jam to pieces and set the logs floating off down the black, sullen river.

"I saw a funny thing while we were breaking that jam," John Locke, who was later general manager of the C.V.L., told me. "The dynamite had frozen, so they built a fire to thaw it out. They shoveled up a bank of earth all around the fire, a foot or two away, and stood the sticks of powder up against the inside of the bank. They left a young fellow in charge of it who didn't know much about the vagaries of dynamite. One of the sticks happened to slip and fall toward the fire, and he reached over to pull it out. Probably someone had told him that dynamite wouldn't explode unless it was jarred. At that precise moment old Win came striding up to see if the powder was ready, and just as the youngster reached over the embankment, Win reached one paw and wrapped it around his short ribs and flattened him on the ground like you would a doll.

"Boom! And that stick of dynamite exloded all over the adjacent territory. But nobody was hurt. Win got up and brushed himself and says to the lad, 'G'acious! G'acious, sonny, you must learn to be more careful.'

"Dan Bosse was doing the shooting. He was a good man with powder. I saw him put in one blast that didn't do any good. He'd tied two sticks of powder onto the end of a pole and swum out with a lighted fuse and stuck it into a hole of the jam. When it didn't go off correctly, he was a little bothered. He wrapped some more dynamite around the end of a pole about fifteen feet long and skipped out onto the jam and pushed it into a hole he'd selected, and stood there watching to see what would happen. It happened all right. The whole front of the jam came loose, and I'll swear it looked as if Dan went up in the air more than ten feet. But when he came down he was standing with both feet on a log and headed downstream."

The drive got down to Fitzdale (today they call it Gilman), and the owner of the mill and the dam there wouldn't let them sluice through the dam. The Stone and Webster people were first-rate engineers but didn't know much about logging, so they had brought in a man from down country named D. J. MacDonald to be general manager. MacDonald, who accompanied the drive in a Buick touring car, advised waiting. Big 'Phonse, who had been brought up under Van Dyke, saw the water dropping ever day, scowled, and said nothing, but he took it upon himself to go and call on the millman.

The tall, slim walking-boss strode into the office, his spiked boots gouging little triangular holes in the polished hardwood floor.

"You open up those sluices," he said, "or God have mercy on you when I turn these rivermen loose. There'll be nothing left of you, your mill, or your dam."

He meant what he said, and the other man knew he meant it. The drive went through.

Just below Fitzdale began the "Horse-Race," a quarter of a mile of rock-toothed rapids that were the start of the Fifteen-Mile Falls. Sam Martin, one of the rivermen, had managed to get drunk, and now, full of bravado and Old Grand-Dad, he got into a bateau all alone and started down through the Horse-Race. A hundred yards down, the boat hit a rock and turned over, leaving Sam out in the middle of the rapids, clinging to a boulder and sober as a preacher.

No man had ever ridden a log through the Horse-Race, and eventually a bateau would have been procured to rescue Sam, but some playful riverman bet Bill Bacon ten dollars he couldn't ride a log down past Sam and pick him off that rock. Bill ran out over the surging logs, picked a big spruce, and stayed on it through the white water. As the log drove past the rock, barely missing it, he grabbed Sam by the collar, hauled him clear, and brought him safely through.

Down the drive went, down and down. The wangan transported in high-wheeled wagons drawn by eight horses each, kept up with it. It's quite a trick to drive eight horses. Next to rivermen, teamsters were the most highly paid men in the woods. In the early days, selecting a campsite was a rather hit-and miss affair, but as drives got better organized, the custom was for the cook to pitch his tent handy to the river and to the most rivermen. John Pattee, a North Stratford storekeeper, was charged by the company with sending a man on ahead to choose good sites and to buy milk, eggs, and other fresh food for the rivermen, and hay for the horses.

Wherever they camped, near the little country villages, all the kids would come down and help dig the beanhole, and then they'd stand around the cook tent and watch the cook mix his biscuits in a pan as big as a bushel basket, and he would give them immense great sugar cookies and gingersnaps to eat, and they would fairly worship him. They watched the rivermen tramp down the board sidewalks with their fine, free gait, gouging out splinters at every step, and while other kids might want to grow up and become locomotive engineers or join a circus, all those lads firmly determined to grow up and be rivermen some day.

I was a boy myself then, living with my uncle on the Fifteen-Mile Falls. He was a farmer, but in his younger days he had worked for the C.V.L. in the great north woods, and he too had "gone down the river." The river-drivers always put up their wangan on his meadow, beside the old toll-bridge, over which "only rivermen and dogs" went free, and if the water was low they would camp there for three weeks while they were picking the log jams off the rocks.

That spring the wangan did not come until some days after the logs had begun to run past beneath the bridge. A man who happened to drive by the schoolhouse at afternoon recess told us the drive was coming. The teacher knew that no more work would be done that day, so she dismissed the pupils, and we went racing down to the bridge. Sure enough, the logs were coming, not many yet, but steadily growing thicker and thicker, rubbing and nosing softly against each other as the swift current urged them on.

We stayed there until suppertime, fascinated by that vast, silent army of marching wood, and after supper we went back again, accompanied by our elders. The bridge was lined with people who had come to see.

Presently, as we stood there leaning on the plank railing, with the cool breeze rising from the river and the sun setting behind us, from upstream around a bend a solitary riverman came straight into the red beams of the dying sun. His peavey point was stuck into the big log on which he rode, and both his hands were clasped around the top of the heavy handle. Seemingly oblivious to the slippery, unstable quality of his steed, poised in a splendid attitude of indifference to the many admiring eyes he knew were fixed upon him, he came whirling down the river, the twenty-foot spruce surging and lunging through the white water. By a miracle of good luck the log avoided all the rocks and the upright riverman swept grandly beneath us, so that we got a good view of him.

His sweaty suspenders were crossed over a red woolen shirt; his heavy black trousers were stagged off about the tops of his spiked boots. A torn, gray felt hat, its tattered brim turned up in front, revealed his eyes, watchful as any cat's, and by the look in his eyes and by the little bend in his knees we knew that while he appeared so nonchalant as he leaned there upon his peavey-handle, he was tensely alert. We almost wished that his log would strike a rock, so we might see what he would do, but really we were glad that it did not. So he went on, the vanguard of the drive, and disappeared in the fading light.

After all the timber had surged past us and on down the river and the wangan had departed southward, the walking-boss, a tall, slim man with keen black eyes and a graceful way of carrying his body (half a dozen years later he gave me a job and I went to work for the company myself) came and paid my uncle for milk and hay the rivermen had bought. They talked a little of the old days in the woods and on the river, and of how this was the last drive. After the boss had gone away, my uncle took a spotted red handkerchief from his hip pocket and blew his nose very loudly. Then he looked at me. His eyes were very bright and I remember I asked him why he was crying, and he said:

"I guess the wind makes my old eyes water, Bobbie."

The drive went down, over Mulliken's Pitch and past the Twenty-Six Islands, and came at last to the Narrows at Woodsville, opposite the Vermont town of Wells River. There was always much rivalry between the two communities. A Woodsville bard once composed a poem of which the refrain goes:

Oh Woodsville is the doughnut,
Wells River is the hole . . .

which did not help promote friendship.

It was the last time they ever put the old *Mary Ann,* the raft or scow that carried the cook's equipment from Woodsville down, into the water. There used to be a "little" *Mary Ann* that they launched below the rips at West Stewartstown and ran over the Guildhall dam and broke up at

Fitzdale, since it could not survive the Falls. It was also the last time they built the horse rafts. There were several of these great affairs which, after 1900, were built on a scow, like the *Mary Ann,* with a hitching rack along one side and a railing at each end. Before 1900 they carried eight horses each, tied head to head. They were used to haul stranded logs into the water. The work was dreadfully hard on the animals, who often had to swim for their lives. Fresh replacements were constantly being walked down from West Stewartstown, while the worn-out nags were taken back up north and turned out to pasture.

Before 1900 the rafts were simply logs fastened together. . . .

Win Schoppe was well over sixty years old that spring. For many years he had been a woods boss and a dam-builder for the C.V.L. He was an immensely powerful man, but he had never had a fight in his life. Indeed it was because he was always good-natured that his nickname was Grinner. His strongest oath was "G'acious!"

Vern Davison, who worked on the drive, told me that there was one man, a mean-tempered, red-headed bruiser working on the rear, who for some reason had it in for the old man. He used to talk loudly to the others about what he would do to Schoppe if the latter ever tried to ride him.

"This fellow came into the tent one night at Brattleboro, noisy and drunk," Vern told me, "and Win told him to shut up, the men needed their sleep. He called Win a son of a bitch, and proposed to give him a licking. He made a pass at him, but Win reached out one hand and took him by the throat and laid him on the ground and bore down. When the fellow came to, Win said, 'G'acious, I hope I haven't hurt you. But really, you shouldn't go around calling people sons of bitches.' The fellow took his turkey and got out of there as fast as he could caper."

And so the drive went down and down. The old men showed the younger ones where the great jams of former years had piled up, where men had been killed, and where some especially pleasant fight had taken place. Finally they came to Mt. Tom, and the last long-log drive on the Connecticut River, the longest drive in the whole United States, was over.

When the Drive Comes Down

ANONYMOUS

Come all ye gallant shanty boys and listen while I sing,
We've worked six months in cruel frosts but soon we'll take our fling.
The ice is black and rotten and the rollways are piled high;
So boost upon your peavey sticks while I do tell you why:

For it's break the rollways out, my boys, and let the big sticks slide!
And file you calks and grease your boots and start upon the drive.
A hundred miles of water is the nearest way to town;
So tie into the tail of her and keep her hustling down!

When the drive starts down, when the drive starts down,
Oh, it's every lad in heaven he would swap his golden crown
For a peavey stick again and a soaking April rain,
And to birl a log beneath him as he drives the river down!

When the drive comes down, when the drive comes down,
Oh, it's then we paid our money and it's then we own the town!
All the gutters run with whiskey when the shanty boys so frisky
Set their boot calks in the sidewalks when the drive is down!

There's some poor lads will never lift a peavey hook again,
Nor hear the trees crack with the frost, nor feel a warm spring rain.
'Twas falling timber, rolling logs, that handed them their time;
It was their luck to get it so—it may be yours or mine.

But break the rollways out, my lads, and let the big sticks slide,
For one man killed within the woods, ten's drownded on the drive.

So make your peace before you take the nearest way to town,
While the lads that are in heaven watch the drive go down!

What makes you lads so wistful-eyed as we draw near to town?
Other eyes is soft and bright, like the stars of a June night—
Wives and sweethearts, praying, waiting, as we drive the river down.
God bless the eyes that shine for us when we boil into town.

Pulp at Lyman Falls

FRED COWAN

IT BEING A COOL day and with the high price of fuel oil it seemed to be a good time to warm up the old wood stove in the den. As I was separating and wrinkling up a few pages from a recent copy of the St. Johnsbury paper to put under the kindling, a previously unnoticed item caught my eye.

The story, on page A3, informed us that, along with other things, an agency of the State of Vermont has made a grant of $93,500 to be used to purchase land on the Bloomfield side of the Connecticut River adjacent to Lyman Falls. With an additional sum of $23,100, apparently to be raised from private sources, 41 acres of land will be acquired and administered by the Vermont Department of Forests, Parks, and Recreation jointly with something called the Vermont River Conservancy.

This purchase will ensure that the public will have access to 3,200 feet of river frontage which is, to quote from the item, "recognized by the Connecticut River Joint Commission Headwaters Subcommittee as one of the best cold water fishing areas in the eastern United States."

Now, I am not an expert on the subject of cold water fishing such as the Commission claims to be, but I am at least fairly well acquainted with the

From Fred Cowan, "Stump to Mill," *Colebrook (N.H.) News and Sentinel,* 7 March 2001.

subject of cold water. Specifically, during the late 1940s, I was acquainted with cold water at Lyman Falls. The Lyman Falls Dam, which used to be situated at this location, was one of the obstacles that made driving pulpwood down the Connecticut interesting. Furthermore, the shallow water and rapids just below the dam always seemed to trap large parts of the wood, which we managed to steer into and through the narrow sluice located on the top of the dam.

Lyman Falls was not a serious obstacle back in the days of most of the long log drives. It originally consisted of a small falls followed by a longish stretch of boulder-strewn rapids. The river dropped a total of a little more than 20 feet in about a half mile. On the easterly side and above the falls, the original river bank was low and quite flat but bordered by a steep high bank, partly a glacial deposit of gravel. The westerly bank was a little higher, but with gently sloping land extending for quite a distance downstream. The Upper Coö's Railroad, later a branch of the Maine Central Railway, was quite close to the river on the New Hampshire side just below the falls, but on a small terrace well above the water.

I never investigated enough to determine just who had the idea that this could be a suitable place to develop hydro-electric power. It may have been a man by the name of F. M. McDonald. Anyway, in October of 1903 an organization called Lyman Falls Power Company purchased some lands on both sides of the river from McDonald. The land on the New Hampshire side had formerly been owned by the Lyman family, which gave that name to the falls, a brook that enters the Connecticut a short distance above the falls, and a cemetery. In my days, the dam and power plant belonged to the Public Service Company of New Hampsire, which had purchased it in 1935.

I suspect that the dam, which was largely of rock-filled wooden construction, was built soon after 1903, although the following years saw additional land and flowage purchases both above and below the dam. The dam was 18 feet high from sill to spillway and about 400 feet long. An additional 300-foot length of dike or bulkhead was built at some time at the eastern end, extending almost to the railroad. This was concrete in my days, but was perhaps originally built of wood.

The penstock, which carried the water to the turbine at the generating plant, began at the Vermont end of the dam and was about 1800 feet long. Beyond the powerhouse, a tail-race canal continued on down more or less parallel with the river for another 1,200 feet or so. In doing so, it necessitated the rerouting farther downstream of the lower end of Mill Brook, which otherwise would have interfered with the flow of water from the turbine.

The location of the entrance to the penstock and the combined length of penstock and tail-race caused a lot of grief for those trying to float wood down the river. The sluice in the top of the dam was placed about at midpoint and could be opened just enough to permit passage of a few sticks of wood at a time. The main current, during periods of average water level, flowed toward the penstock, the mouth of which was protected by a grate.

The two rows of piers and booms, making a path and presumably guiding wood toward the sluice, were out in mid-river, but not in the path of the strong current flowing to the penstock. To this, add the wind that always seemed to blow upstream. When wood was being passed over Lyman Falls Dam, two or three men with pike-poles, running around on the booms, pushing and pulling the wood, were necessary to keep things moving.

Once the wood was through the sluice, more trouble was at hand. Unless there was more water coming down the river than the penstock could handle, the only water below the dam was that small flow that carried the wood through the sluice, or that leaked around flashboards, if any were in place on top of the spillway. This meant that the next 3,500 feet or so of river channel often appeared to be covered by boulders and smaller rocks rather than water.

The rest of the water, of course, came back to the river eventually from the tail-race. The pulpwood was left in the booms above Lyman Falls Dam, whenever possible, until there was sufficient water to float most of it past this section. At the season's end, the shallow rapids below the dam had to be swept clean of wood. If we had not sampled the cold waters of Lyman Falls a few times earlier in the year, we were certain to do so each fall.

Most of the dam was removed a few years ago, leaving a lively run for canoes down over the little falls and the rapids below. I have not made the trip through there recently, but I suppose the water is still cool. I do wonder just who will have the right-of-way, now that these waters and shores are under government control. The fisherman, casting his fly to the fish, or the canoeist, trying to keep from running into those rocks on which logs and pulpwood once lodged?

It is interesting to note that the lowest temperature officially recorded in all of New England, fifty degrees below zero, was registered on the thermometer at the weather station next to the Lyman Falls Dam tender's house in Bloomfield on the morning of December 30, 1933.

Chapter 6

RAMPAGE

What man was doing to the environment through his abuse and neglect was in a way equaled by nature itself. There had been heavy floods in 1854, 1862, 1866, and 1913, but during the second quarter of the century, a series of floods and hurricanes brought to the area disasters unparalleled in modern times.
—*The Connecticut River* by Edmund Delaney

If log driving was drama imposed on the river by man, then floods have always been drama the river has provided on its own. There have been many punishing floods over the years, from the first recorded hurricane in 1635, to Hurricane Carol in 1954. And not just hurricanes bring floods; record rainfall, often combined with melting ice upstream, is the other main culprit.

Flooding has resulted in many deaths, though over the years the main victims seem to have been bridges. Scan the archives, and you realize the fate of Connecticut River bridges was, quite simply, to collapse or to burn; included in this chapter are the stories of several of these. Bridges, of course, take on paramount importance on a river the size of the Connecticut; they become not only the focus of transportation, but also symbols of linkage and connection, so the death of a bridge has always been more than the death of wood and steel. A surprisingly large body of the river's literature deals with just such catastrophes.

The 1927 flood was one of three that came within eleven years of each other. This account is taken from a book put out immediately after that flood, and shows how the waters, starting high up in the tributaries, swept down the valley causing havoc as they roared. In 1938, the famous New England hurricane (this was before hurricanes were named) raced directly up the river and singled Hartford out for special attention.

Everett S. Allen's account, from his excellent A Wind to Shake the World, *is a classic of storm reportage.*

Katharine Blaisdell lives in the Upper Valley and has spent many years compiling local history; she epitomizes the committed local historian who can be found in almost every river town to this day.

And, speaking of rough weather, included here is Mark Twain's famous diatribe on New England weather, often quoted, but rarely printed in full. It was a speech delivered to a gathering of Hartford businessmen and civic leaders, and helps explain his legendary reputation as America's favorite raconteur.

When it comes to the Connecticut, Twain is somewhat disappointing. He mentions it in A Connecticut Yankee in King Arthur's Court, *but other than that, seems never to have written about it at all, despite living by its banks in Hartford, in his famous Victorian Gothic house, between the years 1871 and 1896.*

A little rivulet used to run past the Twain house on its way to the Connecticut. The Clemens (Twain) family enjoyed skating on it, as mentioned in the author's entirely characteristic letter to W. D. Howells in 1874:

> *I've been skating around the place all day with some girls, with Mrs. Clemens in the window to do the applause. There would be a power of fun in skating if you could do it with somebody else's muscles. There are about twenty boys booming by the house now, and it is mighty good to look at.*

The First Hurricane

NATHANIEL MORTON

"THIS YEAR, ON SATURDAY, the fifteenth day of August, was such a mighty storm of Wind and Rain, as none now living in these parts, either English or Indian, have seen the like, being like unto those Hirricanes or Tussins that writers mention sometimes in the Indies. It began in the morning a little before day, and grew not by degrees, but came with great violence in the beginning, to the great amazement of

From Nathaniel Morton, *New England Memorial* (n.p., 1635).

many; It blew down sundry houses, and many more in extream danger. It caused the Sea to swell in some places . . . twenty foot right up and down, and made many of the Indians to climb into Trees for their safety: It blew down all the Corn to the ground and never rose more . . . and had the wind continued without shifting, in likelihood it would have drowned some part of the Country. It blew down many hundred thousands of trees, turning up the stronger by the roots, and breaking the high Pine Trees and such like in the midst, and the tall young Oaks, and Walnut Trees of good bigness were wound as a Wyth by it; very strange and fearful to behold: It began in the Southeast, and veered sundry ways. . . . It continued not in extremity above five or six hours, ere the violence of it began to abate; the marks of it will remain . . . many years in those parts where it was forest. . . ."

The '27 Flood

LUTHER B. JOHNSON

THE GREAT VERMONT FLOOD of November 3d and 4th, 1927, came unheralded. There was no prediction of the unprecedented downpour which caused the catastrophe. Indeed, all the signs favored by weather experts presaged a dry late fall and early winter. Under the theory of averages it should have been so. There had been more than the usual amount of precipitation during the summer and autumn of 1927 in Vermont. In October particularly the rainfall had been excessive. The official record for the month at the Northfield Weather Bureau station showed 5.64 inches, the normal for October being 2.48 inches. Naturally, then, an early cessation of wet weather was anticipated.

Due to the plentiful rainfall, the soil was thoroughly saturated and the streams were running quite full when November arrived. There had been overflows and high water at two periods during the preceding month, which caused damage in some localities. While the great rainstorm that ushered in the flood was quite out of the natural order, conditions already

From Luther B. Johnson, *Vermont in Floodtime* (Randolph, Vt.: Roy L. Johnson Co., 1928).

existent paved the way for the calamity. The soil could not absorb the heavy precipitation to any considerable extent, nor could the water courses, already filled, carry the tremendous downpour away without rising to high levels and sweeping beyond their banks.

Although regarded as relatively free from flood visitations, the steep and narrow valleys of central Vermont especially, through which descend the streams that drain the Green Mountain uplands, are open to danger of this kind whenever violent rainstorms break. The waters rush down swiftly from the high levels, and leap their shallow beds, overflowing onto nearby lands. Ordinarily this is all, but under conditions prevailing at the time of the great flood the sudden unleashing of vaporized moisture, which amounted to eight or nine measured inches within a little more than 24 hours, proved altogether too much for the usual watercourses. Brooks became torrents and rivers roared along in height and volume appalling. . . .

Some day some skilled painter will depict in historical pageant form the Great Vermont Flood of 1927. It will begin with a scene of marvelous enchantment—a beautiful valley basking in sunlight; a background of wooded hillsides resplendent in autumn foliage; here and there in the foreground a well-kept farm with sleek cattle in fall feed and barns filled to overflowing from an abundant and well-matured harvest; splendid roads over which are motoring delighted tourists from distant states; a placid stream meandering through and in the near distance hurrying to turn the wheels of industry for a flourishing town built on its banks.

Next will follow a scene blurred by a deluge of rainfall, merging into one showing the earlier landscape in process of dissolution—torrents leaping from every declivity of the hillside; the placid stream in the foreground changed to a thing of might and dread, grown into a dark, turbid, angry monster, tearing through the meadows, snatching up the cattle, bearing away the homes and barns, disrupting the factories, submerging the town. Heroic rescues of those imperilled will be seen, with now and then a corpse borne away. Darkness, murky daylight, again darkness and again daylight will indicate three days covering this violent period.

Then will come a sad scene of silent disaster and destruction—the river retired ashamedly to a course quite changed in many places; new channels dug here and there through fertile lands; former ones choked with gravel and wreckage; barren silt hiding the meadows; cellar holes marking the place of farm dwellings; lines of debris far back from the watercourse; in the distance the town disorganized; huge rents in the streets, buildings partly gone, partly standing in tipsy fashion, slime everywhere.

And finally the painter will add a scene showing over the lapse of years a gradual transformation, beginning with the first work of relief extended in abundance from outside; the American Red Cross Mother, early and active in aid; and then the stricken Vermonter, rising slowly to his knees, to his feet, dazed at first but soon with senses cleared, a look of determination on his face, seizing axe and saw, shovel and hoe, and going to work to redeem his beloved state, while the world looks on in wonder and admiration. This allegory will end with Vermont restored materially and her men and women shown to be more vigorous, more self-reliant, more self-respecting than ever—tried as by flood.

Upper White River Valley

Following the course of the flood down the main White River, it is noted that destruction began almost at its source. The lovely Gulf road between Warren and Granville, with the dashing stream alongside, is there no longer. Over much of its distance the roadway became the bed of the torrent, necessitating its abandonment for travel until restored. The iron bridge at the Warren Ford place went downstream, as did the old Company dam. Residents of Granville Corner left their homes, expecting everything to be washed out.

Hancock lost heavily in bridges and highways washed away, from farm lands devastated and from landslides. The cement dam at Camp Killooleet gave way and the waters of the pond rushed through the village, carrying off the iron bridge and damaging the abutments of a new cement bridge. Homes were invaded and people fled to safety. The mountain road to Middlebury was blocked by landslides. P. H. Eaton lost 45 sheep by drowning.

As the flood rolled on through Rochester, its toll increased. The meadows suffered severely. In the village, the yards of the hotel, John Foley and Arthur Jones were covered nearly five feet deep with stones, large and small. Cellars were filled and barns wrecked. The creamery ice house and the iron bridge nearby went out. The White River Railroad freight house and passenger station and tracks nearby were undermined. The river cut a new channel through the farms of C. E. Martin, Carroll Alexander and George Bailey.

Below Rochester village all bridges over the White River went out except the Severy bridge, which was weakened, but immediately repaired. With temporary bridges put in toward West Rochester, this enabled communication to be established over the mountain to Brandon, while the town was entirely cut off from the valley below. At the site of the Liberty

Hill bridge a most unique passenger service was rigged up—a sap pan suspended from a cable, the passenger himself furnishing the motive power.

The lowlands between Rochester village and Stockbridge Common bore striking evidence of flood damage in washed and silt-covered meadows, railway embankments destroyed and buildings submerged. The pretty White River Valley Inn, with its riverside golf course, presented a sorry sight.

Pittsfield, located on Tweed River, five miles above its junction with the White at Stockbridge, furnished one of the fatalities of the flood. About 4 p.m. Thursday the Charles French farm, just above Pittsfield village, became surrounded by water and help was sent for. A truck backed up as near the dwelling as possible and a line was thrown to Mr. French. He tied this about himself, took his wife in his arms and signalled to pull. In the rush of the current Mr. French lost hold of his wife and she was swept away. Her body was found in the bushes the next day.

In the lower part of the village people were driven from their homes and much damage resulted. The stream from "Michigan" washed out part of the Barrows dam and filled the street with debris.

The fine clapboard and turned stock mill of W. K. Barrows, located over the Stockbridge line, suffered severely. The Tweed washed around the end of the dam, partially undermined the mill, turned around a 170-foot dryhouse and tore away a 70-foot storehouse. Much finished stock was lost at this mill, the largest manufacturing plant in the town.

At the home of John Durkee, the oldest resident of Stockbridge, seven persons were marooned all night with the water up to the kitchen floor and the current so swift that they could not be reached for rescue.

Cobb bridge, between Stockbridge and Gaysville, went out and this break, together with a huge washout on Whitcomb hill nearby, severed the main route up the valley, pending extensive reconstruction work.

Gaysville Almost Obliterated

One scene is that of a quiet little Vermont village, mostly occupying a small plain reaching across the bottom of a narrow valley. A street with stately old homes, pretty lawns and gardens and an abundance of shade trees extends from one main highway to the other approaching the village. Along this street besides the homes are one of the churches of the village, a store building, postoffice and railway station. Turning onto it off the state road one crosses an iron bridge beneath which bubbles and ripples the clear White River. Nearby and a little above on this side is the power station and above that rises the high dam utilizing a waterfall that had been employed in various ways for a hundred years. Above and beyond the village the state road ascends sharply and from the top as it curves around to descend on the other side the traveller often turns to look back at a scene of surpassing beauty almost directly beneath. This is what was.

Another scene is that of the same plain—we must believe it such, despite our eyes, because of its setting—revealed as a mass of bare, gnarled, pronged bedrock, swept clean of every vestige of human habitation, every home, every building, every bit of green or even soil, every tree—desolation. Off across the broad reach of rocky fangs one sees a few buildings perched on the brink of a sandy precipice. On the other side, along the main street, some of the homes and buildings are gone. The river no longer purls its way nearby but has swung quite to the other side of the valley in places. The dam and the power station stand, only to be mocked by the stream that no longer approaches them.

And between these two scenes so vivid by contrast—the flood. Nobody dreamed that a downpour of rain, however heavy or prolonged, could bring such ruin to this little village. When late Thursday afternoon the tiny brook which flowed under the end of Leon Perkins' woodshed suddenly became a torrent, poured through the house and proceeded to dig a huge chasm across the street men gathered and turned the course of the stream, saving the house, but the street was gone nearby.

At dusk the water flowed over the top of the big ledges at the head of the island as it never had done before and the river roared appallingly. Soon afterward, in the inky darkness, the dreadful work of obliteration began. The bridge went, the station was flooded, the barns at the Dana place and at Alfredine Hassam's went and Leon Perkins' storehouse also.

The river flowed in a torrent over the roof of the power house. It washed the foundations of the town clerk's building. All night long the roar continued, punctuated by an occasional crash, the meaning of which the fear-stricken people forced from their homes sensed only too well. Lights flashed here and there, but only imagination could attempt to picture what was taking place out there in the turmoil of waters.

How inadequate this was the grey light of early dawn revealed. From hill to hill the valley was filled with a raging torrent. Gone were the railroad station, the old boarding house, the Blair home, the fine residence of Dr. F. C. Fletcher with barn and garage, Will Flint's house and barn, Harry Allen's house and barn, the house and barn of Mrs. George Mills, the store of Guy Hodgkins, all gone.

The people first driven from their homes moved their goods into the Methodist church but at daylight the church fell and the things once saved went with it. Followed in steady succession before the hungry torrent the

Safford mill, piece by piece, then Mrs. George Martin's house and barn, then the Safford barn, the long henhouse and the house itself. Next the Nelson Gay house, occupied by Mrs. Waldo Perkins, disappeared. Then Emma Nye's house and barn and a small house halfway up Leonard hill, all slipped into the river's maw. The Vail house slid down the bank till its corner touched the water but the last onrush of the receding river just failed to carry it away.

On the Main street side of the river Alfredine Hassam's house fell at noon. In all, 30 buildings were destroyed and 28 persons rendered homeless in this tiny village, besides the loss of the iron bridge and the destruction of the railroad line.

"Bit by bit the river ate its way across the valley," writes Mrs. Flora W. Chase, "not flooding it so much as undermining it. A lawn looking fresh and green, with its house standing serenely, safely, far above the swirling flood. That is what we saw. Suddenly a few feet from the edge a crack would show, pause a moment, then a clean cut to the water and that land was gone; another followed and another, the house undermined a little, in a minute more no house, no rubbish even, no land. When the houses touched the water it was as if they had dissolved; they were engulfed and nothing more was seen of them.

"As the water receded a strange and desolate scene was presented. The place where the village stood is an incredible mass of rocks and gravel. The rock formation reminds one of the Giant Causeway. There is absolutely not one foot of anything left resembling soil, not a sign that any building ever stood there, not a stone that looks like a foundation wall.

"There are absolutely no words with which to paint the picture. We who knew it so well and loved it can hardly convince ourselves that on that wild waste once stood houses, shade trees, green lawns, fertile gardens. Where the lovely green island stretched its fifteen fertile acres, fringed with trees and bushes, there is nothing now but sand, gravel and stones. Only three trees are left standing, elms with their long roots, and these stand forlornly, their trunks battered and scarred, branches broken. All that saved the buildings on this side is an underlying ledge which proved a harder bit for the river to bite than the sand and gravel on the other side of the valley."

Not only was Gaysville decimated but practically cut off from all communication outside for some time, the highways and railroad being severed above and below in many places through the valley. Shelter and aid had to be extended to the homeless. The Red Cross and other agencies acted as speedily as possible to relieve the distress occasioned by the worst calamity of the flood in White River valley. . . .

Hartford and White River Junction

Nearing its junction with the Connecticut, the White River, in dimensions never before seen, swept out early Friday morning the bridge at Hartford village, said to have been the longest bridge wholly within the state of Vermont. The piers remained. The mill of the Hartford Woolen Company and a number of dwellings at low level were flooded, some being undermined.

White River Junction sat in a sea of turbid water. Hardly had the fire apparatus been removed from the station when the latter fell into the undermining river. Basements on Maple and Hazen streets were filled with water, mud and debris to the first floors. The White River, rising more than two feet an hour Thursday night, finally submerged in its swift current the deck of the highway bridge leading to the business section of the village. The water poured from both ends of the bridge and both banks into the streets, flooding a wide section. The bridge performed the seemingly impossible, withstood the enormous strain of the current and debris piled high against it and became the only remaining highway link over the White River for many miles.

Public edifices, stores, business places, residences on both sides of the White and along the bank of the Connecticut, probably two hundred buildings in all, were surrounded or invaded by water, with great damage resulting, principally from the heavy deposit of filth left behind. Some dwellings were undermined and several washed away. The Nutt meadow section saw several narrow escapes as people in marooned homes were taken out in boats. Few saved anything but what they wore, sometimes only their nightclothes. The powerful current of the Connecticut here necessitated the use of ropes to keep the boats from being carried away. Rescuers even swam to some of the beleaguered houses.

During the work of clearing the tons of wreckage from the railroad bridge over the Connecticut, two men, Edward McGee of West Lebanon and Lawrence Laroe of Enfield, slipped from the girders, fell into the whirling waters and were drowned. . . .

Bellows Falls and Vicinity

Much anxiety was felt throughout the state for Bellows Falls and its environs. Located where the Connecticut River—at flood level carrying an immense volume—passes through a narrow channel and over high rocky falls, with the village on its banks important as a manufacturing and railway center, this locality was known to be greatly exposed to the flood danger. While the worst fears were not realized, Bellows Falls and its suburbs, Walpole and North Walpole, on the New Hampshire side, suffered very heavy property losses. The water level rose above all previous marks, reaching a height of 25 feet and 8 inches above the level of the old dam. At this height all bridges were threatened and likewise the Boston & Maine railroad tunnel under the business section of Bellows Falls. At the entrance to the tunnel on the canal a sandbag blockade kept the waters from surging through, thereby saving the Adams grist mill and the International Paper Co.'s buildings below the hill.

With knowledge in advance of the heavy water flow coming from upstream, there was time in which to strengthen and prepare for it. This proved invaluable, as the event showed. The huge electric power development in progress above the falls engaged immediate attention. Efforts were made to strengthen the double coffer dam at the north end of the canal and at about 9 o'clock Thursday evening all tools and equipment were ordered out of the canal. This work had barely been completed at midnight and plans had been laid to relieve pressure on the coffer dam when a part of it gave way. Filled to overflowing, the stream divided as it struck the power house at the lower end of the canal, the major portion turning to the right and battering against the east wall of the Babbitt-Kelley paper mill at a lower level and to the right of the power house. The other part of the stream turned to the left, running along the tracks past the Moore & Thompson mill and again to the river over the old Rockingham paper mill site, flooding in its course the several floors of the Moore & Thompson mill.

At noon Friday Canal street was flooded four feet deep and about this height of water covered the bridge itself, against which debris of tremendous weight had gathered. At this hour the railroad bridge entering the tunnel was covered several feet deep and was weighted down by heavy coal cars to withstand the pressure. The equipment and personnel of the construction company engaged on the power project, supplemented by many volunteers, were very effective in fighting the flood at all the danger points.

The new cement bridge on Bridge street withstood the strain, but the waters began to wash out past the west end shortly after noon, endangering the Fall Mountain Electric Co. office and the old I. P. Co. storehouse on the bank of the canal. Fifteen dump trucks were immediately put into action. A steam shovel crept up Rockingham street to a gravel bank and continued to feed the fleet of trucks throughout Friday afternoon and night, with the result that the washout was slowly checked and further damage avoided.

The water reached its highest level at about 1:30 o'clock Friday afternoon. Between 12 and 1 o'clock the river had swollen exactly one foot over the dam and from 1 to 2 o'clock an additional rise of eight inches was registered.

With the water at its highest point the entire Rutland Railroad yard about the depot was flooded to a depth of three to four feet. Deep washouts at each end of the large steel railroad bridge from North Walpole to the depot constantly threatened that structure. A washout at the south end of the stone arch of the Boston & Maine bridge above the wooden toll bridge caused a sag in the railroad tracks at this point. The toll bridge escaped with the least damage, showing no danger of going out at any time.

Friday forenoon North Walpole came into the danger zone. The increasing height of the river caused it to overflow the east bank near the log yard, allowing the muddy waters to sweep through streets next to the river. This soon grew into a wide, deep channel, which plowed past the east end of the arch bridge, carried away two houses nearby and cut off access to both the arch and railroad bridges, greatly endangering them until the water subsided.

The Babbitt-Kelley mill, employing about 60 hands and with an estimated value of $200,000, was a complete loss; $25,000 worth of new machinery and about 100 tons of pulp were carried away from this mill.

Damage in excess of $100,000 was estimated in the case of the Moore & Thompson paper mill. Property loss in North Walpole, damage to the numerous bridges and the loss to the New England Power Co. probably totaled close to $1,000,000.

In Westminster and vicinity, the Connecticut, reaching far back, surrounded or invaded many homes. The Sandy Hill schoolhouse and the Lewis wayside grocery were both completely covered with water. A number of cattle perished in the barns before they could be moved to safety. Several families were driven out. Much tobacco in drying sheds was spoiled.

The Race to Save Hartford

EVERETT S. ALLEN

AND THERE WERE THE rampaging rivers, already bursting from days of rain. It was at Hartford where man and river fought their fiercest, most prolonged, and most costly battle; the roily, swollen Connecticut provided disastrous counterpoint to the hurricane.

Howling out of the southeast at four in the afternoon, an 80-mile-an-hour wind, the highest ever recorded in Hartford, spread death and destruction, ripping off roofs, toppling buildings, uprooting trees, disrupting traffic and communications, shattering brick walls, and tearing up fences, which one resident described as "floating in the air like paper." Rain was driven through the city in great sheets, and the *Courant* noted that "few people ventured on the street to brave the wind; at times, their feet were whipped away from under them. . . ."

The clock in the Old State House stopped at 4:10. Pigeons, unable to fly with their beaks to the wind, were smashed against the windshields of automobiles. Store windows buckled in the wind and shattered. Simultaneously, the Connecticut River was rising at the rate of 4 inches an hour; by midnight on Wednesday, it had reached 24.7 feet and was expected to crest at 28 feet by Thursday noon. As rain continued to spill out of gray skies, the residents of the lower East Side stolidly watched their old river foe lapping upward to threaten their homes and their well-being. They made their preparations. Chairs and couches were taken to second floors. Pictures were removed from the first floors. Clothing was packed in case evacuation became necessary.

One woman on Potter Street said, "I was born in a flood and so was my mother. I lived here during the 1936 flood. I'm not afraid. They come every so often." Bushnell Park became a watery wilderness; by night, the lamp-post bulbs glowed like floating Japanese lanterns. But the critical points as the rain-swelled Connecticut rose were at the dikes.

From Hartford's Travelers Insurance Company Tower at noon on Thursday, the view presented a stark contrast.

Overhead shone a benign September sun, and a hazy blue sky dotted with white cloud puffs. Below, the landscape had two faces. One of them complemented the sky. West, southwest, and northwest lay a landscape full of calm and peace, mellow in the mood of early autumn. The other half of the horizon was menacing, and from north to south there stretched a scene of desolation.

The inexorably rising Connecticut River seemed to lie within its banks as it rounded the bend near Windsor, but then, like the contents of a broken paper bag, it sprawled in unsightly disarray over miles of lowlands. The brown, swiftly moving flood, thick with its freight of half-submerged trees and the wreckage of Wednesday's hurricane, stretched from the new concrete Windsor Street extension on the west to the distant meadows of South Windsor on the east.

A few strings of freight cars, temporarily abandoned, stood in the vast lake which covered the freight yards north of the city. To the east of the Willimantic railroad bridge, a foundationless building squatted in the flood, and a long line of coal cars held down the East Hartford trestle.

The entire western section of East Hartford, with the exception of the boulevard, lay inundated by river waters, which had crept to the sills of first-floor windows. Several scores of dwellings, a school, and an apartment house were cut off entirely from the rest of the town, and there was no sign of life about them. Prospect Street, north and south of the boulevard, was the "beach" of a rapidly advancing shoreline. The pier and the gasoline pumps of the Hartford Yacht Club had gone down the river at 9:45 A.M., carrying with them a private craft. Other boats, huddled in awkward clusters, were flanked by driftwood in the upper branches of trees which stood where the river's edge had been only a few days ago.

Memorial Bridge was covered with black crawling lines of slow-moving cars and trucks; the urgent blare of automobile horns below the Travelers Tower indicated the anxious feelings of the drivers, pushing toward the remaining route to their homes east of the river.

A deserted barge loaded with scrap iron, perhaps bound for some foreign war, stemmed the river's current; once it had been berthed alongside the dock at the foot of State Street. Now it was more than 100 feet from dry land.

Here and there in the streets between the Travelers main building and the western rim of the flood, the scars of Wednesday's storm were apparent. The yellow boards of roofs whose shingles had been ripped off by the hurricane and the white jagged points of shattered tree tops reminded one acutely that the city had barely had a chance to draw its breath after the impact of one catastrophe before it was being forced to face another.

There was a reassuring sight in the southeast, where Brainard Field, a pale green oasis, stretched dry and unscathed, protected by its wide encircling dike and by Colt's dike to the north, which, while its durability was in doubt, still held back the river to this moment.

Reporting from what he called, with wry humor, the "East Side Gulf," T. H. Parker patrolled those city streets where deepening water was forcing the people to leave. "The National Guardsmen standing along the road stopping traffic halfway down all streets leading toward the river; neat, new uniforms; night sticks twirling at the end of rawhide loops, and each man with a pint of water in a hip flask while uncountable millions of gallons flow by at their feet," Parker wrote.

"A sign at Grove and Market streets barely above water, reading 'Stop: Through Traffic.' A motorboat being rowed by a man making little progress. And a skiff tied to a sign: 'No Parking.'

"The grandstand seats afforded by window ledges of tenements on side streets off Front. Women yelling down and children shouting back up. A man seated on a doorstep wearing a yachting cap, watching a four-year-old child fish with a string hanging from a twig. A Police Department boat run up on the asphalt shore with youngsters clambering in, quarreling shrilly for a place on the bow.

"Talk is of business, small business in distress. 'Everything gone. Couldn't get it out. We thought it wasn't coming up so high. Well, how much did you lose? 600 cases? 1,000? You asked me, I'd say 1,000 cases.'

"Trucks disappearing down warehouse alleys amidst loud blowing of horns. 'Get the hell out of the way. Don't you see we got to get in there and get that stuff out?' Same trucks reappearing, crammed with goods and being chased by a man trundling a hand dolly. 'Wait! Wait! You gotta take it this time or it's no good by the time you get back!'

"Water, water everywhere. In the kitchen. In the parlor. In the bedroom. Rowboats tied up to porches. A church dismantled. St. Anthony's on Market Street, ruined two years ago, and recently remodeled in such outstanding interior design as to be described in *Liturgical Arts*. Everything taken out; altars, pews, lined in rows on the sidewalk. The fixtures taken to safety from water already running in. Children sitting in the pews, laughing and playing games. Nothing left in the church but the floors, walls, ceilings, and pillars. A novena begun this morning and then canceled, and all hands, clerical and lay, turning to carry out every last object. Water pouring down a flight of steps into the church and disappearing with a sucking sound down the drain pipes. . . ."

All day, tensions over the flood increased. When the relentless upcoming of water caused street after street to be inundated, and hundreds to be homeless, predictions of the crest changed several times and always to a higher figure. Boat patrols were set up and took many to safety. Workers in threatened industrial plants, fighting against time, moved millions of dollars' worth of property to higher ground.

And now began the struggle by 1,200 WPA workers, World War I veterans, college students, and other volunteers in the southeast section of the city to save the homes of 5,000 and to protect the semi–industrial area, where two-thirds of the $6 million damage occurred in the flood of 1936.

This is Thursday night:

A thousand men crack their backs to keep a million tons of water out of the south end of the city. A hundred trucks slam over the pitted, pitch-black roads. They dump bags half-filled with sand along the Colt and Clark dikes, raising the low spots, stopping up the street ends.

Under the hiss of flares, a hundred crews grunt to throw the fifty-pound sacks in place. "Place 'em right; pack 'em carefully," the foremen shout.

On the land side, there is furious work, shouting, din, and sweat. On the other, no haste. Just the river, leisurely climbing up and up, seeping through, no more noise than an occasional, ominous lapping. The water creeps up over the 33-foot mark. Three square miles of a city is imperiled; if this army of a thousand is defeated, if the dikes go out with a roar for the second time in two years, the whole of that three square miles will be the scene of flood, devastation, tumbled wreckage, and ruin.

From Springfield, Massachusetts, where the river has been at a standstill for three hours, comes bad news; the water is rising again. In Hartford, the American Red Cross headquarters, already caring for 1,500 evacuees at six relief stations in the city, is notified by the city government to prepare for 3,000 refugees, ordered to evacuate their homes in the area back of the dikes south of Sheldon Street and east of Main Street. Some go fearfully; some debate going; some have to be forced out of their homes.

All during the evacuation, the diking goes on. The people may not be gotten out in time. Even when they are moved to safety, there are still millions of dollars' worth of property, thousands of homes and businesses to be protected, if protection is possible.

A crest of 34.5 feet is predicted for sometime Friday morning. At Springfield, the upsurge of water accelerates to a rate of one-tenth of a foot an hour. U.S. Army Engineers say there is only a fifty-fifty chance that the Hartford dikes will hold.

All night, the engineers roar in automobiles along the dike areas from Commerce to Sheldon Street to Wawarme Avenue, evaluating the constantly changing situation, ordering quick countermeasures against the creeping waters. As early as 9:30 P.M., the two most critical spots are obvious: the junction of Sheldon and Sequassen, near the Colt Firearms

Company office, from which the battle against the water is directed, and at Sheldon and Commerce; here at the low levels of these street ends, the river makes its major threat to overwhelm the city's south end.

Sandbags are piled, quickly, surely, with tireless haste, into the depressions made by the low roadways. A triple row for a foundation, and then a single row. Bag upon bag, a slender buttress, half a bag wide against infinite pressure of water. Where the water does not simply press, quiet and deadly, it seeps, and by 11 o'clock, small streams ooze from the sandbagging, trickle across Sheldon and spill into the gutters on the sharp declines of Sequassen and Commerce, the perimeters of the great three-square-mile area that is menaced.

It is more than a mile over pockmarked roads to Brainard Field airport, where a roaring digger throws up earth at the "burrow" and sweating men shovel it into bags. Squads of trucks are backed to the spot, and none waits to be more than half-filled. Time is precious. A few bags can do a lot of good if rushed to vital spots. The trucks bound over roads as black as the inside of a pocket. They dodge between red lanterns and shoot by trooping workers en route from one bad spot to another. The workers scuttle out of the way, their electric torches flashing, as they make their way past holes in the road and tangles of tree branches sent down by Wednesday's storm.

Slam-banging into the lower end of Sheldon Street, the trucks slow down into single file and as they pass the laboring crews, the foremen cut them out as needed. With shouts, they are guided up close to the sandbag walls, the dump body rises with a roar of gears, the bags of sand slide to the ground and without stopping to lower the dumpers, the trucks charge down the side streets and off to the pit for another load.

After each clatter that announces the arrival of a truck, after the noise of unloading, silence once more falls over each crew, broken only by an occasional order barked by the foreman. These men work without talk, in part because they were hours ago tired enough to rest, yet there is no time for rest; they work tensely, but without excitement, to bag up each dangerous spot, higher and higher. They work swiftly but with deliberation and care; one sack out of place and enough water might seep through to start the fatal breach.

When each truckload of bags has been laid, they walk back and forth over the tops of the bags, settling them into place; the foreman watches with a critical eye; this bag needs readjustment, square that one up. Now the water is rising at the rate of two-tenths of a foot per hour. Opposite the Colt office and about twenty feet beyond the dike there is a white post nearly covered with water. It is a stake marking the 35-foot level. There are 800 men working in this area; the call goes out for 200 more. Thomas

F. Foley, local WPA representative, is the man in charge of the battle. Sleepless and with a sprained right ankle, he answers a battery of phones in the Colt office, patrols endlessly between the Commerce and Sequassen weak spots, receives half-hour readings from the yellow-chalked post in the swollen stream just beyond the soaked sandbags, and is grimly noncommittal.

Beyond the stake, the murky expanse of rampaging river stretches away into the dark. Some small buildings can be seen dimly in the flickering lights, water halfway up to their single-story roofs. The water makes no sound, and as you look over the top of the sandbagging, it hardly seems to move. It is a sullen river, brown with churned-up earth, and the smell of oil rises from it.

There is some little talk to break the silence when the reserves arrive, with truckloads of shovels. They line up on the porch of the Colt building, waiting to be assigned to gangs. From the dark, there is a loud halloo from some distant foreman, calling for trucks. The wind off the water is cold; it is more comfortable to stand near the flares—at least they give an impression of warmth. By midnight, the water has reached to within a few inches of the tops of the bags in some places and 200 nearby Legionnaires are trying to persuade remaining residents to leave and to assist those who are willing to go.

At 10 o'clock Friday night, the Connecticut River gave up its fight. Reaching a height of 35.1 feet, it began to recede. The U.S. Army Engineers, who had taken over direction of the defending forces, under Colonel John S. Bragdon of Providence, reported that the first recession of the water had been noted and that the level was then 35.09, a drop of 1/100 of a foot. By midnight, the reading was 35.02. The little army, blistered and exhausted, watched by thousands, including the refugees, and prayed for by thousands more, had won the "Battle of Colt's Dike."

It was not until Sunday, when all danger was past, that Mayor Thomas J. Spellacy disclosed that an emergency plan had been set up to dynamite the Clark dike along Brainard Field and the South Meadows at the moment that the Colt dike or its long Sheldon Street emergency sandbag extension gave way. The theory was that if the sandbagging effort had not been successful and the water had broken though, the force of the pent-up river, unless relieved by immediate creation of another outlet to the south, might have swept away the Colt factory buildings and all other structures in its path. City officials anticipated it would have torn oil storage tanks in the area from their moorings and slammed them against the South Meadows generating plant of the Hartford Electric Light Company, and hoped that the dynamiting would have prevented this.

In all of this time of crisis, the most extraordinary phone call received by the Hartford *Courant*—one among a bombardment of hundreds made by those concerned about roads, property, missing persons, and the state of the Connecticut River—came Wednesday night as the city lay shocked and battered after the hurricane. "Can you tell me," the caller asked, "on what date the blizzard of 1888 occurred in Russia?"

Requiem for a Bridge

GEORGE E. WRIGHT

THE BURNING OF THE BRIDGE, which had spanned the river for seventy-six years, occurred Friday evening, May 17, 1895, and was one of the most spectacular fires ever seen in the Connecticut valley. The fire started sometime between 6.30 and 7.30 o'clock, a still alarm from No. 3's engine house sending a hose cart to the East Hartford end of the bridge, where the fire first appeared. Later, about 7.15 o'clock, an alarm was rung in from box 29, Morgan and Front streets, calling out the entire department. Obviously but little could be done, as it was impossible to get upon the bridge without the greatest danger, the fire running rapidly through the pine timbers which had been seasoning for three score and ten years. As it was, the hose cart and horses belonging to Engine Company No. 3, which attempted to get across, were lost through the burning wreck, the driver and firemen barely saving their lives. More than 20,000 people witnessed the fire, which took on the form of gigantic fireworks, the skeletons of the arched framework standing out in bold relief entirely across the river in a line of brilliant fire.

IN MEMORIAM

Farewell, old bridge! Thou monarch of the past.
Thy sheltering arms are laid to rest at last.

From George E. Wright, *Crossing the Connecticut* (Hartford, Conn.: The Smith-Linsley Co., 1908).

No more will travelers thy ancient roadway tread,
For thou art numbered now among the honored dead.

Our fathers braved the winter's snow and summer's sun
To hew from the forest primeval, one by one,
The grand old sentinels that Time had long preserved
For the great purpose thou so well hast served.

They reared thee, with a just and honest pride,
To bear them o'er the swiftly running tide
That holds the Indian title, "River, Great,"
And gave the name to our historic State.

From winter's blasts and summer's torturing sun
Thou didst long protect the weary traveling one;
Nor could the Icy King or sullen rising flood
Swerve thee from where thou hast in duty stood.

Against all elements but one hast thou prevailed;
But when that one thy bulwarks strong assailed,
Though thou didst struggle hard, thou had to yield,
Defeated—not dishonored—on a well-fought field.

And now above thy grave and in thy place
A monument we'll rear that Time cannot efface—
A bridge of stone, from which posterity shall learn
It is not death to bravely die—or burn.

The Bedell Bridge

KATHARINE BLAISDELL

Bedell ferry and bridges

The recently renovated Bedell Bridge, listed in the National Register of Historic Places, is the second-longest two-span covered bridge in the country, the longest being a few miles down the river at Windsor. Bedell Bridge is 396 feet long.

Ferries. Uriah Stone built a log cabin near this site (on the New Hampshire side) in 1763 or 4, and may have also operated a ferry here, using a ferryboat he had hand-hewn from logs. His cabin was swept away by a flood, probably in 1771, landing on Moose Meadow in Piermont, where he rebuilt, and is known to have operated a ferry service for many years.

Moody Bedel chartered a ferry from Haverhill to South Newbury in 1791, near his later bridge site. His ferry was large enough to accommodate teams of horses or oxen with loaded wagons, by means of large flatboats which were poled across the river.

Series of bridges. In 1802, Bedel and others formed a corporation and obtained a state charter for a bridge at this location.

By the way, "Bedell" has become the accepted spelling for the bridge name—perhaps because George Washington spelled it that way.

The first Bedell bridge was built in 1805—a series of open spans built on a light wooden framework. In 1823 it was severely damaged by a flood and had to be rebuilt. Eighteen years later, the second bridge also was swept away, and for ten years travelers had to revert to ferry service until a new bridge was completed in 1851. This, too, was carried away by a spring flood in 1862. The present middle pier was built that fall, and the first covered bridge at this site was completed the following year.

This fourth bridge fell victim to a sudden storm on the Fourth of July in

From Katharine Blaisdell, *Over the River and Through the Years*, The *Journal Opinion* (1983).

1866. They say that a group of people had gathered for a holiday picnic near the New Hampshire end of the bridge, when a sudden thunderstorm drove them to seek shelter inside the bridge. The wind was so strong that the bridge was blown off its foundations and landed on its side in the river. In those days, the river at that point was quite shallow, so nobody inside the bridge was drowned or injured, as far as we know. For the rest of the summer, people crossed the river by walking on the side of the overturned bridge.

A fifth bridge—the present Bedell Bridge—was built in 1866, using much of the timber salvaged from the blown-down bridge, as revealed by old "trunnel holes" (holes for wooden pegs, or "tree nails," used in the old bridge). The new bridge was constructed in a more modern way, using iron bolts. The bridge was built of "Burr truss" design. It is said that its curved arches were hand-hewn from curved trees.

Toll houses. The first toll house was in Haverhill at Moody Bedel's residence at the foot of Powder House Hill. The exact location is hard to identify, because Bedel lived in several different houses while he was in Haverhill, and because there have been changes in the main road through Haverhill, it formerly passing up the west side of Powder House Hill, where an old road can still be seen.

The second toll house is still standing at the Vermont end of the bridge. It was evidently built after the bridge was, because it is positioned so that from the front window the toll-keeper had a clear view through the length of the bridge to watch for traffic.

Reminiscences. Around 1900, the LaFrance family lived in the toll house. Mary LaFrance Millette says that they had the house rent-free for collecting the toll. Someone came around once a month to take the toll money to the bridge owners. Mary remembers there being light blue toll tickets in use.

Mary says her grandfather used to sit in the little enclosed front porch or "cupola" and receive toll through the window, then pull the rope to open the gate. Toll was 2 cents for a pedestrian, 5 cents for a single team, etc., but the bridge was free overnight from 6 p.m. to 7 a.m.

In the summertime, large groups of "bloomer girls" used to get off the train at nearby Conicut Station and walk across the bridge on their way to Camp Tahoma and Camp Serrana, girls camps near Lake Tarleton. The girls would make a great fuss over Grandfather LaFrance, every time they came by.

Queenie LaFrance remembered the first automobile that ever came across the bridge: "It was Dr. Russell's from Haverhill, one of those stick-steering two-cylinder affairs with a spring board. We all ran after it and helped push it up the grade. He was headed for Happy Hollow, but he'd-a never got there if we hadn't helped him push it! We couldn't figure out how much toll to charge, so he said he'd pay when he got back. We talked it all over and decided 25 cents would be about right."

There was always a degree of public opposition to having to pay toll. Sometimes protestors even tore down the toll gate. There was also competition from nearby Haverhill and Piermont bridges, which had been freed earlier, so finally in 1916 the towns of Newbury and Haverhill acquired title to the Bedell Bridge and freed it.

Mary remembers that when she was a little girl, they used to play ball in the bridge on rainy days. The bridge was also a good vantagepoint during the annual log drives, as well as a mooring spot for the cook raft, the "Mary Ann", famous locally for its "beanhole beans." There was always a likelihood of log jams at the bridge, so the rivermen used to hitch one end of a log boom to the middle pier of the bridge, and the other end to a tree upstream on the New Hampshire side, to keep the logs moving down the swiftest part of the river and to protect the bridge.

Every summer a band of gypsies used to camp near the New Hampshire end of the bridge, usually a troop of about forty. Queenie said they used to stay all summer, mostly buying and selling horses—and stealing vegetables. Nobody's garden was safe. Otherwise, they pretty much minded their own business.

Mary says that there used to be a lot of tramps passing through, who would stop at the bridge looking for a handout. Her mother used to tell them that she would give them a meal if they would chop some wood to earn it. Mary remembers one time when a tramp decided he would chop for his supper, and after awhile asked Mary's mother whether he had chopped enough yet. "I'll tell you when it's enough," she replied. It wasn't long before he disappeared and never came back.

Gilbert McClintock says that some years ago, Fred Spear of Newbury—on a ten dollar bet—drove his road grader and four horses onto the bridge, turned around inside, and came out again on the Newbury end!

Dr. Edwin Blaisdell (my husband) used to use the Bedell bridge frequently on his veterinary calls. He remembers having seen as many as three cars on the bridge at one time. Sometimes if he could spare a few minutes in the middle of the day he would stop at the bridge to eat his lunch and drop a fishing line over the side, where there was a board missing—but it was a hard place to land a fish from and they would usually fall off the hook.

Bedell Bridge was seriously weakened by the 1927 flood, so that additional arches had to be installed and the bridge anchored more securely to its abutments and pier.

Buster Carbee of Newbury says that during the 1936 flood, water rose in the bridge as high as a man's head. An ice jam formed above the bridge, the ice reaching almost up to the eaves. Bridge engineers advised Mr. Carbee, who was the town road commissioner, to dynamite the ice to release the icejam—but he refused because he knew it would destroy the bridge. The ice jam itself was already shunting additional ice across the flooded meadow, so the jam wasn't getting any worse, and by the next day the water had gone down and the ice had broken up. The bridge was bowed a little by the pressure, but remained standing.

Old age. In spite of reinforcement by heavy iron rods, age gradually took its toll, and when one arch cracked and the downstream Vermont corner dropped about a foot, the bridge was closed to traffic by joint vote of the two towns in 1958.

Persistent travelers. But—it's hard to convince the public that a bridge is really closed and to prevent "just one little car" from going across. Bart Mann says that while he was a Haverhill selectman, the Bedell Bridge was really a headache. They blocked off access to the bridge every way they could think of—put up a barricade of planks, but people tore them out and carried them off—put heavy chains across the entrance, but someone cut them down and stole them.

When Stub (Arthur) Bigelow was road agent, his men dumped four loads of gravel in front of the bridge, but people drove right over it with jeeps. Then Roland McKean's crew with a payloader blocked the way with an enormous boulder—which by the next morning had been pushed aside and rolled into the river, where it can still be seen when the water is low. Roland says the final and successful barricade was a tangle of logs and stumps.

In state hands. Periodic attempts to restore the bridge failed and demolition seemed certain until 1967, when Haverhill and Newbury took joint action to save the bridge by quitclaiming it to the State of New Hampshire, with the understanding that the state was to repair the bridge and incorporate it into a river wayside park, for which the state purchased 71 acres of adjacent meadow land.

While awaiting funding for repairs, the bridge suffered severe damage in the spring and summer floods of 1973. By that time, Wilder Dam had raised the average water level by five feet, and produced frequent changes in the water level, causing increased erosion of the embankments at the ends of the bridge. The flood of July 1, 1973, was intensified in this area by extra water having been let out of the up-river dams over that weekend. In addition, water flow at Wilder was impeded by debris remaining from spring high-water.

As the water finally went down, Maarten Smit, who lives in the former toll house, could hear a continual creak-creak-creak coming from the bridge. After listening to this ominous sound for four days, Mr. Smit took his life in his hands and went out onto the bridge to find out where the noise was coming from. He found a broken queenpost, which with every creak was separating a little more from other parts of the bridge structure. He wrapped a cable around to anchor it to the next solid part of the bridge, and as the cable tightened and slippage stopped, the creaking stopped—and the bridge remained standing.

As a result of the flood damage, experts considered the bridge to be beyond repair; in fact, collapse seemed imminent. When state officials heard reports that canoeists were stopping to eat their lunches under the precarious bridge, they hastily dispatched work crews to put up signs warning everyone to stay a safe distance away.

The state, being liable for any damage caused by the bridge, signed a contract for the bridge to be demolished in October, 1973.

Last minute reprieve. A storm of public protest to the Governor resulted in hasty scheduling of a meeting in North Haverhill on October 22—the night before demolition was to begin. There was a "stay of execution" of four days, then another week, while the "Save the Bedell Bridge Committee" formed a corporation to assume responsibility for the bridge.

During a period of five years, "Bedell Covered Bridge, Incorporated," under the presidency of Stephen Wellington of Pike, raised bridge repair funds of over $250,000 through sizeable grants from the National Parks Service and charitable foundations, added to the generous donations and untiring efforts of local citizens and friends of the bridge throughout the country.

Reconstruction. Milton S. Graton of Ashland, the ranking covered bridge restoration expert in the Northeast—and perhaps in the world—was quickly engaged for both emergency repairs and restoration of the bridge.

In early December he set an enormous post on the river bottom and equipped it with a cross piece and tackles to support the weakest part of the bridge—but within a few days, skim ice coming down the river shook the crossbeam loose. In an emergency late-Sunday-afternoon repair, Mr. Graton and Mr. Wellington stepped very carefully onto the bridge and reattached the crossbeam to the post. A few days later, an unseasonal flood carried away the entire rig, letting the damaged span drop even lower than before.

Working quickly, Mr. Graton and his crew strapped broken joints to sound ones with steel cables, then set a timber frame and tackle over the center pier to support the sheared arch ends.

Suspension cables. To lift the bridge to its desired position and to remove tension while repairs were being made, they created a temporary suspension bridge within the covered bridge. Steel cables were anchored on each shore by means of "dead-men"—immense oak logs deeply buried, well back from the riverbank. The cables passed over cribwork towers at the ends of the bridge and at the center pier, then looped under the center of each span, supporting its weight. Hydraulic jacks on the towers permitted regulation of the tension of the cables as necessary, while work progressed on repairing damaged parts of the bridge.

On November 15, 1978, the suspension cables were removed and the bridge stood on its own, probably stronger than ever before. . . .

Dedication of Bedell Bridge State Park

On July 22, 1979, there was a festive celebration of the restoration of Bedell Bridge and the dedication of the state park, attended by an enthusiastic crowd of 2500 to 3000 people. . . .

For many people, the highlight of the day was the parade—through the bridge—of many of the kinds of vehicles and travelers who had passed through the bridge during its long history. . . .

Bedell Bridge destroyed by windstorm

On September 14, 1979, less than two months after the festivities of dedication day, Bedell Bridge was completely destroyed by a violent windstorm, a remnant of Hurricane Frederic—the same as had happened to the previous bridge on this site, 113 years earlier.

There was to have been a wedding on the bridge the following day. Bedell Bridge had always meant a lot to Winifred Welch and Richard Patten, so when they decided to be married they made arrangements to have their wedding on the bridge. The night before the wedding, they came with friends to the bridge to make preparations, putting up decorations for the festive occasion—but then about 7:00 the storm hit. They started out of the New Hampshire end of the bridge to go to their cars, but when they saw that the wind was knocking down trees, they decided to stay within the shelter of the bridge. As the wind increased, the bridge started swaying—then what seemed like a giant tidal wave of wind wrenched it from its foundations and dropped it into the river.

Five of the people leaped off the end of the bridge before it collapsed, but two more had to crawl out between the beams—fortunate to escape with only cuts and bruises. The eighth person, Ellen Wheelock, was pinned in the wreckage—and it would be nearly two hours before rescue teams could succeed in releasing her.

One of the party ran across the meadow and up the hill to Lavoie's Garage to get help—with immediate response by the Haverhill Corner Fire Department, soon followed by other emergency groups. Rescue efforts were hampered by fallen trees blocking the road across the meadow. CB requests for chainsaws brought abundant help. Robert Gilbert, chief dispatcher of the Grafton County Sheriff's Office said, "A small army of people showed up to help. We'd put out a call for a backhoe and get three of them. We'd ask for a chainsaw and get 15. What amazes me is the way people turn out around here when you need them."

Finally reaching the bridge, about ten men worked to free Ellen Wheelock, using chainsaws, handsaws, and jacks to cut and move the wreckage. It was a delicate process, because cutting one beam could have caused another to collapse—and the whole end of the bridge might have slid into the river, carrying rescuers with it.

Haverhill police officer Charles Nelson said that Miss Wheelock remained very calm during the whole procedure, which was a great help. Norman Demers, local fire warden, climbed down into the wreckage and stayed with her the whole time. Dr. David Frechette was on the scene for emergency treatment of the victims.

Cheers went up from the crowd when Miss Wheelock was finally released from the wreckage. She was taken by ambulance to Cottage Hospital, where it was determined that her main injury was a broken ankle.

Everyone rejoiced that no lives were lost, and the wedding took place on schedule—not at the bridge, but at the 111 Club in Woodsville.

The bridge is so completely destroyed that reconstruction is impossible, but it is hoped that there will be some kind of structure built in the park to house an exhibit of bridge memorabilia.

Speech on the Weather

MARK TWAIN

I REVERENTLY BELIEVE THAT the Maker who made us all makes everything in New England but the weather. I don't know who makes that, but I think it must be raw apprentices in the weatherclerk's factory who experiment and learn how, in New England, for board and clothes, and then are promoted to make weather for countries that require a good article, and will take their custom elsewhere if they don't get it. There is a sumptuous variety about the New England weather that compels the stranger's admiration—and regret. The weather is always doing something there; always attending strictly to business; always getting up new designs and trying them on the people to see how they will go. But it gets through more business in spring than in any other season. In the spring I have counted one hundred and thirty-six different kinds of weather inside of four-and-twenty hours. It was I that made the fame and fortune of that man that had that marvelous collection of weather on exhibition at the Centennial, that so astounded the foreigners. He was going to travel all over the world and get specimens from all the climes. I said, "Don't you do it; you come to New England on a favorable spring day." I told him what we could do in the way of style, variety, and quantity. Well, he came and he made his collection in four days. As to variety, why, he confessed that he got hundreds of kinds of weather that he had never heard of before. And as to quantity—well, after he had picked out and discarded all that was blemished in any way, he not only had weather enough, but weather to spare; weather to hire out; weather to sell; to deposit; weather to invest; weather to give to the poor. The people of New England are by nature patient and forbearing, but there are some things which they will not stand. Every year they kill a lot of poets for writing about "Beautiful Spring." These are generally casual visitors, who bring their notions of spring from somewhere else, and cannot, of course, know how the natives feel about spring. And so the first thing they know the opportunity to inquire how they feel has permanently gone by. Old Probabilities has a mighty reputation for accurate prophecy, and thoroughly well deserves it. You take up the paper and observe how crisply and confidently he checks off what to-day's weather is going to be on the Pacific, down South, in the Middle States, in the Wisconsin region.

From Mark Twain, *The Complete Short Stories and Famous Essays of Mark Twain* (New York: P. F. Collier & Son Co., 1923).

See him sail along in the joy and pride of his power till he gets to New England, and then see his tail drop. *He* doesn't know what the weather is going to be in New England. Well, he mulls over it, and by and by he gets out something about like this: Probable northeast to southwest winds, varying to the southward and westward and eastward, and points between, high and low barometer swapping around from place to place; probable areas of rain, snow, hail, and drought, succeeded or preceded by earthquakes, with thunder and lightning. Then he jots down this postscript from his wandering mind, to cover accidents: "But it is possible that the program may be wholly changed in the mean time." Yes, one of the brightest gems in the New England weather is the dazzling uncertainty of it. There is only one thing certain about it: you are certain there is going to be plenty of it—a perfect grand review; but you never can tell which end of the procession is going to move first. You fix up for the drought; you leave your umbrella in the house and sally out, and two to one you get drowned. You make up your mind that the earthquake is due; you stand from under, and take hold of something to steady yourself, and the first thing you know you get struck by lightning. These are great disappointments; but they can't be helped. The lightning there is peculiar; it is so convincing, that when it strikes a thing it doesn't leave enough of that thing behind for you to tell whether—— Well, you'd think it was something valuable, and a Congressman had been there. And the thunder. When the thunder begins to merely tune up and scrape and saw, and key up the instruments for the performance, strangers say, "Why, what awful thunder you have here!" But when the baton is raised and the real concert begins, you'll find that stranger down in the cellar with his head in the ash-barrel. Now as to the size of the weather in New England—lengthways, I mean. It is utterly disproportioned to the size of that little country. Half the time, when it is packed as full as it can stick, you will see that New England weather sticking out beyond the edges and projecting around hundreds and hundreds of miles over the neighboring states. She can't hold a tenth part of her weather. You can see cracks all about where she has strained herself trying to do it. I could speak volumes about the inhuman perversity of the New England weather, but I will give but a single specimen. I like to hear rain on a tin roof. So I covered part of my roof with tin, with an eye to that luxury. Well, sir, do you think it ever rains on that tin? No, sir; skips it every time. Mind, in this speech I have been trying merely to do honor to the New England weather—no language could do it justice. But, after all, there is at least one or two things about that weather (or, if you please, effects produced by it) which we residents would not like to part with. If we hadn't our bewitching autumn foliage, we should still have to credit the weather with one feature which compensates for all its bullying vagaries—the ice-storm: when a leafless tree is clothed with ice from the bottom to the top—ice that is as bright and clear as crystal; when every bough and twig is strung with ice-beads, frozen dewdrops, and the whole tree sparkles cold and white, like the Shah of Persia's diamond plume. Then the wind waves the branches and the sun comes out and turns all those myriads of beads and drops to prisms that glow and burn and flash with all manner of colored fires, which change and change again with inconceivable rapidity from blue to red, from red to green, and green to gold—the tree becomes a spraying fountain, a very explosion of dazzling jewels; and it stands there the acme, the climax, the supremest possibility in art or nature, of bewildering, intoxicating, intolerable magnificence. One cannot make the words too strong.

Chapter 7

THE CLASSIC GUIDES

Whether we see the Connecticut at Haverhill, Northampton, or Hartford, it still possesses that gentle aspect; and the imagination can scarcely conceive Arcadian values more lovely or more peaceful than the valley of the Connecticut.
—"Essay on American Scenery" by Thomas Cole

Guidebooks have a double readership—those who use them for their travels, and those (a much greater number, publishers believe) who read them simply for the delights of armchair travel, and never visit the places described. It's the enthusiasm of that second group that's honored here; the Connecticut has been blessed with some excellent guidebooks over the years, and they allow the modern reader to travel vicariously, not only through the valley, but through the reaches of time.

Guidebooks also testify to the changing role of the valley corridor over the years, as railroads, state highways, and the interstates became the successive modes of travel. In 1901, the Boston and Maine Railroad issued a guide to their route along the river, which recaptures the golden age of guidebook writing, with its innocent hyperbole, even the most humdrum scene becoming, in the anonymous author's prose, a vista of absolute splendor.

By the time the Works Project Agency (one of the New Deal's most successful make-work agencies) commissioned its series of excellent guidebooks to the states, a much more sober, much more informative style was called for. The excerpt here, from the "Connecticut" volume, gives a good idea of what it was like to drive along the river before the hurricane hit in 1938.

An untold number of canoeists have been introduced to the river by the Appalachian Mountain Club's canoeing guide. I've included an excerpt from the second edition of 1968. As well as providing a vicarious float down the river, it points out that these were still the dark ages of river pollution.

People are still finding original ways to write valley guidebooks. One of the most innovative of recent years is Bradford B. Van Diver's Roadside Geology of Vermont and New Hampshire, *wherein he describes, in epochal terms, what you can see out your window as you drive north on I-91. While it's hard to say anything good about the interstates (the way they cut off both Hartford and Springfield from the river is criminal), this kind of guide at least helps to make the drive interesting.*

The River by Rail

PASSENGER DEPARTMENT, BOSTON AND MAINE RAILROAD

PICTURESQUE NEW ENGLAND HAS no more alluring gateway than that which tourists, bound from New York and the South for the glorious summer playground of the White Mountain region or Northern Vermont, are ushered through when they reach the far-famed Connecticut River Valley.

Mere printed words are inadequate to depict the ever-changing beauties of this long and majestic highway of travel; and portly, indeed, must be the volume that could picture and describe in detail the charms of the multitude of interesting stopping-places scattered through the section to which it gives such easy access.

The good people who dwell near the Atlantic coast, and make their summer journeys to the country by wholly different avenues, are in this respect less favored than their neighbors in New York, Philadelphia, and Washington: for it is through this royal road to a princely domain that these must necessarily travel. There is not, it may be repeated, a more delightful way of reaching this enchanted land of Vacation, from whatever

From *Valley of the Connecticut and Northern Vermont* (Passenger Department, Boston and Maine Railroad, 1901).

point of compass the excursion may be essayed; and it is in thorough harmony with the fitness of things that the journey over the Boston & Maine's portion of the railroad stage of the trip should begin at the prosperous and attractive city of Springfield, Mass.

From the handsome union station, into and from which nearly two hundred trains roll every twenty-four hours, the rails of the Boston & Maine Company's Connecticut and Passumpsic Division stretch northward like silver ribbons for 250 miles, linking together a grand out-door mosaic of the loveliest scenes that eye ever feasted upon. . . .

Meanwhile, the fast flying express has brought the traveller into close connection with other railroads, at South Deerfield, Bellows Falls, White River Junction, and Wells River, and with other branches of the Boston & Maine at Northampton, South Vernon Junction, Wells River, and St. Johnsbury, opening up to those who would wander thither the central portion of Massachusetts, the Ashuelot valley and the Monadnock country of southwest New Hampshire, the Sunapee region, the Pemigewasset and Winooski and Passumpsic valleys, the White and the Green Mountains, Lake Champlain, and the Memphremagog section of Northern Vermont.

Could a more intoxicating vision of varied lake and river and mountain landscape be possibly conjured up by the most romantic tourist, as, seated in a comfortable railroad coach, he sets forth upon his long anticipated and much too short vacation?

Springfield is a city whose importance is vastly out of proportion to its size. It has been the theatre of stirring events of history, the nursery of men and women who have made great names in literature, politics, and industrial endeavor.

Far more to the present point, it is a city of beautiful surroundings, with its noble river, gliding majestically to the Sound, its encircling highlands, its fertile meadows and its rural parks and drives.

The visitor who tarries here for a time will find much to interest and instruct, including the famous United States Arsenal, which played such an important part in the late war with Spain; the Federal building, Forest Park, St. Gaudens' statue of "The Puritan," the Public Library, and many other institutions in which Springfield takes a just pride.

The city has many fine churches, a metropolitan standard of journalism to which it owes much of its intelligent progressiveness, and a group of manufactories, notably in the industry of paper making, that are famous the country over.

It is from the observation tower of the Arsenal, located on the highest elevation in the city, that the best view of Springfield and the surrounding country is to be had. The view includes the adjacent cities of Chicopee and Holyoke, the latter about eight miles distant; West Springfield and

Agawam, the church spire in Longmeadow in which swings the old bell that "rung the Lexington alarm and echoed the Declaration of Independence"; the site, nearby, of the ancient Indian Fort of King Philip's day; the "Indian leap," the fertile meadows of Agawam, and, best of all, the lovely hills of the Mount Tom range that make the panorama perfect.

Leaving the union station, where intersect the trains from Boston, the West, New York, and Montreal and the mountains,—the converging point, as it were, of a continent,—the traveller is quickly transported to Holyoke, the famous "paper city," many points of interest being noted ere the eight miles are traversed. The noted Hampden trotting park of Springfield gives way to a soul-stirring view of the noble Connecticut, seen here in the fulness of its power and impressiveness, and scarcely to be absent from the delighted gaze of the tourist until many, many miles of its sinuous course have been enjoyed.

The first local station passed by the train is Brightwood, once the abiding place of Dr. J. G. Holland, the gifted poet and journalist, who did so much to perpetuate in verse and prose the beauties of this charming region. There is a large car-building plant in this place.

Next on the time-table comes Chicopee Junction, which gives rail communication with the busy Massachusetts city of Chicopee, two and a half miles away. Willimansett and Riverside follow and give notice that Holyoke draws near. The train glides over a splendid bridge spanning the river, and the amazed tourist shortly finds spread out before him one of the most wonderful spectacles to be seen in the world,—the famous Holyoke dam.

The wide spreading Connecticut pours over this stupendous structure a perfect waste of waters, and the sight is one worth going many miles to see. This great triumph of engineering skill is owned by the Holyoke Water Power Company, capital $1,200,000, and furnishes about 30,000 horse power. It is over one thousand feet in length and about thirty-two feet in height.

There are no less than twenty-six paper mills in Holyoke, with a combined capacity for producing more than five thousand tons per week of fine paper stock, mainly writing and envelope paper. Four thousand persons find employment in these mills, and an equal number are kept busy in the numerous other manufactories that go to make up the city's prosperity.

It was in Holyoke, by the way, that the first lock and canal system in America was attempted, the settlers in the early days finding it necessary to overcome in some way the insuperable barrier to rafts and boats presented by the falls in the Connecticut. Of late the possibilities of reviving, in some measure, the old time river navigation from this point to the Sound is being discussed.

Just now, however, the Connecticut hereabouts is monopolized mostly by the devotees of canoeing, and it is one of the most famous rendezvous for canoeists in the United States. More ideal conditions for this splendid pastime are scarcely to be imagined.

Another pastime is fishing for shad in the river, a sport that is sometimes carried on by moonlight, under most romantic conditions. The streets of Holyoke are busy and interesting, and it contains some very handsome public buildings. What will interest the tourist most, however, is the glorious hill range near the city, especially Mount Holyoke and Mount Tom. . . .

The extent to which the canoeing fad prevails here is exemplified in the cluster of canoe lodges maintained by the members of the local canoeing associations, noticed as the train draws out of Holyoke and begins to speed for the next stopping place.

Smith's Ferry, a name so suggestive of the "good old times" when river ferries were more primitive institutions than they are now, dawns upon the vision almost as soon as does the entrancing prospect of the hill sentinels of Holyoke and Northampton, Mount Holyoke on the right and Mount Tom and Mount Nonotuck on the left. Visitors from the great metropolis, while tolerably familiar with the sight of canal boats, may perchance raise their eyebrows in surprise at the discovery that Smith's Ferry actually is equipped with the old-fashioned, flat-bottomed ferry boats, propelled by pulling on a wire stretched across river, and transporting both man and beast. This picturesque accompaniment may seem quite the thing to expect in the far south, where a civilization's strides have not been so rapid, but it certainly looks very romantic and "remote" right here at the doorway of bustling cities.

South Hadley, in which is located Mount Holyoke College for young women, lies not far distant, its spires being visible from Smith's Ferry. Next comes that unique little hamlet, Mount Tom Junction, nestling at the gateway of the hills and watched over with jealous care by Mount Tom. The view from here is panoramic and beautiful, taking in the distant city of Northampton and giving the traveller a foretaste to a feast of color and beauty that is to come.

Near Mount Tom Junction is a restful grove and a once busy boat landing. It is possible from this point to reach the summit of Mount Holyoke, over 950 feet above the sea level. It is accessible either by carriage road or mountain railway. The prospect, taking in as it does velvety meadows, rolling hills, fertile fields of grass and grain, lakes, streams, hamlets and cities, is one of the finest in all New England. The picture is that of New England's natural beauty and agricultural richness personified, and, on the authority of no less distinguished an observer and traveller than Agassiz, "the finest cultivated view in this part of America."

Mount Nonotuck, not as high as Holyoke by about one hundred feet, but affording almost as superb a view, may also be reached from this point, and without crossing the river as in the other case. Easthampton, a beautifully-located town with important manufacturing interests, can also be reached by a three-mile journey over the branch road. Williston Seminary, a well-known preparatory academy for boys, is located there.

Winging its way northward again, the train soon brings its passenger in full view of the famous Ox-Bow of the Connecticut River, an example of Nature's vagaries which is familiar in pictured reproduction to many thousands who have never seen it. Time was when the Ox-Bow was the main channel of the river itself, but the narrow neck of land that separated the ends of the bow was eventually invaded by the force of the current and the river took the "short cut" it had been cheated out of for so many years, the whilom peninsula being converted into a small island. It is interesting to know, even if one cannot stop to enjoy it, that at certain times there is excellent muskalonge fishing in calm waters of the old channel.

THE WPA GUIDE

WORKERS OF THE FEDERAL WRITERS' PROJECT

TOUR 8: *From* OLD SAYBROOK *to* MASSACHUSETTS LINE *(Springfield)*. *62.2 m.,* State 9 and US 5A.

Via *(sec. a)* Essex, Haddam, Middletown, Cromwell, Rocky Hill, Hartford; *(sec. b)* Windsor, Windsor Locks, Suffield.

Local and interstate busses travel the route between Middletown and the Massachusetts Line. The N.Y., N.H., & H. R.R. parallels the route.

Concrete highway with short stretches of macadamized road.

Excellent accommodations of all types.

Sec. 1. *OLD SAYBROOK to HARTFORD*, 41.2 *m.,* State 9.

FROM Old Saybrook, this route traverses a wooded area to Essex.

From Workers of the Federal Writers' Project, *Connecticut* (Boston: Houghton Mifflin Co., 1938). This project was part of the Works Progress Administration for the State of Connecticut.

Beyond Essex the highway, State 9, leads close to the Connecticut River past very old towns where shad fisherfolk haul their nets as they have for almost three centuries, where shipyards once launched sturdy craft of native oak that sailed for the West Indies with cargoes of onions, staves, cattle and other products from the back country. At the confluence with the Salmon River below Haddam, the Connecticut river flows from the narrows southeast of Middletown. The route follows the broad Main Street of Middletown which appears more like a mid-western town than a New England community. North of Middletown the highway enters a residential and market-gardening area, passing the largest greenhouse and cut-flower plant in central Connecticut at Cromwell. Through the peaceful countryside of Rocky Hill and Wethersfield this route proceeds over straight, good roads to Hartford.

Leaving US 1 (*see Tour* 1) at Old Saybrook this route follows State 9 to the junction with State 9A at 1.7 *m*. . . .

At 2.7 *m*. (R) stands the *William Bower House* (1720). Succeeding generations of carpenters have 'improved' this dwelling until little that is typical of its age remains, with the exception of large flaring corner posts, old ovens both upstairs and down, and the unmistakable proportions of an early house.

At 3.4 *m*., across the meadows, to the right of the highway, is *South Cove*.

At 4 *m*. is the junction with an asphalt road.

Right on this road is the *Pratt Smithy, 0.6 m.* (L) established in 1678, which has been handed down from father to eldest son for eight generations, and is the oldest business in the country to be continuously conducted by the same family. The ivy-clad smithy stands on the site of the early wooden structure that was torn down in the middle of the 18th century. *The Smith's House*, second to the west of it, has an ell said to have been the homestead of the founder, John Pratt (1679). As the town flourished with its Colonial shipbuilding and West Indies trade, the smithy prospered and a larger, more elaborate house was added to the older one, with handsomely paneled rooms, corner cupboards, and well-designed hinges and latches wrought by the smith himself.

Near-by lived Phineas and Abel Pratt, father and son, who invented the first successful machine for cutting comb teeth and who here produced combs in 1799.

ESSEX (alt. 40, town pop. 2777), 0.8 *m*., a river town of old Connecticut, which reached the height of its shipbuilding prosperity about 1840, remains little changed through the years, despite the growing number of summer residents. The houses of sea captains line Main St., leading down to the landing-place. The long rope-walk, once busy outfitting the many vessels built here, has long since gone, but pleasure craft are still built at the boat yards and sail lofts are redolent with aromatic hemp.

Settled in 1690 by residents of Old Saybrook who were attracted to this area by the excellent agricultural prospects offered by the sandy river plain, Essex was incorporated in May, 1852. The 'Oliver Cromwell,' commanded by Commodore Theophilus Morgan, and mounting 24 guns, was launched here in 1775 for the Colony of Connecticut; it was soon transferred to national service. During the War of 1812, Essex's importance as a center of maritime trade marked the town for an attack by the British. Sailing up the river on April 8, 1814, the invaders raided the yards in the Middle and North Coves and burned 40 ships. Among the many ships laid down in local yards, the largest was the 'Middlesex,' 1400 tons, which was launched in 1851.

At the center is the *Osage Inn* (R), a summer hotel, named for the ship 'Osage,' which was burned to the water's edge during the British raid in 1814. For many years the charred ribs of the rotting hull lay near the shore at North Cove. Recently the chestnut timbers were salvaged by residents, who now occasionally offer for sale a chair or some other small piece of furniture made from the old ship.

Ye Old Griswold Inn (R), 48 Main St., 1 *m.,* erected in 1776, has been a tavern for more than 150 years since it was first kept by Ethan Bushnell. Diagonally across the street, surrounded by giant maples and a white picket fence, is the dignified *Captain Lewis House* (1760 or later), a large two-and-a-half-story dwelling with a well-designed entrance. Above the doorway, which is flanked by fluted pilasters and has a delicately leaded fan-light, a Palladian window carries out the lines of the door and entrance frame. In the rear of the house the old fashioned garden of the prosperous sea captain still perfumes the air with a spicy odor of mignonette, rosemary, and lemon verbena.

The last house on the right is the former *Hayden Tavern* (1760). The building, a two-story and basement, white clapboarded house with a broad porch, is now occupied by the Dauntless Club. On the door is a fine old knocker and a hand-wrought latch made many years ago at the Pratt Smithy. Uriah Hayden, original owner of the tavern, one of the leading shipbuilders and merchants of his day, was the builder of the ship 'Oliver Cromwell.' His warehouse on the river, close by, filled with sugar, molasses and tobacco brought in by the West Indian trading vessels, sent goods by river boat and overland carts to inland villages. The old tavern sign, said to have been made in England, bears a picture of a full-rigged ship and the legend '*U* and *A* 1770,' the initials standing for Uriah and Ann Hayden.

The house nearest the river on the right, locally known as *The Beehive,* was built in 1730 by Robert Lay, a prosperous West Indies merchant. The exterior of this old, peaked-roof, two-and-a-half-story house has been altered by renovations, but within are elaborately carved mantels and fine paneling.

Here, along the river front are boat docks, marine railways, and gasoline pumps. In summer, young people, gay in sport clothes, are busy with boats and fishing tackle at the landing place that once swarmed with dark-skinned men of the sea, unloading elephant tusks for the ivory shops and molasses barrels heavy with amber syrup from Cuban cane. The fumes of gasoline replace the pungent tar and the sharp odor of rum; the chug of motorboats takes the place of chanteys and the creak of gear from schooners in the West Indian trade making ready to sail.

Ely's Ferry to Hamburg (*see Tour 1E*) can be boarded at this point; excellent service is maintained by a new gleaming white craft with a tri-colored stripe at the waterline.

At 4.3 *m.* is the red *Factory of the E. E. Dickinson Company* (L), one of the world's largest distillers of witch-hazel, whose bright blue barrel heads are seen in medicinal warehouses around the globe.

At 4.8 *m.* is the junction with State 144; a *Congregational Church* of 1790 stands at the crossroads.

Left on State 144 is the village of IVORYTON (Town of Essex), 1 *m.*, a community that clusters around the former *Comstock-Cheney and Company Plant,* a piano-action concern that at one time used so much ivory that the scrap from the great mills was shipped to Japan to be carved into novelties. This concern did not survive the depression. A recent merger has been completed between this firm and the Pratt Read Company of Deep River. The summer *Repertory Theater* in Ivoryton presents plays with casts of New York professionals.

DEEP RIVER (alt. 60, town pop. 2381) (Town of Saybrook), 7.3 *m.*, was formerly in the township called Old Saybrook and was first settled by white men from the parent Colony between 1663 and 1700. Locally the town is called by the name of its center, Deep River, to avoid confusion with Old Saybrook which is usually called 'Saybrook.' The town had been known at different times as Eight-Mile Meadow and Potopaug Quarter.

In 1809, Phineas Pratt employed about 20 artisans in the production of handmade combs, and the present piano-action *Factory of the Pratt Read Company (open on application at office),* established in 1866, is a direct outgrowth and development of the comb shop. Ivory is imported from Kenya Colony of British East Africa, and from Zanzibar, which produces the best grades of ivory for piano keys. At the factory the ivory is cut from the tusks and is then bleached in glass-covered frames that look very much like ordinary hotbeds. The sunlight bleaching process assures a uniformity of color and texture in the finished keyboard that cannot be secured in any other way. The ivory strips are cemented into place on carefully selected and machined wood, then the completed keyboard is cut into proper shape for piano keys, and the black keys are fitted into place. During the depression this organization made small boats to keep their woodworkers busy. Alive to change in their industry and in styles, the Pratt Read Company is now busy on the production of small piano actions.

At Deep River is the junction (L) with State 80 (*see Tour 1D*).

At 9 *m.*, high on a crag, diagonally across the river (R) is the piled-up masonry of the *William Gillette Castle* (*see Tour 1D*), the model of a Rhineland castle adapted to the Connecticut hills for that whimsical actor (1855–1937). The stone blends well with the browns and grays of the hilltop, and only the skyline silhouette makes the passer-by aware of the great castle standing, sentinel-like, above the waters.

At 9.2 *m.* is the junction with State 148.

1. Left on State 148 is CHESTER (alt. 80, town pop. 1463), 0.9 *m.* Originally the Pattaconk Quarter of Saybrook, the town of Chester was settled about 1690; the parish was named and set aside in 1740, and the town incorporated in 1836. Later a small part of the area was re-annexed to Saybrook

Chester young people introduced a style of singing in church that is mentioned in histories as 'newfangled.' The lack of harmony between these young voices and the voices of their elders is typical of the stormy character of the entire parish.

Russell Jennings, an early preacher (1800), invented the first extension bit in America and laid the foundation for a business that still makes bits, that find a ready market anywhere in the world. Despairing of making an impression on the hardheaded, quarrelsome churchfolk of his parish, the Rev. Mr. Jennings turned inventor with more satisfactory results.

Round brushes are also made in Chester; a factory on the brook turns out tool handles of native hickory and ash, and another mill produces manicure sets of gaudy hues and odd shapes. Needles and novelties are made in the town, as are bright wire goods and many hundred gross of bits annually; nail sets and augers are forged and packed along Deep Hollow Brook that drains Hoophole Hill, Hearse House Hill, and Flute Hill.

Shipbuilding once flourished here. Governor Winthrop obtained a water-power right in the area and precipitated the first of several boundary disputes between Chester and the neighboring parishes and towns. At one time large numbers of sheep were raised here and often came during services to the square in front of the church where they set up such a bleating that men had to drive them off.

The marshes blaze with color and resound to the boom of the duck hunter's gun; a fish peddler hawks 'Shad, fresh shad!' as a fat tomcat follows his wagon along the quiet Main Street and purrs with anticipation.

Granite was an important building stone in Chester. The most conspicuous building at the center is the *Old Stone Store* (R), built about 1809, now a beer parlor. The building has fluted stone pillars and more the appearance of a church or a bank than a tavern. The *Stone Hotel* (R) was built in the same year. Two old millstones are used as the steps of the *Chester Savings Bank* (R).

2. Right at the junction with 148 to the old *Chester Ferry* (*see Side Trip from Tour 1D*) which still crosses the river for customers at the signal of a motorist's horn (7 A.M. *to* 7 P.M.; 25¢ *for car and driver,* 5¢ *each additional passenger*).

From 10.6 *m.* to 11.3 *m.* the highway travels close to the river with many views of the broad stream and the rolling wooded ridges along its eastern bank.

At 11.6 *m.* is the junction with State 82 (*see Tour 1D*) in the tiny side-of-the-road settlement of TYLERVILLE (Town of Haddam).

At 12.6 *m.* is a junction with a dirt road.

Right on this road to the *Adventist Camp Ground,* 0.8 *m.,* a settlement of cottages grouped on the bank of the Connecticut River.

At 13 *m.* there are beautiful views across the Connecticut River (R) to the mouth of the Salmon River, which flows into the larger stream around the end of Thirty Mile Island. Shad run up Salmon River to the first dam, where they are taken with flies. Here the State maintains a hatchery.

At 14.2 *m.* State 9 passes through SHAILERVILLE, a rather drab little village, where the 'New Lights,' or 'Separatists,' as they were first termed, formed the *Baptist Church* (R) of Shailerville. This section was formerly the 'Lower Plantation' of the 'The Plantation of Thirty-Mile Island,' as Haddam was known in the older records. The town mill was once operated here in a gloomy dell beside a stream.

HADDAM (alt. 200, town pop. 1755), 15.2 *m.,* chief center of the only town in the State bisected by the Connecticut River, was, according to local tradition, purchased from the Indians for thirty coats. Surrounded by wooded hills, the quiet village, back from the river front, still retains an atmosphere of early fishing and seafaring days. Nets drying in the sun and signs reading, 'Shad for sale,' are reminders of the days when the village was the center of extensive salmon and shad fisheries. Shad, salted, smoked, pickled and served fresh, was a staple food in this region. Farmhands tiring of the diet, often specified in their contracts that shad was not to be served to them more than five times per week. In years when the shad run was especially large, Connecticut roads were often crowded with fish peddlers' carts, hurrying to their home towns where they made the welkin ring with blasts on their tin horns and shouts of 'Fresh shad for sale.'

Shad were often used for fertilizer; many a good crop was raised as a result of 'a fish in every hill of corn,' a practice learned from the Indians. The present-day run of shad is not very large, although limits placed on the catch may increase the future haul.

According to a legend of the local Indians the Shad Spirit yearly led the shad from the Gulf of Mexico to the Connecticut River.

The AMC Guide

CANOE GUIDEBOOK COMMITTEE, APPALACHIAN MOUNTAIN CLUB

THE CONNECTICUT LAKES. From its source at Fourth Lake, the Connecticut is a tiny trout brook to Third Lake. From Third Lake to Second Lake it is still too small and steep to canoe, and from Second to First Lake it is too difficult to canoe. Although both Second and Third lakes offer pleasant canoeing, fishing, swimming, and other water sports, the canoeist wishing to run the river will probably start at the head of First Lake. A side road leading from Rte 3 to Mettaluk Point offers easy access to that end of the lake. There is a launching area at the foot of the lake near the dam. Below First Lake the stream becomes canoeable for the first time, but as the level of First Lake is controlled by a dam there is apt to be insufficient water unless some is being let through for power. Water releases are, however, posted daily at the dam. Below the dam the

From *The AMC New England Canoeing Guide* (Boston: Appalachian Mountain Club Books, 1968).

river is very rough and steep for 1 mi., then easier rapids follow for 1/2 mi. to the entrance of Perry Stream *(q.v.)* on the right. These easy rapids continue another 1 mi. to Lake Francis, which is an artificial lake over what was formerly a less attractive stretch of river through farm lands. Below the Lake Francis dam there is less than 1 mi. of rapid river to the bridge and dam at Pittsburg, where one must take out. CAUTION: Take out above the dam as there is an impassable gorge for 1 1/2 mi. below to a covered bridge. It is possible to line down this gorge in low water, but if a car is available it is much easier to carry and one must carry at medium to high water.

Although the river itself through the Connecticut Lakes offers little to the canoeist, all the lakes except Fourth Lake are accessible by car and are pleasant for both paddling and sailing.

Pittsburg to West Stewartstown, 9 mi. Put in at the covered bridge 1 1/2 mi. downstream from Pittsburg, below the impassable gorge. The river is rapid but easily passable all the way to Beecher Falls. In 2 mi. the mouth of Indian Stream *(q.v.)* is passed on the right and nearby is the Indian Stream School camping area. Another 2 mi. farther down is the New Hampshire-Vermont boundary marker. Below this point the river becomes the boundary between the two states. It is another 3 mi. to the mouth of Halls Stream *(q.v.)* which enters on the right after forming a long portion of the Canada-United States boundary farther north. It is only a short distance to Beecher Falls, where there is a sharp rapid below the green steel bridge. This rapid should be scouted, and the best vantage point for this is the left bank. If a portage is necessary, the carry can be made on the right bank. There then follow 1 1/2 mi. of easy rapids to West Stewartstown and Canaan, where there is a carry of nearly 1/2 mi. around the dam and mill on the west side of the river.

West Stewartstown to North Stratford, 26 mi. The river now becomes mostly smooth, winding through open pasture lands. It is 10 mi. to the bridge at Colebrook, 1/2 mi. above which the Mohawk River *(q.v.)* enters on the left. There are fine views of Monadnock Mountain in Vermont along here. The first 2 mi. are smooth and then the current quickens for the following 2 mi. with some riffles. Shortly above Lemington, there is a sharp bend and a narrow chute of 100 yds. easily passable at most water stages. In another 1 mi. the town of Lemington, Vermont is passed and the Lemington-Columbia bridge reached. The next 3 mi. are mostly smooth and are followed by 2 mi. of fast water. In this stretch about 2 1/2 mi. above the old Lyman Dam, there is located the Countryside Campgrounds in Columbia, N.H. on the left bank. Above the former Lyman Falls Dam there are some log cribs in the center of the river. This section should be examined before running. Most canoeists will probably choose the Vermont side as easier, but at low water a portion may have to be carried because of the remains of the dam and rocks. One can also run close to the New Hampshire side but should watch carefully the section below, where the dam was formerly located as there are a number of large boulders and rocks in the river and the channel is difficult to find. At low water it may be necessary to line down here. There are moderate rapids for the 3 mi. to North Stratford, where just below the bridge the Nulhegan River *(q.v.)* enters on the right.

North Stratford to Guildhall, 25 mi. About 1 mi. below North Stratford is the pitch known as the Horse Race, sporty but not difficult. The river is placid with wide meanders from here to the dam at Guildhall. It is 4 mi. to Stratford Center opposite which Paul Stream *(q.v.)* enters on the Vermont side, and another 6 mi. to the bridge at Stratford. It is then 11 mi. with wide meanders on a flat river plain with fine views of the mountains to the confluence with the Upper Ammonoosuc River *(q.v.)* at Groveton, where the river becomes badly polluted by the paper mill. Only 3 mi. farther on, the bridge and dam at Guildhall is reached. Although this dam, which is sometimes known as the Northumberland or Wyoming Dam, is 12 ft. high, it has been run by canoe at high water. As water is spilled over the top at all times this dam should not be approached too closely without checking, especially at high water when one might easily be inadvertently swept over. The portage trail is on the Vermont side just to the right of the power house, but less experienced canoeists may prefer to take out farther upstream to avoid the risk of being swept over.

Guildhall to Gilman, 23 mi. The placid water continues for the next 23 mi. to the dam at Gilman, but the river is less pleasant paddling because of the pollution from the pulp mills at Groveton. It is 10 mi. to Lancaster, where the Israel River *(q.v.)* enters 1/2 mi. below the bridge, near which is located on the left bank Treffrey's Campgrounds with good facilities. There follow 7 mi. of winding river to the bridge at South Lancaster and another 3 mi. to the next bridge at South Lunenburg, where the Johns River *(q.v.)* enters on the left. About 1/4 mi. below the R.R. bridge one should watch carefully for large boulders just beneath the surface, which could easily overturn a laden canoe. From there it is only 3 mi. more to the dam and bridge at Gilman. One can easily take out on the New Hampshire side at the end of the boom above the dam. If prior arrangements are made with the Gilman Paper Co., a vehicle can sometimes be made available for the carry to the gravel pit on the Vermont side below the bridge.

Gilman to East Ryegate, 30 mi. The beautiful Fifteen-mile Falls section of the river formerly began at Gilman, but these fine rapids, the best on the river, are now completely inundated by the Moore Reservoir and the Comerford Reservoir, although when the former is low there are still a 1/4 to 1/2 mi. or more of fast water with rocks and boulders. The New England Power Company, which operates these two dams and the McIndoe Falls Dam below, has provided a number of boat launching and picnic areas on the reservoirs, but no overnight camping is allowed at these points. One can put in at Gilman on the Vermont side jut below the bridge. From here to the Moore Dam are 12 mi. of paddling, mostly lake travel on the reservoir, although when the water level is low there may be as much as 1/2 mi. or more of easy rapids. Care should be observed, however, if the water volume is large as the waves can be high. Once on the reservoir the going is very pleasant but a head wind can make progress a strenuous affair. It is, therefore, usually best to start this section early in the morning before the wind rises. There are three boat launching and picnic areas on the south shore of the reservoir and one on the north bank in Waterford near the dam. The carry at the Moore Dam is on the Vermont side, about 1/2 mi. long and well marked by signs. The bank at the put-in place is somewhat unstable so that care should be taken.

As the backwater from the Comerford Dam comes practically to the Moore Dam, the 7 mi. between the dams is practically all lake paddling. There is a boat launching and picnic area just below the Rte 18 bridge on the New Hampshire side and another one on the Vermont side not far above the dam. The carry at the Comerford Dam is on the New Hampshire side, about 1/2 mi. long, and marked by signs.

The 7 mi. from the Comerford Dam to the McIndoe Falls Dam can be very interesting. If the Comerford Dam is discharging water the current will be swift and the paddling easy although there are some large boulders about 1 mi. below the dam which present hazards to navigation. In another 1 mi. the Passumpsic River *(q.v.)* enters on the right and the river turns to a southerly course. The next 5 mi. are though a narrow wooded valley with high hills in either side most of the way. The portage at the McIndoe Falls Dam, on the New Hampshire side, is easy, about 200 yds. long, and well marked.

The narrow wooded valley continues for the next 4 mi. to the Ryegate Paper Company's dam at East Ryegate. This 15-ft. high dam should be approached with caution as water is often spilled over the top. It is just below a left bend in the river and as the carry is on the New Hampshire side it is best to approach it along this bank. Several portage routes are available varying from a few hundred feet if the current is slow to several hundred yards if the current is fast and one cannot approach the dam closely.

East Ryegate to Hanover, 51 mi. This is one of the more interesting and picturesque sections of the river and one on which one will find a certain amount of canoeing and boating, especially in the lower portion. Below the dam at East Ryegate there is some fast water and the best channel is usually on the New Hampshire side. It is 4 m. to Wells River-Woodsville, where the Ammonoosuc River *(q.v.)* enters on the left and 1/4 mi. below the Wells River *(q.v.)* enters on the right just below the Rte 302 and railroad bridges. There is a short but easy rip just below these bridges, then 10 mi. of shallow, winding river to the bridge at Newbury and another 2 mi. more to the next bridge at South Newbury. The valley has now become wider with farm lands in the level areas and views of the mountains appear in the background. The current now begins to slacken as the water backed up by the Wilder Dam 37 mi. below is reached. This section is now known as Wilder Lake and provided with boat launching ramps and picnic areas. There is little perceptible widening of the river for many miles. It is 6 mi. to Bradford and the entrance of the Waits River *(q.v.)* on the right bank. In another 1 mi. one passes under the Rte 25 bridge and in 4 mi. more the bridge from Fairlee to Orford. Here it is that Samuel Morey tested his steam propelled vessel in 1792–3. There are two private campgrounds in this section: one at Bugs Island, Piermont, N.H. and another 2 mi. below at Bradford, Vt. Both are owned by Lloyd Bugbee of Lower Plains, Vermont, from whom permission to use them should be obtained. At Orford, N.H., there is a municipal boat-launching area where one can camp with the permission of the selectmen. It is then 6 mi. to the next bridge at North Thetford and 2 mi. more to that at East Thetford. By now the river is obviously becoming wider. Here on the New Hampshire side, in Lyme, are the River Landing Campsites operated by Ralph Fisher of Lyme, N.H., with all kinds of supplies including rental canoes. In 5 mi. one passes the mouth of the Ompompanoosuc River *(q.v.)* on the right and in another 5 mi. the bridge at Hanover, below which it is only 2 mi. to the dam at Wilder. This whole section has considerable boating and is used by the Dartmouth College crews for practice.

The cruise from Hanover, New Hampshire, to Long Island Sound is called the Ledyard Cruise after the trip made by John Ledyard in 1772, when as a freshman at Dartmouth, he hewed a canoe from a large pine and paddled down the Connecticut to Hartford. The voyage is now made annually by Dartmouth students, principally members of the Ledyard Canoe Club, a part of the Dartmouth Outing Club, in April, a poor time to be on the river unless speed is the primary consideration. Recently other college teams have been making the cruise, adding an element of competition. The present record is 33 hours, 50 minutes, set in 1960 by Pete Knight and John Fairbank.

Roadside Geology

BRADFORD B. VAN DIVER

THE CONNECTICUT VALLEY MARKS an important plate tectonic boundary as well as the political boundary between Vermont and New Hampshire. It also contains a wealth of depositional and erosional features related to Wisconsin glacial recession. The Connecticut Valley is historically important as a corridor for settlement of New England, and it is one of the most beautiful regions of the northeast.

Between the Massachusetts border and Lancaster, New Hampshire, the river follows the western margin of the collapsed Bronson Hill island arc complex, that formed in the early stages of the Taconian mountain-building cycle and later collided with the continent. The river thus separates two radically different terrains, the ancient basement and younger metasedimentary cover of ancestral North America on the west and island arc on the east. If that interpretation is correct, much or all of New Hampshire east of the narrow arc complex is "exotic" terrain, formerly a piece of Africa or Europe.

South of the border in Massachusetts the river occupies a somewhat different bedrock environment where it meanders over the floor of the Connecticut Valley basin. This is one of many linear fault-block basins

From © Bradford B. Van Diver. *Roadside Geology of Vermont and New Hampshire.* 1987. Missoula, Montana: Mountain Press Publishing Co.

near the east coast of North America that contain distinctive red sediments and basalt lava flows of Triassic-Jurassic age. All of the basins are products of crustal stretching that began about 200 million years ago and eventually led to the separation of the Americas from Eurasia and Africa, with the opening of the Atlantic Ocean basin. This happened more than 200 million years after the collapse of the island arc that became the Bronson Hill complex.

Most of what we know today as the Connecticut Valley was here before Wisconsin glaciation. Ice crowded into the valley and moved southward along it, gouging it deeper and wider. As the glacier finally melted, the valley held a lake, called Lake Hitchcock, that gradually lengthened upvalley as the ice receded northward and at one point stretched from Middletown, Connecticut, to the Canadian border. Kame terraces formed as "strip deltas" alongside the ice as it retreated.

Copious quantities of sediments released from the melting glacier and washed from the barren lands newly freed of ice piled up under water on the valley floor. The deposits include the famous varved clays that have yielded so much information on the timing of glacial recession from this region. Each lamination in the varved clays grades from light to dark gray upward and represents one year's accumulation. The lighter material is rock flour released from the melting ice during the summer; the darker, thinner layers built up under the lake ice in winter.

Studies of the Connecticut Valley varves by Ernst Antevs (1922) revealed that it took 4300 years for the Wisconsin ice front to recede from Middletown, Connecticut, to St. Johnsbury, Vermont, a distance of about 200 miles and an average recessional rate of about 245 feet per year. Much glacial study in New England has focused on varved clay because there are so few moraines to mark various stands of the ice terminus.

Working out the timing by Antevs's method assumes first that varves were constantly being formed as the ice front moved northward. Thus, the earliest varves formed in the south, while the land to the north was still under ice. Secondly, it assumes that varves formed in the same sequence of years can be matched from one exposure to another. Only in this way would it be possible to total up the years involved because the varved records are everywhere only fragmental. The method also assumes that the varves would everywhere be thicker in warm years when more rock flour sediment would be shed from the melting ice. Individual varves, thick or thin, could not, by themselves, be matched from place to place; but records showing thickness fluctuations over scores of years could be. So Antevs simply made graphical records of each exposure, showing varve thicknesses measured one by one from the base to the top of each exposed section. Then he placed pairs of graphs side by side, and shifted them until he found matching segments. When records overlapped or correlated only partially, the earlier years of one and later years of the other could be added on to the overlapping part. The lowest varve at a particular site marks the first year of accumulation after the site was freed of ice. By repeated correlations, Antevs was able to construct a continuous record.

Most rivers in the glaciated regions of North America have eroded their channels deeper during postglacial time. The enormous mass of the glacier deeply depressed the land, but it sprang back up after the ice melted, thus causing the rivers to cut downward. The amount of rebound increased northward where the ice was thickest, and it was minimal at the southernmost stand of the glacier margin, where the ice was thinnest. The plain of Lake Hitchcock has been particularly useful in charting the rebound in Vermont and New Hampshire. The method involves measuring the present altitudes of numerous preserved Hitchcock shoreline features such as beaches, sand bars, and wavecut benches, all of which formed at the same level. When these were graphed according to elevation with the proper horizontal spacing between them, a profile of a tilted lake plain emerged, in which the northern end at the Canadian border is now 700 feet higher than the southern end at the Massachusetts border.

The river cut into the valley fill during the rebound, creating river terraces as it meandered back and forth, and exposing cross sections of varved clays and other valley-fill sediments. The flat-topped terraces are now visible in many parts of the valley, although vegetation makes many of them difficult to identify.

Between the Massachusetts border and Brattleboro (8 miles), several roadcuts expose the Devonian Littleton formation. The rocks are generally rather dark gray phyllites with lustrous cleavage surfaces formed by low-grade metamorphism of shales with thin interlayers of white quartzite formed from sandstone. The Connecticut River in this section is a few miles to the east and out of view.

North of Brattleboro, the highway remains close enough to the river for more than 100 miles to provide many good views of the valley. The valley floor at river level is locally quite broad and everywhere very flat. This is the flood plain of the modern river on which it continually meanders back and forth. It is also working downward into the valley fill, although the rate of downcutting is very slow. As the river works its way deeper, the active floodplain will be carved at an ever lower level, but some of the current floodplain may survive the erosion as a terrace. This has been going on for thousands of years, since some time after Lake Hitchcock was drained; and that's why there are now river terraces at several levels on the valley sides in addition to the surviving kame terracing above them. The road lies atop the terraces in many places; and many villages, including Brattleboro, are built on them, or on the floodplain. It will take a little practice to recognize the terraces. They are most conspicuous where they have been cleared for cultivation. The higher ones, being older, are often more deeply dissected by tributary streams than the lower ones.

As you drive this route, note that most of the small tributary streams are entrenched into narrow, steep-sided valleys. This is also a product of the post-glacial downcutting of the main stream. In general, the Connecticut River has controlled the leveling of the land because it carries the most water; and is thus the base level for regional erosion. The tributaries keep the downward pace, but have so little energy to cut sideways that the results are narrow valleys. A good example is Mill Brook by exit 4 to Putney; but there are many more. The entrenched character is not always obvious close to the master river; you need to look up the valley where the streams have cut deeply into bedrock, in some places carving narrow gorges. Shorelines of glacial Lake Hitchcock extend far up into West River valley which the highway crosses by exit 3 north of Brattleboro.

A good exposure of varved clay at Putney, is in the banks of the small creek that intersects US 5 by the entrance to Interstate 91. This clay so far from and so high above the modern river gives a good impression of the large size of Lake Hitchcock.

At Putney (exit 4), you cross the axis of an anticlinal fold with roadcuts exposing the Ordovician slates and phyllites of its core. The rocks resemble those of the Littleton formation, but lack the white quartzite interlayers. Between Putney and Bellows Falls (exit 5—10 miles) are cuts in gently dipping, or sloping, layers of slate and phyllite near the crest of a large anticlinal fold that trends from north to south. Elsewhere the layers of the fold limbs are steeply inclined. Actually, this fold is only a wrinkle on the much larger Brattleboro syncline. The syncline consists of tightly folded strata between the collapsed Bronson Hill island arc complex, and the domes of eastern Vermont, upfolds shaped like overturned bowls. This, in turn, is only a small part of the much larger Connecticut Valley-Gaspe syncline that extends into Canada. Simply put, the rocks of the Brattleboro syncline were caught in the vice [*sic*] between the great masses of the ancestral continent and the island arc as the proto-Atlantic basin closed. The constriction is narrowest between Putney and Ascutney (exit 8—34 miles), where the Athens dome on the south, and the Chester dome on the north, each cored with Precambrian basement rocks, lie only 5–10 miles west of the river. Note the roadcuts in this section display somewhat more severe deformation.

Mount Ascutney, at 3144 feet with the tower on top, is the prominent summit visible from many points between Bellows Falls (exit 4) and Pompanoosuc (8 miles north of White River Junction exit 12), a distance of 50 miles. The highway skirts the base of the mountain just north of Ascutney (exit 8). A paved road in Mount Ascutney State Park leads to the summit and provides scenic views of the surrounding country, including the Connecticut Valley. The mountain is an isolated peak that stands nearly 2000 feet above the surrounding terrain, and is held up by a small, isolated igneous pluton of the White Mountain magma series. Practically all of the other members of this series are in the White Mountains of New Hampshire. Here the rocks are of variable composition, ranging from dark gabbros to pale granites. The relatively small Cuttingsville pluton, which intrudes the Precambrian core of the Green Mountains 20 miles west of Mount Ascutney, is another small member of the White Mountain series exposed in Vermont.

The village of Windsor, on a river terrace 5 miles north of Ascutney, is called the birthplace of Vermont. The state constitution was signed there on July 8, 1777. Meetings of the General Assembly were held there until Montpelier was established as the permanent capital in 1805.

Between Ascutney and White River Junction (18 miles) are many large roadcuts in phyllites and mica schists of the Devonian Gile Mountain formation, most of them with nearly vertical lustrous cleavage. The North Hartland Dam on the Ottauquechee River is visible west of the highway near White River Junction. This section of the Connecticut Valley is particularly broad, well-terraced, and dotted with many, very large sand and gravel quarries. Erosion of one 2-mile long segment of terrace near Hartland left a ridge of sand and gravel that rises 60–80 feet above the highway and separates it from the river.

Chapter 8

ON THE RIVER

One of the main vacationers was Albert Einstein, who visited Old Lyme in 1935. Einstein, having sailed on a small inland lake near Berlin, decided to rent a Cape Cod Knockabout to sail on the river. Unfamiliar with the intricate currents and sandbars, he spent more time aground than afloat. The New London Day wrote about his adventure with the headline "Einstein's Miscalculation Leaves Him Stuck On Bar of Lower Connecticut River!"
—Edmund Delaney in *The Connecticut River*

Anyone who knows the Connecticut intimately knows it's two very distinct rivers, one seen from above, another experienced when you're actually on it or in it. Memoirs of the river refer again and again to the surprising difference that comes from being on the river, the solitude, the secret quality—starting back in the nineteenth century when people began viewing the river, not just as a partner in work, but as a resort for their leisure hours. Partly this comes from topography—the Connecticut is steep banked almost all the way along its course, so, when you're on the river, you feel protected and enclosed by a verdant tunnel—but it also speaks volumes about the way people have neglected the river over the years. When they venture out onto it on a boat, they immediately fall head over heels in love with a beauty they didn't suspect was there.

Lyman S. Hayes shows that the river was the locus of fun and games, even as early as 1859. The next selection is by John Boyle O'Reilly, a charming Fenian who wrote frequently of American rivers; his work was known and admired by Walt Whitman, among others. This account of a Connecticut River canoe trip dates from the late nineteenth century.

The Voyage of the Ant is one of my personal favorites. James Dina, who as a young man became fascinated by the river he lived beside, decided not only to build a birch bark canoe, not only to build it using the tools and methods available to the Indians, but to take his creation, The Ant, all the way up the headwaters, or at least to the spot where the river becomes so shallow he had to walk on foot to the source.

Oliver Allyn headed in the opposite direction with his homemade sailboat, sailing downstream from Hartford toward the mouth; as with many boaters, he finds beauty, unexpected beauty, even in the heart of the river's busiest stretches.

The Early Boat Clubs

LYMAN S. HAYES

IN 1859 BOTH BRATTLEBORO and Bellows Falls had active boat clubs that had much enjoyment from their experiences on the water. In May of that year the Green Mountain Boat Club of Brattleboro made an excursion up the river to Bellows Falls. They started from there at 5 o'clock in the morning and landed at the old canal locks here about one in the afternoon, having rowed about 27 miles. A number of Bellows Falls citizens dined with them here at the old Bellows Falls Stage House, the party comprising some of the most prominent citizens of both villages.

Each of the Brattleboro men wore a sailor's shirt neatly made of blue flannel. Their standard colors, then recently presented to them by the ladies of Brattleboro, were of tasty design and made quite a show as the party came up from the river. The boat was named "Swift Water" and was 42 feet in length. . . . They started on their return trip a little past 4 o'clock, giving three cheers for Bellows Falls, which was immediately responded to by a large number of our citizens who lined the shore.

During that season the Swift Water Boat Club was challenged by the Wantastiquet Boat Club, also of Brattleboro, for a boat race to Bellows

From Lyman S. Hayes, *The Connecticut River Valley* (Rutland, Vt.: The Tuttle Co., 1929).

Falls for a purse of $400, each party to contribute $200 of it, and the whole to go to the successful boat. Considerable discussion arose over the terms and conditions of the challenge. Until the building of the Vernon dam, Bellows Falls had the advantage of Brattleboro in the matter of about 15 miles of comparatively still water above the dam here, but at the present time the facilities for this sport are about equal.

In the year 1909, and for several years before and after, motor boating was enjoyed here to a great extent, there being that year 47 such craft in active commission, 12 new power boats having been put on the river that season. A large boat club was enjoying the river here and they had a well equipped club house just above the Vermont end of the steel arch bridge, with a large hall for dancing, and the basement was used to store the boats. Each evening, and Sundays, the river was alive with boats and throngs of people watched them from the shores and the bridge. The interest has gradually waned, until for the last few years only one or two pleasure boats plow the waters, and the same is true at Brattleboro.

The river falls 52 feet here where it passes from the north to the south end of the village. Because of the rapidity of the current, and the jagged rocks, it is often said no boat ever successfully passed through these falls, but that statement is erroneous. August 11, 1876, a party of river-men who were handling one of the large drives of Ross & Leavitt's logs then passing down the river, did the stunt. Five different boats passed through the entire length of the falls, each manned by two men. The men in boat No. 1 were Henry Davis and William Doane; No. 2, Gorham Spencer and Frank Dudley; No. 3, Ben Mitchell, John Murphy; No. 4, Frank Mohawk, Joseph Swartson; No. 5, Henry Wadleigh and John Murphy. The last boat went down twice, and Henry Davis did the same. Three of the boats dipped some water, but two went over dry. Each man handled one oar, guiding the boat from both the prow and stern. The water was very low at the time and the river-men became daring and conquered.

A few of the present residents remember the incident of Capt. Paul Boyton passing through the falls and under the toll bridge in his rubber floating suit. He was on a pleasure trip down the Connecticut and arrived at the dam just at night, October 29, 1879. During the evening it became known that he would go through the falls the next morning and it was estimated that a crowd of 2000 people gathered to watch the feat. So many occupied vantage places on the toll bridge that fears were entertained for its safety and some were ordered off. The water was somewhat high and rushed through the gorge with mighty force.

He went into the water just below the dam and with his paddle struck out for the center of the current, being carried swiftly down. He was caught a number of times in the eddies and carried round and round, giving him a hard pull to get out into the current. When at last he went through the place where the water rushes with the greatest force, just above the Fitchburg bridge, he went out of sight and did not appear seemingly for some minutes; the hair of the spectators stood on end with horror.

He, however, soon appeared a long distance down the river and came out of the water from the eddy below. At Town's hotel that evening in discussing the day's experience he stated that it was the worst in his life, and that nothing would ever tempt him to try these falls again. He said the water bore him down with a terrible weight to the bottom of the channel, and for a few moments he confidently expected it would hold him there to his death.

Canoeing circa 1888

JOHN BOYLE O'REILLY

SO WE TOOK OUR little boat farther up, till we came to a favorable spot for launching, and there we slid her into the river from a marvelous white sandbank, which ran into the deep, slow stream, and from which we took our first glorious "header" into the Connecticut.

All along the river, down to Middletown, hundreds of miles away, we found, at intervals, this remarkable kind of sandbank on which one may take a race, and dive directly into deep water. And yet the bank is not straight, under water, but a rapid incline, easy and pleasant for landing.

What need of details? Miles in a voyage are of no more account than years in a life: they may be filled with commonplace. Men live by events, and so they paddle.

We had ten, fifteen, twenty days ahead, if necessary! We were rich in this. Hundreds of miles of beautiful water, splendid days, a new moon, a well-stored locker, and a boat that danced under us like a duck! So we started, dripping from the embrace of the sweet water.

From John Boyle O'Reilly, *Athletics and Manly Sports* (Boston: Ticknor & Fields, 1890).

We paddled about fifteen miles, when we saw a tempting nook, a pine grove above a sandbank, with a dashing stream; and, not far withdrawn, a comfortable farmhouse, where we might buy milk and eggs and bread. As we had started late, we landed for the night, and one set off for the farmhouse, while the other made ready for supper.

We had a copious larder. We carried too many things, observers said. So we did; but we both liked many things when we stopped for meals. Our table was the sandbank, with a rubber blanket spread. Olives, cheese, sardines, bacon, Liebig's extract of beef—these looked well. Then came the farm supplies—quarts of rich milk, a dozen eggs, two loaves of bread, and a lot of cooked green peas, thrown in by the farmer's wife; a bottle of good claret. What a dinner and supper in one! Then coffee, then a cigar, then the philosophies—quiet talk as we sat looking at the river with the darkness coming down, the frogs sounding resonant notes over on the New Hampshire side, and the white light of the young moon trembling up over the dark pine hills. Then we wrapped ourselves in our blankets, and slept till morning.

We had no tent; we two had discovered that we needed no tent in July or August, though we do not advise others to follow our example. Fortunately for us, we wake in the early morning with the same feeling of refreshment—our lungs full of the delicious air, and our faces wet with dew. On this first morning, I leaped up at sunrise, shouting, "This the way Nature meant men to live and sleep and wake!"

I shall never forget that first glorious morning. For an hour before rising, I had lain awake looking out at the river, and listening to the strange country sounds around me. All over the grass and low bushes the spider's webs were stretched, glistening with dew. What a wonderful night's industry! Those webs were nearly all, or quite all, new. The little night toilers had woven them over our olive bottle, over the gun, over ourselves. The field above us was white as snow with this incomparable cloth-of-silver.

As I lay and looked at one of those webs close to my face, I saw a strange thing. A little gray-and-black spider ran up a tall grass blade, rested a moment, and then ran off, through empty air, to another blade, six inches off. I looked closer; surely he must have a fine line stretched between those points, I thought. No; the closest scrutiny could find none. I watched him; he was soon off again, straight for another point, a foot above the ground, running on clear space, and turning down and hanging to it, like a monkey, but still going ahead. I called Guiteras, and he came and saw and examined, and smiled in his wise way when he doesn't know. We could not see the little fellow's cable, or railway, or bridge. He was as much finer than we as we are finer than mastodons.

And the birds, in that first rich morning speech of theirs, full of soft, bubbling joy, not singing, but softly and almost silently overflowing. Two little fellows flew rapidly down to a twig near us, and began bubble-bubbling as if in a great flutter and hurry; and immediately they flew far and high, as for a long journey; at which my philosophic friend moralized:

"Those little fellows are like some canoeists who wake up, and don't wait for breakfast; but bubble-bubble, hurry-hurry, get-afloat, we-have-a-long-way-to-go! Now, we don't do that."

Indeed, we do not. This is what we do. We light our little alcohol stove, and boil two quarts of the rich milk, into which we put our prepared coffee (Sanford's—a great and precious compound, which we heartily recommend to all men fond of outing). Then we plunge into the river for a good swim, getting the first of the sun as he comes over the hill. The sandbank is soft to land on; and so up we go to the meadow above, for a four-round bout with boxing gloves; and, when this is done, we are in good trim for breakfast.

Here let me say that we were never sorry when we selected a white sandbank or a pine grove to sleep in; the latter to be preferred, on account of the soft pine needles, the healthy fragrance, and the absence of mosquitoes. If the sandbank is chosen, first scoop out a hollow for the hips and shoulders; spread the rubber blanket, and then the woollen blanket; turn the latter bag-like up from the feet, and draw the rubber over all. Then your couch is as soft as a feather bed, and a hundred times healthier.

After breakfast, two hours of easy paddling, during which we keep the gun ready, and usually kill about a half dozen birds to enrich our dinner. Then follow two hours of hard paddling, which prepares us for dinner and a rest. After this, two hours of easy paddling, and two hours of hard paddling. Then supper; after which, a slow and easy, meditative paddle in search of pine grove or sandbank. This was our regular daily program, and its worth was shown by our excellent condition when we reached the end of the river.

Events by the way—how shall I recall them, crowded as they are? We were upset: it was in this way. We had carried our boat round a fall, where the logs ran so furiously that nothing else had a chance to run. At about eight o'clock in the evening we floated her, below the falls, intending just to paddle down till we found a place to sleep. We did not know, from the dusk, that the rapids extended for miles below the falls. We soon found the water extremely strong and swift, full of eddies and whirls, and mixed up with tumbling and pushing logs. It was the ugliest race we had seen or did see on all the river. We swept down like an arrow for about half a mile, and then a thunderstorm of extraordinary violence and continuity burst. The night became pitch dark. We could only see the black river, running like a wolf at the gunwale, and the lightning zigzagging the night above. Suddenly we realized that the logs on our left were stationary, while those in the stream on our right were tearing down like battering rams. So long as you go with the logs they are gentle as friendly savages, just rubbing you softly like living things, and movable with a finger. But get fast, and let them come down on you, and the ribs of a boat will smash like a matchbox under their brutal drive and the jagged fibers of their tapered butt ends. The logs on our left were stationary; but the rapid water boiled up between them. We ran swiftly along two great logs—then suddenly stopped. An immense log had been forced up and across its fellows, and as its farther end was driven swiftly forward, its heavy butt came straight for the canoe. Dr. Guiteras got the first blow, on the head and shoulder, which rather keeled us. Then the log took me fairly on the chest, and over and down we went. For some seconds, Guiteras's feet having got fast somehow in the boat forward, he was in a bad way; but he soon kicked free, and we swam at our ease with the boat down the river. . . .

As we came down the river one thing was noticeable and very enjoyable—the courtesy and kindness of every one on the banks. At Brattleboro we found two gentlemen who owned canoes . . . who lent us a pair of single paddles, and who were otherwise exceedingly kind.

At Springfield we stopped long enough for me to lecture in the evening (by previous arrangement). There was a large audience, and Guiteras sat on the platform, brown as an Indian, and fell asleep. Fortunately he was shielded by a large tropical plant. . . .

We had been told that the beauty of the Connecticut ended at Springfield; but it is not so. Indeed, one of the loveliest stretches lies between Hartford and Middletown, though the river under Mt. Tom and Mt. Holyoke is surpassingly beautiful. I never saw more delightful scenery than in the river valley just above and below Northampton. . . .

From Hartford to Middletown is one of the finest stretches of the Connecticut, and it is by no means low-banked or monotonous. One of the peculiarities of the river is that it is almost as wide and apparently as deep at Hanover as in this latest reach.

It is not necessary to go a great distance up the Connecticut to find splendid canoeing water. If one had only a week's time, and entered the river at Brattleboro, or below Turner's Falls, he would find enough beauty to remember for a lifetime.

The distances on the river appear to be quite unknown to residents on the banks, who evidently judge by road measurement. We found, in most cases, that the river distance was at least a third to a half longer than the road.

One of our rarest pleasures came from paddling for a few miles up the smaller rivers that run into the Connecticut. They are invariably beautiful, and the smaller ones are indescribable as fairyland.

One stream, particularly (I think it is a short distance below White River Junction, on the New Hampshire side), called Bromidon, was, in all respects, an ideal brook. It had the merriest voice; the brownest and most sun-flecked shallows; the darkest little nooks of deep, leafy pools; the most happy-looking, creeper-covered homesteads on its banks. We could hardly paddle into it, it was so shallow; or out of it, it was so beautiful. Guiteras wanted to write a poem about it. "The name is a poem in itself," he said; "any one could write a poem about such a stream." All the way down the river his muttered "Bromidon!" was like the self-satisfied bubble-bubble of the morning birds.

Voyage of the Ant

JAMES DINA

EACH STROKE OF THE cedarwood paddle inches the canoe upstream against an unrelenting current. Each stroke is a single effort, yet it merges with an endless sequence of strokes, past and yet to come. Each stroke is an exercise in rhythm, endurance, even monotony.

I watch the water passing under the bow—a bow of bark, roots, and pitch put together by my own hands. The streamlines turn to eddies as the bow cuts them cleanly and sends them along the gunwales toward my paddle . . . another stroke, as some inner discipline suggests the fine difference between achievement and futility. The eddies swirl astern, anxious for the sea. Another stroke, and yet another . . .

A swallow darts across my intended course and my eye follows her to shore. The spring floods have receded by now, leaving sandy terraces at the river's edge. The bank steepens near the top and there the swallow finds her nest, a cubicle among thousands bored into the sandy wall. I

From James Dina, *Voyage of the Ant* (Harrisburg, Pa.: Stackpole Books, 1989).

must imagine what lies above the grassy lip of the riverbank as my canoe sits low in the water beneath. But this part of the Connecticut is familiar to me and the panorama forms instantly in my mind. I see the tops of tall poplars and maples that mark the courses of smaller streams joining the great river. Between are marshy meadows of cattail and water lily. The firmer ground supports carefully tilled plots of corn, beans, and squash. The highest places are home to the people—the Newashe. Copper-skinned and black-haired, they move across the rich earth in their timeless way, not owning the land but of the land. Bound by Nature's whims, they are never her servants, as it is their custom to accept whatever little she offers without complaint. The mouth of the great river is three days' paddling downstream to the sea and five days back against the current to this place they call Podunk. I feel the presence of kindred spirits.

The cedar paddle pulls against the current once more, almost directing itself in this contest with the river. I watch the water again. It bears a shining object toward the bow. As it approaches my paddle, an inscription becomes visible along its edge. It is suddenly familiar—an aluminum can. I don't want to admit its existence, but it breaks my trance of endless stroking. The next stroke pushes it astern. I press onward. Soon a faint rumble reaches my ears. It is still distant but continues to grow as I move northward. I see the river bend, and beyond, a great span arching above the river—Route I-91. My reverie is broken once again as I continue to ascend the Connecticut toward its source. To expect anything else in the twentieth century would be unrealistic.

The Connecticut Valley is populous, but that was so, in relative terms, even before Europeans arrived. This stretch of river may have supported several thousand inhabitants in the sixteenth century. Theirs was an agrarian society dependent on corn and many other native crops. Fish and game rounded out the diet in the south and became more important northward, where farming contributed a decreasing share. Major settlements were not far apart—probably as close to one another as the present-day riverbank communities I would pass through.

This valley's primitive character still lingers. The land on either bank is often floodplain extending more than a mile from the river. Once the spring floods have receded, the fertile land is used only for farming and grazing. Buildings are absent for long stretches. Often, even the faintest hints of the modern world disappear. Indeed, much of what I see is as it once was: meadowlands, cornfields, poplars and maples, and the river itself, even though sixteen dams span its waters. The native inhabitants are long since gone. I am the only person here. I am a modern white man, not a primitive American. But my canoe is fashioned entirely of natural materials, with tools of stone. My gear is primitive: I have no metal, no matches. My food stores of dried meat and corn are insufficient for the trip upriver and back. I must supplement them with wild plants and animals, or abandon my quest.

Another stroke of the cedarwood paddle. Another small gain against the pressing river. The highway bridge is far behind now, the offending beer can well on its way to the sea. My daydream returns by degrees, as the modern world slips astern. I am alone again with my vision, with the river. I am of this land, but not of this time; I am here, but not now . . .

The first miles on the river were filled with experiment. I had little time to practice in the finished canoe before departure, and it was just revealing its idiosyncrasies. Some of its little quirks were due to the materials of its construction. A large patched knothole in the bark sheath increased underwater drag on the port side. But the slight lack of symmetry was the result of my rustic workmanship. When I sat exactly amidships, the freeboard was different on each side. The stem piece was slightly off vertical, so the course heading wasn't quite what the centerline suggested. All birch canoes are keelless and turn easily; short length aggravated the problem in my case. The canoe was tippy as well, even though I had made the bottom reasonably flat. I planned to compensate for the equipment's shortcomings by sharpening my own skills. When that wasn't sufficient, I hoped I could live with things as they were.

My inventory of styles and strokes was short, even though canoes in general were not new to me. That mattered little here, as the Connecticut was wide and deep. Perseverance, not precision, would be the rule of progress.

I knelt Indian-style as I paddled, a position I never found comfortable. The canoe was down by the stern, which reduced speed. I attempted adjustments between strokes but never allowed the canoe to slip downstream. I set this standard of self-discipline at the beginning, and I was determined to maintain it until I headed back downriver.

A hint of mist still on the water defined the fore and aft limits of my world. Dense stands of trees on the banks deepened my physical isolation. The only tense was the present, compressed between a past and future that knew no date. The sun would do little more than distinguish morning from afternoon. What I was doing at the moment was the only important thing.

Twin islands with tall trees loomed ahead. An osprey flapped from its perch there and floated out of range. I decided to land and find a more comfortable stowage for the gear and myself. After unloading, I checked for leaks. There was very little water in the canoe, and most of that had probably dripped off the paddle tips. Good so far! I repacked the basket in front of the main thwart, with the water container and food even farther ahead. This meant I would now have to land and get out for a drink of water, but that was a necessary compromise. The only gear aft was the sleeping bag. I tied a length of deerhide around the rear thwart to cushion my spine, sat on the duffel, and leaned back. Trim was nearly level; I was lower in the canoe and more comfortable.

The sun had crossed the river by now and was leaning west. Sometime before day's end I would encounter the first major obstacle to navigation, Enfield Rapids. Quickly I checked my Connecticut River Watershed Council guidebook. It was superb in every respect, save one—it was written for *downstream* travelers. Enfield Canal was the suggested detour around the four-mile stretch of rapids. The guidebook pinpointed the canal's north entrance at one-quarter mile below the Route 190 highway bridge. I hadn't reached that bridge and needed the south entrance, not the north.

A few days ago someone mentioned a canal access pathway just above Dexter's. The name had registered dimly, but I was too preoccupied to ask for details.

A strange smell permeated the air at the next river bend, and curiously, made me think of Nova Scotia. A large industrial building stood on the west bank. I made no connection between the two. Water trickled into the river through a masonry sluiceway below the plant—industrial waste, no doubt. This was the first sign of civilization since morning. To avoid it, I changed course toward the far side of the river. Current picked up under a rusting railway trestle—probably just a shallow spot near the footings. It slacked off momentarily, then returned with new force around the next bend. From bank to bank and as far north as I could see, the river was filled with white water flecks dancing to the atonal din of water on stone. A disturbing sight. I pulled harder, leaning heavily into each stroke. The paddle blade bent and shuddered; the canoe crept forward at an ever-slowing pace. The sun still scorched my back and a mist distorted my vision as I thrust into the white water. I pictured Enfield Dam and the quiet canal that would take me around it. But I could see neither one ahead as I blinked to clear my eyes. Something was terribly wrong. The canoe was standing still and I was tiring fast. There were no options left.

With my last effort I pulled toward the west bank, grounded on a large island, and sagged to the earth exhausted. Enough for one day. A distant church bell pealed six times. Nearly three hours had passed while I struggled through the last watery mile! Perhaps I was a victim of the late-afternoon hydroelectric discharge up at the Holyoke generating station. If I started out at first light, I could beat the morning water discharge.

Dusk approached as I stretched out on the sandy island. This was a disappointing end to my first day. I was a mere eight miles from home. The two major cities on my route still lay to the north. I wanted to get beyond them, bound toward more pristine country. Now it would take that much longer. I was also uncertain about getting through the rapids immediately above. I hadn't seen another soul since morning; there was no one to talk it over with now, except the Ant. Perhaps this was just the first of many lessons in acceptance I would learn from the departed Newashe.

I looked around: firewood, edible plants, the shelter of tall trees. It was tranquil. Only the breeze and sounds of rushing water intruded on my privacy. I rolled over and burrowed deeper into my sandy bunk, probing for a position that suited my aching shoulders. The canopy of heart-shaped poplar leaves grew dim. A mockingbird sang the last of its cyclical tune as the fire's embers burned to white ash. I closed my eyes and heard an echo of the song that awakened me at dawn. How different was my perspective then! I groped to measure the intervals: one day and eight miles, a different world and another time.

Feelings of anticipation had urged me out of my comfortable bed at home. But I lingered for a moment to fix in my mind the images of my surroundings, and my wife's slender form—a quiet shadow beside me. My breakfast was a simple affair that would be typical on the upcoming voyage: a handful of corn kernels boiled to softness, washed down with sassafras tea. My travel gear was packed. The canoe was ready, with paddles tied in lengthwise for carrying across the meadows to the launch site. My wife and children were up, enjoying a more substantial breakfast while I made dozens of last-minute checks. Like all travelers, I was concerned about forgetting something. Given the survival nature of this trip, such worries were out of place. What I needed or didn't have I would find or make along the way. But old habits die hard.

This was not just the beginning of an ordinary canoe trip. As a boy of twelve, I had dreamed of such a voyage, filled with the fantasy and adventure of fairy tales. I might have undertaken it at twenty, for the sheer love of nature and unrestricted life. But in the intervening years I had developed an unquenchable passion for knowing, in a most fundamental way, who I was and what it was that made me so. I hadn't been able to extract the answers from the routines of modern living. Now I was convinced they lay buried somewhere in the past. There was no way to know for sure without going back for a firsthand encounter. Now, I was past forty; a sixth sense told me this was the last chance to make the voyage.

The planning and building had been a fairly private affair until a local newspaper article announced a "Back-to-Basics River Journey." Friends and neighbors, and people I had never met, stopped by to see the nearly completed canoe. There was a flood of questions: Did I really make all of this stuff? Where did I get the materials? Handicraft people were interested in the baskets and pottery: Where did I learn my primitive crafts? Were the designs my own? A Boy Scout troop was most impressed with the stone tools: How did I make the big arrowheads I was using for knives? Could stone axes really cut down trees? How big a tree? Did I plan to take a bow and arrows? Motherly concern showed in the questions of neighbors' wives: How did I intend to keep clean? to shave? Where would I sleep? A glance about the yard showed that I had mastered many primitive crafts. Here were an authentic canoe, paddles, and a variety of survival gear. The equipment itself was the answer to most of these questions.

Tim Shepard, the president of the local chapter of the Connecticut River Watershed Council, strutted into the yard, an unlit cigar stuck between his teeth. He was enthusiastic. "Are you really going upriver?"

"Yes," I answered.

"Good. I'll call ahead to the council offices in Easthampton and Hanover and tell them to expect you." He made it sound like I was halfway there. I felt tired at the thought of it.

My father called from Arizona. "I had a vision about you and your canoe," he announced. "I can see you launching into the river, pointing the bow upstream and then drifting backward as you paddle the water to a froth." There was more. "Meanwhile you sink lower and lower until only your beak is showing." We laughed together.

A canoeing enthusiast from Simsbury had read the paper and wanted to see the canoe. He asked the questions I would expect from an outdoorsman: What speed did I expect to paddle against the current? How far upriver would I go? How did I plan to get around Holyoke Dam without a second person to carry the gear?

A close friend spoke his mind without reservation. "What happens when you get a hundred miles from home and this canoe starts to fall apart?"

For these questions I had no ready answers. I was counting on a little romance and adventure to offset the drudgery of daily paddling. I looked forward to feeling a bit like a pioneer when I reached obstacles like Enfield Rapids and Turners Falls.

The questions and comments and suggestions kept my mind racing while my hands were busy with dozens of last-minute details. There remained one question, a question of the most fundamental nature, that no one had asked. Eventually, someone did.

An elderly lady stopped me on the street the day before departure. I knew her as the unofficial Main Street historian. Her pluck more than compensated for her diminutive stature. She stared up at me from a few inches away and launched in: "I want to know what it is that makes a man leave home and paddle miles and miles up the biggest river around."

My best reason was the oldest and simplest: I loved nature and always had. Wild places were magnetic to me. They retained hints of the pioneers—native American and European—who first trekked across land. They were still populated by wild creatures. I knew each of these animals before I was thirteen and never tired of watching their moves. Being close to the natural world offered a touchstone for my own sense of being. It was at balance, with no unresolved conflicts. I thought that its lessons ought to apply equally to everything humans did, whether in city or in forest.

I enjoyed manual craftsmanship nearly as much as the outdoors. I sought a balance of function, beauty, and dependability in all my projects, modern or primitive. Quite naturally, this trio soon became fundamental to my way of living as well as building.

Through the years, I tried to get a small daily dosage of my ideals. I never lost touch, but always the contact with the outdoors was at the periphery of my life. I wanted it to be the focus.

Although I was patient, certain small things about modern life always annoyed me. I couldn't tune up my car anymore; an engineering degree from M.I.T. wasn't enough without another thousand dollars of sophisticated equipment. The battery was dead in the electric pencil sharpener, but the model with the hand crank had been thrown away. The maxim "simple tools for simple tasks" was fast giving way to a preoccupation with intricate solutions. Modern technology shouldn't have disturbed me, as I understood it thoroughly. None of these things, taken singly, were very important, but together they were symptomatic of a larger malaise. I was losing control over things that affected my everyday life, and with that, I was losing a little of my personal identity.

A quiet revolution had been ongoing in the New England countryside for nearly a century. The hardwood forests were returning. Since the mid-1800s farmers had been abandoning exhausted plots for the promise of free land in the West. Overcutting the forests for charcoal ended, too, as coal and oil became more popular fuels for the furnaces of the industrial revolution. Countless hillsides were left fallow, and the hardwoods moved in to reclaim them.

A not-so-quiet revolution had begun on the fringes of our largest cities. Suburban sprawl was on a direct collision course with the recently matured forest land. Not in two or three centuries had the countryside looked more primeval, and never before had it been threatened with so complete and final a change.

Each of these factors increased my feeling of urgency about making firm contact with a way of life that seemed to have disappeared. The connection didn't need to be permanent, but it needed to be complete and intimate. My incurable sense of romanticism complicated the search. It's easy to sit in the real world of today, annoyed by noise, pollution, and the pressures of modern living, and lament the passage of those pure and pristine times when man lived in idyllic balance with his surroundings. Much of what I believed in arose from this perception of man's former states, which might be as imaginary as a Greek myth. I needed to make real contact with the past to know for certain. I wanted not only to see and hear, but to touch and feel the reality. I wanted to experience everything relevant to that reality, the pain along with the ecstasy.

The Connecticut River flows southward a scant half-mile behind my home. From there it is just fifty miles to the river mouth in an arm of the Atlantic called Long Island Sound. Northward the river bisects Massachusetts and then becomes the common border between Vermont and New Hampshire. The uppermost thirty miles of river are entirely in the little hump of New Hampshire that stands above Vermont. There is a puddle just short of Canada called Third Lake. It is the river's source, three hundred and sixty-one miles from home. The Connecticut is the natural gateway to New England. It is the watery thread that ties together four states. It defines the region in a very real sense by draining its heartland. Although not as wide and deep as New York's Hudson River, it is longer. Four hundred and eleven miles from source to sea, it is large enough to be majestic and commanding, yet small enough to be personal and inviting.

I visited the river often, watching it rise and fall in response to the seasons. Broken stone tools and potsherds from another age dotted the sands at low water. I picked up the artifacts and enjoyed the tingle every archaeologist feels when he unearths a piece of the past. But I also felt something missing. Living human beings had produced these items. The pieces remained as evidence of what they had done, and from them the archaeologist could even recreate their life-styles. But the testimony of silent stones left me cold. It told me nothing of what the people felt or who they were. I needed to know. Ten years of walking the riverbanks hadn't given me the answer, but it *had* made me realize how little the river and local surroundings had changed since those artifacts sustained the lives of real people. Here was a setting that was still relatively remote, with traces of the primitive world strewn about. This was the right place to make contact even if the time was wrong. Echoes of the past were faint but persistent. It was like listening to voices through a closed door that I couldn't open. There had to be another entrance.

There was. It came in the form of a gift, a thin book. The elegant profile of a birchbark canoe glided across the front cover. Thoughts of making such a canoe had crossed my mind over the years. The little volume in my hand wasn't an instruction manual for building canoes. It was John McPhee's book about Henri Vaillancourt of Greenville, New Hampshire, who makes fine birch canoes. Immediately, I knew that this book was the second key to my quest, like a small spark falling on dry tinder. This canoe was the obvious vehicle I needed to become a time traveler into the Connecticut's past.

The combination of river and canoe mandated a primitive voyage. It also dictated a third element: a primitive voyager, a canoeist from the past who could be totally at ease with the unknowns of a primitive river and the quirks of the primitive canoe he would propel. I wanted desperately to be that canoeist. But how? I was still a product of this century. To announce that I was going primitive after work on Friday, then return for Sunday supper was too shallow to be convincing. A week-long camping trip to the Maine woods wasn't likely to do it, either. I needed another way to access the primitive mentality required of this canoeist. I lacked blood ties or direct cultural connections to native Americans and their past. There was only one other point of entry I could think of.

Ever since childhood I had dabbled in native American crafts. Arrowheads, hatchets, and the stuff of TV Westerns were among my first efforts. The results had been crude, and by the time I was midway through high school, the interest had become dormant. One summer, as an adult, I began making stone arrow points again—beautiful pieces this time. I turned them out by the dozens. I had no idea why. One type of primitive manufacture followed another. Bit by bit I was accumulating a complete array of wilderness survival gear.

Building the canoe and voyaging in it would be a major undertaking. Still, I was confident that I could produce a serviceable craft. In New Hampshire, Henri Vaillancourt was building better canoes. Somewhere in Canada, native American descendants were doing the same with steel tools. Merely reproducing their efforts at lesser quality would provide me with a canoe but little else. As far as I knew, no man living today had built a birch canoe with *stone* tools. Limiting myself to the tools and materials available to primitive Americans would require me to rediscover ways of thinking and doing that had disappeared centuries ago, and would admit me into the world of the past. The river waited. The canoe would speak for itself when finished. It was my great hope that I could recapture the spirit of those lost times in the process.

I pulled another armful of sand under my head. During this single day, philosophical thought had been displaced by immediate necessities. The river was a beautiful adversary. Already it was taking control, dictating my moves.

The river crashed throughout the night. The sound of rushing water became an obsession as I half-dreamt and half-heard the force that had fought me to a standstill. It droned on into the grayness of dawn without change: clearly not hydropower. I rekindled the fire and splashed cold river water on my face. As my head cleared. I reread the river guidebook, picking up on a detail I had missed. The canal's lower entrance was supposed to be just above Dexter's *mill.* Mill? The Nova Scotia smell . . . paper pulp! Yesterday's industrial building was Dexter's Paper Mill, and the masonry sluiceway was an overflow from the canal. I felt like a fool. I had paddled right by it into Enfield Rapids. Here I sat on an island fifty feet off the west bank. Inland, just another hundred feet, was the placid canal.

Getting off the island and into the canal was a chore that exceeded the distance between them. My gear—two paddles, bark rope, ash splint pack basket, sleeping bag, ground cloths, hickory bow with stone-tipped arrows, three birchbark containers with water and food—all had to be packed and loaded into the partially floating canoe. Drifting across to the mainland took only a few seconds on the current. Then the procedure was reversed: beach the canoe, unload, and haul everything inland. The effort of scouting ahead to find the easiest path is usually repaid when one is carrying a canoe. The ground rose quickly away from the river. I stopped in the underbrush at the sight of familiar foliage and dug up an edible tuber as large as my fist. There was no hurry about reaching the canal. Nor was any moment of contact with the earth to be wasted. Almost every task I performed could suffer interruption here.

A moist air mass was settling over the region and the sky had remained gray since first light. The brush thinned a few yards ahead where the ground flattened; mist filled the open area. I stepped out onto a bicycle path and looked down into the canal.

The masonry walls on both sides were still level and square after a hundred and sixty years. Back in 1824, Yankee ingenuity had tackled the problem of getting flatboats above the rapids without the time and toil it took to rope and pole through. Labor arrangements included the importation of twelve hundred Irishmen enticed by the prospects of lodging and steady work. They toiled for sixteen hours each day. By the time the newly completed canal collected its first toll a year and a half later, many of them were dead of overwork and disease. I appreciated their sacrifice as I paddled through the slack water.

Another cycle of unloading, carrying, and reloading put me back in the river just above Enfield Dam. It hadn't aged as well as the canal. Today it was little more than broken rubble, strewn diagonally across the river. White water pours through the gaps and down into the rapids. In the old days it wasn't uncommon for downstream cargo boats to risk shooting the dam in high water. If they made it, they saved time and the canal toll. I winced at the thought of plunging over the nine-foot drop in my birch canoe.

Everything was ready, yet I hesitated with one foot in the canoe, the other on dry land. The gray river and even grayer sky ahead looked uninviting. I should have been standing here yesterday in the bright afternoon sun, with an easy three hours of paddling time left. The Ant, my symbol of perseverance, stood silently etched on his headboard. I didn't want to see him right now.

Forcing myself, I shoved off and took a tentative stroke at the water. The current here appeared to be light. This heartened me a bit. As I reached midstream, two young men with fishing rods spotted me from shore.

"Homemade?" one called.

"Yes," I called back. They smiled and signaled me a thumbs-up. I nodded in thanks, wondering whether they were aware of the extent to which my canoe was indeed homemade, from scratch. Their admiration reassured me nevertheless, urging my paddle to a more confident pace.

The air was warm and oppressive although the sun was still hidden behind a thick sky. Gentle rain began to fall sometime during the next hour. It was a welcome relief to the humid stillness. The droplets patterned the smooth river with rings that interlocked, then encroached on their neighbors. A single heavy cloud boiled up along the west bank. It would pass soon, I thought. A sandy island with stunted willows hugged the east shore. I was just rounding its upper end when I felt the hair on the back of my neck rise. A strange crinkling sound filled the air, then a shocking glow as a deafening roar rushed past my ears. A second electrical discharge followed, even closer. Heavy rain hissed out of the turbulent cloud as I beat a hasty retreat to shore. Without pausing to unload, I dragged the canoe under tall oaks, then overturned it quickly to protect the gear. Rain began to pierce the heavy canopy of oak leaves as I tied the paddles and a ground cloth into a shelter around the trunk. I was wet to the skin but it didn't matter; my equipment was safe. Without delay I collected a stack of dead wood before it soaked through. Soon I was drying my clothes and heating water over a crackling fire. I sipped sassafras tea slowly and tried to reckon the day's progress: something under four miles—less than yesterday. At least the cause of the present delay was obvious and there was nothing I could do about it. The ground cloths insulated me from the wetness but not from the effect it had on my spirit.

Something happens when one is continuously out of doors. The grass and trees are not a relief to other surroundings; they are all that exists. The ancient Greeks were the first to describe man's connection to nature. They organized the earth's diversity into four all-embracing categories: fire, air, water, and earth. Their model was simple and practical, and I adopted it for my river-bound world. My intent was not to achieve control over the elements, but to interact with them. The realms of earth, air, and water accounted for the majority of things I would encounter. . . .

Walking was something I thought I could depend on. Although it rises and falls, earth at least stays put—it doesn't slip downstream against a traveler. The variable quantity that had made the river an enchanting but whimsical mistress had just been removed.

I tried to dismiss my regrets over abandoning the waterway that had led me three hundred miles from home. This was a journey, a quest, not just a canoeing trip. In the old days the river was the most practical road into these parts, but as George had pointed out, many travelers had turned inland well below here, using tributaries, then forest paths. Footsteps were not out of place then or today. Briefly, I entertained the thought that I could have walked all the way here. The straps of the pack basket began to dig into my shoulders, convincing me otherwise. I couldn't have carried much more than a musket or a hunting bow in my free hand. Everything I needed for current travel was in the pack, but carrying anything else for trade or starting a homestead in the wilderness was out of the question. The canoe had been the best option until the river gave out.

The blacktop turned to hard-packed earth a short distance out of Bloomfield. Much of the road ran parallel to the river, allowing me a firsthand look at what I was missing. The stream twisted its way through the narrow flats that were all that remained of the valley as the encroaching hills pressed it more tightly with each mile.

As with paddling, the first day of walking was an experiment in locomotion. After so many years it would seem that there was nothing left to discover. By midmorning I was stumbling under the weight of the pack. Fortunately, I had selected the deerhide as essential gear for overland travel. I twisted it lengthwise and wound each end around a pack strap. The middle of the soft hide roll fell across the back of my neck. The load on my shoulders lightened as I leaned forward and to one side, hauling on the dangling ends of the hide with my right hand. I wrapped the fingertips of the other around the base of the birch canteen, swinging it in slow cadence to my lopsided gait. Onward I went, hunched over, the Quasimodo of northern Vermont. Each footstep was a metered push, not so different from the effort of paddling. The vistas crept by at the meagre two knots of my previous canoeing: a faded farmhouse by the road, followed by a weed-choked family graveyard; a clear-cut hillside across the river; pink wild raspberries; then the river again, boiling down its little trough, barely resembling the broad stream that passes my home so many days south.

By afternoon I was at the covered bridge that crosses to Columbia, New Hampshire, eating the last of my maple sugar rations as I soaked my aching feet in the chilly river. Large blisters were beginning to form. As daylight faded, I saw spruce-clad Mount Monadnock towering to the west. A small stream passed under the road, tracing its way to the Connecticut. I followed it down to look for a place to spend the night.

For the last time I dig groundnuts. As I do so, I think that I would gladly shed the thin cloak of intellect that every action wears, and become a creature of the earth, seeking a simple subsistence of roots and browse like a primordial forest ungulate. I would eat the succulent green leaves, pulling them from their branches with my teeth and devour them straightforward, with no intervening niceties between discovery and nourishment. Then I would sit satisfied on the ground with no particular thoughts to occupy my mind during the brief period of contentment before hunger's next call.

Then I think that I would cast off my mortal half, leaving only an intellect free from the requirements of biological maintenance, free to indulge itself without regard for the consequences. But I am the imperfect synthesis of those two more perfect extremes. Somehow the smelting of beast and god has run awry, as one nature too often argues with the other in the depths of man's breast.

My hands move forward on their own, more slowly while my mind considers the complexities of human nature. I stop digging and return to the water's edge to muse over the beauty of day's end. My thoughts follow the sun westward, and beyond, wondering where and when the spark of all life originated, how it happened or who caused it to happen. The question grows too large. A stirring in my middle brings me swiftly back to the cold earth of the riverbank, where I must sustain the very life whose origin I have been seeking. Soon I will withdraw the fire sticks and produce the most godlike creation of which I am capable: a feeble spark for roasting tubers, which would have been more numerous except for my mental flight through the heavens. When they are done I will return to the task that always seems to come first and last—feeding the beast.

Dawn came in like most others in the upper valley. I picked my way through the dripping grass and started down the road; it was as misty as the river. I moved slowly, favoring yesterday's blisters. Once the haze burned away, the air turned suddenly hot.

Flat water, the first I had seen in four days, appeared at intervals. It would have been easy work in the canoe, if I could have gotten it up here. But it soon disappeared again as the stream shrank and turned white between the stones. Robert was right: the river had indeed given out.

Time and distance had insulated me effectively from home and many twentieth-century habits, making both convincingly remote. The miles had accumulated slowly, allowing me to adjust to each new place. I was never far from the previous night's camp. I left nothing there but cold ashes and a depression in the grass; I arrived with everything I was accustomed to.

I laughed inwardly at the thought that I had come to conquer this river. It had affected me far more than I had affected it. My wake, if it was still on the river, would soon be part of the sea. The headwaters of the Connecticut were the point of aim, not the goal. I had really come to answer burning questions of identity: who am I? What was it that made me so? As much trouble as it had been, the second had been easier to answer. Being a part of my race's genetic memory wasn't good enough. I wanted it as part of my own conscious memory, reliving in a small way every minute of man's ascent: foraging like a beast in the meadow, cracking two stones together at the dawn of history, preparing for the hunt atop an Ice Age flint mine, planting the first corn and the seeds of civilization, building a boat of birch to carry me against a river that defied time. Each man alive—red, white, or otherwise—is what he is because of these things. I had experienced equal portions of pain and ecstacy in coming to know them; it had been worth every effort. But that other question: *Who?*

As I trudged along under the pack basket, I felt as though I were outdistancing the answer. Ahead I saw only bright sun with shimmering heat on the road, and a shrinking river that threatened to evaporate before I knew.

Canaan, Vermont, seemed to come up fast, then Beechers Falls. A sign at the center of town read CANADA, with an arrow pointing left. I followed it, biting my lower lip as I saw the crimson maple leaf fluttering on its field of white at the border crossing. Two guards were on duty, a balding gentleman who looked like an aging Dudley Dooright, and a pretty French woman who spoke English with a heavy accent.

Dudley was cordial and friendly. "Where are you headed?" he asked.

"Nowhere, just here," I told him. "I need to make a phone call."

"It's cheaper just over on the American side," he suggested.

"I'd rather make it from here."

I rang Annie from the outdoor phone booth. She was at home.

"Where are you?" she asked.

"Quebec."

"Quebec! It sounds so far away. How are you?"

"Fine, but my feet hurt. I've been walking the last two days."

"Why did you have to pick such a long river?"

"I didn't; I think it picked me. Either way I'm sure it was the right river."

"Well, I'm glad you have it out of your system at last." She paused as though expecting an answer. But I didn't have one. My mind was preoccupied with the fifty miles of river between home and the sea. Later this summer I would finish that, too; it would be easy—downstream. With that done I would have paddled every passable mile on the river, many of them in both directions, five hundred in all.

I hung up the phone and sat down on the grass. After pursuing this goal for so long and reaching it, I didn't know what to do with myself. A feeling of pointlessness settled over me. Walking over the land had been a psychological relief from paddling, but a presence I always felt on the river was missing. I thought back to Robert's shed, where the canoe was stored. Its every detail was still etched in my mind from the labors of building and endless paddling: thwarts worn smooth with use, muddied ribs, root lashings bleached white by water and sun. I traced its gunwales forward until they swept upward to meet the stem piece, to the Ant on his headboard. He rested at last. There would be little for him to see in the quiet dimness, but I was sure he could hear current passing through shallows in the nearby river. I pictured him from afar, but saw him more clearly than I could have from within the confining world of an eleven-foot canoe.

Once this project had seemed endless. Now I could safely admit things that would have exhausted my strength before. Some forces are too powerful when taken in a single dose; the Connecticut, upstream at least, is one of them. I had needed this silent, stoical ant. Now I could let him go, back away, see him in perspective. For the first time, I could acknowledge who he was. I realized I had known him all along, and known him well. I looked closely, seeing more clearly than ever. And I knew: I was the Ant.

Sailing the River

OLIVER ALLYN

I HAD BEEN WAITING a long time to begin my journey, waiting to start the boat, waiting to finish her, then waiting for the perfect weather that might never come. Finally, not even the scorching heat and the nearly flat calm could prevent me from starting out. *Emma,* riding with happy anticipation on her trailer, had been brought down to the launching ramp in Riverside Park on the north edge of Hartford. Mary and Emily came along to wish me bon voyage and to drive the empty trailer back home. I had no way of knowing where and when they could pick *Emma* and me up again.

What an inauspicious place to start my journey. The City of Hartford had forgotten that it is on the banks of one of the country's greatest rivers. Riverside Park was nothing more than unmowed brown grass where high tangled weeds clutched the litter that was everywhere. Nothing was going on—no baseball games, no picnics, no lovers. At the edge of the trash-strewn road an occasional person slumped in an old car, and stared into emptiness. The pitted asphalt of the launching ramp was covered with mud and flotsam left over from the previous spring's high water. Off to the side of the ramp a single desultory fisherman whiled away the hot sunny morning. The river banks were covered with weeds and undergrowth so high they screened any view of the river except where the ramp temporarily pushed them aside.

Excitement, anticipation, flashes of trepidation were quickly followed by an underlying confidence . . . a moment of unsureness, then barely suppressed childlike exuberance. Along with the flickering emotions was the beginning of a sense of quiet pleasure deep inside, kept just under the surface by the bustle and confusion of final preparation.

I was trying to keep calm. Everything had been checked and rechecked, stays tightened, sails ready to be pulled up, anchor line firmly shackled to anchor, oars at hand, and rudder and leeboard on, but tipped up for launching. Finally the ice chest was fastened down with shock cord just aft of the mast step.

At last we backed the trailer through the caked mud and shoved *Emma* gently out onto the river.

From Oliver Allyn, *Dreams of a Landlocked Boatman* (Exeter, N.H.: J. N. Townsend, 1998).

Monday, July 30, 1979, 11:30 a.m. I felt like I should say something grand, something profound that would give this great adventure of mine meaning to the rest of the world—at least to my wife and daughter standing there at the edge of the forlorn, forgotten park. In reality I probably said something like, "See you later."

With a last wave I turned downstream. Silently and very slowly I was carried along by the vestigial current, the slightest breath of wind, just enough to fill out my sails. I drifted under Bulkeley Bridge and then Founders Bridge, slowly making my way past the city skyline. Hartford, actually so close, seemed more like a mythical city on a far distant horizon, of no concern to me, exerting no influence on my passage downstream. The river became everything. Its banks defined a long narrow world that absorbed my presence and removed any need beyond its confines. Any signs of civilization out there somewhere were only those signs that were directly linked to the river. The occasional log jetties for small oil terminals were there because of, not in spite of, the river. Red and green channel markers became friendly signs, welcoming me to their water road. Even the few small airplanes flying low toward Brainard Airport became great humming dragonflies, saying hello to this new inhabitant of the river.

By midafternoon the current had stopped entirely and although the breeze was a little stronger, it came from dead ahead. I started tacking back and forth across the river, each tack bringing me a few yards farther downstream. A particular overhanging branch might be my goal for the port tack, and then a small rock outcrop the challenge for the starboard. By the time I reached the entrance to Wethersfield Cove I realized that I was not only bucking a head wind but also a head current. A good tack then, meant not losing any ground. Opposite the mouth of the cove the current was very strong, sweeping in through the narrow entrance, very nearly sweeping me in with it. Fortunately, I managed to reach shore and tie up before I got in any real trouble. A small boy and an even smaller girl, both wearing muddy rubber boots, stood fishing on the flats at the cove entrance. The little girl said in a happy sounding voice, "Tide's comin' in. What kind of boat is that?" I told them about the boat and my trip. They thought this was a perfectly natural and wonderful thing to do.

The boy said, "You're going to have to row for a while though." So row for a while I did.

The 1974 edition of the Connecticut River Guide, published by the Connecticut River Watershed Council, mentions that there is a tide as far as Hartford but that it isn't really a problem. Obviously, they weren't thinking of sailboats with no wind. After I rowed for a short distance, little puffs of good wind sprang up. There is nothing more frustrating than to feel a puff of wind, run up the sails, ship the oars, have the wind disappear and then find yourself drifting backwards. A number of people have been quoted as the author of a very wise saying: "Getting anywhere in a small sailboat is largely a matter of patience." I am not normally an extremely patient person, but that late afternoon of my first day on the river I had a lovely time alternately rowing and sailing very slowly down the Connecticut River.

I decided to spend my first night on the river at a nameless cove two and a half miles below Wethersfield. About 7:30 in the evening I rowed around Crow Point and cut in through the narrow entrance. Even though I had the idea that the cove was the result of digging for fill when Highway 91 was built, it still looked as if no man before me had ever seen it. The oddly rectangular sides of the cove, nearly a half mile long, were lined with dense high trees, effectively hiding any signs of civilization. There were no people, no buildings, no roads and no noise. This was just the way it should be. In the early evening light the smooth surface of the cove was the color of blue-green slate.

The light was fading fast and there was a lot to do to get ready for the night. After a quick supper of peanut butter sandwiches, a couple of cookies and a can of orange soda, I checked the anchor and started to prepare my bedroom suite. In my tiny boat this meant first moving all the daytime sailing gear and bulk supplies to new positions in order to make room for the air mattress. I seemed to have so much gear that it was impossible to get at one thing without moving three others. Retrieving necessary articles was a lot like finding a sock in the bottom of an army duffel bag. Sailing required one batch of gear, cooking dinner required another and when I got myself and my boat ready for the night I needed to move everything all over again. After each change, it all had to be properly stowed away or lashed down in its new position. The whole gear and stowage problem needed a lot more thought. I shuddered to think of what it was going to be like with a rocking, pitching boat in the wind and rain.

I unlashed and moved the cooler to get at the boom tent and mattress. Any unneeded gear went under the fore deck; the cooler was lashed back in place and emergency things like flashlight, life jacket, and horn were put in their plastic dishpan, handy under the aft deck. The air mattress was laboriously blown up, puff by puff (there ought to be a better way) and then spread out with the sleeping bag on top.

Rigging the boom tent was the last thing to do. Adjust the boom to the right height, put the boom tent over it, tie the tent fore and aft, snap it along the sides just under the rubrails, unsnap the sides, readjust the boom, snap the sides again.

Fastening the mosquito netting over the after-end of the tent always made me a little bit uneasy. What if, half asleep, I had to get out of the cockpit in a hurry. The thought of the boom tent become a shroud passed through my head.

At 9:30 p.m., after a last peer out from under the boom tent at the still, charcoal-gray cove, I stretched out on top of my down-soft sleeping bag, rested my head on the spare-clothes pillow and listened to the stillness. Occasionally, a tiny creaking sound in the rigging or the gentlest pat of a ripple on the hull broke the silence, as if to remind me that I was in a boat. A fish jumped after a bug or just from the joy of a lovely night. *Emma* and I were enveloped by a blue-gray, misty peace.

My second day started early. I woke up at 5:00 a.m. to a hazy persistent light, but lay there for a while luxuriating in my floating cocoon. After rowing the fifty feet to shore, I stretched my legs with a walk along the sandy cove of Crow Point and then cooked breakfast on the narrow strip of beach. I probably would have been better off clearing the bottom of the boat and cooking there because, as it was, I ate scrambled eggs, seasoned with salt, pepper, and sand. By 7:45 a.m. I was ready to sail.

Again there was no wind, but there was no upstream current or midday heat either, so I started to row. I don't know how far, maybe a couple of miles, before the strengthening morning breeze allowed me to raise the sails. It was a very quiet breeze, just ruffling the surface of the water, but blowing fairly steadily from the south. The river took a looping turn toward the east, so I could silently ghost along on a close reach with the sails pulling smoothly, the board down all the way, and everything working just as I knew it could. It was a beautiful summer morning—hot but not too hot; sun almost audibly tinkling on the tops of tiny wavelets; blue, blue sky reflected in the deeper parts of the water. The feeling of being in another world was even stronger than before—a different world; a constantly changing world; a world creating different sights, sounds, sensations. Slowly sailing along, occasionally tacking to adjust to bends in the river and subtle shifts in the wind, I became more finely tuned to this new world. In some places trees on the river bank arched over the water, making patches of shade, which were lovely and cool to sail through. The water in these shady places was sometimes the color of old bronze, dark but with a life-giving patina of its own. In the pebbly shallows of the opposite shore, the sun polished the bronze until it glittered with gold and white and touches of green.

As I sailed through long narrow channels I began to pay more attention to the red and green channel markers. I was gradually beginning to do a better job of relating the markers to the river charts I had cut into manageable sections and folded into clear plastic zip-lock bags. Long ago I had studied the charts over and over again, but they always remained just charts without much real meaning. Now the same charts had become a series of long narrow pictures of my future in this new world of the river. These aids to navigation, like the river itself, had become peculiarly and personally mine.

Suddenly, I was no longer the only traveler down the channel. Just as I slowly passed marker 120, midway along the east side of Glastonbury Upper Bar Channel, an automobile tire intrusively swept up alongside, interrupting his purposeful journey just long enough to examine the interloper on his river. He wore a covering of green algae like a blazer of crushed velvet, and sported a piece of frayed waterlogged rope like a badge of high office. Of indeterminate age and origin, he nevertheless exhibited infinite self-esteem and confidence, so imbued with his own supremacy that he did not need to be boastful or overtly display any signs of conceit. Apparently I was not worth any more of his scrutiny because, with not so much as a bob, that old tire oh-so-haughtily moved downriver ahead of me.

I have never been interested in racing but I just couldn't let this slime-coated example of circular self-assurance outdo me in our passage along the river.

"I challenge you to a race down to the ferry dock at Rocky Hill."

No response at all. But he seemed to be going just a bit faster! How could that be? If he had a current I surely had a current too. Even though there was very little wind, there was some now and then. I had sails and supposedly knew how to use them. Slightly falling off the wind and letting the jib out just a bit, I gradually began to catch up to that self-important circular freeloader. Up ahead I could see that the river made another looping turn to the west, so that soon the faint breaths of wind would be more across my beam. The tire, now just ahead of me, began to angle off to the left, following the outside curve. A flash of brilliant strategy hit me. I would sail more of a straight line across the curve, thereby lessening the distance to travel. That plus better wind should help me pass my adversary.

One of the many reasons I am not a racer is that I don't concentrate very long on the race. There are too many things that steal my interest, too much else to be aware of, to feel, and to see. As I slowly cut across the bend in the river just above Glastonbury Two Piers Bar Channel, I became increasingly aware of the beautiful colors and reflections in the water. In places I could see the bottom, the bronze turned to gold, here and there sparkling silver. The water was much cleaner; the pebbles and shells on the bottom made interesting wavy images in the filtered light. Suddenly, just as I realized that the reason I could see the bottom so clearly was that the bottom was so close to the surface, I ran aground. Even though the leeboard flipped up as it was supposed to, I still had enough momentum to scrape on the bottom pebbles. The bow swung slowly around until it was facing directly upstream and the boom complained loudly as it swung over and whonged against the port shroud. That slimy tyrant of a tire would get way ahead of me.

For a few moments I had been so intent on the race that when I got the bright idea to cut across the river's bend (shortest distance between two points and all that), I forgot to look at the chart. In so doing, I not only didn't check the depth numbers, I completely missed a real milestone of my trip. I had just passed on to a new chart section—Rocky Hill to Middletown.

Once I really hit bottom, I worked fast, freeing the sheets, grabbing the gaff and pushing the bow around into the wind, and then giving a mighty shove from the stern. By sheer luck the cross wind momentarily died so I had no trouble poling myself far enough out into the river so that the leeboard and rudder would go down again.

I'll never know, but I think the tire may have been coming over near me, probably so he could gloat over my misfortune. In any case, he must not have been watching what he was doing either, because he ran smack into a big log semi-submerged just off the channel, and had to bounce and drift and roll around it in that peculiar way of tires.

The tire was only about ten yards ahead of me. I could see one side of the Rocky Hill ferry slip up ahead, just at the beginning of the next bend. For once the wind cooperated. It kept blowing very lightly but steadily, so that I was sure I could actually sail most of the way to the finish line. But never did anyone sail so slowly. The wind was so gentle that I discovered we would move better if I sat on the leeward side of the boat. The tire had moved back out near the center of the river, instinctively knowing where the best current was. He was not more than three yards off my port bow when we made the last bend, heading due south again. I had to tack. With perfect timing, if I do say so myself, I swung across right behind him and, as a gust of unusually strong wind came, swung back across the river so I could make one final tack toward the finish line. The boom swung over for my final turn—we were bowsprit to bowsprit (if he had had one) and that is the way we stayed, right across the line. A draw, a tie, a dead heat. No winner, but no loser either. As I sailed back toward a little pier on the Rocky Hill side that perhaps lonely, sailing circle continued downstream to wherever old river tires go. I'm sure I saw him give a couple of quick little bobs and dips. Whether to say, "You'd never keep up all the way to the Sound," or just, "Goodbye," I'll never know.

Chapter 9

POETRY

Still it sings the same sweet song
And still it tells its tale.
Complaining of commercial wrong
To forest, hill and dale.
It longs for freedom from the mills,
To be forever free,
To sweep unharnessed through the hills
From cataract to sea.
—"The Song of the River" by Joe Cone, 1901

Next to love, water must form the most popular subject for poets through the years. Clouds, raindrops, lakes, ponds, surf—and, most common watery subject of all, rivers. Aside from their intrinsic loveliness, rivers look like poems, being relatively narrow, confined within definite bounds; like poems, they are fluid, starting at one specific point and, like the better poems, ending in a larger, general merging.

The Connecticut has inspired more than its share of poetry over the years, a great deal of it simply awful, a surprisingly large amount memorable, worth reprinting. Joel Barlow, the Connecticut statesman and "wit," was one of the first poets to achieve a national reputation in the early years of the nation; he wrote an epic poem about Columbus's discovery of America, in which, so chauvinistic was Barlow about his native river, he couldn't resist giving Columbus a vision of a river he never got close to.

Thy stream, my Hartford, through its misty robe
Played in the sunbeams, belted far the globe.
No watery glades through richer vallies shine.
Nor drinks the sea a lovelier wave than thine.

A nice touch, that last verse ("The Vision of Columbus," 1787). Actually, there was a great deal of such rotund versifying. Here's an example drawn from the work of John Gardener Calkins Brainard, an editor who lived and wrote in Middletown; it's from his poem "To the Connecticut River" (circa 1832):

From that lone lake, the sweetest of the chain,
That links the mountains to the mighty main,
Fresh from the rock and swelling by the tree,
Rushing to meet and dare and breast the sea—
Fair, noble, glorious river! in thy wave
The sunniest slopes and sweetest pastures lave.

And so on and so on, for hundreds of heroic couplets, but no rhymes quite match that last one! Amusing stuff—but some of the early poetry can still charm with its detail. Josiah Dean Canning (1816–1892), who spent most of his life in Gill on the lower Connecticut, was the self-styled "Peasant Bard," and his poem in the Longfellow mode, "The Shad-Fishers," is a souvenir of the time when much of river life revolved around the annual shad run; an excerpt is included here.

The twentieth-century poets had their eyes on the river, too, if looking toward it with less sentimental, less chauvinistic purpose. Reuel Denney's "The Connecticut River" was esteemed enough to make it into the Modern Library's Twentieth Century American Poetry as late as the 1963 edition. I've included it because it represents the very last time the subject of "New England," where it fits into contemporary American culture, could still be considered a monumental issue.

Two poets of genius lived along the river in the 1950s. Wallace Stevens was an executive in the insurance industry in Hartford, and it's said he liked to walk the banks of the river during his lunch hours; the river, in his day, was at its most polluted, so, lovely as it looked from afar, it may have contributed to some of the darkness here. Sylvia Plath went to college in Northampton, and the two poems included here, while not her best-known work, give off a youthful intensity that the river is lucky to have won.

Richard Eberhart was an excellent poet who taught at Dartmouth and obviously knew and loved the river. And let's not forget Robert Frost, who mentions the river at least once in his complete poems ("New Hampshire," 1923):

New Hampshire raises the Connecticut
In a trout hatchery near Canada,
But soon divides the river with Vermont.

Oddest story of all among the poets is the fact that Rudyard Kipling, that genius of muscular British imperialism, married a Brattleboro girl and lived near that river town for four productive years in his mansion called Naulakha. The jungles and plains of India were on his mind here, not the Connecticut River—and yet the river, or at least the river towns, managed to force their way into one of his poems, "Pan in Vermont," in which an itinerant seed salesman makes his way around the countryside.

He's off the drifted track to catch the Windsor train,
And swindle every citizen from Keene to Lake Champlain;
But where his goat's-hoof cut the crust—beloved, look below—
He's left us (I'll forgive him all) the may-flower 'near her snow!

The Shad-Fishers

THE PEASANT BARD

All in the merry month of May,
When snowy shad-trees blossomed gay,
To tell the fisherman the time,
When fish were plentiful and prime:
All in the merry month of May,
Where TURNER'S pouring waters play,
And lash, and dash, and roar, and bray,
Were wont to gather, there and then,
All in the merry month of May,
Back many years on Time's highway,
Fishers of SHAD, and not of men.
Upon old-time "Election Day,"
I've heard gray-headed worthies say,
Not only fisherman, so wet
With sweeping seine and scooping net,
But other folk would muster there
As now they gather at a Fair.

From Josiah D. Canning, *Connecticut River Reeds* (Boston: Joseph George Cupples, c. 1838).

From all the region round about
They came, the gentleman and lout;
The yeoman, whose spring-work was done,
Resolved to have one day of fun;
The peddler with his gew-gaws fine,
And ballads, dog'rel, not divine;
The bully of the country-side
In all the swell of hero pride;
The gamester who was skilled to know
The science of a lucky throw;
The loafer, whose "chief end of man,"
Was, Go it, cripples! while you can;
The verdant youth from hill side green,
Come down to see what might be seen,
And treat the dolse whom he led
To penny-cake and gingerbread;—
A motley crowd of beings, wishing
To see each other and the fishing.

Now, ye who read these truthful rhymes,
And life in these noise-making times,
When dams, and mills, and paddle-boats
And other craft the water floats,
With all their din and clickmaclaver
Scare off the red-fins from the river,—
Can scarce conceive what schools of shad
Made our old fisher fathers glad.
Their numbers did exceed almost
The rapt one's countless heavenly host.
Upon the bottom of the river
Their fins like leaves were seen to quiver:
And leaping salmon, tho' less plenty,
Were grand as royal One-and-Twenty.
A single haul would bring ashore
Some forty, fifty, sixty score;
The fisher who the scoop would duck
Would get St. Peter's sacred luck;
A few hours' toil and you might heed
Shad piled like hay-cocks in a mead.

Then, some facetious ones have said
That folk so much on fish were fed,

One scarce could draw his shirt o'er head:
His skin with fish bones bristly grew,
And held the garment as he drew.
They must have been most scaly persons,
Themselves, to venture such assertions;
And all of us would now be glad
To "make no bones," had we the shad.

. . . .

Those fishers were a race of men
Whose like we ne'er shall see again.
Creative WISDOM seems to give
Men for the times in which they live,
Born in the days of "hoddin gray"
When Fashion's walks were far away;
Bred in the days when hardest toil
Was needful to subdue the soil;
Their school-house was the broad, green sod;
Experience with her rule and rod
Taught them the lessons Science spurned;
But Science claims not all the learned.—
Strong, brave and forceful; earnest hearted;
With them the rope drew, or 'twas parted;
When unoffended, very clever;
But wrath aroused, was wrath forever.
They loved their day and generation;
They loved the creature, and creation;
They loved life's cheer, they bore its burden,
And all have traveled over Jordan,
And low away at rest were laid
Long while before my pen was made.

. . . .

So while these scenes were going on,
The scoops were plied, the nets were drawn.
Swift shot the row-boat from the shore,
As lively played the flashing oar;
And as it darted circling round,
By skillful hands the net was drown'd.
Next came the pulling, long and strong,
Like sailors warping ship along;
The low, but animated cheer,—

(Fishers aye deem the fish will *hear;*)
Till landward as the meshes drew,
The prisoned fish appeared to view,
And now grown conscious of their trouble,
Made the fenc'd water boil and bubble.

Just so, 'tis said, mankind will let
Themselves be snared in evil net,
And make no effort for exemption
Till in their case there's no redemption
Next, by the father of all fish!
To have been there you well might wish,
When, for some two-and-seventy pence,
You might have drawn a cart-load thence
Of just the finest shad that ever
Swam this, or any other river.

The Connecticut River

REUEL DENNEY

I

This land whose streams seem as the lives of men,
Birched with the Indian blood and pale with snow
Whose random sheens of spring beneath the sun
Rise in a hilly glitter like words of Emerson;

Land of the barn handhewn, and firmly made
Of some such silent form where hope may stay
Not lush in heat like grapes of sun-warmed towns
But short of season as sweet mountain hay;

From Reuel Denney, *The Connecticut River and Other Poems* (New Haven: Yale University Press, 1939).

Dictionary maker, schoolroom of the Iowa town,
The shining coast turned toward the Opium Wars,
The churched hills and the cotton mills,
And the nasal A's of tottering country stores;

It is the province honored and mistrusted,
Much spoken of in Cleveland, but not understood,
Taking the country home and the summer tourist
As if they knew it—though they never could.

As made for a museum its blades of water
Call and enclose the temper of its skies
Whose chanting blue from the tempestuous mountains
Sharpens the view where charming pasture lies.

And the ladies making tea in governors' mansions
Speak soft the Indian names, the adulteries.
Honey and rum, the captain's nightly bottle,
Are sunk at last in the oriental seas.

2

When commerce sailed a well-clewed gleaming yardarm,
Drove drunken privateers and reeled the foam,
They smoothed the highway for the bonded blackman
And brought the fans but not the hold-stench home.

Nothing they did salt failed to purify,
Making the son forget the sultry trade
That sent the congo gods to dream on cotton
And sing so sad all since have been afraid.

Night. The fortieth parallel. The stars.
The bark lies singing on a tack long held from dawn
Whose pace derives the beneficent westerlies
Still scented with the Azores, spiced and warm.

Or morning, and the horrid Horn behind them
Like gateways where the oceans lean to plunge,
And under the bows the urgent dolphin's fins

Fly frothing, and the Massachusetts towns
Die in the past like words forgot in hymns.

Farmer and herder did not bow to train,
To rail and steel more painful than the crows.
Tea and the supper light were all they needed
Of China, and the surge where right whale blows.

Those mountains blessed with rigid loneliness
And duties hardly said but always known,
And the early dawns of those dissenters showed
Farms all their own, and righteously alone.

3

What hope now in the country and the towns
Whose sons lie in Chicago and whose words
Hover a steel-grey plumage, sober song,
On western towns, whose ears are not on birds?

Blood of jurist and parson, shouting Webster,
The proper people properly tight at fairs,
The stars that J. Q. Adams held in sight,
The strength withheld, the shy and powerful airs;

Are they the hostage of the village mansion
Whose mill-bred beauties ape the former times,
While enterprise is wary, and the bedroom
Fastens the madness of the ancient crimes?

Those things that made a people all themselves
Fight terror in the rooms where madmen lie.
The manias for collection and dissipation
Point out an identical way for men to die.

Neurosis and division feed upon
Aristocrat and the people of the town,
Whether it is known or whether still unknown.
The awful smile of some deserted farm.

4

Milk sold by monopoly, feed at higher prices,
The cost of machinery on farms not made for it,
The west beyond its boom and yet still fruitful,
Closed mills, and a crazier history yet.

Luther and Calvin knew the difficult way
And ships taught others of a wilder kind
How men whose priests held back the western day
Could wake and know, and measure, seek and find.

Now that the order's broken and the hill
Lies curving shadow to the bomber's wing,
Concrete bursts through in rivers fit for wheels
And song delays to hear what air may sing.

What's left to teach a people how, together,
Land and the factory might shake hands,
Not war, as at the edge of rivers, cities
Die slumward where the workless fisher stands?

Hawthorne's fear found, traveling in the mountains,
In hemlock passes Salem-drunk with spice,
The silent girls who knitted at machines
Whose turning wheel drove from the melting ice;

He saw beyond congruities fantastic
Made out of books by Alcott and some others,
And heard what glacial silence would be pressed
On tongues that meant these men should act as brothers.

5

Or, in the spring, it's time to bring our hatred
And sympathy for those granite banks and laws
Our fathers quarried deep from the mothering hill
As children walk in the thunders of divorce.

Led by the rain gone ghosting down the valley,
Our sorrow follows, hovering on the roads

That married once the landscape and the man,
Past streams expressed in reeds and singing toads;

We find the spring shine pale on cellar-holes
And shells of ice along the upland waters;
Husband and child at once of the glistening pasture,
We breathe above the poisons of the motors.

Some dream combines the climber's respiration
With grassy sounds, and motions underhill
As if, where factory chimneys are not seen,
Man and the birch sucked at some single will,

Or, in the liquid voices of that season,
Green ocean greys, wet whisperings of birth,
Both shuddered in the shock of generation
When lifting fogs disclosed both man and earth.

Our bride is the river in the valley
And all the hills around that did not die
When father moved his office into death
In the grey vault in the slope where pheasants fly.

Two Poems

WALLACE STEVENS

THIS SOLITUDE OF CATARACTS

He never felt twice the same about the flecked river,
Which kept flowing and never the same way twice, flowing

Through many places, as if it stood still in one,
Fixed like a lake on which the wild ducks fluttered,

Ruffling its common reflections, thought-like Monadnocks.
There seemed to be an apostrophe that was not spoken.

There was so much that was real that was not real at all.
He wanted to feel the same way over and over.

He wanted the river to go on flowing the same way,
To keep on flowing. He wanted to walk beside it,

Under the buttonwoods, beneath a moon nailed fast.
He wanted his heart to stop beating and his mind to rest

In a permanent realization, without any wild ducks
Or mountains that were not mountains, just to know how it would be,

Just to know how it would feel, released from destruction,
To be a bronze man breathing under archaic lapis,

Without the oscillations of planetary pass-pass,
Breathing his bronzen breath at the azury centre of time.

THE RIVER OF RIVERS IN CONNECTICUT

There is a great river this side of Stygia,
Before one comes to the first black cataracts
And trees that lack the intelligence of trees.

In that river, far this side of Stygia,
The mere flowing of the water is a gayety,
Flashing and flashing in the sun. On its banks,

No shadow walks. The river is fateful,
Like the last one. But there is no ferryman.
He could not bend against its propelling force.

It is not to be seen beneath the appearances
That tell of it. The steeple at Farmington
Stands glistening and Haddam shines and sways.

It is the third commonness with light and air,
A curriculum, a vigor, a local abstraction . . .
Call it, once more, a river, an unnamed flowing,

Space-filled, reflecting the seasons, the folk-lore
Of each of the senses; call it, again and again,
The river that flows nowhere, like a sea.

Two Poems

SYLVIA PLATH

IN MIDAS' COUNTRY

Meadows of gold dust. The silver
Currents of the Connecticut fan
And meander in bland pleatings under
River-verge farms where rye-heads whiten.
All's polished to a dull luster

In the sulfurous noon. We move
With the languor of idols below
The sky's great bell glass and briefly engrave
Our limbs' image on a field of straw
And goldenrod as on gold leaf.

It might be heaven, this static
Plenitude: apples gold on the bough,
Goldfinch, goldfish, golden tiger cat stock-

Still in one gigantic tapestry—
And lovers affable, dovelike.

But now the water-skiers race,
Bracing their knees. On unseen towlines
They cleave the river's greening patinas;
The mirror quivers to smithereens.
They stunt like clowns in the circus.

So we are hauled, though we would stop
On this amber bank where grasses bleach.
Already the farmer's after his crop,
August gives over its Midas touch,
Wind bares a flintier landscape.

ABOVE THE OXBOW

Here in this valley of discreet academies
We have not mountains, but mounts, truncated hillocks
To the Adirondacks, to northern Monadnock,
Themselves mere rocky hillocks to an Everest.
Still, they're our best mustering of height: by
Comparison with the sunken silver-grizzled
Back of the Connecticut, the river-level
Flats of Hadley farms, they're lofty enough
Elevations to be called something more than hills.
Green, wholly green, they stand their knobby spine
Against our sky: they are what we look southward to
Up Pleasant Street at Main. Poising their shapes
Between the snuff and red tar-paper apartments,
They mound a summer coolness in our view.

To people who live in the bottom of valleys
A rise in the landscape, hummock or hogback, looks
To be meant for climbing. A peculiar logic
In going up for the coming down if the post
We start at's the same post we finish by,
But it's the clear conversion at the top can hold
Us to the oblique road, in spite of a fitful
Wish for even ground, and it's the last cliff
Ledge will dislodge our cramped concept of space, unwall

Horizons beyond vision, spill vision
After the horizons, stretching the narrowed eye
To full capacity. We climb in hopes
Of such seeing up the leaf-shuttered escarpments,
Blindered by green, under a green-grained sky

Into the blue. Tops define themselves as places
Where nothing higher's to be looked to. Downward looks
Follow the black arrow-backs of swifts on their track
Of the air eddies' loop and arc though air's at rest
To us, since we see no leaf edge stir high
Here on a mount overlaid with leaves. The paint-peeled
Hundred-year-old hotel sustains its ramshackle
Four-way veranda, view-keeping above
The fallen timbers of its once remarkable
Funicular railway, witness to gone
Time, and to graces gone with the time. A state view-
Keeper collects half-dollars for the slopes
Of state scenery, sells soda, shows off viewpoints.
A ruddy skylight paints the gray oxbow

And paints the river's pale circumfluent stillness
As roses broach their carmine in a mirror. Flux
Of the desultory currents—all that unique
Stipple of shifting wave-tips is ironed out, lost
In the simplified orderings of sky-
Lorded perspectives. Maplike, the far fields are ruled
By correct green lines and no seedy free-for-all
Of asparagus heads. Cars run their suave
Colored beads on the strung roads, and the people stroll
Straightforwardly across the springing green.
All's peace and discipline down there. Till lately we
Lived under the shadow of hot rooftops
And never saw how coolly we might move. For once
A high hush quietens the crickets' cry.

Three Poems

RICHARD EBERHART

JOHN LEDYARD

Only death remains
To tell us
How great we were

Great with life,
The stone entablature
By the river

Tells us
Of a youth who made a canoe
From a cedar,

Descended the Connecticut,
Discovered far places,
Died the great voyager

Far from home,
Lost in Africa,
Youthful, valiant, destroyed.

That was in another century.
The incised bronze fades,
His name only remembered

By insignificant lovers in the Spring
Who read his story
And clasp each other,

Amazed at intrepidity
For all they want is themselves,
His valiancy hallucinatory,

His trial of the world incredible,
Their heroes themselves,
They only want to clasp each other.

Only death remains
To tell us
How great we were

Speaks the voice of the voyager
From fading bronze letters,
Great with desire.

RIVER WATER MUSIC

With the sun half way down the tall pines
Heading for the earth of Vermont,

I sit in New Hampshire high over the Connecticut
Listening, eskered, to electronic music expand,

High decibel, confronting nature with man's extravagance.
Power burst of electronic music burst over the hills,

A kind of gigantic extravagance unknown to earlier ears
Which hear the rich slight wind whisperings of near sun-down.

Brisk, strong, air-penetrating reverberances
Fan out into the innocent air for miles around,

Man denting the idea of ideal silence
With power gestures waking the ears to new feeling

While all over heaven flaunt the claps of electronic aggression
Saying the mind may be old but the sound is new.

AT THE CANOE CLUB

(To Wallace Stevens)

Just a short time ago I sat with him,
Our arms were big, the heat was on,
A glass in hand was worth all tradition.

Outside the summer porch the viable river
Defied the murmurations of guile-subtle
Truths, when arms were bare, when heat was on,

Perceptible as picture: no canoe was seen.
Such talk, and such fine summer ease,
Our heart-life against time's king backdrop,

Makes truth the best perplexity of all,
A jaunty tone, a task of banter, rills
In mind, an opulence agreed upon,

Just so the time, bare-armed and sultry,
Suspend its victims in illusion's colours,
And subtle rapture of a postponed power.

Chapter 10

THE FISH

Smallmouth bass. It's their inhabitance that fascinates me, their pursuit that lures me out. The river is full of them here, fish that take on the same green-gold darkness as the water, so you can say of them what Thoreau said of Walden's pickerel, that they seem the animal nuclei of the river—Connecticut all over and all through.
—*Upland Stream* by W. D. Wetherell

It's my hunch, my strongly self-serving hunch, that fishermen and fisherwomen are the ones who know the river the best. Out in all weathers, studying the water's depth, temperature, currents, probing, always probing, constantly asking the river questions—those who fish get to know and understand a river in a way few others can.

The river has seen its ups and downs as regards fish and fishing. Everyone commented on the massive runs of salmon and shad that met the first settlers; everyone bemoaned their loss with the building of the first dams at South Hadley Falls and Turner's Falls. Now the fishy life, the bio mass in the river, seems to be on the rise again, with a healthy shad run, and, if not a healthy salmon run, something of a miraculous one, that any salmon have been coaxed back to their ruined home at all.

Jack Noon gives an excellent summary of the fishy history of the Connecticut. Leslie Thompson's is a charming reminiscence of fly-fishing the Upper Connecticut trout water circa 1927 in the area now flooded by Lake Francis. My own contribution continues the story of my infatuation with the Connecticut begun in the introduction to this anthology and tries to explain something I wholeheartedly believe: that fishermen, when it comes to rivers, see a lot more than anyone else.

History of a Fishery

JACK NOON

THE CONNECTICUT RIVER SOUTH of New Hampshire's border with Massachusetts flows on for about 135 miles down to the river's mouth at Saybrook, Connecticut. North of the border twice as much of the river, or about 270 miles, has belonged to New Hampshire since 1764. In that year King George III ended a long dispute between New Hampshire and New York by setting the west bank of the Connecticut as the boundary between the two provinces. As Vermont emerged from her own squabble with New York into independence and eventually into statehood, the boundary endured—the west bank of the Connecticut. The upper river and its fish have officially been New Hampshire's for well over two centuries.

Native fish that spent their entire lives in New Hampshire's portion of the Connecticut included a variety of warmwater species—pickerel, yellow perch, various cyprinid minnows, sunfish, suckers, horned pout, and a few others—in addition to brook trout. Cusk were also reported in the Connecticut River and its tributaries. Silver eels ranged as far up as the Connecticut Lakes and at the ends of their lives swam down to salt water and to the Sargasso Sea to spawn. Northern pike and smallmouth bass introduced themselves into the Connecticut by escaping from where they'd been stocked: the pike in 1840 from the ponds in Plymouth and Ludlow at the head of Vermont's Black River; the bass from Livingston Stone's ponds in Charlestown in 1867 and from Lake Sunapee after 1868. Brown and rainbow trout, walleyes, largemouth bass, carp rock bass, and landlocked salmon are all among the introduced species.

Whatever anadromous fish reached New Hampshire's portion of the Connecticut on their spawning runs had first had to ascend both South Hadley Falls and Turner's Falls, which served to slow and concentrate the fish and provide good fishing. The Massachusetts dam constructions at South Hadley Falls in 1794 and at Turner's Falls in 1797 killed the spawning runs on the upper Connecticut half a century earlier than the dam at Lawrence, Massachusetts, killed them on the Merrimack.

When Adriaen Block sailed up the lower reaches of the Connecticut in 1614, the river held a natural-state abundance of the same anadromous fish as the Merrimack: Atlantic salmon, Atlantic sturgeon, striped bass, shad, alewives, and lampreys.

Documentation is scanty for just how far up the Connecticut the anadromous fish traveled on their spawning runs. Shad, however, almost certainly stopped in the eddies below Bellows' Falls, as local historians recorded. Suggestions that shad may have been much further north and that shad perhaps reached Lancaster are speculative and misleading and not to be taken seriously. Until such time as contradictory hard proof comes to light, Bellows' Falls should be accepted as the upper limit for shad on the Connecticut.

Salmon kept on into northern New Hampshire, are documented to have been at least as far up as Colebrook and Stewartstown on the main river, and almost certainly reached Pittsburg in northernmost New Hampshire. They ran up the Ashuelot and the Ammonoosuc as well, but, as far as the other New Hampshire tributaries of the Connecticut go, I've been unable to find unequivocal accounts of their presence. For the Ammonoosuc, Lucy Crawford in her 1846 *History of the White Mountains* reported that ten-pound salmon had been taken fifty years earlier from near the river's source in Crawford Notch. Her fifty-year claim coincides with the time just prior to the dam constructions in Massachusetts. Salmon would have spawned in the uppermost reaches of the Connecticut and its tributaries wherever gravel bottoms of brooks and streams offered them suitable spawning grounds, probably including such places as Indian Stream and Perry Stream in Pittsburg and perhaps a score or more of other tributaries downriver that we'll never know about.

A 1794 history of Vermont, published at Walpole, New Hampshire, gave an account of the Atlantic salmon just before the first dam had been completed across the Connecticut down in Massachusetts:

> In the spring, about the 25th of April, these fish begin to pass up Connecticut river, and proceed to the highest branches. . . . When they are going up in the spring, they are round and fat, of an excellent taste, and flavour. From the first week in May to the second week in June, they are taken in great numbers. . . . Some of these salmon in the spring will weigh thirty-five or forty pounds.

Sturgeon were reportedly speared as they attempted to run up South Hadley Falls. For the ones which may have succeeded in getting above those falls, there was certainly the physical capability (if not the instinctive inclination) to run up Turner's Falls and Bellows' Falls as well. However, there is no documentation for the presence of sturgeon in the Connecticut upriver from the Massachusetts border other than for one highly anomalous, 37-pound specimen found floating and dead in the canal above the hydro-electric plant at Bellows' Falls in 1938. The presence of this fish more than 140 years after dams had stopped the spawning runs was almost certainly the result of some experimental stocking project.

In the Connecticut River above the Massachusetts border striped bass and alewives aren't mentioned in historic accounts. Most probably they had never been present in western New Hampshire. I have yet to find any eyewitness record of lampreys above Bellows' Falls, but lower down in the watershed they were reported to have been numerous in the Ashuelot River along with salmon and shad and were commonly used for food by early settlers.

The upper Connecticut's white settlers, in contrast with their counterparts on the Piscataqua and the Merrimack, had only a comparatively few years to take advantage of the annual spawning runs before the salmon were gone. On the Connecticut white settlers were at Bellows' Falls about fifty years before the Massachusetts dams were built, but probably fished commercially only for two or three decades. On all three rivers Yankee thoroughness likely resulted in severe overfishing of anadromous species well before the erection of dams killed the spawning runs completely.

When the first English settlers arrived at the lower Connecticut River in the 1630s, they had little interest in fishing. David Field, writing in 1819 about the abundant fish in the Connecticut River from Middletown, Connecticut, down to the river's mouth at Saybrook, supposed that "little effort was made to take them for more than a century after the county [Middlesex County, Connecticut] was settled. Within the memory of persons living, there was very little demand for salmon, and as for shad it was disreputable to eat them. But as this prejudice gradually died away, and as profitable markets for fish were opened, fishing became an important business thirty or forty years ago [between 1780 and 1790]."

The lower Connecticut is wide and slow and lacks the falls and constructions that on the Merrimack served to concentrate the fish and identify the best fishing sites. In Connecticut dip nets would have been useless anywhere on the main part of the Connecticut River. The best fishing sites for the efficiencies of seine fishing were just below the falls considerably upriver: South Hadley Falls and Turner's Falls in Massachusetts and Bellows' Falls in New Hampshire. Dip nets or spears could have been used effectively in the natural fish passageways at the falls themselves.

In the commercial fishery that was developing a century after the first English settlements, Sylvester Judd judged in his 1905 History of Hadley that shad were more important than salmon. This claim of the greater importance of shad, however, isn't a clear indication of local preference. Judd doesn't mention that for many years there was a steady demand both for New England shad and for the poorer grades of codfish because they were about the cheapest food that could be fed to slaves on the sugar plantations in the West Indies. In Northampton in 1733, according to Judd's research, shad were sold for a penny apiece—a price which held in that part of Massachusetts for about forty years—and in 1736 barreled Connecticut River shad were being advertised in Boston. Salmon were used by many families in preference to shad. People probably brought them fresh from fishermen and salted most of them to preserve in barrels for home consumption. Salmon cost a penny a pound in Hartford in 1700 and had risen to about two cents a pound by the time of the Revolution. Within her own borders Massachusetts regulated the fish dams and weirs, which were primarily used to catch salmon. Official permission to erect dams and weirs had to be granted by the "court of sessions." Petitions for weirs in Hampshire County, Massachusetts, began in 1729.

An account of the commercial fishery at South Hadley Falls that was underway after the American Revolution came largely from two old men, Joseph Ely and Justin Alvord, who'd been interviewed in 1848. Judd reported their recollections:

> Fishing generally began between April 15 and May 1, very seldom as early as April 15. The best fishing season was in May. Shad were caught in seines below the falls, and in scoop-nets on the falls. Boats were drawn to places on the rocky falls, fastened, and filled with shad by scoop-nets; then taken ashore, emptied and returned. A man in this manner could take from 2,000 to 3,000 shad a day, and sometimes more, with the aid of a boatman. These movements required men of some dexterity. There were some large hauls [with seines] of fish at the wharves below the falls. The greatest haul known was 3,500, according to Ely, and 3,300, according to Alvord. It was not often that 1,500, or even 1,200 shad were taken by one sweep of the net. Salmon were taken on the falls in dip-nets, and below in seines with shad. Before their day, salmon had been taken at the foot of the falls in places called pens. Ely had never known a salmon taken at the falls that weighted above 30 pounds; some weighed 20, and many from 6 to 10 pounds. They were always few in number compared with shad. The river seemed to be full of shad at times in some places, and in crossing it, the oars often struck shad. Ely and Alvord, like other old men, related that fishermen formerly took salmon from the net, and let the shad go into the river again, but not in their time; and that people in former days were ashamed to have it known that they ate shad, owing in part to the disgrace of being without pork. Alvord sold thousands of shad after the Revolution for three coppers each, and salmon were sold from two to Three pence per pound. It was more difficult to sell salmon than shad.
>
> Some [striped] bass were caught with hooks after shad time. Sturgeon were taken on the falls with spears. Lampreys, called lamprey-eels, had long been plenty on the falls, and many were taken at night by hand, by the aid of torch-lights. Some were eaten in a few towns in old Hampshire [County], but most were carried to Granby, Simsbury and other towns in Connecticut.

Shad seasons brought to the falls, on both sides of the river, multitudes of people from various quarters. Some came from Berkshire county. All came on horses with bags to carry shad, except a very few who had carts. Some, intending to purchase two loads of shad, led a horse. For some years there were only two licensed inn-keepers at the falls—Daniel Lamb and widow Mary Pomeroy, but every house on both sides of the river was full of men, and some lodged in shelters and out-houses. Horses filled the stables and many other places. It was estimated one day, that there were 1,500 horses, on both sides of the river; this estimate is not reliable. A great number of the men brought victuals with them; many cooked shad, and other brought food at the houses. Many were detained one day or longer. They indulged in plays and trials of skill. Where there were so many men, and rum was plenty, there was of course much noise, bustle and confusion. The greater part were industrious farmers, and after leaving the falls, they wound over the hills and plains with bags of shad in every direction. They were plainly dressed, according to their business. There was another class at these gatherings, composed of the idle, the intemperate and the dissipated. They came to drink and frolic, and some to buy shad if their money held out.

Lampreys came above the falls in great numbers, and entered the streams that run into the Connecticut, until the Holyoke dam was built in 1849. They were very numerous in Fort River in Hadley . . . and were caught by the light of torches, sometimes several hundred in a night. Men waded into the streams, and grasped them with a mittened hand and placed them in a bag. . . . In a dark night, men might be seen in the river, clasping now and then with one hand a squirming lamprey, and holding in the other a birchbark torch, which threw light on the river and on all objects on its borders. Very few [lampreys] were cooked in Northampton and Hadley; many were given to the hogs. Some were conveyed to other towns in Massachusetts but most to Connecticut. None are now [1905] caught above Holyoke dam.

Another account of the fishing at South Hadley Falls comes from an unidentified 1801 eyewitness:

The salmon and shad fishery had of late become a great object in the vicinity of the Lower Canals. The people living in that neighborhood have built as many as fourteen wharves in the river, at the foot of the South Hadley Falls, where they fish for about three weeks in the month of May. They draw up their nets against those wharves, and catch sometimes as many as twelve hundred fish at one haul, which, it is said, will fill twenty barrels. It is also said that the owners of one of these wharves caught fish in one season, to an amount which, after deducting all the expenses, cleared them the sum of four thousand eight hundred dollars!

At Walpole, New Hampshire, the first white settlers arrived in the middle of the eighteenth century before the end of the French and Indian Wars and settled near the Great Falls, later known as Bellows' Falls. Then after Wolfe had defeated Montcalm at Quebec in 1759 and after the

French had surrendered Montreal and all of Canada in 1760, the threat of deadly, French-led or French-inspired raids was no longer a deterrent to the settlement of the upper Connecticut River Valley. Settlers flocked north, and until the first dams on the Connecticut were raised about thirty years later, had the chance to take advantage of as pristine a fishery as any non-Abenaki would ever see on the upper Connecticut.

The local claim that the Great Falls (Bellows' Falls) was the best fishing spot on the entire Connecticut, though it would certainly have been disputed by Massachusetts fishermen at South Hadley Falls or Turner's Falls, could easily be defended. The Great Falls was the reported and probably upper limit of shad on the Connecticut, and vast throngs of the fish milled around in the eddy below the falls where they could be netted in large numbers. Lyman Simpson Hayes, a local historian writing in the earliest years of the twentieth century, reported on historic commercial fishing practices at Bellows' Falls:

> The shad nets were often nearly half a mile long and from eight to twenty feet deep. To each end of the net was attached a long rope. . . . The net would be taken up the river, upon one side, . . . then, striking out into the stream the fisherman would row across, paying out the net, and return . . . with the other end of the rope and wind up the two ropes as rapidly as possible by means of a windlass, drawing the net over a large space of the stream. Shad in great numbers were caught in this way. Drawing nets in this manner was continued to a later date further south than at this point, and one record shows over two thousand shad taken at a single drawing of the net.

The white settlers at Bellows' Falls likely used the same kinds of fishing gear as salmon fishermen over on the Merrimack, but they also added a pair of innovations. After Colonel Enoch Hale built the first bridge across the Connecticut in 1784 right over the fast water at Bellows' Falls, some enterprising soul rigged a chair to hang from the bridge for salmon fishing. A fisherman in the chair speared salmon as they struggled up through the white water beneath his dangling feet. Other fishermen reportedly fished out over the fast water "with dipping nets" from chairs at the ends of long, counterpoised logs.

Above Bellows' Falls the anadromous fish history to focus on is that of the Atlantic salmon. Unfortunately, among the upper river's historic fisheries claims from local sources there are only scraps of factual information to go on. Many writers of town or regional histories simply ignored or glossed over the topic of early fish and fishing. Others got some of their facts right, but also repeated oral-tradition inaccuracies or made unwarranted suggestions based on fragments of old accounts they'd stumbled across.

Because of the comparative lateness of white settlement in the uppermost part of the Connecticut River valley, most of the settlers had had thirty years at best to catch salmon before dams in Massachusetts stopped the spawning runs. Locally surviving claims cited Connecticut River "salmon holes" at Stewartstown, "in the great eddy at the head of the Fifteen-Mile falls, in Dalton, near the mouth of John's River," and "at the mouth of Israel's River in Lancaster." In addition the history claimed, as had Lucy Crawford, that salmon had ascended the Ammonoosuc River, one of the longest Connecticut River tributaries, all the way up to Fabyan's near Crawford Notch. The name of Salmon Hole Brook, a tributary of the Ammonoosuc, still appears on maps about two centuries after salmon were last caught from the salmon pool at its mouth.

The great stumbling block in assembling a fishing history is the problem of the reliability of collected accounts. Oral traditions can very quickly drift away from actual historic conditions. Yankee storytellers instinctively add their improvements from generation to generation, and facts may be well evolved into fiction by the time that some second or third generation descendant is either writing a local history or else being interviewed for contributions to one. Pride in family roots and the ego satisfaction of speaking with authority about the world of personal ancestors can result in quite inaccurate accounts finding their ways into print at early dates. The mere age of the accounts and the lack of readily available alternative sources suggest a reliability to later researchers and writers who, in turn, compound the difficulties by passing on the shaky accounts as authoritative.

To show how quickly oral traditions can drift, I'll offer an illustration from an article in an 1881 publication of the Connecticut Valley Historical Society. A Dr. Alfred Booth was attempting to deal with conflicting oral traditions on early sales of shad and salmon in the lower Connecticut Valley: whether people buying shad had been forced to take some salmon along with them in their purchases or whether people buying salmon had had to take some shad. From whatever the underlying facts might once have been, both versions were current. Dr. Booth located very old eyewitnesses of the early fishing and, in attempting to form his own opinion and gather corroborating support for it, interviewed octogenarians and recorded their round-number, childhood memories of "seeing flat-bottomed boats on the river containing perhaps twenty tons, or 20,000 shad . . . at South Hadley falls" and about a hundred salmon "near the mouth of Agawam River . . . thrown on the grass under an apple tree' and five hundred shad taken at one haul of a seine. He also mentioned the conflicting versions of whether "Agawam pork" referred to salmon or to shad; the storyteller's cuteness of expression probably copied from the conventions of "Albany beef" to designate Atlantic Sturgeon up the Hudson and "Derryfield beef" to signify lampreys at Amoskeag Falls.

On the upper Connecticut, in light of the tendencies of storyteller Yankees to improve their material, the late nineteenth-century and early twentieth-century locally recorded accounts about early fishing are of questionable accuracy. The most reliable sources of surviving salmon information about the upper Connecticut and its New Hampshire tributaries are the earlier contemporary records of the New Hampshire legislature: the petitioner of complaint submitted to the legislators and the laws that the petitions inspired.

In 1786 the legislature passed "An act to prevent the distruction of salmon in Ammonoosuck River." This potential "distruction" had taken the form of gill nets, weirs, and mill dams. The act prohibited all salmon-catching whatsoever within one hundred rods of the mouth of the Ammonoosuc. An additional fine would be levied for the use of a gill net in the proscribed area. All mill dams across the Ammonoosuc were to "leave proper passage for said Salmon," and fishing was prohibited within fifty rods of every such mill dam. Finally, it was declared illegal to "erect any ware in said River & thereby obstruct the passage of said Salmon."

Dams across the Ashuelot River drew legislative attention in 1789 because they had blocked the passage of "Salmon, Trout, Shad, and other Fish" to the extent that "the said Fish are Intirely hindered in their course up the River Ashuelet." The towns of Hinsdale, Winchester, Swanzey, and Keene, one of the preamble clauses of the law claimed, had formerly gotten great benefit from the presence of these fish.

Seven men from the upper Connecticut petitioned the legislature in a letter from Lancaster dated May 17, 1788, to do something about fishing abuses on the Connecticut River itself. They complained about the virtual or actual net-barring of the river with seines and weirs "Perticularly in the Grete falls at Walpole" and "That those Parsons among us who used to Stabb with their Spears 18 or 20 Salmon in a Neight, they can now scarcely see a Salmon to Catch."

In response to this petition and probably others, the legislature passed a law on February 6, 1789, in plenty of time for it to be in effect before the next fishing season. This law contains a treasury of contemporary information about the salmon fishery on the upper Connecticut River which has slipped by all writers of town and county histories during the past two centuries. Its opening passage confirms the problem of overfishing to the point of extirpation:

> Whereas by reason of the great number of seines Nets and Machines which are Constantly used during the fishing season, In taking Salmon & shad in Connecti-

cut River, they have decreased for a Number of years past, and there is great danger that the fishing in said River will be destroyed . . .

The law limited all fishing to three days a week, "from Sunrise on Tuesday to sunrise on Friday." It cited the particular problem spots for overfishing of "Bellows's Falls Quechae Falls White River Falls and fifteen Mile Falls" and for emphasis repeated the same provisions of the law as applying to those specific spots. Because shad, and perhaps lampreys too, weren't found above Bellows' Falls, the fishermen at Quechee Falls, White River Falls, and Fifteen Mile Falls had all been fishing for salmon seven days a week during the spring runs with as many salmon-catching devices as their inventive Yankee minds could come up with—small wonder that the fishermen above those falls could "scarcely see a Salmon to Catch." New Hampshire fishermen on the Connecticut weren't allowed to "drag any seine or drag net or use or set any scoop net or any other net or Machine for the purpose of catching any of said fish" except on those three days of fishing allowed. Final requirements of the law banned the use of nets or seines more than twenty rods long and prohibited, from the first of May to the last of October, "any Mill dam, ware or other Obstruction whatever" that would interfere with the passage of fish up and down the Connecticut.

This response of the legislature had recognized the problems and had attempted to eliminate them. The effort failed, however, and whether the new laws had been strictly enforced or not enforced at all ultimately made no difference. The 1791 and 1795 changes in the laws attempting to protect the Connecticut River fishery were also irrelevant: for the laws passed by the New Hampshire legislature had no effect whatever in Massachusetts, and Massachusetts was where the dams were being built. The salmon of the Connecticut River were doomed.

An undocumented, second-hand report claims salmon lingering in the upper Connecticut as late as 1808, more than a decade after the dams had been completed at South Hadley Falls and Turner's Falls. After that date the native Atlantic salmon in the upper Connecticut were unequivocally gone; their restoration a pipe dream for future optimists—salmon restoration biologists, fishermen, and writers of fishing histories. Many thousands of Atlantic salmon there had been netted or speared as subsistence food. They'd been a commercial commodity, too, for a few decades after the white settlers had arrived. Quite ironically sportfishing, which is the primary support behind modern-day efforts at salmon restoration, probably never found its way to the upper Connecticut when the salmon runs were in their glory.

Fishing the Vanished River

LESLIE P. THOMPSON

ON THE MORNING OF 6th July 1927 I was driving north on the west bank of the Connecticut above Colebrook Bridge. Here was a beautiful river flowing through a beautiful valley, but to my eye it was not ideal trout water. Long winding reaches of a big slow-moving stream which at long intervals broke into shallows and runs from which in the near future I was to take fine rainbow trout. How was I to know that? Of the river's possibilities I knew scarcely nothing. The vaguest king of a rumor—whispered, oddly enough, years before on Cape Cod—had led me on this tour of exploration, and I continued to drive up the valley stopping here and there at farm houses and country-stores; but the information gathered concerning fish in the river was meagre and unsatisfactory. Following the main highway I finally arrived at the dam at the foot of the first Connecticut Lake. On the shore above the dam stood Stewart Young casting a fly. "Yes," said Stewart, "there are good rainbows in the river below the dam; at Judge's Pool the other evening I caught a three and a half pounder." He advised me to start fishing the next morning three miles below at Archie Heath's farm.

At eight o'clock the next morning I was standing in the river below the old covered bridge on Heath's Farm. The water was low and clear, the weather hot and sultry threatening rain. No fly on the water but the first cast of a small Red-Palmer-Badger rose a bright twelve and a half inch rainbow, and he was brought to net. To the same fly floated under the bridge a larger fish showed, and a half hour of careful fishing was spent to no effect. Above the bridge a quarter-mile of pocket and ripple was covered—I'm afraid rather hurriedly, for it had commenced to drizzle and I was anxious to see what the water up-stream had to offer.

Coming to a slow-moving run there were four fish rising to tiny iron-blues. I stood in one spot, rose, hooked and netted three rainbow trout—two of a pound each and one of one pound three ounces. A smaller fish a few yards above was allowed to feed unmolested, and I continued up the shore passing another quarter-mile of fast water.

Before me was a pool of quite different character from the one below. In a swift current, swirling and eddying among rocks and boulders, six

From Leslie P. Thompson, *Fishing in New England,* New York: D. Van Nostrand Co.; 1955.

fish were showing. I cast to No. 1 but could not touch him, there was a bad drag. Ditto No. 2. Casting over No. 3 a fourteen-inch brown trout came to a floating hackle—he went three ounces over a pound. While resting the pool I saw at the top the head and tail rise of a very large trout—probably feeding on small gnats of a sort—and I worked over him with greatest care. It was now raining great guns, and a wet line did not help in placing the fly to advantage. Finally the water bulged in a short rise to a very small Alder semi-submerged. My watch said one o'clock, the two remaining fish had gone off the fee, and I drove down river to the village.

The heavy rain continued, but fortified with strong tea and lemon pie I returned to the river and labored up-stream through two miles of wet brush. Time and labor were well spent, for stopping from time to time I noted many a pool and pocket well deserving careful attention in the future.

On the way over the Dixville Notch, returning to join my family at Shelborne in the valley of the Androscoggin, I reviewed the events of the day. I had seen two miles of good trout water. Here the river had left the broad meadow-lands above Pittsburgh and had become a rough tumbling stream, not easily waded, to be sure, with its slippery black rocks, but narrow enough to be covered in most places by a long cast. I had fished three pools and had seen ten feeding fish, over four pounds of which were in my bag. I could not rate my performance high, but I had fishing the like of which I'd never dreamed and had it *alone*—not another rod appeared on the stream. It was good fishing but not the best; the best to my mind is never hurried. I do not like the "crowded hour" and better a quiet meadow pool than noisy foaming rapids. It was a little *too* good to be true, and it was not entirely true as events in the near future would prove.

One week from the day when I had first cast a fly below the old covered bridge I was again standing in the same spot. It was hot and muggy and during the day one shower followed another. Conditions were nearly the same as they were a week ago, though the water was a trifle lower. But where were the fly and fish? For two long days I covered two miles of water, rose and set free two very small trout. The river was *dead,* and I was completely baffled; had all the fish left this piece of water? Yes—most of them had, but I did not know that until later when I discovered that the big trout from the miles of flat meadows below came up on high water and remained in the upper rocky reaches for a few days only.

In 1927 an old-fashioned dam held the waters of the lake. When power-plants far down the river required water, several boards were lifted and down rushed a young flood—bank high. Enough water down river and down drop the boards for a "shut-off." That's the moment for the fisherman's attack, the big fish are up from the meadows feeding greedily on hatches of fly which a sudden drop favors. Why this condition produces a hatch I do not know, but such is the case for I have seen it happen many times on this and other rivers.

To return to the fishing. The next day was a very hot one. I was puzzled and at high noon was beating a retreat when, in the meadow below the bridge, I saw the tall grass bent by a faint foot-path. The path led to a beautiful pool. It was a slow-moving meadow pool fringed with alders, and the current swung to a focus over deep water. Not a sign of fly or fish, but if there was a fish in the river he would be lying here. With this in mind I broke out a new leader and to the 3X point tied a Red Palmer Badger No. 4 (new style). The fly was floating down the current, it was there and then it was not there, it had disappeared by magic and into the air goes a high-colored three-pound rainbow. The pool was free of ledges and snags, and soon the trout was safely in the net. I wonder—perhaps that may have been the rear guard of a good company returning to the meadows below.

That was the beginning of several seasons of glorious fishing enjoyed by myself and a few old friends. Having discovered the secret of the upper waters, we planned as best we might to be present directly after a "shut-off." But after the building of a new dam at the foot of the first lake, the fishing was never the same. The flow of water appeared to be constant, holding a low level in the rocky reaches below the dam. No longer was the river subjected to bank-high floods with low water following directly, and with the new condition the phenomenal fishing which I found on my first visits to the river never returned. Heavy rainstorms, even sudden cloud-bursts in the hills, never caused the sharp and sudden contrast of high and low water produced by artificial means.

But while it lasted the fishing was *good,* not only in the swift rocky runs and adjacent meadow pools of the upper river but for many miles below where the river shallowed between long stretches of slow-moving water through farm lands and open meadows. When conditions were favorable, hatches of fly in great variety were abundant, and fine rainbow trout from a pound weight to two pounds and over were often in our landing nets. . . .

. . . Now, alas, the old covered bridge, the rocky run above and the meadow pool below, lie many feet under the sparkling waves of Lake Francis.

The New River

W. D. WETHERELL

SINCE THAT FIRST AFTERNOON on the Upper Connecticut, in the ten years since, I've been back well over a hundred times—a statistic that probably carries no significance for anyone but me, yet one I'm childishly pleased with as a mark of my devotion; it's as though I've entered upon a marriage so perfect I renew my vows every chance I get. And—why not admit this?—I'm head over heels in love with the river still, think about it often while I'm away, pine for it, dream about it, rave about its virtues to family and friends, soberly come to terms with its imperfections (which in any case are of a kind to make me love it all the more), take solace from the memory of past assignations even as I find excitement in plotting my next. When it comes to infatuation, the Connecticut and me, it's the heart's whole nine yards.

And it's remarkable, looking back on that first introductory season, how fast the routines started to form that have served me well in the years since, with little variation. The early-morning start, often in darkness, the stars bright out the window as I go around the kitchen on tiptoes trying to bag together a lunch. Tom driving up in his pickup right on schedule, or maybe Ray in his little Volkswagen—the quick stowing of rods, vest, and waders, the brief remarks about the weather, always putting a good face on it, at least at this stage, when even snowflakes on the windshield can be given a propitious slant. The drive up the interstate, high on its ridge overlooking the valley, the two of us talking over prospects, all but rubbing our hands together and chortling in anticipation of the swath we'll cut among these trout. The sunrise over the White Mountains to the east, the summits capped by lenticular clouds that multiply their dimensions in purple-gray swellings. . . . The radio, the news, fading out in static, the last noisome whispers of the world we're leaving behind. . . . Breakfast at our favorite truck stop, the eggs and home fries and homemade toast appearing so fast on our table it's as though the short-order chef has gotten word of our coming through CB radio, anticipated our order well in advance. . . . Leaving the interstate for slow, stately old Route 2, route of the logging truck, the school bus, the moose.

From W. D. Wetherell, *One River More* (New York: The Lyons Press, 1998).

The first view of the Connecticut near Lancaster, giving us a clue as to what kind of water level we'll be fishing in—the banks sandy here, the water slow, but a reliable guide all the same. On through Guildhall, the neat, compact little village where the road cuts north. The vexing question of whether to continue up the west, forgotten side of the river or cross over to busier New Hampshire for the added speed . . . Northumberland, Groveton, North Stratford. . . . Trout water at last, the river not slow, sleepy, and deep anymore, but fast, broken, and rushing, so even through the window glass, in the eight A.M. sunshine, it gives the effect of well-shaken champagne poured down a silver-bronze chute. Fishable? Yes! A bit high, but not too high, and transparently clear from bank to bank, the boulders on the bottom doubled by their own blue shadows. . . . The talk about where to start in, not abstract and hypothetical like it was two hours ago in the darkness, but urgent now, needing a fast decision. Trophy Hole? Perfect. Slug our way up to it while we have all our energy, fish it while the sun has the stoneflies rock and rolling up a storm, then the current on our backs for the long wade back. . . . Parking, unpacking, getting dressed—stopping now and then to blow on our hands, our breath in front of us in crystal balloons that pop apart on anything but the softest syllables. Socks on, waders on, vest on, rod strung up—the ritual that is so important a part of the fly fisher's start. . . . And then the river itself, stepping into it—hardly feeling anything at first, not even coolness, not until we're well out into the current and sense that old familiar pressure on the back of our waders, like a reassuring pat on the rump as the river welcomes us for the 101st time.

There are other rituals in the course of a fishing day, but it's the river that's setting the agenda now, with much more variation, so things never again become quite so formalized as they are when starting out. I've gotten to the point where I need every one of those steps along the way, feel, rightly or wrongly, that if one or two are left out then I won't be able to catch as many fish, or at least not quite as much enjoyment—that substituting apple jelly for marmalade at breakfast will result in botched casts, missed strikes, and overall futility. In life, ritual seems to work best in small things and big things, coffee breaks or weddings, and for me, fishing the river is a mix of both—and yet the small comes first, to the point where I think a fishing day could be described not in terms of fish landed, but solely by all those small, dearly loved familiarities woven into the fabric of a fishing life. The downward, not unpleasant tug a fishing vest gives on the shoulders when you first put it on; the sharp taste of split shot as you bite it closed; the gossamer shine of tippet material blowing in the wind; the fine, almost invisible spray of wetness that comes off a fly line as it shoots forward and drops. "All this is perfectly distinct to the observant eye," Thoreau wrote of delights just as small, "but could easily pass unnoticed by most."

With all this by way of introduction, starting now on the second stage of my exploration, it's time to come forward with what is simultaneously the most extreme and yet sincere bias in my entire arsenal of fishing beliefs: that the most important factor in fly fishing for trout is not casting ability or streamcraft or entomology, but coming to appreciate and understand something of the landscape, terrain, history, and culture of the region through which your river flows.

This is heresy of course—suggesting that anyone setting out to fish the Henry's Fork might do better to bone up on local history than consult guidebooks to the various pools; that sitting in bars and diners listening to the locals talk weather, politics, or crop prices ultimately might be more useful than hiring a guide; that time spent loafing beside a river looking out at the distant views is in many respects even more valuable than time spent studying the water. All this not only flies counter to prevailing wisdom, but hardly makes up a corner of it at all—and yet I'm absolutely convinced it's true.

Why? Remember, we're talking bias here, personal hunch and intuition, and it would be hard to isolate the direct causative factors between understanding the region and understanding the fish. Certainly, to try to come to an appreciation of the larger scape a river runs through demands of a person a certain investment of time and attention—and it's exactly the ones who are willing to do this who are most likely to bring the same qualities to their fishing. Then, too, it slows a fly fisher down, looking outward like this, and in fishing, slowing down is half the battle. Too often we come to the river caught up in the fast, frantic pace of the artificial world we're seeking to escape, and this man-made schedule is the first and most onerous burden we must shed. A river can't be rushed—this is the first rule of fishing, the second, and the third—and so any time spent along its banks *not* fishing is a worthy investment, slowing, quite literally, the speeding hands of our inner, overwound clocks.

Listening to the locals, trying to learn who they are, what their lives are like, pays off, too, since these are the people you will encounter along the stream, and there is simply no talking to them unless you're willing to make some effort to share their world. Fly fishing is more art than science (although fully neither), and one of the criteria for being good at it is the ability to take into simultaneous consideration many varied threads. Local knowledge is one of the most important of these elements—and how else to tap it except by meeting it halfway?

I could back up my theoretical arguments with a more pragmatic one, point out that the best fly fishers I know happen to be the ones who have an instinct toward the elusive "feel" of the region they fish in. I could also point out examples of fly fishers for whom none of this counts—those who are too wrapped up in their own passion to focus on anything but the fish there in front of them. Not understanding the country's rhythms, they're locked into the rhythm they bring from home, so there's a clash right from the start; not catching very much understanding, they will not catch very many trout. Not catching many trout, they will hire a guide next time, or buy yet another book on fishing how-to, and, because they are mistaken in their basic assumptions, the river will always run away from them and never be grasped.

This kind of larger understanding and empathy is even more important when the region through which the river flows is an unusual, even quirky one, not at all what it first appears. The Connecticut River, starting as a small beaver pond only a few yards from the Canadian line, flows through a series of four mountain lakes of increasing diameter before spilling through Murphy Dam and becoming a full-fledged trout river in the town of Pittsburg, New Hampshire. Little bigger than a good cast across, fast, weed-slick, and rapid, it's not until it reaches Stewartstown and works the west out from its southwest trending that it becomes prime fishing water; from here on in, for the next 235 miles, it forms the border between Vermont and New Hampshire, though in a compromise that goes back to the former state's admission to the union in 1791, New Hampshire law still governs the river itself. Between Pittsburg and the vicinity of Lancaster the valley remains in the same overall pattern and can be spoken of as one; this is the region, the hard, gritty, difficult region, that in the course of my fishing trips I gradually began to know.

There's no shorthand name for this land, or rather, there are two names, both of which testify to the fact that it's a world apart. The Vermont side of the river, not without some irony, is called "the Northeast Kingdom"—a broad upland of granite hills and boreal forest, with a sparse, hard-working population settled in a few, well-scattered villages. Across the river in New Hampshire it's called "the North Country"—a similar landscape, only with higher, steeper mountains and, if anything, even poorer, more nondescript towns. The river valley proper, the broad floodplain, manages to seem as pastoral and gentle as anything further south (the white farmhouses, the old ones, are the most prosperous looking, best-kept buildings in sight and have been for two hundred years); a mile from the river on either side it's a different story. Here the upland begins, and it gives a rougher, grittier kind of feel, both in the landscape and in the habitation. Trailers covered in plastic; log cabins that are never quite finished and look horribly out of place; suburban-style ranch houses built from kits; sagging tourist cabins long since gone bust. This is as far from the familiar Currier & Ives stereotype of New England as it's possible to be, and much closer in feel to Appalachia, or timber country out West. Many of the towns, even in summer, manage to give off the worn, tired feel of perpetual November; Colebrook, the market town in the region's center, has the wide main street and slapdash, unfinished feel of a small town in Wyoming, though its origins date back two centuries. Like the river, the money has always flowed south here and probably always will.

An intimidating land, in the end—a region everyone agrees is "different," though without any of them quite agreeing where exactly the difference lies. Some would point to the terrain, those mountains that aren't as high as the Whites or as approachable as the Greens, but humpbacked and shaggy, less visited, more remote. Others might point out that, geographically speaking, this is very much a dead end—all the roads seem to end at border crossings which, for lack of traffic, always seem to be closed. There's the prominent French influence, or rather the Quebecois; the convenience stores have names like DeBannville's, the tackle shops Ducrets, and the churches are more apt to be cement, workaday Catholic ones than the stately Congregational churches associated with townscapes further south. Others, the wiseacres, might have fun with the moose, point out that moose-watching is the favorite (some would say the only) after-dinner activity. Sensitive observers, those who like to gauge a region in the faces of its inhabitants, might point to the people you see in diners or waiting by their trucks as they fill up with gas—their beaten mien and shabby clothes, the hill-country strength that stays hidden from strangers, yet you know must be there.

The difference is as much good as it is bad—people who linger here, make the attempt to know the region intimately, agree on this, too. There's the Connecticut, of course, its winding beauty, the locus for all that is soft and easy in the landscape, at least in summer. The beaver ponds lost in the ridges near the Quebec line, the brook trout lost and lonely in their centers, splashing to a fly like drowning swimmers to a life ring. Those moose that are everywhere—the wildness that clings to them like a second, more exotic pelt. The sense the surrounding forest gives of true northing—of boreal spareness and boreal flint, hills scraped as clean of ornament as the people who by stubbornness or inertia make it their home. The fact that it's a yuppie-free zone and always will be—that even its lakes haven't been gentrified or tamed.

You can take the difference even deeper. Living in most parts of America is like living on an inclined plane or gigantic slide, one that's tipped in only one direction, toward the great American middle ground—middle in jobs, middle in culture, middle in aspirations—so all you can hope for, growing up in it, it to drop pinball-like into one of several inevitable and ready-made slots. Here in this forgotten corner, up high on the height of land where the watersheds begin slanting over toward the St. Lawrence, the sense is of sliding away from America altogether, lives running in a totally opposite direction. Those radio talk shows in French. The poverty so pervasive the Depression is remembered as a prosperous time. The legends of bootleggers, draft exiles, and smugglers. The roll call of hermits and loners and misfits who have fit in here and nowhere else. The old communes and forgotten marijuana fields rotting away deep in the woods. The cranky politics. Yes, in a nothing direction entirely.

Cranky politics? For anyone driving through the region this is most apparent in the local custom of planting your property every four years with an orchard of campaign signs, one that, once staked, are only reluctantly removed, so, feeling in something of a time warp already, seeing those signs, you're apt to think Ford/Dole is still running against Carter/Mondale. The shabbier the house, the more likely it is these signs will be for Republicans, though many are hand-lettered and crude, warning the U.S. out of the U.N., or vowing fidelity to guns. This is your basic old-fashioned cranky New Hampshire reactionary right, the kind you might have thought had crept up here to Coos County to die, were it not for the fact it seems to be spreading. There's an anarchistic flavor to it all; you get the feeling, talking to them even casually, that what these people really hate is any government interference whatsoever, though in the same breath they're berating it, they complain about how the state government down in Concord (or Montpelier) hardly seems aware of their existence. . . .

There's tourism here, of an old-fashioned blue-collar sort—northern New Hampshire is one of the last refuges of your basic $28-a-night tourist cabin—but nowhere near the kind that overwhelms the White Mountains every summer. Over on the Vermont side of the river there's even less in the way of visitors, and it's possible to drive the roads in October at the height of foliage season and never see another out-of-state car. What the region does experience in the way of mass invasion comes in appropriately bizarre fashion; the biggest event of the year in Colebrook, for instance, is the "Blessing of the Bikes" in May, when thousands of motorcyclists from all over New England drive their machines past a Catholic shrine set in a little grotto off Route 3. The shape of the two states accounts for a difference in the tourist flow; when you drive north in Vermont, you're driving toward the broad base of its inverted triangle, spreading everyone out; when you drive north in New Hampshire, you're driving into the apex, so everyone becomes concentrated.

Logging is the main industry here and always has been. It's an important part of the economy in the lower parts of both states, but up here it's the only industry and so it's more visible, with logging trucks as common as cars, tote roads going everywhere, scars on the mountainsides from recent cuts, and, in mill towns like Groveton, mountains of sawdust and the sweet, heavy smell of boiling pulp.

Skidders, forwarders, and whole-log "harvesters" have made logging into a humdrum, brutally efficient business, though one that still carries with it more than its share of danger. It has its romance, too, or at least its history of romance. A hundred years ago the Upper Connecticut was the starting point for the great logging drives on the river (still the longest in world history), wherein the timber cut from the surrounding hills was sledded over the snow every winter, piled on the river's ice, then—with the help of a great deal of manpower—floated on the springtime head of water down to the mills in Massachusetts, three hundred miles to the south.

Log driving was one of those hard, miserably paid jobs that, like cow punching and whaling, seems more glamorous in retrospect than it probably did at the time. Look closely at those old photos of rivermen posing by their bateaux or waist-deep in a river full of logs: along with the pride and cockiness, you see a great deal of plain old bone-weary exhaustion. For logging was a brutal way to make a buck, one requiring agility and great strength, accomplished by a mix of Yankee woodsmen, immigrant Finns, and itinerant Quebecois. Rising before dawn to spend fourteen hours up to their waists in forty-degree water, ordered about by dictatorial woods bosses, preyed upon by hustlers of every stripe—it's no wonder rivermen were famous for their brawls (caulked boots festooned with case-hardened spikes three-quarters of an inch long were their weapon of choice, the flying leap toward the face their favorite tactic); the not uncommon murder (Canaan, Vermont, once had a lawless, rock 'em-sock 'em reputation to rival Abilene's or Dodge's): the devil-may-care attitude that made them spend their money as fast as they took it in (brothels, even up here at the drive's start); their chilblains, lumbago, and TB. . . .

There remain few visible traces of those days. At Lyman Falls you can see what's left of an old wooden dam and sluice; detouring into the woods to get to better fishing positions, you'll sometimes stumble upon the rusty old cables that held boomed logs in place . . . but that's about it. At least once during my fishing day I find myself wondering what the river looked like full of logs (and what it did to the trout—did they just hunker down until all the confusion swept past?), but it's a tough feat for imagination to pull off. Partly this is due to the fact that my fishing is in the clement months, so the river seems too relaxed and gentle to have ever been involved with anything so chaotic; partly because, on this side of the mythic enlargement time brings, the river now seems far too small.

But there are other moments when I can picture the log drives perfectly—autumn days, for instance, when the water is high and the leaves are gone from the trees, when the water seems darker, more furious, capable of something mighty, waiting only its chance. You can also sense something of the atmosphere of log-drive days just by cruising the roads, looking at the hardscrabble towns, sensing the feeling that something essential about the region, its very heart, has long ago been swept downstream.

The kind of man who found the log drives his escape—you can picture him, too. Earlier this season, after fishing just above the covered bridge at Columbia, climbing back up to my car, I discovered my keys were missing. I gave myself the usual frantic shakedown, then, thinking I had left them locked in the car, started prying at the window trying to get my hand far enough in to pull up the lock.

I had just found them (in the most obvious spot, naturally—the toes of my waders) when a pickup pulled over and young man in a T-shirt and jeans jumped out, ready and eager to help. He was no more than nineteen, short and wiry, with a large French nose, bright blue eyes, and a restless, blinking kind of expression that couldn't stay fixed in one mood for long.

"Stupid of me," I said, holding up the keys. "Thought we were going to have to smash that window."

The young man grinned. "Why I stopped! Wouldn't have been the first time I smashed one."

I pointed to the chainsaw and gasoline cans in the back of his truck. "Looks like you're pretty busy in the woods."

"Nope. Not anymore. Got laid off"—he glanced down at his watch—"two hours ago."

"Christ. Sorry."

He grinned even wider. "No problem. They'll hire me back if I want. Old man Toller, he lays off everyone after nineteen weeks so we don't get enough consecutive in for unemployment. Then he hires us back, starts it over." He looked toward the river, spat without any particular malice, added by way of after-thought, "He's a bastard. Anyway, it don't matter. This time Sunday I'm out of here."

I played a hunch. "Army?"

"Marines."

Well, there it was, the North Country's other industry, the export trade that works full-time in so many of the forgotten places of the world, the beautiful places—sending its children to places less beautiful, less forgotten, less hard. With time, if he serves enough years for a pension, perhaps he will come back again to hunt and fish out his retirement, be able to enjoy the land without having to wrest a living from it, fight that particular battle at such long odds.

But he was excited with the future the way any young person gets excited when it comes time to tell the place you grew up in to go to hell. He pointed to the river, bent his head over so he could peer under the first tree limbs upstream.

"Always wanted to try a fly rod, see if I can keep myself from strangling in all that line. But up there's where you want to be fishing. Base of that little island, current scrapes out a big hole. Go there at night sometime. That's my secret spot, and here I am handing it over free of charge." He shook his head, ruefully this time. "What good is it to me? Hell, you can have them all. Up there by the town hall—good spot, too. You go down to where you see those cows, there's a little sandbar that'll take you right out in the middle of the river like a causeway. Rest is mud, so that's the only way. Good spot for browns. You know the old gravel pit down by the airport?"

On and on he went—my brain raced to take all this down; I kept wishing I had a tape recorder—going over his favorite spots, all the stories that went with them, so it was as if this were another part of the burden he had to shed before he could be free of the place and leave. Light, wiry, tough already at nineteen—it was easy to picture him growing up by the river in the days of the great drives, begging each year to go, being reined in by his mother as long as possible, until finally come the day—and off he goes with his stagged kersey pants cut short in riverman fashion, the black felt hat, the peavey or cant dog, the spiked boots . . . and with a last farewell glance or, more likely still, without any backward glance whatsoever, away he floats down that river, never to return.

If getting to know a region helps you to get to know the fishing, the converse is true as well—there are few better ways to get to know a region than spending your time fishing it. Out in all weathers through six months of the year; poking your nose into all kinds of unexpected venues as you seek out new water; spending long hours in what is often someone's backyard; relaxing on the bank near a road, watching the traffic stream past; helping yourself to wild raspberries; learning where the old apple trees are that still bear fruit, if only by snagging your backcast on their branches; having the local flotsam and jetsam drift past your waist (red Frisbies, a blue Styrofoam "noodle"—whatever water toy is currently the rage); sliding down the midden heaps that river banks often become, so the archaeological perspective comes into play; talking to the local fishermen, the occasional duck hunter, the kids who come down to the river to throw stones in the current or hunt crayfish; being involved in a common pursuit people enjoy asking you about; making friends in the diners where you break for coffee or the bars where you go to celebrate your success. After a while, all this adds up. This is even more true if you go about your fishing quietly and modestly, so you all but become a part of the riverscape yourself—a tree, a willow, albeit one with eyes and ears and understanding.

I've often thought a good book could come out of this—a collection of tales on the order of Ivan Turgenev's *Sportsman's Sketches,* changing the hunter into a fly fisher who in the course of his or her exploring learns much about the local people and their customs, their heartbreaks, and sadness, their losses and their loves (Coos County, New Hampshire, badly needs its own poet or novelist; Frost never got this far north, and all the fiction writers seem to be concentrated on the Vermont side of the river). Just last week, fishing the river in the course of a long June day, I came away with enough locales to fill the book's first half. I started fishing behind the county old folks home, a Gothic pile straight out of Dickens, where people in wheelchairs sunning themselves on the terrace waved as I waded past; a hundred yards downstream (the state liking to put all its institutional eggs in one convenient basket), I passed the county "farm" that serves as the reformatory—young men this time, too busy piling up hay to wave, hardly noticing as, right below them, I landed a good brown. A little later, driving upstream, I fished behind some abandoned factories, had my thoughts filled with a *temps perdu* kind of moodiness that made me think again of the region's boom-and-bust history. In late afternoon I was caught in a sudden hailstorm, took shelter in De Bannville's, where French mémeres in curlers shook their heads and clucked in sympathy as the ice melted down from my hair. At dusk, waiting for the sulphurs to get going, I ran into a ninety-two-year-old bait fisherman, pumped him shamelessly, not only for information about the fishing, but for his memories of the old days (these took a morbid turn; most of his stories were of young men and women who had drowned in the Connecticut and people he knew who had helped pull them out).

And, just for the record, it's the bait fishermen you want to talk to if you're interested in learning equally about the fish and the region. Too many fly fishers these days are too narrowly focused on their pursuit, too businesslike and competitive to spare much time for my random kind of sightseeing; then, too, fly fishers you see on the river are apt to be from elsewhere, without much in the way of local knowledge. Spin fishermen, many of them, are pretty much just out for the afternoon, and when it comes to learning about the river, few have paid the requisite dues. No, what you want is the classic worm-chucking old-timer (by old-timer I mean anyone between the ages of fourteen and a hundred who fishes alone and obsessively and ponders the implications of what they discover), though once upon a recent time, to fly fishers with illusions of purity, these were apt to be viewed as our enemy. Secretive when they're fishing, they're talkative when you catch them at ease, and, like the teenager leaving me his secrets or the old man with his tragic stories, they're invaluable sources of information on the river you're trying your damnedest to figure out.

The hatch I was waiting for has started now right on schedule—little sulphur duns whose color is halfway between the white of a Cahill and the yellow of a daffodil just past its prime. The pool I'm fishing is a slow, even one, where the current, running broken along the Vermont bank, slides to the east, widens and slows, creating a living-room-sized terrace (with boulders for armchairs) that is almost always dappled with feeding trout. Catchable trout—for a change I feel pretty certain of this, and thus take my time getting ready, giving me the opportunity to go back again to one of the points I made earlier.

It concerns the river being the one locus of beauty in an otherwise hard-pressed land. Fishing the tributary streams, hiking the woods, driving the back roads, spending much time in town, you get the feeling that there is indeed much in the way of beauty here in this northern wedge of land, and yet it seems to come at you through a gauze, a scrim, that all but makes you rub your eyes in bewilderment, trying to clear them so you can see things plain. It's partially a scrim of poverty: the sense you have, even today of what brutalities can be inflicted upon a land where the growing season is six weeks too short; a recognition that *beauty* is not a word that can be tossed around lightly in this kind of world, not with the shortcuts, stopgaps, and scraping that is visible on every hand. And yet, go down to the river, spend your days in its pastoral corridor, and the scrim literally dissolves; words like *lush* or *lovely,* prissy absurdities when applied anywhere else in the north country, suddenly become fully applicable, so it makes you see not just the Connecticut, but the entire region with a gentler, more forgiving kind of appreciation.

Wading out toward those fish, tugging line down from my reel preparatory to casting, picking out my spot, I'm aware not only of the merging cobalt rings spread across the current by the trouts' inhalations, not only the yellow-blue surge of water where the lowering sun hits the river and thickens it, but the tall, seed-heavy meadow grass that begins on the bank, the bristly hedgerow of sumac, black cherry, and ash, the first sloping esker with its birch and white pine, the staircase of spruce-covered mountains that leads toward the coral-dark sky—Vega at the top of it, the high steady beacon of a midsummer's eve.

"What a land!" I say to myself, not for the first time. "What a river!" and I want to shout.

Ten minutes left of dusk in which to appreciate it all—just time enough to end on a personal note, expose to light what my mind kept chewing over when it should have been concentrating on those trout. It was about the boy I met earlier in the season, the logger who was bailing out for the Marines. I thought of him, and in a strange way that surprised me; I realized I envied him, and not just a little.

What's going on here? A dead-end job, telling the boss to shove it, going off to the tender mercies of boot camp—no, it wasn't envy of any of these. Envy instead of what he probably hated most in himself: of having this hard, bitter land as the place he grew up in, the region he will—for better or worse—compare every other with for the rest of his days. I suppose it's a mixed blessing—mixed for those who leave, just as it is for those who hunker down and stay. Live your whole life in such a landscape and between tears and exhaustion and familiarity, the beauty disappears; it's someone like me, neither local nor stranger, who, when it comes to appreciation, has the priceless vantage point of standing halfway in between.

In this respect—and here again I'm speaking most personally—almost anything would be better than being from the suburbs. When that boy searches his memory one day it will be of dark forests and impetuous rivers and snowstorms in October; when I search mine, it's of patios and split-levels and manicured front lawns, spiced with nothing more romantic than the occasional vacant lot. I think of Chekhov, born into a family of peasants, vowing to squeeze the serf from his soul drop by hateful drop—and remember as a young man vowing in much the same way that I would force everything suburban from my soul or die trying. Hence, I suppose, those long hours on the river in all kinds of weather, fishing long past the point of exhaustion, dreaming about the river when I'm away, coming back every chance I get. Much has changed in my life—and yet the cleansing still goes on.

And maybe all this helps explain the feeling that comes over me sometimes that this hard northern land, with the river as its mouthpiece, is speaking to me quite plainly and directly—that if I haven't succeeded in articulating its message here, it's my own fault, not the region's. Certainly, having this feeling . . . of embrace, of acceptance, of an odd and powerful kind of pity . . . is a good, reassuring sign that I'm that much closer to understanding the river, making it, in the vain way we speak of such things, mine. If stage one was that first specific reconnaissance, then stage two is this working toward a more general, wider appreciation . . . and this is what I flattered myself that I had now, as a tall shadow in a forest of round ones, I climbed out of the current, reached the crest of the bank, then turned my head quickly back toward the river like a man trying to catch it unawares.

Chapter 11

GLEANINGS

The Springfield Canoe Club is one of the most thriving of local institutions, having increased its membership in a couple of years from 35 to 100, while it has one of the handsomest, best arranged clubhouses and a fleet that is not equaled in the country. The young people are beginning to realize the delights of our convenient river, and it has become quite the fad to join the Canoe Club, have one's own private canoe, and take one's best girl out paddling.
—Springfield Graphic, 11 June 1892

Anyone compiling an anthology has to make wrenching decisions about what to include, especially since his or her first temptation is to include everything. Photocopies are reluctantly pulled from the accumulating pile, put back in again, edited and shortened, finally, the stack of pages growing too high, yanked out again with a vicious act of will.

I quickly discovered that selections that didn't make the cut, for one reason or the other, made an interesting anthology of their own. Here they are, the gleanings from a year's worth of reading, little excerpts that, interesting in themselves, testify to the depth and variety of Connecticut River writing.

Even with gleanings, I'm aware most of all of how much space I'd still like to have. How good it would be, for instance, to include in all its mind-numbing detail and difficult legalese, the Clean Water Act of 1965, which, in terms of its beneficial effect on the river, is the most important single piece of writing ever devoted, in any way, shape, or form, to the river.

Naming the River

JEROLD WIKOFF

WHEN THE DUTCH NAVIGATOR Adriaen Block discovered the river, he named it De Versche Rivere—the "Freshwater River." This name was used by the Dutch for over thirty-five years, until they were forced by the English to abandon the river in 1650. English settlers never used the Dutch name. Instead, its name for them was always the Connecticut, taken from the Indian name Quinni-tuk-ut, meaning "long river." The "tuk" apparently signified a river whose waters are driven in waves by the tide or wind.

Although Connecticut was the name used by the English, there was little agreement as to its spelling. Governor Winthrop did use the spelling Connecticut seven times in his 1633 *History of New England,* but in the same book he also wrote Conecticot and Connecticott. William Bradford of the Plymouth Colony spelled the river's name at various times as Conightecute, Conightecut, Conightecutt, Coonightecutt, and Conightecute. Rogers Williams spelled it Quonihticut, Qunnihticut, and Qunnticut.

All told, more than forty spellings of the river's name were recorded in early histories, including Quinetucquet, Quenticutt, Quoncktacut, Canedicott, Canetticut, Connectecotte, Conectigus, Conittekock, Conitycot, Countticott, Conecticot, and Conite Cock. Why Connecticut came to be the preferred spelling is unknown. Perhaps it was simply that over the years this spelling seemed to conform most to the way people pronounced the name.

From Jerold Wikoff, *The Upper Valley* (Chelsea, Vt.: Chelsea Green Publishing Company, 1985).

Dinosaur Tracks near Holyoke

GEORGE W. BAIN AND HOWARD A. MEYERHOFF

PEOPLE STILL WRITE FROM as far away as the Rocky Mountains to ask if the dinosaur footprints beside the Connecticut River are still in place. They are. Anyone may see them in that triangular area between the Boston and Maine tracks and Federal Highway 5 about one-quarter mile north of the entrance to Mountain Park. Marvelous as their preservation from the assaults of man may seem, it is even more amazing that they should have been preserved in rock at all.

The footprint beds are shaly sandstones about thirty feet above the Granby tuff—a bed of volcanic ash formed in late Triassic time. They are inclined 15° towards the river, and even the higher strata which form the "Riffles" are footprint-bearing. The sandstones are ripple-marked, and they contain worm trails and a few casts of salt crystals. Some beds have impressions of gymnosperm leaves resembling firs and cordiate leaves resembling reeds. The footprints range from half an inch to ten inches in length, and the stride of the larger animals was from five to eight feet. Most of the tracks are headed up the present slope, but a few are going in the opposite direction.

The Deerfield Captives

JOHN DEMOS

THERE IS ONE DAY of respite: the captors order a "rest" on the Sabbath. John Williams leads an impromptu worship service for his Deerfield flock. His sermon text is drawn from the Book of Lamentations:

From George W. Bain and Howard A. Meyerhoff, *The Flow of Time in the Connecticut Valley* (Springfield, Mass.: Connecticut Valley Historical Museum, 1963).

From John Demos, *The Unredeemed Captive* (New York: Knopf, 1994).

"The Lord is righteous, for I have rebelled against his commandment . . . My virgins and my young men are gone into captivity." And the group sings a psalm (44:9–14) on a similar theme: "Though hast cast off and put us to shame . . . and has scattered us among the heathen." The Indians look on with bemused curiosity, and "upbraid us because our singing [is] not so loud as theirs." Still, the captives find comfort—even "revival"—in their wilderness devotions. The site of all this is the confluence of the Connecticut and a west-side tributary; in subsequent years the latter will be named Williams River.

Account of Eight Enemy Indians Killed by Caleb Lyman

CALEB LYMAN

SOMETIME IN THE MONTH of May, 1704, there came intelligence from *Albany,* of a number of enemy *Indians* up *Connecticut River,* who had built a fort and planted corn, at a place called *Cowasauck*. On the fifth of *June* following, we let out (by order of authority) from *Northampton,* and went nine days journey into the wilderness (through much difficulty, by reason of the enemy's hunting and scouting in the woods, as we perceived by their tracks and firing) and then came across some fresh tracks, which we followed till we came in sight of the abovesaid river. Supposing their might be a number of *Indians* at hand, we being not far from the place where the fort was said to be built, here we made a halt, to consult what methods to take. And soon concluded to send out a spy, with green leaves for a *cap* and *veste* to prevent his own discovery, and to find out the enemy. But before our spy was gone out of sight, we saw two *Indians,* at a considerable distance from us, in a *canoo,* and so immediately recalled him. And soon after we heard the firing of a gun up the river. Upon which we concluded to keep close till sunset; and then if we

From Samuel Penhallow, *The History of the Wars of New England, with the Eastern Indians* (Boston: n.p., 1726).

could make any further discovery of the enemy, to attack them, if possible, in the night. And accordingly, when the evening came on, we moved towards the river, and soon perceived a *smoke,* at about half a miles distance, as we thought, where we (afterwards) found they had taken up their lodging. But so great was the difficulty, that (though we used our utmost care and diligence in it) we were not able to make the approach till about *two* a clock in the morning, when we came within twelve rods of the *wigwam,* where they lay. But here we met with a new difficulty, which we feared would have ruined the whole design; for the ground was so covered over with dry sticks and brush, for the space of five rods, that we could not pass without making such a *crackling,* as we thought would alarm the enemy and give them time to escape. But while we were contriving to compass our design, God in his good Providence so ordered, that a very small cloud arose, which gave a smart *clap of thunder,* and a sudden shower of rain. And this opportunity we embraced, to run throw the thicket; and so came undiscovered within sight of the *wigwam;* and perceived by their noise, that the enemy were awake. But however, being unwilling to lose any time, we crept on our hands and knees till we were within three or four rods of them. Then we arose, and ran to the side of the *wigwam,* and fired in upon them. And flinging down our *guns,* we surrounded them with our *clubs* and *hatchets,* and knockt down several we met with. But after all our diligence, *two* of their number made their escape from us: one *mortally* wounded, and the other not hurt; as we afterwards heard.

When we came to look over the slain, we found seven dead upon the spot: *six* of whom we *scalpt,* and left the other unscalpt. (Our *Indians* saying, They would give one to the country, since we had each of us one; and so concluded we should all be rich enough.) When the action was thus over, we took our *scalps* and *plunder,* such as *guns, skins,* etc. and the enemies *canoos;* in which we came down the river about twelve miles, by break of day. And then thought it prudence to dismiss and break the *canoos,* knowing there were some of the enemy betwixt us and home.

Rogers Arrives at Fort Number Four

KENNETH ROBERTS

THE DOOR AT THE END of the room burst open. A stolid-looking man in a wrinkled blue uniform peered at us, blinking. "Which?" he asked. "Which one?" He came to us. "They said Major Rogers! None of you are Major Rogers!"

"I'm Rogers," the Major said. "Now here: write down what I say. I can't repeat. What's your name?"

"Bellows," the officer said, "in charge of King's stores." He clapped his hands to his pockets, looked confused, then hurried from the room. When he returned he had pencil and paper. "We didn't know——" he stammered. "We heard—where did you——"

"Get canoes," Rogers said. "Load 'em with food. Send 'em up river. Mouth of the Ammonoosuc."

"These men are Provincials," Bellows said apologetically. "They're bound home. There's only——"

"Get settlers," Rogers said. "Good canoemen. Hire 'em!"

"It's pretty bad weather," Bellows said doubtfully. "Maybe when it clears off——"

Rogers rose wavering to his feet, then straightened himself to his full height and seemed to fill the room. In a strained, hoarse voice he said: "Today! Today! Now! Can't you realize there's a hundred Rangers at the mouth of the Ammonoosuc, starving! Get men and pay 'em! Get all the settlers into the fort! Call 'em in! Drum 'em up! I'll talk to 'em! For Christ's sake, get started!"

From Kenneth Roberts, *Northwest Passage* (Garden City, N.Y.: Doubleday, Doran & Company, 1937).

A Visit from Washington

GEORGE WASHINGTON

MONDAY MAY 19TH, 1789. We arrived at Middletown, on Connecticut River, being met two or three miles from it by the respectable citizens . . . I took a walk around the Town, from the heights of which the prospect is beautiful. Belonging to this place, I was informed (by a Genl. Sage) that there were about 20 vessels. . . .

Having dined . . . passing through a Parish of Middletown and Weathersfield, we arrived at Hartford about sundown. At Weathersfield we were met by a part of the Hartford light horse, and a number of Gentlemen from the same place with Colonel Wadsworth, at their head, and escorted to Bub's Tavern, where we lodged.

Another Bridge Disaster

WALPOLE (N.H.) POLITICAL OBSERVER

[15 December 1804]

"On Thursday, the 8th [December], Isaac Grant, one of the workmen completing the flooring of the new bridge connecting Brattleboro and Hinsdale fell backwards from the center of the western arch into the river. He fell about 30 into about 25 feet of water. He could not swim but on rising to the surface he was told not to struggle against the current which being swift carried him some rods below the bridge where he was saved by the exertions of two men who came to his assistance. He was so exhausted that it was some hours before he was restored to his senses.

"The humane activity and determined presence of mind of those who

From *Diary of Washington* (Original manuscripts first printed New York, 1858).
From The *Political Observer* of Walpole, New Hampshire, 1804, 1805.

saved the life of this valuable citizen had they lived within the notice of a humane society would doubtless have been honored with a medal. It is only in our power to notice their merit by inserting the names of Jacob Locke of Walpole and Lewis Brewer."

[16 February 1805]

"We learn that on Thursday last the new bridge lately erected across the Connecticut River between Brattleboro and Hinsdale fell, and was crushed to ruins. The cause is said to have been the great weight of snow lodged on it. The private loss must be heavy and the public inconvenience not small."

A Boy in Cromwell

JOHN HOWARD REDFIELD

THE COMPLETION OF A vessel ready for launching was a great event in the quiet village, and to us youngsters was a holiday of delight. The newly painted hull, with its dark sides relieved by a strip of white, blue or red, the national colors flying above, the "ways" on which she was to glide into the river, and which were slippery with grease and flax-seed, the resounding blows of the hammers and axes, as the wedges forced up the cradle to receive the vessel's weight as the shores which had previously supported her were successively knocked away, then that last anxious moment when the final order to "knock away the quick-shore" was shouted, then the watching for the first slow movement announced by cries of "There she goes!" the quicker and quicker motion of the huge mass until its plunge into the water; then the rise of the stern and the descent of the bow, as the vessel came to her level in the new element, all her former supports flung aside and floating away like useless husks, the cracking of the bottle as the vessel made her plunge and received her

From *Recollections of John Howard Redfield* (1900).

name, all these were fascinations no boy could resist, or could ever forget. Happy was the urchin who had the unspeakable privilege of launching in the vessel, a privilege rarely granted unless to some one nearly connected the owner. At a much later date I had the joy of launching in a freight barge built for my father, and still later in a ship built in Guidersleeve's yard at Portland opposite Cromwell.

The Golden Age of Purple Prose

HARPER'S NEW MONTHLY MAGAZINE

IT IS A WINSOME village in all its details, no less than in its healthful picturesque seat, terraced high above the river shores. . . .

Brattleborough is, after Northampton, the most popular summer residence of ruralizers and invalids in the Valley of the Connecticut. Its mountain proximity gives greater piquancy to its temperatures than the lower latitude affords, while its great water-cure hotels are scarcely less famous. If these Priessnitz places here should be Erricsonized a little in style and title, and called air instead of water cures, the truth would be more nearly told. With the two magic agencies united, both pure, fresh, and sparkling, fair Hygeia would be sure to work wonders before the season waned.

The broad and verdant lands of the Vermont Lunatic Asylum, spreading away on the northward to the banks of West River, look, in their quiet summer beauty, like a fitting domain for a "Castle of Indolence," where this busy world and its cares might be easily and happily forgotten. Surely in such smiles as Nature here puts on, their [sic] must be balm for mind diseased.

From *Harper's New Monthly Magazine* (August 1856).

Augustus Saint-Gaudens, of Cornish, Says Goodbye

WALTER HARD

FIRST IN THE OLD barn and later, after a disastrous fire, in his new studio, Saint-Gaudens turned out sketches, heroic statues, bronzes, designs for United States coins, and medallions and reliefs in marble and in bronze.

He loved the river and the surrounding hills. "It is very beautiful," he said a few days before he died, as he looked out at a sunset behind Mt. Ascutney, "but I want to go farther away." . . .

Tri-State Points

GEORGE CALVIN CARTER

FROM A NUMBER OF hills in Vermont and New Hampshire near their southern boundaries, local and summer residents may look upon the alluring vistas of three states, while from some of the elevations south of the northern Massachusetts line, both Vermont and New Hampshire may be viewed, none of them can see the exact point at which the three states meet. It gives one a real thrill to visit that spot.

One noted writer refers to "that cryptic and elusive spot, where one can stand with both feet in Massachusetts and, leaning forward place the left hand in Vermont and the right in New Hampshire." This sounds both sensible and feasible, but the simple fact that it can't be done shows that

From Walter Hard, *The Connecticut* (New York: Rinehart & Company, 1947).
From George Calvin Carter, *Samuel Morey* (Concord, NH: privately printed, 1945).

the writer was never in that immediate vicinity, much less actually attempted the feat so beautifully described.

The author has been there and found that a copper spike had been set in a granite post, the latter deeply inbedded in the very slippery clay and silt bank of the river. At the time of call the top of this marker was about eighteen inches under water and was visible only when the lights and shadows were just right. However, the visitor had been made ready for the ordeal and by some very crude, but none the less effective methods, was able to touch the copper spike and get a real thrill in the realization that he was walking around in three states all the time, although at no time more than a few inches from the center of the marker.

This was accomplished by stringing a double line of telephone wire around a tree on the Vermont side, knotting the wire at frequent intervals to hand holds, and gradually leading down the steep and very slippery bank, whether out of water or under it, very much as a lineman would use rope or wire in climbing up a slippery steep, or letting himself down into a dangerous abyss. The "trip" was successful, but is not recommended. If anything had gone wrong, as, for instance, a broken wire or a slip in making a hand hold, the visitor would have been taken care of by the rapidly flowing river in short order.

Because this tri-state marker is sunk in a rapidly descending mud bank, it is called "The Mud Turtle Monument." It marks the southeastern corner of Vermont and the southwestern corner of New Hampshire as they meet on the Massachusetts line. The copper bolt is set in a granite block marker, itself set in a mass of concrete, set feet square, at low water mark of the Connecticut River. The letters "MASS" are cut on the south face, "VT" on the west face, "1895" on the north face, and "N.H." on the east face. The elevation at top of copper bolt is 177.017 feet. Latitude, 42,—43' 37.21. Longitude, 72,—27' 32.08. . . .

Now for the "cryptic and elusive" Tri-Town, Tri-County, and Twin Country marker. Going upstream with the Connecticut to find its source, it has suddenly veered to the right at its juncture with Hall's Stream and continues toward its four lakes of origin through the very heart of Western Coos County. The northern tri-state boundary, therefore, is to be found in Hall's Stream at a point where are joined the farm lands of Austin Hann, Pittsburg, New Hampshire, and Mrs. Nate Beecher, Canaan, Vermont. Here again, the normal low water mark becomes the boundary, which is designated by an appropriate marker set in cement. At low water it is here possible to stand with one foot in Vermont, another in New Hampshire and throw a stone into Quebec, for the other side of the stream is, of course, Canada.

The northeast corner of Vermont has a fine large reference monument, on one edge of which is a vertical line indicating Pittsburg, New Hampshire, to be on one side and Canaan, Vermont, on the other. On the broad face of the monument is this inscription: "Supreme Court of the United States, Boundary Commission, 1934. North East Corner of Vermont is a point at low water mark on the west side of the Connecticut River in Lat. 45,—00, 49.20, Long. 71,—27, 57.48, N,—89, 40' E. 314 ft. from this marker. Low water elevation, 1,001 feet."

The Last Drive

KATE MEADER

THE SHOW BEGAN ONE sultry June evening while the family was gathered on the back verandah to catch a cool breeze, when, straight out of the heart of the sunset, rounding the curve of the Big Oxbow, came the first boat of the log drive. Its solitary occupant stood high in the narrow pointed prow with one foot on the gunwale, and a long blue oar lightly poised paddlewise over his knee. We wondered whether he knew how much like a Viking of old he looked in bold relief against the evening sky, or, as he came nearer, what a charming bit of color his red shirt and blue oar made in contrast to the dusky green of the willows on the opposite bank.

But looking neither to right nor left, apparently as unconscious of his own picturesque attitude as our admiring gaze, he floated down with the current and silently faded from our sight . . .

From *The Granite Monthly* of Woodsville, New Hampshire, 1919.

Candy on Ice

JOHN HAURILICK

BACK OF MY FATHER'S place, they put up a six-foot chicken wire fence, because my folks didn't like to have me associate too much with the French people. You know, it kept us more to home. I can remember one winter, it was a particularly cold winter, and in the spring the river kept raising up higher and higher. Ice got to be that thick.

Well, anyway, the ice starts to moving one day—if you ever hear a river with the ice going out it would be like a freight train going by—you can't hear yourself talk, it makes that much noise. That's an experience you should have. Well, anyway, standing on the bank one day and the water was about three feet below us, and the river is grinding away and all of a sudden this great big cake of ice gets shoved out and it kept coming down. It came up there and it shave about two feet of dirt from the bank, took the fence and everything. After it went past the neighbors it just slid out of sight. Just as if Nature said it was going to take the fence.

I almost got drowned. The last building on the left as you go across the river, was an ice cream and a candy store. A fire broke out and after the fire a lot of the candy was supposedly bad. So they threw it out of the first porthole—the first porthole in the bridge—they threw it out on the ice.

We used to walk between Acme St. and the bridge because there is a path following the river, and we heard about the fire. And we heard about the candy. So we decided we'd get some of it. It was out there on the ice, laying in the boxes. I was about the biggest one of the bunch, so I went out and got some. Old Nick it was, and it tasted just as good as new.

I decided I'd get the box that was furthest out and all of a sudden the ice gave way. I went into the water and I was hanging onto the ice, hollering my head off for help. The woman at the gate heard us kids screaming so they came down with some clothesline and rope, and they threw it through my arm. Of course, in the meantime, the current was pulling on me. Course I had all my clothes on you know.

From Suzanne Nothnagle, "An Oral History of the Connecticut River" (Ph.D. diss., Dartmouth College, 1997); interview with John Haurilick of Windsor, Vermont.

I was scared to death. I had pictures of being under the ice and going down the river. They pulled me out and all I can remember was how bruised my ribs were when they were hauling me out. I was on the edge of the ice and got ripped up.

I went to the first house on the end of the street. Mrs. Barnes took me in and let me go into the bathroom. We tried to dry my clothes as best we could.

I never told my folks about it. Didn't dare.

Balky Bill

KEN ULINE

MY GRANDFATHER ON MY mother's side, who lived here, was a river driver. He came here on the last river drive on the Connecticut River. This was his place. He was a big man—a real big man. His name was Melvin DeWitt, and they called him Bill, but most of the people in the town of Lyme called him Balky Bill, because he'd balk about almost anything. He worked in the woods most of the time, and then finally he went helping around on the farm. He told me he went on the river drives. He come out of St. John's when he was twelve years old. One time he was telling me about coming down the Connecticut River, and when he get down to the town of Lewiston—that's across from Hanover—and the guys would have their tents. The students would come over and they'd sing to 'em and all that. There was a covered bridge across the river. Then when it was time for the men to turn in, they'd thank them and the guys would get in their tents—and the Dartmouth students would throw stones on them! So the next year when they come down through the logs, the boss of the logging crew, one of the drivers, he picked out his men and he wanted ones that could fight. So they come down here to Lewiston again and the students come over. So they did their singing and all that stuff, and the boss thanked 'em. And he told the river drivers, when they

From Mary Daunbenspeck and Judith G. Russell, eds., *We Had Each Other: A Spoken History of Lyme, New Hampshire* (Lyme, N.H: Friends of the Lyme Library, 2000); interview with Ken Uline of Lyme, New Hampshire.

got in the tent, not to take their cork boots off. And pretty soon the stones started in again. So they took after 'em, and he said going through that covered bridge some of them would get knocked down and they'd jump on top of them with their cork boots. He said they put quite a few of them up in Hitchcock Hospital. That ended the trouble with the students on the river driving. But those river drivers, they were pretty tough guys. This drive here was on the Connecticut, but he drove on the St. John's, on the Maine, oh, all over because he'd been at it for years.

A Boy's Bridge

CARLTON BACON

WELL, MOTHER DIDN'T WANT us, when we were kids, anywhere near [the East Thetford bridge]. But we used to go down there and climb all over that bridge, underneath it and over the top of it, and everything else. And when we lived in the bridge house down there, before they raised the dam, there used to be sand bars down there. Right north of the bridge there used to be two or three, and south of the bridge. Dad would take us kids down there, take us one at a time, 'cause next to each shoreline it went down deep and then it leveled up. So he would take us out and set us on that sand bar, one by one, until there was four of us out there, and then he'd come out. We were content to play in the middle of the river. And down there where Dr. Glass is there, we used to swim under the bridge; that was before they raised the dam. After they raised the dam 'course the water was dirty, and it never cleared up. Back when I was a kid you could walk across Thetford Bridge and you could look down and see bottom anywhere. Now you look down and it's the color of this [table]. It's never cleared 'cause it keeps washing the banks, but back then you could walk across that river the whole width and it would never come above your knees. One time we throwed a bicycle frame off

From Mary Daunbenspeck and Judith G. Russell, eds., *We Had Each Other: A Spoken History of Lyme, New Hampshire* (Lyme, N.H: Friends of the Lyme Library, 2000); interview with Carlton Bacon of Lyme, New Hampshire.

the bridge, for the fun of it, being kids. It landed on one of them old piers. We could look down and see it. We had to get that out of there, so we borrowed Georgie Stevens' boat, two or three of us kids, and we rowed out there and pick the frame right up, that's how deep it was.

Peace Comes to the Valley

WILLIAM H. MACLEISH

IN THE SUMMER OF 1945 I heard a train whistle going crazy down in the Connecticut Valley: three shorts and a long, three *shorts* and a long, on and on, warbling with wind, rising and falling with the Doppler effect. Everyone knew what that meant. It meant V, and it meant Victory. That is how I learned the war was over.

The Prettiest Landscaped Sewer in the World

BEN BACHMAN

BY THE LATE 1950S and early 1960s, when I was growing up in West Hartford, . . . the Connecticut River was taken for granted . . . , on those occasions when it intruded into my consciousness, which was not often. I remember a visit to the Mark Twain House, probably on a Cub Scout field trip, during which we were told that the famous author's

From William H. Macleish, *Uphill with Archie* (New York: Simon and Schuster, 2001).
From Ben Bachman, introduction to *The Connecticut River* (Boston, Mass: Bullfinch Press, 1989).

residence had been built to resemble a Mississippi River steamboat. No mention was made of the long and glorious history of steamboating on the lower Connecticut (although Twain took an interest in it), or of the fine square-riggers that slid down the ways of the shipyards in Portland (opposite Middletown), Connecticut, or of the fact that the Royal Navy had attacked Essex, Connecticut, during the War of 1812. There was a lot that could have been said and was not. When it came to the river itself—I don't think I'm exaggerating this a great deal—we simply assumed that if it was a familiar part of the southern New England landscape, then it could not be worth very much; certified scenic wonders were to be found out West. Further, it was assumed that the sad, neglected condition of the Connecticut was equivalent to a fact of nature and, therefore, irreversible.

The Dark Water

TRACY KIDDER

IN THE MIDDLE OF the night years ago, Tommy parked his cruiser near a dirt road to the Meadows, and in a moment, to his surprise, a prominent citizen, an older man, appeared out of the dark, walking east toward the great river. Tommy called to him. Tommy knew him well enough only for hellos and weather conversation, but the man stopped and climbed into the cruiser and started talking. On and on he talked, about nothing that seemed very important to Tommy, but, his radio being silent, small talk seemed as good a way as any to pass the dead hours of the night. Tommy thought he sensed a hint of urgency in the man's voice, but then again this guy was known to be a bit eccentric. He talked to Tommy for almost two hours. The next day he showed up at the station, handed Tommy his rosary, and said, "You saved my life last night." Then it all seemed clear. The man had planned to drown himself in the Connecticut. Just by chance Tommy had intervened. He knew it for a certainty.

From Tracy Kidder, *Home Town* (New York: Random House, 1999).

The Lag in Appreciation

CONNECTICUT RIVER WATERSHED COUNCIL

A REVERSAL OF THIS long slide downhill was born in the environmental awakening of the late 1960s and 1970s. This report documents the money, effort, care and concern that have gone into improving the Basin's environment. While this is a success story in itself, general public opinion about the Connecticut River has not yet caught up. So long was the river regarded a cesspool that it may well take another decade—or even a generation—before the bulk of the people living near it appreciate its grandeur.

Peyton Place sur le Connecticut

GRACE METALIOUS

ALLISON AND NORMAN PUSHED their bicycles ahead of them, for it was too hot to pedal uphill. The bicycles were heavy because the baskets attached to them were loaded with the picnic hamper, a six-bottle carton of Coca-Cola, a cotton patchwork quilt, two bathing suits, four towels and a thick volume entitled, *Important English Poets*. Allison and Norman pushed and panted, and the July heat rose, shimmering, from the highway that led away from Peyton Place. . . .

"We wouldn't be able to get near the water at Meadow," said Allison, raising one hand from her bicycle handle bars to lift the heavy hair that clung to her damp neck. "Every kid in town will be at Meadow this afternoon. I'd rather stay home than go there."

From Connecticut River Watershed Council, "Recovering the Valley" (1983).

From Grace Metalious, *Peyton Place* (Boston, Mass.: Northeastern University Press, 1999).

"It can't be much farther," said Norman philosophically. "The bend in the river is exactly one mile beyond the hospital, and we've certainly come almost that by now."

"It's not much farther," agreed Allison. "We passed the mills ages ago."

After what seemed an eternity in the summer afternoon, they came at last to the bend in the Connecticut River. Gratefully, they pushed their bicycles into the shade of the giant trees that grew close to the water's edge, and sank down on the soft, dry pine needles that covered the ground.

"I thought we'd never get here," said Allison, puffing out her bottom lip and blowing at a strand of hair that fell on her forehead.

"Neither did I," said Norman. "It was worth it, though. There isn't another soul around for miles. Listen to the quiet."

Chapter 12

THE LONG RIVER

Is the Connecticut worth saving? I need not offer an opinion. I need only mention that I have seen rather more of the world's surface than most men ever do, and I have chosen the valley of this river for my home.
—Roger Torey Peterson, quoted in *The Connecticut River,* by Evan Hill

Anyone who thinks of an anthology as a dusty repository for writing that would otherwise be forgotten has it wrong. A good anthology, a vibrant anthology, not only brings to life work that deserves a second chance but points to the future, documenting an impulse, a literary flowage, that is far from spent. Reading about the river, marveling at how much good writing it's generated over the years, I was struck most of all by the fact that the golden years of Connecticut River writing still lie ahead—that as the river is rediscovered, reclaimed, restored, more and more talented writers will find it a compelling subject to tackle. I predict that within ten years this anthology could be doubled with writing published since 2000 alone.

This last chapter points the way, with some extraordinarily varied work by writers focusing on the river today.

In a moving essay, poet Sydney Lea shows what a thinking man's hunter can do with the river, the river's bounty; you get the sense, reading his work and that of his contemporaries, that it's his generation, men and women in late middle age, who have rediscovered the river, turned back to it, after too many generations of those who found the river, not to mince words, foul. Michael Caduto, who lives downstream from Lea in Norwich, writes about the delightfully nutty yet valuable work a local town accomplishes on one of the most beautiful stretches of the river. My own short story, "The Bass, the River, and Sheila Mant," is a contemporary love story, with the river as a central character. Bill McKibben writes of plans for the Silvio Conte refuge—still in the future when he wrote this, but now very much a reality. And finally, Richard J. Ewald brings the anthology full circle with a vivid epiphany at the river's source.

Mussel Defenders

MICHAEL J. CADUTO

"RESOLVED, THAT THE TOWN of Plainfield, N.H., designate the Dwarf Wedge Mussel—a rare bivalve for which Plainfield provides one of the last remaining habitats—The Plainfield Town Mollusk."

With a flourish and show of hands the several hundred Plainfield residents who attended the business portion of town meeting on the 14th of March in 1987 passed this resolution. Following the adoption in 1986 of another endangered species—the cobblestone tiger beetle *(Cicindela marginipennis)*—as its town insect, it would seem that Plainfield has come out of its shell as a leader in grassroots endangered species preservation. As endangered species, the cobblestone tiger beetle and dwarf wedge mussel may not be as spectacular as the peregrine falcon or California condor (which has recently become extinct in the wild), but the Plainfield species are endearing themselves to an ever-widening circle of people.

There was little opposition to the dwarf wedge mussel adoption, although a few townfolk seemed to think that adopting the "ancient floater," as the mussel is also known, was a bit frivolous. In fact, Nancy Mogielnicki, a Plainfield resident who works as a physician's assistant when she's not out crusading for endangered species, proposed this sincere resolution tongue in cheek, making reference to possibly designating the mussel's home in the Connecticut River as "mussel beach," and naming the Plainfield athletic teams the "musselmen" and "musselwomen." One town resident added to the occasion by asking: "If I inadvertently use one of these (mussels) for fish bait would I go to jail?"

Said Mogielnicki, "If you can't appeal to peoples' sense of conservation ethics you can appeal to their sense of humor or sense of pride in adopting a town endangered species. By the way," she added, "the dwarf wedge mussel is not good to eat." Even the native Abenaki Indians who lived along the Connecticut River are not known to have consumed its freshwater mussels.

Another factor working to the mussel's advantage was that the adoption resolution requested no funding. In fact, the proceeds from T-shirt sales and other fund-raising activities by the Society for the Preservation of the Cobblestone Tiger Beetle, which evolved in 1986, raised $500 for the town's conservation work and additional money for environmental education programs for Plainfield elementary school children last year.

The beetle's adoption also supported other conservation efforts, such as the designation of the beetle, in August of 1986, as Vermont's first officially protected state insect. Clearly these adoptions have increased local interest in conservation. As Nancy Mogielnicki's husband, Peter, a physician at the Veterans Administration Hospital in White River Junction and co-leader of the species adoption efforts, pointed out, Plainfield residents "have reacted very well. They're aware of the value of the beetle and mussel in protecting the open land in the valley."

Mogielnicki observed that "the conservation-oriented people reacted very positively to the resolutions, as did those who reacted well to the jokes. There's an awareness of the Connecticut River and its values." She added, however, that "there are also people in Plainfield interested in hydroelectric power and who see the link between the species adoptions and the dam." Some people consider the species' attractiveness as a "warm fuzzy" disguising a conservationist's hardball.

Since the late 1700's dams have eliminated most of the free-flowing waters needed to maintain the beetle's cobblestone beaches and the mussel's rapids. In recent years there has been an on-again/off-again proposal for a hydroelectric dam to be built on Chase Island just downstream, which would flood the endangered species' habitats. The future of this proposal is uncertain, but the heightened awareness of the species' presence, the stewardship role now adopted by Plainfield, and the endangered status of the two species will help to preserve this stretch of the Connecticut River from further development or pollution. Taken singly, the species' adoptions may seem like an aside in the history of this small town of 1,850 people set in a rapidly growing area, but it is one way that Plainfield's residents are protecting their natural heritage.

The beetle and mussel also serve as living populations that can be studied to learn about managing other endangered species and populations in the Connecticut River's last remaining stretches of free-flowing water. In addition, the Plainfield town insect and mollusk are good indicators of pollution because they are sensitive to it; are pretty—aesthetically pleasing; and have intrinsic value because they are alive.

The presence of the dwarf wedge mussel is an indication that this stretch of the river has remained relatively unchanged by human activity, for the mussel is an ancient species that cannot adapt well to changes in water temperature, flow, or presence of pollution. "The mussel needs clean, fresh, oxygenated water that moves fast," said Phil Hoose, past director of the Nature Conservancy in New Hampshire.

Viable populations of *Alasmidonta heterodon,* as the mussel is known to scientists, may now be found in as few as three locations: in the Ashuelot and Connecticut Rivers in New Hampshire and the Choptank River in Maryland. The mussel may soon join the litany of endangered plants and animals that are disappearing forever from the earth at an estimated rate of three species every day. The federal government is considering the mussel for designation as a threatened species, and it has been proposed for the endangered species list in New Hampshire. Vermont now lists the mussel as a threatened species.

Douglas Smith, senior technical assistant and acting curator of invertebrates at the Department of Zoology, University of Massachusetts, Amherst, noted that, "The mussels are so hard to find that it's hard to get a large enough population to study. When I find a large enough population where the loss of a few females won't affect the population I will conduct an extensive study, but not until then."

These unassuming mollusks live in the roiled water at the base of a waterfall. Beds of the nearly 2-inch-long, greenish-brown, iridescent mussels anchor themselves in the bottom sediment where they filter tiny plants, animals, and pieces of debris from the water for food. The minute larvae of the dwarf wedge mussel spend their first days attached to the fins of a fish. They're so small that the fish is unaffected, but those larvae that fail to find a suitable host fish don't survive. Soon, the larvae grow into small versions of the adult state and drop off to live on the river bottom. Since the adults move about very little once they settle in, the juvenile period of hitchhiking on fish is important to help the mussel disperse.

Individual mussels are either male or female. In mid-to-late July the males shed sperm into the water and females pick up the sperm to fertilize the eggs which are carried in the females' gills. The fertilized eggs develop into larvae which overwinter in the protection of the females' gills. When the larvae are released in April or May only a few are able to find and attach to a suitable host fish on which to metamorphose into an adult. It is a long and tortuous route from egg to adult and the few surviving mussels need all the help they can get.

"Sumner's Falls is a famous historic site where the dwarf wedge mussel was first discovered in the 19th century," said Smith. The mussel is gone from most of its original habitats, but not from Sumner's Falls. Smith added: "It is very important to preserve the natural character of that part of the river, keeping it clean. Not only are we concerned about supporting the mussel but also the population of the host fish." The exact identity of the host fish, or fishes, has not yet been determined.

The Conte Refuge

BILL McKIBBEN

IN THE WINTER OF 1991 Silvio Conte, a genial congressman from western Massachusetts, introduced legislation to create a federal wildlife refuge along the Connecticut River, which bisected his district. Several days later, he died. Tactically, it was a brilliant move. Swept up by affectionate memories of the Berkshire Republican, his House colleagues acted quickly to found the reserve, now named in honor of its proponent.

Only one problem: Conte hadn't told anyone *where* in the four states the Connecticut traverses he wanted the preserve. Had he lived, he undoubtedly would have had a good deal to say about its future. But as it turns out, there is only a video of a speech he gave dedicating a fishery research laboratory to offer any clues to his thinking.

"Silvio Conte was a visionary," says Larry Bandolin. "The only trouble is, we don't have him to talk to. We've had to set our own vision—and *I'm* not a visionary." Maybe not—but Bandolin, a career fisheries biologist plucked from the ranks of the U.S. Fish and Wildlife Service to establish the new refuge, is setting his sights on something brand-new for federal land managers. Call it a refuge without borders; call it a preserve of the mind; call it one of the clearest examples of that sizzling buzzword *ecosystem management:* For better and for worse, the Silvio O. Conte

From Bill McKibben, "On the Connecticut River," *Audubon* (January–February 1995).

National Fish and Wildlife Refuge may well turn out to be the model for how the nation protects its great treasures in the years to come.

"The Conte is of real national importance," says Bandolin's boss, Fish and Wildlife director Mollie Beattie. "This is the crucible of experimentation for landscape-scale conservation that does not depend on federal acquisition or regulation—and may not depend on acquisition or regulation at any level at all."

Up and down the 407-mile length of the Connecticut, Bandolin and his planners may find a few acres here and there of critical habitat to purchase and protect. But after the Fish and Wildlife Service announces its plans this summer, there won't be the usual visitors' center, six green pickups, and five miles of barbed wire separating a "refuge" from the harsh world outside. Instead, there will be people and expertise and money—a small bureaucracy designed to provide technical assistance to local governments, working side by side with regional land trusts, paying farmers small sums to protect their riverbanks, and running nature-education programs for everyone from schoolkids to sewer engineers.

"It's true that the legislation creating the Conte was written for a classic refuge," says Bandolin. "But we're learning that we can't only look at little areas. We've failed in many cases with a single species on a single area." The river's watershed covers 7 million acres in New Hampshire, Vermont, Massachusetts, and Connecticut, he points out. "We'll never *own* enough land to make a real impact on the fish and wildlife of this basin. And from a purely pragmatic standpoint, we've had to fit in, as a federal agency, to this infrastructure of local sportsmen's clubs, town wetlands commissions, national conservation organizations. It would be criminal, from a taxpayer's standpoint, to duplicate work that's already being done. We have to find a niche."

In search of that niche, the planners have already exhibited what a biologist studying the federal beast would call aberrant behavior. From the mouth of the Connecticut to the headwaters, they've held more than 160 meetings over the past two years with anyone who would talk. Some conservationists, convinced that only strong federal management will save the Connecticut's fish and bird life, say they've gone much too far in addressing the concerns of property rights groups and "wise use" activists. Others, mindful of the difficulties in working on a river with a run of shad that can top a million but a flock of people twice that large, praise the compromising and consensus building. All agree that, like it or not, they just may be looking at the future. "If we're going to do any conservation at all in the twenty-first century," says Mollie Beattie, "this is how it's going to be done."

The U.S. border with Canada, usually a line running with happy diplomatic precision across mere geography, actually makes some sense where northern New Hampshire meets Quebec. If you park at the border crossing and walk for about a mile along the mowed strip of electronic sensors that follows the high ground, you'll eventually reach an arrow pointing south. There, about a hundred yards away, sits the source of the Connecticut River—Fourth Connecticut Lake, a moose-tracked beaver pond less than two acres in size quietly catching all the water that falls on the American side of the hill.

Like most rivers, the Connecticut has changed its character completely by the time it flows, broad and wind-chopped, into Long Island Sound near the town of Essex. Piping plover have replaced loons, and great sea runs of herring have taken the place of trout. Its exquisite tidelands are well preserved in part because, unlike other eastern rivers, the Connecticut has no major port squatting at its mouth. Along the way, the river cuts through many strata of biology and history and economy—small farms, old mill towns dating back to the zenith of New England's industrial revolution, small cities slowly rotting.

A few things unite the beginning and the end of the river, however, and one of them is clean water. In most places that's a recent development—as late as the 1960s, the factories and city sewers discharging into the river gave it a reputation as "American's best-landscaped sewer." Jeanie McIntyre, associate director of the Upper Valley Land Trust, grew up on the river's central stretches. "There was a man in my town who swam across the river every day, and everyone thought he was crazy. They'd always say to him, 'Keep your mouth shut when you're in there, man.'" The Clean Water Act of 1977 and its transfusions of federal cash shut down the open sewage and industrial-waste pipes, and the river quickly cleansed itself. Geoff Dates, New England's coordinator of the River Watch Network, still worries about the possibility of heavy metals and toxins, but he says the ordinary sewage is nearly gone, except when heavy rainstorms overwhelm municipal treatment plants.

It's a Lake Erie–type resurrection that still has some of the locals amazed. "When I first came to Vermont in 1953, I had a dairy farm close to the river," says syndicated nature broadcaster Will Curtis. "You didn't even think of canoeing on it then—mattresses would float past you. But time went on and we all got together and now it's relatively clean. I was just doing a TV show on the river, and to show people that you really could swim in the Connecticut, I just stood up and jumped out of the canoe."

For a century, along most of its polluted length, people had turned their backs on the river—all that Day-Glo factory waste made it a de facto wilderness, lined in most places by a strip of hardwoods and then a farmer's field. "On the river it's always been surprisingly remote," says Bill Bridge, who is putting together a chain of canoe campsites in Vermont and New Hampshire for the Upper Valley Land Trust. "I paddled through White River Junction and West Lebanon yesterday, and all I saw were the backs of a couple of industrial buildings."

Most residents of the Connecticut Valley see the river only in brief glimpses through the guardrails as they drive across its many bridges. But as the water has become cleaner, people have begun to return. "There's been a lag time of at least ten years in perception," says Bridge. "It was really cleaned up in the seventies, but people are only now waking up to the fact that it's a great place. You see more docks out in the river all the time." Months earlier, as he pounded in the sign for the last of his eight canoe campsites, a party of 12 paddlers had suddenly swung into view.

On many stretches of the river, canoe gridlock is the least of the emerging tensions. The urban sprawl that has long marked the Hartford area has begun to spread north into Massachusetts, as corporate headquarters and condominium developments replace old fields of shade-grown tobacco and truck-farm vegetables. "These are some of the richest soils in the world—you'd think that would keep the farms stable," says Whitty Sanford of the nonprofit Connecticut River Watershed Council. "But what's best to farm is also best to build—that's what the developers say."

The new developments bring not only more pavement—and with it increased pollution threats from surface-water runoff—but also hundreds of new users to what was once a wallflower of a river. Sanford's husband and Watershed Council colleague, Tom Miner, shows me a photo on the front page of the week's Northampton, Massachusetts, newspaper: A dense knot of pleasure craft bobbing at the local yacht basin makes it hard even to see the water. The council, in fact, has just finished a long fight to reduce motorboat speeds over one particularly sensitive stretch of the river in Massachusetts. "There were good scientific reasons, good cultural reasons," says Miner—but there was also stiff resistance from the marinas. Finally everyone compromised: 15 miles an hour, max, and no Jet-Skis.

But the battles will likely get harder, not easier—they're no longer the simple sorts of environmental fights, like cleaning up dirty water, that everyone can agree on. "It's easy to deal with a discharge pipe. You know the specific things you can do," says Sanford. "But now it's the type of land use, what runs off the land; and that's much harder to deal with because it gets to the whole question of planning, of land-use regulation, of property rights."

Larry Bandolin, who is walking head-on into this collision of values, drives me to the remains of the Enfield Dam, just south of the Connecticut-Massachusetts border. Over the past decade the dam has been slowly washing out, till the roar from the first real rapids on the river is loud enough to drown out everything on Interstate 91 except the largest tractor trailers. Our heads surrounded by a darting hatch of zebra caddis flies, we stand staring out at the white water, now a prime spot for striped bass fishing.

"Nature is restoring itself," Bandolin says. "This is no longer a major barrier to migration for the shad and the herring." There are those who want to rebuild the dam, however; it would raise water levels upstream, making boating easier and perhaps permitting riverboat gambling from docks in the depressed city of Springfield, Massachusetts. "I know that there's an economic argument, I know that there's maybe a recreation argument—but I just don't think that's a wise use of the river," says Bandolin.

Most of the time, however, Bandolin sounds deeply cautious, radically moderate. It's the effect, most likely, of spending a lot of time talking to people up and down the Connecticut River, which runs through a political terrain at least as varied as its geography. Near the mouth it's easy to find people excited about conservation efforts. "People love the idea that these marshes have been designated one of our 'last great places,'" says Juliana Barrett, who coordinates the Nature Conservancy's tideland programs on the marshes near Long Island Sound. Susan Merrow, first selectman in East Haddam, Connecticut, enthuses that the Conte plan could represent "the ultimate greenway."

Farther north, however, attitudes shift. Sharon Francis, executive director of the Connecticut River Joint Commissions for New Hampshire and Vermont, says, "I was very enamored of the idea of a greenway, too. I learned pretty quickly, however, that as you went north people thought a greenway was a kind of green monster that would swallow up their way of life. We quickly dropped it; we don't even say it anymore. It's the G-word." The property rights movement has been strong in the area in recent years; Cheryl Johnson of the New Hampshire Landowners Alliance, which led a successful battle to prevent listing of the Pemigewasset as a federal Wild and Scenic River, says her greatest wish for the Conte refuge is "that it would just go away."

Across such varied political topography, Bandolin and his crew have won high praise for getting out and talking. "They're doing a damn good job of getting in front of the public, I'll give them that," says Johnson.

Fred King, a state senator from New Hampshire's Coös County, which includes the headwaters of both the Connecticut and the Androscoggin rivers, says, "It's completely different from when they established the Umbagog Refuge on the Androscoggin. Then they just had a meeting and told us what they were going to do."

To further allay fears, the Feds have all but promised that they'll avoid using eminent domain to take land for the refuge. Instead they are emphasizing the unthreatening—the nature-education centers that may be built in each state, the technical assistance to local sewer departments. "For better or worse, we'll be going to a lot of meetings," Bandolin says. "The people working for me will be working eight to five some of the time, but they're going to spend a lot of time working with the seven-to-nine conservationsists, the people who go out to a land-trust meeting after supper."

Bandolin can point to some concrete examples of the small-scale approach he has in mind. Driving one day along a stretch of road in northern Massachusetts, he pulls over to show me a stream, "a classic little native brook trout fishery." As we follow it downstream toward the Deerfield River, a major tributary of the Connecticut, it crosses a dairy pasture, where cows have caved in the banks going after water. "For a few hundred dollars, perhaps the farmer would be willing to fence most of the stream and give his cattle just a little access," says Bandolin. "That would save the stream for spawning fish—I know a guy who hooked an Atlantic salmon on the Deerfield two years ago!"

Far upstream, in Colebrook, New Hampshire, a series of dairy farms provides grassland habitat for harriers. King, the Coös County legislator, suggests paying farmers for their land and then letting them keep farming. "Maybe we'll just act as a bank for local communities," says Fish and Wildlife director Beattie. "Perhaps we'll have a pot of money that we can match with land trusts or conservation commissions so they can acquire lands that meet certain criteria, purchase conservation easements on lands that meet other guildines, and so forth."

Some of the collaborative projects may protect places like the home of the rare dwarf wedge mussel; others will be on a vastly bigger scale but involve no funding. For instance, in Hartford, the largest city on the river, residents have been cut off from the water for a generation by Interstate 91. "If you want to take your lunch there from downtown, you can't do it," says Joe Marfuggi, director of the city's Riverfront Recapture program. "You almost can't see it unless you're in one of the taller office buildings."

But that is starting to change: By 1996 Marfuggi's nonprofit group plans to have an esplanade built across a newly depressed section of the highway, giving access to six miles of public parks and river walks. Some of these new facilities got a tryout in September, when the Bassmasters fishing tour made the Connecticut the first-ever northeastern stop on its professional circuit.

Inner-city kids are already rowing donated eight-oared shells on the river. "Hartford Public High School, which serves one of the poorest populations in the Northeast, is rowing against places like Greenwich," says Marfuggi. Both public funds and private donations fund Riverfront Recapture; but Marfuggi says he looks forward to the help the Conte refuge will provide, noting that the river "doesn't work for recreation unless it's clean."

Such quiet and cooperative efforts already have a history on the Connecticut. The upper river's joint commission, for instance, has been handing out small grants for the past few years for many small projects, from canoe campsites to farms that grow hops for the local boom in microbreweries, and it has been working with committees up and down the northern stretches of the river to develop river-corridor management plans. "Too much of our drive for environmental quality," says Francis, "has relied on confrontational mechanisms—lawsuits, regulations. And we're experiencing a backlash because of it. Those things are sometimes necessary, but here the commitment to the environment is pretty near universal."

Some conservationists, however, say the all-carrot-no-stick approach to environmental protection is an abdication of federal responsibility. "If no one's bothered by the Conte plan, that shows it's probably lacking vision," says David Carle of RESTORE the North Woods, an upstart group based near Walden Pond in eastern Massachusetts. Carle has been battling with the Fish and Wildlife Service, demanding protection of the Connecticut's Atlantic salmon population and stronger measures to prevent the fish from being cut to shreds in dam turbines as they swim downstream.

Instead of mandating costly springtime spills over the dams, though, the Fish and Wildlife Service has worked with utilities to design high-tech fish tunnels—described as "guide walls," "experimental weirs," and "vertical venetian blinds"—that guide the fish safely back to the ocean. Though the service's Ted Meyers says he is "pretty confident" that the technical measures will increase survival rates, it should be noted that after 28 years of trying, last year the Feds managed to lure just 318 salmon upriver as far as Holyoke, Massachusetts.

In general, says Carle, the government should be getting tougher, not looser: "Cooperative agreements and so forth may be fine for buffer zones, but at least the core areas should be under one management agency with a clear statement of purpose and clear, enforceable guidelines. Planning boards and zoning boards at the local level are only as strong as the people on them."

Which gets to the heart of the matter. What environmentalist, committed to the notion of acting locally, would want to argue against the people who live in a place taking care of it? But what environmentalist, worried about losing some plant or animal forever, is willing to trust local powers to set aside gains in tax dollars or jobs for the future of a short-nosed sturgeon?

Yet nurturing political maturity—the willingness of local communities to say no to short-term benefits if they come at some larger cost—may be easier in places where much has already been despoiled. Near the river's mouth, says the Nature Conservancy's Barrett, some local officials welcome suggestions about where to channel development in order to decrease runoff. Upstream, where there have been fewer mistakes to learn from, development is the thorniest issue, according to John Harrigan, editor of the *Coös County Democrat.* "Zoning and so on—that's where we have the greatest political growing up to do," Harrigan says. "I have a deep, gut aversion to telling my neighbors how to behave."

Mollie Beattie, who led Vermont's fish and game bureaucracy before moving to Washington, says, "It's hard living in a rural area that hasn't changed in two hundred years and accepting that it could change very fast. There's always an isobar of people fifty or a hundred miles north of where the development is that doesn't believe *their* land could ever change."

In northern New Hampshire, state senator King represents that school of thought. "We had thirty-five thousand people in 1965, we have thirty-five thousand people now, and the state estimates we'll have thirty-five thousand people in 2005," he says, as we gaze out his office window across a cornfield tended by inmates of the county jail to the river beyond. "There've been some second homes, but what's wrong with that? That's healthy growth." In fact, says King, national attention focused on a new wildlife refuge may do more to spur hordes of tourists than anything else—"If they have to stand in line to put their canoes in, how good will that be?"

As a result, while King says he can accept certain features of the Conte plan and would like to see one of the nature-education centers approved under the legislation built in his county, he's clearly not enthusiastic about "a bunch of Feds driving their green pickups up and down our roads and walking on our land."

Still, at a weekend planning retreat organized by Bandolin last spring, King and his Coös County neighbor Jamie Sayen, perhaps northern New

England's most outspoken environmentalist, made a joint presentation arguing that the Conte refuge should form local citizens' advisory committees to oversee the planning. "He was worried that something was going to be imposed on us—and I'm worried about that too," says Sayen.

The joint commission's Francis concedes that people who live along the Connecticut "haven't had to deal with the threats people have dealt with elsewhere." As the water and hence the image of the Connecticut continue to improve, "I can't promise local people will be so high-minded when there's real pressure for development." Still, Francis says, helping communities grow more sensitive to environmental issues is the only real option, at least along a corridor as crowded as the Connecticut Valley. "It may well mean we'll lose some habitat. It may well mean we'll lose a species. But we'll gain more in the long run by taking the partnership approach."

The thought of losing a species or two—even the dwarf wedge mussel—in the process of educating people is sobering. The Fish and Wildlife Service's own record on the Atlantic salmon—where 20 years of collaborative efforts to spare any real hardship to power companies with dams on the river have yielded just handfuls of fish—testifies to the limitations of a policy of making nice.

But federal officials say they see little choice. "I don't think you're going to see any new support for sweeping regulations," says Beattie, who is currently fighting merely to keep the federal Endangered Species Act intact in the face of attacks in Congress. "I don't think you're going to see any big new chunks of money to buy land."

Anyway, as Beattie points out, the traditional federal approach of shopping for choice parcels has a mixed record itself. "Even in a small state like Vermont we were spending millions and millions of dollars," she says, and that was in the heyday of environmental largesse, in the late 1970s. "Despite all that, we've been able to save and conserve very few whole systems. If we really mean to do conservation, we've got to make it possible for the people that own the land to do it themselves."

Already, says Larry Bandolin, he's getting calls from other parts of the Fish and Wildlife Service, asking for advice about his new approach.

As we stand near his office in Turner's Falls, Massachusetts, we train binoculars on a bald eagle chick flapping in a nest a couple of hundred yards from a busy boat launch. "I heard from the people in the Chesapeake region," Bandolin says. "They wanted to know, 'How the hell do you deal with something this big?' And I told them—there's no other way than working together with the people out there and trying to do big things. There's no other way. Uncle Sam just can't do it by himself anymore."

Goodbye, Boy

SYDNEY LEA

ON A CERTAIN MORNING last autumn, I spread my decoys offshore from Grant Balch's pasture. Such a gesture seems almost perverse nowadays, the degeneration of late fall waterfowling on this stretch of the Connecticut River having been catastrophic. If once I could blame a failed duck hunt on a boyish restlessness or bungling, now I can generally blame the simple absence of game. I've become a better retriever trainer, a better duck caller, and a better shot over the years—years that locally reduce these skills to near irrelevance.

Too soon old, too late smart, as they say.

One temptation is to stay in bed, since I might often kill as many ducks from there as from my blind. And yet I continue to go, drawn by the season and the hour. Bumping along in the ruts, my old retriever's head in my lap, my old canoe snubbed in the truckbed, I tune in a particular French Canada radio station; it features archaic rural fiddlers, and comes through clearly before the great interference machine of contemporary life cranks up—hard rock and soft, phone calls and faxes, dismaying news.

By noticing whose lights are on in the village, I can make a crude but authoritative demographic survey, which, to be sure, tells its own dismaying yarn. As the country people perish or are supplanted by refugee professionals, fewer and fewer kitchen lamps shine at 4:30 A.M. After his eighty-odd years, Grant himself is gone. As I drove to that morning's hunt, it was therefore a small reassurance to look through the window and return the wave of his wife Margaret, already at her coffee.

It was likewise fine to see Herefords still in her pasture, no matter that they belonged now to a neighbor. I even rather enjoyed my usual game at the gate: shooing the steers, then racing to get the truck through before they could regroup and race through too, the other way. The one with the scarred shoulder nibbled like a goat at my jacket as I restrung the barbed wire. Finished, I turned and ruffled the thick mane on his boss. We like that.

At river's edge, there was also the plain gratification of being in a beautiful place when the sun first comes to it, a white stain seeping down the high palisade on the Vermont side opposite. The shouts of unroosting crows jostled memories of my boyhood self, crouching in weeds near a papier-maché owl, hoping to outsmart what I then considered the wariest animal on earth. I'd seen so many warier ones since that that old headiness seemed nearly unimaginable. Yet I could and did imagine it after all, together with the pure, youthful compulsion to what I then called success.

Ducks or no ducks, I knew there'd be incidental blessings in this lovely reach of river. When hadn't there been? That astonishing eagle, studying my decoys from a young elm's branch ten feet above my head. That mink who ambled through the blind, climbing nonchalantly over my booted feet. That huge buck who swam from Vermont virtually into the same blind. Graceful passing of countless herons. Comic carryings-on of hooded mergansers—"little dippers," in local parlance which always drive Topper, my ornithologically indiscriminate retriever , to distraction.

I could reasonably look forward to such possibilities; yet recent dawns on the river have left less room for prospects than for retrospects. Compared to other pursuits, of course, this was always so, even back when the shooting was hot. The mere job of busting brush for grouse precludes much soulful study until the sun itself is done. The same, for me, with chasing deer: I'm not made right to linger on stand; I must keep moving and pausing, moving and pausing, a method oddly called still hunting. But it's in a waterfowl blind that I do the only hunting that could rightly be so called. Physically stationary, however, I'm provoked to mental travel; and the fewer the ducks, the farther my range.

The morning I speak of, mild and windless, would have been unducky even in better days. Not that the real cold was so far off: snow buntings plucked at the cattails around me; juncos, flashing that shock of white tail, bounced by every few moments; one nervous gang of pine siskins simultaneously lit and flushed at pasture's edge. I watched a gray squirrel dash from his hole in a moribund pine, dash through a hawthorn hedge to Grant's stubbled corn piece, dash back with a full cheek; he knew what was at hand, and he meant to be ready for it.

A generous chunk of time passed until, away to the east, invisible even in the clear daylight, I heard a flock of geese tending southward. First over Mt. Cube. Then Smart's Mountain. Somewhere near Cummings Pond, I judged, they faded from hearing. Not long ago in this country, we'd have considered them late in migration. But everything changes. It was once a rarity in any time of year to see a few Canadas on a back pond or slough, not to mention on the river itself; now they've become almost common, and they stay longer. The majority are still high-flyers, headed for richer farmland, balmier climate, and it's still for the most part a pretty vain undertaking to hunt them over decoys. Yet there are those who've begun to do so, and the jump-shooters encounter greater success every season.

Some speculate that the Canadas, who already short-stop inland as far north as Massachusetts, will one day stop up here, too. Our winter months seem less and less frigid, often leaving patches of open water, so it does seem conceivable that geese will someday linger year-round in local grainfields (if in fact, such fields themselves endure). Perhaps like the birds themselves, who now thrive on such upland fare rather than stuff from the vanishing marshes, I'll adapt to the change: I will refinish the honker decoys that have mouldered since I quit traveling to the Eastern shore; I will brush up my rusty hail call and gabble; I will start hunkering in pits instead of brush blinds. With those geese flown on, it was easy to ponder all that; but it was hard to *feel* any of it, so different from everything I'd learned to expect.

Was the expectable, however, an automatic virtue? In a way, of course, yes, and my being on the rivershore proof enough. I'd come because this is what I do in that season, part of one autumn merging with its counterpart the next. On the other hand, what would hunting be without a mix of the expected and its utter opposite? That eagle; that mink; that deer; and just then—as if on cue—the watersnake who glided into a pond-lily cluster shoreward of my decoys. Warm though it was, who'd have figured to see such a creature even in a mild November? And indeed, the pretty little thing seemed languid, almost desperately so. When I stood for a better look, he slid off the rotted pads as slowly as a gorged alligator from a mudbank, cruising the surface to another batch a few yards downriver.

Topper watched the snake go, then looked around at me, quizzical. I rubbed his muzzle, clown-white with age, but he suddenly jerked from under my hand. As so often, I followed his stare to birds, though not this time to airborne ones. A pair of drake wood duck, who should long since have been gone from this territory, was paddling in among my blocks; lost in reminiscence and morose prophecy I'd missed their arrival.

Topper's trembling was strenuous yet controlled. Briefly rolling his eye back; as he does for example whenever the little dippers cavort unmolested before us, he mutely questioned me: For God's sake, will you *shoot?*

Just then I mutely answered: No.

The ducks were no more than a dozen yards off by now, the sun dazzling their crests, their inverted reflections exact in the pondlike water.

"Get out of here," I said in a speaking tone.

And out they got, their wake a lather of bubbles that caught the sunlight too. For a moment in flight, hard-edged and clean, the woodies appeared almost stationary against the Vermont cliff. But soon enough they became southerly specks. Only then did Topper relax, his body going loose in a huge, whining sigh.

"They looked too pretty," I mumbled. I could tell as usual that the dog disagreed, and I felt bad for him. A major motive for these unpromising duck expeditions, after all, was my hope of giving Topper some work. However fine his condition, he was ten years old, and he hadn't had a chance to show half his stuff for half his life. There's never been a lovelier pet than he, and I had long loved him in that part; but it wasn't the part his breeder had in mind, nor the one I'd rehearsed him for myself, from a puppy. Probably I should have tumbled at least a single. Too late for that.

Five years earlier, after watching his brilliant retrieves from a Chesapeake cove, a waterfowl outfitter had offered me an immense pile of cash for my dog. I don't miss that money, but to this day I wonder whether I shouldn't have made the deal, granting Topper a more appropriate life.

Yet how appropriate those *ducks* had been to the spangled glaze of the Connecticut.

Downstream a half-mile, Bernard Tullar's milking machines abruptly quit. Their drone is always so much a part of morning there that I never notice it till it's gone. Had an older man once sat in my place, brooding in his own way? Conscious of all that cow-barn mechanism, did he think back on a time when a dairy was more hands-on and human? Maybe. If so, it's unlikely that he'd ever hooked up a milking rig in a mid-winter dawn, any more than I have; and yet, if woods and waters both empower your psyche and exert power over it—if you *need* them as my visionary man and I do, along with their wild denizens—then you'll believe that the primary, tactile experience is at least as important as human convenience. Lacking such belief, who but a madman would be where I was in that November daybreak?

And yes, I had arrived at Grant's field in a four-wheel drive truck, its radio playing tunes from across national borders. I took advantage of a mechanical epoch, which frees us in many ways, which provides us with mobility, which may protract our lives. Still, sometimes I wonder, where is it we will go, and what (to use the ready pun) is the *nature* of our health and our liberty? I'd rather travel a few splendid miles than many a gray one.

Or so I'll often say. My more honest self recognizes the delusion or at least the fecklessness of such nostalgias. Thus I've lately tried to convince myself that under new circumstances I might see through a new lens. Shouldn't that be possible? If the geese are to supplant the ducks, for example, why not be a goose hunter? Failing to adjust, I'll know a future devoid of anything but retrospection, banal and bitter at once. Looking back on that morning at Grant's, for instance, I might easily write, "the skies remained empty," when in fact they were full of motion and light, and even a stoic fall music: all around me, the brave calls of chickadees, just starting to arrive in real winter numbers; from crags on the palisade, the gritty croaks of ravens, scouting for road kill; deep in Grant's evergreens, the pileated woodpecker's flourish.

Why should I be less enthralled by any of these creatures than by a game bird? My answer is scarcely recondite, yet few will grasp it who have not traveled my kind of beautiful miles. And of course, indifferent or plain hostile to genuine hunting, that's exactly what most people will never do. I preach to the small choir. To the great congregation my sermon is either an attentuated frontier romanticism or, more commonly, a bloodthirst tricked up as aesthetics.

It's true enough that I can't evade the fact of blood. A kill *defines* the hunt and all its subordinate objectives and agents, including the hunter: in that one moment, the path of an elusive and superbly equipped prey intersects with a human predatory capacity, both schematic and intuitive, mundane (which boots to bring, which shells?) and superstitious (hunt high ground in an east wind); and for that one moment, the world reveals a gorgeous coherency.

The anti-hunting propagandist is appalled by such a sacramental perspective, precisely because its icon is a bloodstain. Nor will the hobbyist sportsman read me rightly. I speak only to and for the passionate hunter, the one who regards this business as more than mere sport. Surrounded like everyone by a mechanized and abstractive culture, he appreciates how seldom human gesture can be unmediated, literal.

I've always understood all this somewhere in my soul, but I've needed to come this far before bringing it to articulation, however imperfect. Ironically, I worry that such a development may threaten the hunt's very value: if I ever reach a point of rational, self-conscious understanding, then the passional foundation of what I do will have vanished, along with its aesthetic. And its ethical foundation as well, even as vulgarly understood: the fact of blood will no longer mark an unmediated moment; however difficult of achievement, a kill will degenerate into cold-blooded *killing;* at long last I'll be forced to give this dear game up.

None of this has actually happened yet, and I pray it shall not; but I can't deny that certain things do come clearer with age. For example, I understand why with every passing season hunting should seem a greater treasure than fishing, even if I'd not gladly sacrifice either. It's partly of course that hunting is the more fragile resource: I'll be physically able to fish well after I'm all done with hard terrain and icy blinds. But there's more to it than that. Conservation instincts, or plain common sense, dictate that we release the trout, the salmon, and even the bass we now catch. Thus the gesture of angling is ever more symbolic, less what I call a primary act than somehow a charade of the primary. I might say that hunting is to contemporary sportsfishing roughly as the dead black duck at my feet is to the photo of him I might have taken instead. A direct, an undiluted *presence* on the one hand, and on the other a kind of disembodied *re-presentation*.

My craving for the former may seem odd. A writer's traffic is after all in words, and nothing (except perhaps money) could be more abstract or representative. But doesn't a northerner now and then lust for an untracked beach, a sun straight overhead, blue waves wheezing on the shingle? Doesn't he dream that in paradise he'll travel back and forth between such a southern place and the evergreen-dense hills behind the house that he's chosen for his own? My very commitment to a verbal and meditative art may quicken desire for similar vacation, one impulse galvanizing another. If I give words to my vision now, it was without them that it transpired—complete with the northman and the tropical sunlight, the white strand and the hillside house—on the morning I speak of. I remember it well.

Yet even as I remember and write, I must smile at myself. Though I hope that somewhere, sometime such contradictions may disappear, who besides me would all but leave his body in order to ponder the joys of unadorned physicality, would claim the benefits of primary pursuits while elaborating a billowy inward picture of some Eden-to-come? I am tempted to pun on the fact that I was in a blind that morning.

In any case, I hadn't the time for self-irony just then, for my reverie was broken by Topper's romping out of his crouch. I started to hiss him back under cover, but what the hell? There wouldn't be any ducks. Why not put the poor guy at his ease for a spell? Besides, it was getting toward the hour for gathering up decoys. I had projects waiting for me on my desk, and too extensive a voyaging into mental places always entails the risk of not getting back all the way.

The twittering of songbirds, the lisps of the breeze, and the faint hum of the river's current had by now become a sort of silence . . . through which to my amazement, off to northeast above Grant's stubblefield, pumped five soundless geese. It couldn't be, I thought at the same time wondering if I'd ever beheld even a single Canada in such utterly soundless flight. I didn't believe so; still don't. The big birds were well up, and the sun shone frankly upon them. Like the wood ducks earlier, they appeared chiseled, lapidary, but they were moving, right enough—my way, their wings already set.

Surely they'd make one lofty pass over my spread and then travel on, even higher. I didn't of course have a Canada call. I was half out of the blind to boot, and Topper all the way out, bulling through the cattails, on furlough. He hadn't noticed the geese, who remained stone-quiet. And still came straight on.

I'd frozen in a semi-upright posture, imagining the sun's blaze off my balding head, the all-too-human angles and divots of my silhouette.

The geese kept incredibly coming.

I whistled once, curtly. At the signal Topper immediately sat, his hind parts in several inches of cold riverwater. Not that his caution or mine would do any good. By now the birds had certainly spied us: they'd squawk and flare in another few yards.

They flew ever toward us, mute.

The small flock broke the vertical plane of my set and abruptly dropped to the water outside it, facing the breeze. I took the moment to reseat myself. What few geese I'd ever seen in the Connecticut's actual water while hunting over decoys knew how to navigate the river's center, exactly out of shotgun range from either side. These five would of course be no different; they'd swim a half-dozen yards or so further offshore to get it just right.

But no: they turned and sculled in among my blocks, unhesitating, unperturbed, one even dabbling the bar on which at daybreak my canoe had momentarily run aground. I could still see the frail keel-mark in the mud. Topper flattened, his whole belly and chest in the water now. Again his eye rolled toward me in its socket, and again I knew what he was thinking: Shoot, you fool!

But I wouldn't. Not yet anyhow.

I watched for a long spell. There seemed to be a couple of shortneck geese and three longnecks. Two married couples, I figured, and one bachelor or widower. I looked at Topper's clown face, then back at the gaggle. I was trying to determine which were the mated pairs so that I might kill the odd gander out, so that my dog could have *his* defining moment. But my thoughts grew ever more fussy and ludicrous: I recalled a chapter from Lorenz about homosexual goose matings. They lasted for life too.

"Get out of here," I declaimed for the second time.

Now the birds made racket enough, hauling their heavy bodies into air, lashing the slick to froth. My dog jumped instantly to all fours, his ears cocked, not shivering from the chill alone. We followed the Canadas out of sight to southward as we had the woodies.

Topper expelled another great breath, bigger than the earlier one. I broke my gun, unloaded it, and laid it on the dew-sopped vegetation behind me. Then, dropping to a knee and calling his name, I threw both arms around the old retriever's marsh-rank neck. He deserved my apology, had deserved it a long time. And yet shooting a single one of those geese would have been a sin: the word still seems precisely right.

It wasn't the birds' beauty and grace, not their conformity to the land-

and riverscape—even more stunning than the ducks'—that had dissuaded me. Or at least one of these things entirely. It was simply that I'd exercised no skills; rather, the game had atypically failed to exercise its skills, its keen senses, its native wariness. A kill, so far from defining anything, would have done just the opposite, ratifying the accidental, the random. It would have left me no better than the oaf who, driving by in his car, blasts a grouse off a roadside wall, shooting merely because he's happened on something shootable. Or I'd have been the fool who, looking for deer, murders the bear he blunders across. In a child we may partly forgive such moral idiocy, but not an adult.

I had done the right thing. There could be no earthly doubt about it. But I was suddenly overcome by an exquisite melancholy. My logic blamed this blueness on the double disappointment of an aged retriever, but something in my spirit resisted the neatness of that explanation.

By now the sun had melted the thin skin of frost on which my canoe slid so easily at dawn. I tried to drag the boat back to the truck with all my gear stashed on its hull, but could not. I needed to make several trips, fetching my decoy bags, my canvas stool, my gun, my shell bag and the rest. Yet even the weight of an empty boat seemed enormous in my state, which had turned to genuine depression, for reasons I still couldn't name. To name them, I'd have to wait till much later, and in order to make a cautious truce with that morning's emotions, I'd have to discover their relations to some prior emotions.

It seems that for me one retrospect begets another.

Back in the 1960s, I once sat on a shore near the ice-wrecked bridge in Haverhill. That was far upstream from Grant Balch's pasture. It was also a much earlier fall day than the one at Grant's, so the teal hadn't left yet. A bird shy of a limit, and full of youthful avarice, I was waiting well into morning for a straggler.

All of a sudden I heard a pair of near Canadas, who before I knew it had passed outside my decoys and dropped about a hundred yards downstream. After they coasted around a bend, I leapt from the blind and ran after them, my heart a hammer. As I've said, a goose on ground or water was a spectacle in those days.

I tried to judge the distance these two might have swum, hoping they'd strayed closer to shore in the process. In that stretch, the riverbank on the New Hampshire side stands twenty feet or so above the Connecticut's flow; I might just be able to rush to a brink and—if I'd guessed properly—fire my gun. I'd been running along in a punishing half-crouch, and was badly winded; yet my body felt more than ever *alive*.

When I made my dash across a cut hayfield to streamside, I found I'd misestimated. Not by much, to be sure: had I scampered on another twenty yeards, the birds would have given me a pretty decent shot. Indeed, if they hadn't in that uncanny way remained dead-center even in this skinny run of river, I'd still have had a reasonable one. As it was, they lifted off to north, honking, well out of harm's way.

I wasn't surprised, but I was surely disappointed. Or rather, resentful. Like any boy, I vaguely believed the world blameworthy for not accommodating my every craving. Back at the blind, I forgot all about the last teal I'd been wishing for. I jerked the canoe from the cattails and churned out to my spread, where I yanked the blocks on board, half willfully tangling line and anchor so that I could fume and curse even more bitterly.

For weeks and months after, I replayed the whole scene, but supplied a fantasy ending: Monster, my duck dog in those days, presented me with the first trophy, then proudly swam for the second; next came the labor of picking the birds, the pleasure and ardor of cooking them—a jigger of orange liqueur in the stock, shoots of celery in the birds' cavities, wild rice steaming on a top burner. The works.

I compare the breathless, exhilarated pursuit of the geese by a man in his twenties with my almost comic deliberation at Grant Balch's last fall; I compare their aftermaths; and I find that in the years between those two mornings, the hunter himself has changed more radically than his country or wildlife. He is now affected, in the woods and on the waters, less by the thrill of anticipation than the seductions of recall.

Another essay might find an analogous change in a man's sexual career. I'll not take up so complex a matter, save to say that the diminishment of either predatory instinct isn't irredeemably grim nor even sad. For it is compensated, one hopes, by an increase in moral judgment.

And by the putting aside of childish things. For it happens that a child had lingered in my spirit for longer than I ever dreamed he would when I was an *actual* child. The mind is its own place, says John Milton's devil, but I seem always late to arrive there; it's only in writing this that I understand where I have come. To watch those birds disappear below Grant's pasture was to watch a boy disappear as well.

It was goodbye, boy. And perhaps good riddance—at least to his storms, bewilderments, agitations. How wouldn't I mourn his death, though, the one with whom I traveled so many beautiful miles, and whom I had loved, if ambiguously, for so very long.

The Bass, the River, and Sheila Mant

W. D. WETHERELL

THERE WAS A SUMMER in my life when the only creature that seemed lovelier to me than a largemouth bass was Sheila Mant. I was fourteen. The Mants had rented the cottage next to ours on the river; with their parties, their frantic games of softball, their constant comings and goings, they appeared to me denizens of a brilliant existence. "Too noisy by half," my mother quickly decided, but I would have given anything to be invited to one of their parties, and when my parents went to bed I would sneak through the woods to their hedge and stare enchanted at the candlelit swirl of white dresses and bright, paisley skirts.

Sheila was the middle daughter—at seventeen, all but out of reach. She would spend her days sunbathing on a float my Uncle Sierbert had moored in their cove, and before July was over I had learned all her moods. If she lay flat on the diving board with her hand trailing idly in the water, she was pensive, not to be disturbed. On her side, her head propped up by her arm, she was observant, considering those around her with a look that seemed queenly and severe. Sitting up, arms tucked around her long, suntanned legs, she was approachable, but barely, and it was only in those glorious moments when she stretched herself prior to entering the water that her various suitors found the courage to come near.

These were many. The Dartmouth heavyweight crew would scull by her house on their way upriver, and I think all eight of them must have been in love with her at various times during the summer; the coxswain would curse at them through his megaphone, but without effect—there was always a pause in their pace when they passed Sheila's float. I suppose to these jaded twenty-year-olds she seemed the incarnation of innocence and youth, while to me she appeared unutterably suave, the epitome of sophistication. I was on the swim team at school, and to win her attention would do endless laps between my house and the Vermont shore, hoping she would notice the beauty of my flutter kick, the power of my crawl. Finishing, I would boost myself up onto our dock and glance casually over toward her, but she was never watching, and the miraculous day she was, I immediately climbed the diving board and did my best tuck

From W. D. Wetherell, *The Man Who Loved Levittown* (Pittsburgh: The University of Pittsburgh Press, 1985).

and a half for her, and continued diving until she had left and the sun went down and my longing was like a madness and I couldn't stop.

It was late August by the time I got up the nerve to ask her out. The tortured will-I's, won't-I's, the agonized indecision over what to say, the false starts toward her house and embarrassed retreats—the details of these have been seared from my memory, and the only part I remember clearly is emerging from the woods toward dusk while they were playing softball on their lawn, as bashful and frightened as a unicorn.

Sheila was stationed halfway between first and second, well outside the infield. She didn't seem surprised to see me—as a matter of fact, she didn't seem to see me at all.

"If you're playing second base, you should move closer," I said.

She turned—I took the full brunt of her long red hair and well-spaced freckles.

"I'm playing outfield," she said. "I don't like the responsibility of having a base."

"Yeah, I can understand that," I said, though I couldn't. "There's a band in Dixford tomorrow night at nine. Want to go?"

One of her brothers sent the ball sailing over the leftfielder's head; she stood and watched it disappear toward the river.

"You have a car?" she said, without looking up.

I played my master stroke. "We'll go by canoe."

I spent all of the following day polishing it. I turned it upside down on our lawn and rubbed every inch with Brillo, hosing off the dirt, wiping it with chamnois until it gleamed as bright as aluminum ever gleamed. About five, I slid it into the water, arrranging cushions near the bow so Sheila could lean on them if she was in one of her pensive moods, propping up my father's transistor radio by the middle thwart so we could have music when we came back. Automatically, without thinking about it, I mounted my Mitchell reel on my Pfleuger spinning rod and stuck it in the stern.

I say automatically, because I never went anywhere that summer without a fishing rod. When I wasn't swimming laps to impress Sheila, I was back in our driveway practicing casts, and when I wasn't practicing casts, I was tying the line to Tosca, our springer spaniel, to test the reel's drag, and when I wasn't doing any of those things, I was fishing the river for bass.

Too nervous to sit at home, I got in the canoe early and started paddling in a huge circle that would get me to Sheila's dock around eight. As automatically as I brought along my rod, I tied on a big Rapala plug, let it down into the water, let out some line and immediately forgot all about it.

It was already dark by the time I glided up to the Mants' dock. Even by day the river was quiet, most of the summer people preferring Sunapee or one of the other nearby lakes, and at night it was a solitude difficult to believe, a corridor of hidden life that ran between banks like a tunnel. Even the stars were part of it. They weren't as sharp anywhere else; they seemed to have chosen the river as a guide on their slow wheel toward morning, and in the course of the summer's fishing, I had learned all their names.

I was there ten minutes before Sheila appeared. I heard the slam of their screen door first, then saw her in the spotlight as she came slowly down the path. As beautiful as she was on the float, she was even lovelier now—her white dress went perfectly with her hair, and complimented her figure even more than her swimsuit.

It was her face that bothered me. It had on its delightful fullness a very dubious expression.

"Look," she said. "I can get Dad's car."

"It's faster this way," I lied. "Parking's tense up there. Hey, it's safe. I won't tip it or anything."

She let herself down reluctantly into the bow. I was glad she wasn't facing me. When her eyes were on me, I felt like diving in the river again from agony and joy.

I pried the canoe away from the dock and started paddling upstream. There was an extra paddle in the bow, but Sheila made no move to pick it up. She took her shoes off, and dangled her feet over the side.

Ten minutes went by.

"What kind of band?" she said.

"It's sort of like folk music. You'll like it."

"Eric Caswell's going to be there. He strokes number four."

"No kidding?" I said. I had no idea who she meant.

"What's that sound?" she said, pointing toward shore.

"Bass. That splashing sound?"

"Over there."

"Yeah, bass. They come into the shallows at night to chase frogs and moths and things. Big largemouths. *Micropetrus salmonides,*" I added, showing off.

"I think fishing's dumb," she said, making a face. "I mean, it's boring and all. Definitely dumb."

Now I have spent a great deal of time in the years since wondering why Sheila Mant should come down so hard on fishing. Was her father a fisherman? Her antipathy toward fishing nothing more than normal filial rebellion? Had she tried it once? A messy encounter with worms? It doesn't matter. What does, is that at that fragile moment in time I would have given anything not to appear dumb in Sheila's severe and unforgiving eyes.

She hadn't seen my equipment yet. What I *should* have done, of course, was push the canoe in closer to shore and carefully slide the rod into some branches where I could pick it up again in the morning. Failing that, I could have surreptitiously dumped the whole outfit, written off the forty or so dollars as love's tribute. What I actually *did* do was gently lean forward, and slowly, ever so slowly, push the rod back through my legs toward the stern where it would be less conspicuous.

It must have been just exactly what the bass was waiting for. Fish will trail a lure sometimes, trying to make up their mind whether or not to attack, and the slight pause in the plug's speed caused by my adjustment was tantalizing enough to overcome the bass's inhibitions. My rod, safely out of sight at last, bent double. The line, tightly coiled, peeled off the spool with the shrill, tearing zip of a high-speed drill.

Four things occurred to me at once. One, that it was a bass. Two, that it was a big bass. Three, that it was the biggest bass I had ever hooked. Four, that Sheila Mant must not know.

"What was that?" she said, turning half around.

"Uh, what was what?"

"That buzzing noise."

"Bats."

She shuddered, quickly drew her feet back into the canoe. Every instinct I had told me to pick up the rod and strike back at the bass, but there was no need to—it was already solidly hooked. Downstream, an awesome distance downstream, it jumped clear of the water, landing with a concussion heavy enough to ripple the entire river. For a moment, I thought it was gone, but then the rod was bending again, the tip dancing into the water. Slowly, not making any motion that might alert Sheila, I reached down to tighten the drag.

While all this was going on, Sheila had begun talking and it was a few minutes before I was able to catch up with her train of thought.

"I went to a party there. These fraternity men. Katherine says I could get in there if I wanted. I'm thinking more of UVM or Bennington. Somewhere I can ski."

The bass was slanting toward the rocks on the New Hampshire side by the ruins of Donaldson's boathouse. It had to be an old bass—a young one probably wouldn't have known the rocks were there. I brought the canoe back out into the middle of the river, hoping to head it off.

"That's neat," I mumbled. "Skiing. Yeah, I can see that."

"Eric said I have the figure to model, but I thought I should get an education first. I mean, it might be a while before I get started and all. I was thinking of getting my hair styled, more swept back? I mean, Ann-Margret? Like hers, only shorter."

She hesitated. "Are we going backwards?"

We were. I had managed to keep the bass in the middle of the river away from the rocks, but it had plenty of room there, and for the first time a chance to exert its full strength. I quickly computed the weight necessary to draw a fully loaded canoe backwards—the thought of it made me feel faint.

"It's just the current," I said hoarsely. "No sweat or anything."

I dug in deeper with my paddle. Reassured, Sheila began talking about something else, but all my attention was taken up now with the fish. I could feel its desperation as the water grew shallower. I could sense the extra strain on the line, the frantic way it cut back and forth in the water. I could visualize what it looked like—the gape of its mouth, the flared gills and thick, vertical tail. The bass couldn't have encountered many forces in its long life that it wasn't capable of handling, and the unrelenting tug at its mouth must have been a source of great puzzlement and mounting panic.

Me, I had problems of my own. To get to Dixford, I had to paddle up a sluggish stream that came into the river beneath a covered bridge. There was a shallow sandbar at the mouth of this stream—weeds on one side, rocks on the other. Without doubt, this is where I would lose the fish.

"I have to be careful with my complexion. I tan, but in segments. I can't figure out if it's even worth it. I wouldn't even do it probably. I saw Jackie Kennedy in Boston and she wasn't tan at all."

Taking a deep breath, I paddled as hard as I could for the middle, deepest part of the bar. I could have threaded the eye of a needle with the canoe, but the pull on the stern threw me off and I overcompensated—the canoe veered left and scraped bottom. I pushed the paddle down and shoved. A moment of hesitation . . . a moment more. . . . The canoe shot clear into the deeper water of the stream. I immediately looked down at the rod. It was bent in the same, tight arc—miraculously, the bass was still on.

The moon was out now. It was low and full enough that its beam shone directly on Sheila there ahead of me in the canoe, washing her in a creamy, luminous glow. I could see the lithe, easy shape of her figure. I could see the way her hair curled down off her shoulders, the proud, alert tilt of her head, and all these things were as a tug on my heart. Not just Sheila, but the aura she carried about her of parties and casual touchings and grace. Behind me, I could feel the strain of the bass, steadier now, growing weaker, and this was another tug on my heart, not just the bass but the beat of the river and the slant of the stars and the smell of the night, until finally it seemed I would be torn apart between longings, split in half. Twenty yards ahead of us was the road, and once I pulled the canoe up on shore, the bass would be gone, irretrievably gone. If instead I stood up, grabbed the rod and started pumping, I would have it—as tired as the bass was, there was no chance it could get away. I reached down for the rod, hesitated, looked up to where Sheila was stretching herself lazily toward the sky, her small breasts rising beneath the soft fabric of her dress, and the tug was too much for me, and quicker than it takes to write down, I pulled a penknife from my pocket and cut the line in half.

With a sick, nauseous feeling in my stomach, I saw the rod unbend.

"My legs are sore," Sheila whined. "Are we there yet?"

Through a superhuman effort of self-control, I was able to beach the canoe and help Sheila off. The rest of the night is much foggier. We walked to the fair—there was the smell of popcorn, the sound of guitars. I may have danced once or twice with her, but all I really remember is her coming over to me once the music was done to explain that she would be going home in Eric Caswell's Corvette.

"Okay," I mumbled.

For the first time that night she looked at me, really looked at me.

"You're a funny kid, you know that?"

Funny. Different. Dreamy. Odd. How many times was I to hear that in the years to come, all spoken with the same quizzical, half-accusatory tone Sheila used them. Poor Sheila! Before the month was over, the spell she cast over me was gone, but the memory of that lost bass haunted me all summer and haunts me still. There would be other Sheila Mants in my life, other fish, and though I came close once or twice, it was these secret, hidden tuggings in the night that claimed me, and I never made the same mistake again.

One Moment at the Source

RICHARD EWALD

ONCE, ON A LATE summer afternoon, after driving several hundred miles and hiking for a half-hour through a forest, I found what I was looking for: the headwaters of the Connecticut River. It's a pond, known as Fourth Connecticut Lake, standing about 1,600 feet above sea level, just this side of the Canadian border.

I was researching a small book on the "cultural landscape" of the Connecticut River Valley. Like many others who have come here, I felt powerfully drawn to trace the river upstream to its source. Perhaps it was something like the same urge that had compelled Adriaen Block, a Dutch sea captain and the river's first documented European explorer in the south, to enter its mouth from Long Island Sound. In their ship named "Onrust," which means "Restless," Block and his crew sailed upriver to the falls at present-day Enfield, Connecticut, in 1614.

Following a path through the woods around the small lake, I came to a short split-log foot bridge over a swampy place. A trickle of water seeped under the bridge and into the marshy upper edge of the lake. With a sense of having come a great distance and found the answer to a very big question, I stretched out on the logs and lowered my face to within inches of the water. Here the origin of New England's largest river is as wide as your finger, its flow no bigger than a faucet left dripping.

The bottom of this crystal-clear, miniature river was light and sandy, flecked with tiny, dark shreds of decaying vegetation. I could see the individual grains of sand shifting along the bottom, tumbling in the current, moving downhill. It occurred to me that some 410 miles to the south, the enormous sand bars at the river's mouth are made of particles like these, some grains from right here perhaps among them.

Suddenly, millions of years seemed to pass before my eyes in a flash, and their vast consequences stood legible in the landscape in the present moment: continents drifting, colliding at the seam the river later found . . . New England's mountain ranges rising up, then gradually sculpted by water and ice . . . the glacial-melt lake that once filled up half the length of the present river valley . . . the receding of the last glacier . . . the slow northward growth of a great forest, its trees now shading me from the summer sun. From these freshwater uplands clear to the tidewater flats at the sea, the intricate arrangement of rock, soil, and plant within these seven million acres seemed held, suspended. Then, with the sound of water running downhill, it all came back in motion, cycle and change, renewal and redispersal, beginning here with this trickle's whisper.

In that whisper spoke the voices of Native Americans, for whom the Connecticut River Valley was home for some 10,000 years before the arrival of Europeans. Then, at a time when most Europeans were clustered in Atlantic coastal settlements, others began to push inland. It was up this long river that American colonists first launched themselves deep into the continental wilderness. Native American voices in the valley were joined by Dutch, French, English, Irish, Scottish, Italian, Polish, German, Scandinavian, Slavic, African-American, Hispanic, and Asian. Each new people arrived, like Block, in the "Restless"-ness of their own ethnic group and era, and made themselves at home in a new place.

Throughout the watershed, they invested themselves upon their page of the landscape, erasing something in order to inscribe new text composed of houses, barns, mills of all sizes, churches, cemeteries, schools, town halls, libraries, general stores, downtown commercial blocks, country villas, apartment buildings, resort communities, housing subdivisions—all in a variety of materials and styles whose details and combinations are distinctive to the region. Footpaths beneath a continuous forest canopy gave way to roads, boat landings, ferry crossings, dams, canals, bridges, railroads, hydropower plants, airports, highways, and computer networks.

Eons ago, this land knew a lush, tropical climate, where families of dinosaurs walked through mudflats; their footprints are visible now in shale. Today, in changing seasons, in drought or flood, it is a temperate river system with diverse human habitats: large cities, a patchwork of towns and village centers, a rural countryside, patterned by fields and woodlands, a sparsely-populated, mountainous forest.

Now, along the banks of a river famous for its log drives, today's settlers drive cars and log on to the Internet. Within the watershed, more than two million inhabitants now take their place in the flow, by the hearth, at the office or shop, at church suppers, town meetings, musical performances, ethnic festivals, school plays, book discussions, club events. We raise families, operate businesses, plant crops, fish, hunt, sing, sew, worship, wash, conceive inventions, paint pictures, build furniture, write letters, cook meals, pay the bills, patch the roof, gaze at the night sky.

All of this, past and present together, shapes up to be the "cultural landscape" of the Connecticut River Valley. It is the terrain we inherit. It is the topography of what we believe our history to have been, and who we imagine ourselves to be. To me, right now as on that particular summer afternoon as I lay staring into a thread of water entering Fourth Connecticut Lake, it is the river that runs through this real estate, this cultural landscape, that connects us. It connects us as beneficiaries and stewards of a watershed, both downriver and upriver from our neighbors. It draws us down to earth and roots us in one place on the planet. It is the flow into which we step, which moves on beyond and without us, but which is altered by the shape of our thought and presence.

A spattering of raindrops brought me back to where I lay. A single cloud hung overhead, backlit by the sun, much lower now in the west. I rose stiffly to my feet and stretched, and looked down one more time at the water. No, I thought, the Connecticut River cannot be said to have one source, but thousands and thousands of sources and "re-sources." They are as various as its micro ecosystems, as diverse as its natural and human history, as numerous as all its inhabitants' needs for, and dreams of, water.

The gathered volume of the river is large, and has a lot to say; that's why its singular mouth is so wide. But the Connecticut has thirty-eight major tributaries, each with its own network of minor brooks and branches, a vast web of gravity depicted. In the damp places where each rivulet rises, in ponds deep in the woods, in back yards where small streams commingle, in cities where tributaries enter the main stem—whether in Connecticut, Massachusetts, Vermont, or New Hampshire—those places, too, are the origins of the great river. No matter where you locate yourself on the map of the physical and the cultural landscape, one of those places is near you, and surrounds you, and is within you.